ip '73   10.00
12

?

UNIVERSITY
OF NORTH CAROLINA
STUDIES IN
THE GERMANIC LANGUAGES
AND LITERATURES

NUMBER TWENTY-ONE

AMS PRESS
NEW YORK

HERMANN HESSE AND HIS CRITICS

The Criticism and Bibliography of
Half a Century

By

JOSEPH MILECK

CHAPEL HILL
THE UNIVERSITY OF NORTH CAROLINA PRESS

Library of Congress Cataloging in Publication Data

Mileck, Joseph, 1922-
   Hermann Hesse and his critics.

   Reprint of the 1958 ed., which was issued as no. 21 of
North Carolina University.   Studies in the Germanic
languages and literatures.
   Includes bibliographical references.
   1.   Hesse, Hermann, 1877-1962.   2.   Hesse, Hermann,
1877-1962--Bibliography.   I.   Title.   II.   Series:
North Carolina.   University.   Studies in the Germanic
languages and literatures, no. 21.
PT2617.E85Z83 1972   838'.9'1209   72-10899
ISBN 0-404-50921-5

Copyright 1958
THE UNIVERSITY OF NORTH CAROLINA PRESS

Reprinted with the permission of the original publisher
First AMS edition published in 1966
2nd printing ,1972
International Standard Book Number :0-404-50921-5
Library of Congress Catalog Card Number: 72-10899

AMS PRESS,INC.
NEW YORK,N.Y. 10003
     1972

Manufactured in the United States of America

UPON THE OCCASION OF HERMANN HESSE'S
EIGHTIETH BIRTHDAY,
JULY 2, 1957

WITH THE SUPPORT OF A GRANT
FROM THE
AMERICAN PHILOSOPHICAL SOCIETY

TABLE OF CONTENTS

Page

Introduction .... **xi**

Part One: HERMANN HESSE **1**

  I   A Bio-Bibliographical Sketch **3**

  II Hesse and his Art **14**

III Hesse and his Age **34**

Part Two: HESSE AND HIS CRITICS **57**

  I   Books **59**

  II Pamphlets **104**

III Articles in Books, in Pamphlets, and in Periodicals **128**

      Preceding 1927 .... **128**

      From 1927 to 1955 .... **133**

         Surveys **133**

         Congratulatory Articles **135**

         Hesse and his Age **139**

         Hesse and Youth **147**

         Hesse and Nature **150**

         Hesse and Music **151**

         Hesse and Psychology **158**

         Geist and *Natur* **166**

         Hesse and Religion **173**

         Glasperlenspiel **178**

         Poetry **192**

 IV General Interest in Hesse **196**

Part Three: BIBLIOGRAPHY **201**

  I   Hesse Archives in Europe **203**

  II Hesse Bibliographies **208**

     Bibliography **215**

         Works by Hesse **218**

         Books and Pamphlets **219**

         Short Stories, Articles, and Poems in Books and
         Pamphlets **224**

         Short Stories, Articles, and Poems in Periodicals **227**

Page

Articles and Poems in Newspapers 231

Reviews 233

Letters 238

Hesse in Textbooks for English Speaking Students 242

Translations of Hesse's Works 243

Works about Hesse 250

Books and Printed Dissertations 250

Pamphlets 252

Articles and Passages in Books and Pamphlets 255

Histories of Literature 262

Articles in Periodicals 265

Articles in Newspapers and Weeklies 285

Dissertations 293

Notes 298

Index 311

INTRODUCTION

This study consists of three sections. Part I deals primarily with Hesse, Part II with his critics, and Part III provides a classified bibliography which includes both the works by Hesse and those about him. Part I is meant to afford a quick perspective as far as Hesse himself is concerned: the "Bio-Bibliographical Sketch" outlines Hesse's life and the chronology of his writings; in "Hesse and his Art," his prose and poetry are briefly characterized; "Hesse and his Age" presents the author's conception of the world of today and its reaction to him.

The large body of critical literature which has already been written about Hesse falls into three distinct periods. The first and least significant of these ended in 1926. The second began in 1927 but soon faltered under the Nazis, and faded away almost completely during the Second World War. The third and most important of the periods has not yet ended; in the wake of Hesse's renewed acclaim in Germany and his greater recognition abroad, more critical material has been published since 1945 than during the combined preceding periods.

To present a well-organized analysis of this literature proved more difficult than anticipated. The strictly chronological approach which these well-defined periods first suggested, soon bogged down in a confusing, disconnected repetition. A purely thematic approach, on the other hand, would have dissected every longer work beyond all recognition. I decided, therefore, to analyze the books and printed dissertations individually and chronologically. The pamphlets which deal exclusively with Hesse have been put into four categories: appreciative surveys of Hesse's life and works, studies centered about single issues, varied composites, and bibliographical supplements. They are discussed individually and chronologically under these headings. The hundreds of articles which have been published in books, pamphlets, and periodicals in the course of fifty-five years presented new difficulties and called for a different approach. Since by far most of the items preceding 1927 fall into the relatively inconsequential category of reviews, it was felt that a general survey with specific attention given only to a dozen or so of the more significant articles, would more than suffice for this early period. On the other hand, the more numerous and much more noteworthy articles which have appeared in the two periods since

1927 lent themselves best to a more thematic approach. Pertinent background information is presented under specific headings, and all the available relevant articles of any consequence are scrutinized in as chronological a manner as the subject permits. Many hitherto untouched aspects of these themes are broached, and bibliographical aid pertinent to the suggested expansions is appended.

No efforts were spared to make this *Stand der Forschung* as encompassing as possible. What I was unable to find at Harvard, Yale, or at the University of California at Berkeley, I generally managed to locate in one of the various Hesse Archives in Germany, or in the Royal Library in Copenhagen. Every available item written in any language and published before 1956 was examined. Needless to say, only the better of the hundreds of entries in my bibliography are touched upon in Part II. All of the seventeen books, and all but one of the forty-one pamphlets on Hesse (Rudolf Adolph, *Hermann Hesse, Schutzpatron der Bücherfreunde* [1952], 23, pp.) were available for analysis. No major article is neglected, although four or five promising but inaccessible items receive only passing notice. The more important of the many minor articles are tended to very briefly, and the multitude of trivial items which have appeared in weeklies and newspapers are almost completely excluded.

In Part III, I discuss the six leading Hesse Archives in Germany and present a detailed description of the nine Hesse bibliographies already in print. The bibliography which follows comprises two major sections, and each of these falls into a number of different categories. "Works by Hesse" includes: books and pamphlets; short stories and articles in books and pamphlets; short stories and articles in periodicals; articles in newspapers; reviews; letters; textbooks for English speaking students; translations of his works. Since most private reprints are of no particular use to scholars, I felt that all but the most significant of these might best be omitted, and I also chose to omit the books edited by Hesse, rather than duplicate the extensive list in Kliemann/Silomon (*Hermann Hesse. Eine bibliographische Studie* [1947], pp. 35-41). Otherwise I have tried to be as exhaustive as possible.

"Works about Hesse" includes: books and printed dissertations; pamphlets; articles and pertinent passages in books and pamphlets; histories of literature; articles in periodicals; articles in newspapers and weeklies; dissertations not in print. Ideally, every item touching upon Hesse should have been included in this list. Practically, however, this could not be done. In certain of the categories selection was absolutely necessary, and in other instances, items had to be omitted for want of adequate bibliographical information. Many Japanese references had to be discarded for this reason. Books and histories of literature which make only casual reference to Hesse have not been included. Of the one hundred and twenty-six periodical articles listed by Ernst Metelmann ("Hermann Hesse," *Die Schöne Literatur*, 28 [1927], 306-310), only forty-six proved to be worth listing again, and to these I have managed to add only eleven other significant early items. On the other hand, the periodical articles from 1927 to 1957 represent as complete a list as I have been able to compile. Of the innumerable articles in weeklies and newspapers, I have listed mainly what appeared to be the better items of the past three decades; except for fifteen important entries, I have not included the seventy-six early newspaper items listed by Metelmann.

Approximately two-thirds of the items under "Works by Hesse" and three-quarters of those under "Works about Hesse," do not appear in any of the bibliographies which have already been published. The entries range from 1899 to the middle of 1957.

Periodically during the past five years, I have received letters from fellow students of Hesse asking for information about certain themes and requesting bibliographical data for others. These inquiries have done much to persuade me that there is a very definite need for a study such as this, which presents the pertinent facts of Hesse's life and art and which makes possible a rapid orientation in the criticism centered about his works. It is hoped that the purposeless duplication of studies, which is far too common in this criticism, will now be curbed, and that the general studies, which have been so prevalent up to now, will soon be supplemented by more investigations of specific themes.

Because the *Gesammelte Dichtungen* of 1952 were too incomplete, and since the more inclusive *Gesammelte Schriften* of 1957 were not yet available, I chose to use earlier editions of Hesse's works for my references. Page indications refer to the following editions:

Hermann Lauscher (München, 1920).
Franz von Assisi (Berlin, 1904).
Nachbarn, 1st ed. (Berlin, 1908).
Gertrud, (Berlin, 1927).
Schön ist die Jugend (Berlin, 1916).
Demian (Berlin, 1919).
Blick ins Chaos (Bern, 1920).
Kurgast (Berlin, 1925).
Bilderbuch (Berlin, 1926).
Nürnberger Reise (Berlin, 1927).
Steppenwolf (Berlin, 1931).
Krisis (Berlin, 1928).
Betrachtungen (Berlin, 1928).
Eine Bibliothek der Weltliteratur (Zürich, 1946).
Narziss und Goldmund (Berlin, 1931).
Weg nach Innen (Berlin, 1931).
Fabulierbuch (Zürich, 1947).
Gedenkblätter (Zürich, 1947).
Gedichte (Zürich, 1947).
Glasperlenspiel (Zürich, 1943).
Traumfährte (Zürich, 1945).
Der Pfirsichbaum und andere Erzählungen (Zürich, 1945).
Krieg und Frieden (Berlin, 1949).
Dank an Goethe (Zürich, 1946).
Briefe (Berlin, 1951).
Späte Prosa (Berlin, 1951).
Hermann Hesse/Romain Rolland. Briefe (Zürich, 1954).
Beschwörungen (Berlin, 1955).

Part One

HERMANN HESSE

A BIO-BIBLIOGRAPHICAL SKETCH

Hermann Hesse was born in Calw, Württemberg, July 2,
1877. That this little Swabian town on the Nagold at the edge of
the Black Forest should have become his birth-place, was sheer
chance. His father, Johannes Hesse (1847-1916), was born a
Russian citizen in Weissenstein, Estonia, where his grandfather,
Hermann Hesse (1802-1896), had established a flourishing
medical practice after leaving his native Dorpat. His great-grand-
father was an enterprising businessman from Lübeck. Hesse's
mother, Marie Gundert (1842-1902), was born in Talatscheri,
India, the daughter of the Pietist missionary and Indologist,
Hermann Gundert (1814-1893), whose family had its roots in
Stuttgart. To this North and South German family stock, Hesse's
maternal grandmother, Julie Dubois (1809-1885), added a French
Swiss element and his paternal grandmother, Jeanette Agnese
Lass, a Slavic.

This ancestry was as spirited and versatile as it was diversified. Hermann Hesse, *Kreisarzt, Staatsherr,* and beloved pa-
triarch of pioneer Weissenstein, was a jovial Pietist who was
still fond of skating at fifty and continued to climb trees and
tend his garden at eighty. Johannes Hesse, although a more
sensitive and retiring person than his father, dedicated himself
to the practical service of Christ at the age of eighteen, and,
following his ordination, served four years as a missionary in
Malabar, India (1869-1873). Brought back to Europe by ill
health, he settled in Calw to assist Hermann Gundert, then director of the *Calwer Verlagsverein.* From 1881 to 1886 Johannes
edited the *Missionsmagazin* in Basel, and taught at the *Missions-
haus.* Returning to Calw, he continued to assist his father-in-
law until he assumed the latter's position in 1893. Fervent though
he was and severe in his demands upon himself and upon others,
Johannes was not the highly emotional and narrow-minded
Pietist one might expect. A cultivated literary taste and intellectual curiosity had taken him far afield. His thought and his
religion evidenced the broadening and tempering effect of Latin
literature, Greek philosophies, and oriental religions.

Hermann Gundert was perhaps the most colorful of Hesse's
immediate forbears. After more than twenty years as a pioneer

missionary in Malabar (1836-1859), he returned to Europe, assigned by the *Basler Mission* to assist the director of the *Calwer Verlagsverein*. He assumed the directorship in 1862 and continued in this capacity until his death in 1893. Like Johannes Hesse, Gundert was no ordinary Pietist missionary. Not only was he completely at home in English, German, French, and Italian, but just as capable of preaching in Hindostani, Malajalam, and Sanskrit. He was almost as fluent in two or three other Indian dialects, and had some competence in at least ten other languages. A scholar at heart, Gundert's world in Calw soon became one of books. Much of his time was devoted to Indological studies, to a Malajalam translation of the Bible; and for thirty years he worked intermittently on his Malajalam lexicon. His home was long a meeting place for scholars, theologians, and exotic visitors from the Orient.

Marie Gundert Hesse was just as exceptional as her husband. She was born in Malabar and educated in Switzerland and Germany. Until 1870, her life was a continual shuttling between Europe and India. Although she was the mother of nine children, of whom six were to survive her, Marie found time not only to help her father and her husband in the *Calwer Verlagsverein*, but also, in the course of endless prayer meetings and countless daily tasks, to master four or five languages, to write verse, and to compose biographies of Bishop Hannington and David Livingstone. It could only be a matter of time before an artist would emerge from such an ancestry.

The heart of Calw, with its narrow cobblestone streets, its closely set houses with their pointed gables and little gardens, is still very much what it must have been in Hesse's childhood. Except for a modest plaque, the house in which Hesse was born stands inconspicuous in the market place opposite the old city hall. The large fountain continues to fascinate urchins, and the old stone bridge with its curious little chapel still spans the Nagold in which Hesse once delighted to swim and fish. In Bischofstrasse across the river, the once imposing *Haus des Calwer Verlagsvereins* is now a textile shop. It was to this house that Hermann Gundert brought his family in the early Sixties, and in which he remained until his death. It was into this house that the Hesse family moved in 1886, after five years in Basel, and where, but for a brief period in Ledergasse (1889-1893), it remained until shortly after Marie's death in 1902. Down the street a little way, the Perrot machine shop, in which Hesse toiled from June, 1894, to the autumn of 1895, is still in operation. A little stone fountain commemorates his apprenticeship.

Calw and its inhabitants left an indelible impression upon Hesse's memory. It is the Gerbersau of his early stories. It was here, in Perrot's machine shop, that Hans Giebenrath found his last refuge (*Unterm Rad*), here that ludicrous little Andreas Ohngelt politely stammered his way through life (*Die Verlobung*). In Gerbersau Walter Kömpff reluctantly tended his shop, got religion, then hanged himself. Here the Kelleresque *Sonnenbrüder* loafed and played their malicious pranks (*In der alten Sonne*), dapper Ladidel fell prey to temptation, and the scamp Emil Kolb pursued his wanton ways. It was to Gerbersau that Knulp returned to die.

A hypersensitive, imaginative, lively, and extremely headstrong child, Hesse was to prove a problem and a constant source of despair both at home and at school. As early as 1881, Marie Hesse sensed that her son's would be no ordinary future: "Bete du [Johannes] mit mir für Hermännle, und bete für mich, dass ich Kraft bekomme, ihn zu erziehen. Es ist mir, als wäre schon die Körperkraft nicht ausreichend; der Bursche hat ein Leben, eine Riesenstärke, einen mächtigen Willen, und wirklich auch eine Art ganz erstaunlichen Verstand für seine vier Jahre. Wo will's hinaus? Es zehrt mir ordentlich am Leben, dieses innere Kämpfen gegen seinen hohen Tyrannengeist, sein leidenschaftliches Stürmen und Drängen . . . Gott muss diesen stolzen Sinn in Arbeit nehmen, dann wird was Edles und Prächtiges draus, aber ich schaudere beim Gedanken, was bei falscher oder schwacher Erziehung aus diesem passionierten Menschen werden könnte" (*Marie Hesse* [1934], p. 208). By 1883, Johannes Hesse was seriously wondering whether it might not be better to put his intractable, precocious child into the care of others: "So demütigend es für uns wäre, ich besinne mich doch ernstlich, ob wir ihn nicht in eine Anstalt oder in ein fremdes Haus geben sollten. Wir sind zu nervös, zu schwach für ihn, das ganze Hauswesen nicht genug diszipliniert und regelmässig. Gaben hat er scheint's zu allem: er beobachtet den Mond und die Wolken, phantasiert lang auf dem Harmonium, malt mit Bleistift oder Feder ganz wunderbare Zeichnungen, singt wenn er will ganz ordentlich, und an Reimen fehlt es ihm nie" (*Marie Hesse*, p. 231).

By 1886, however, when his family returned to Calw, Hesse had become quite manageable. Although school held little attraction for him, and his teachers even less, he was able with almost no effort to stand at the top of his class. It began to appear likely that he would follow in the footsteps of his father and grandfather. In order that he might qualify for free schooling in Maulbronn, Hesse became a citizen of Württemberg in 1890. He then attended Rector Bauer's *Lateinschule* in Göppingen (February, 1890, to the summer of 1891) in preparation for the notorious *Landexamen*, which he successfully passed in July, 1891. Hesse's sojourn in Maulbronn was unexpectedly brief and most unhappy. Determined to become a writer and not a theologian, he neglected his studiès, resisted his teachers, and finally took French leave on March 7, 1892. Two months later he was withdrawn from Maulbronn by his parents and sent for a cure to Bad Boll. The exorcism of the celebrated Christoph Blumhardt proved futile. The patient stubbornly refused to have his will broken. After an attempt to commit suicide on June 20, Hesse was placed in the care of Pastor Schall in Stetten, then of Pastor Pfisterer in Basel. By the end of summer, he finally seemed ready to attend the *Gymnasium* in Cannstatt.

Hesse managed to survive the first year, but hardly had the second begun before he again became delinquent, sold his books to buy a pistol, and was promptly expelled. His subsequent apprenticeship in a bookshop in Esslingen terminated abruptly only three days after it had begun. Returning to Calw, Hesse helped his father in the *Verlagsverein* for about six months, then decided to learn a trade before emigrating to Brazil. However, after sixteen months of manual labor in Perrot's machine shop, he left in October, 1895, to begin a relatively uneventful apprenticeship of four years in the Heckenhauer bookshop in Tübingen.

Although Hesse composed poetry almost before he was able to wield a pencil, these years in Tübingen mark the actual beginning of his career. It was during this period that he wrote his first collection of verse, *Romantische Lieder* (1899), and the romantic prose episodes of *Eine Stunde hinter Mitternacht* (1899).

In the summer of 1899, when he had just finished his apprenticeship in Tübingen and was about to assume a new position in Basel, Hesse spent two weeks in little Kirchheim unter der

Teck. Here, in the Gasthof zur Krone, he and his intimate friend, Ludwig Finckh, comprised the nucleus of a brilliant circle of romantic spirits who paid court to the innkeeper's two charming nieces. Although Hesse's love for the younger niece, Julia Hellmann, proved to be ephemeral, this brief encounter was not without lasting consequences. It was this episode which found poetic expression in "Lulu" of *Hermann Lauscher*.[1]

Hesse's five years in Basel were busy ones. During the first two, he wrote all the *Hinterlassene Schriften und Gedichte von Hermann Lauscher* (1901) except "Meine Kindheit" which was written in 1896. *Gedichte*, poems composed from 1899 to 1902, was published in 1902. By 1903, Hesse was able to leave the book business and to devote all his time to his own work. *Peter Camenzind* (1904) was an immediate success. Hesse became a celebrity almost overnight. That same year, he received the *Wiener Bauernfeldpreis*, the first of many literary awards.

In September, 1904, Hesse married Maria Bernoulli, nine years his elder, the daughter of an old and prominent family of Basel. Soon afterwards, he and his bride left for the village of Gaienhofen on the German side of the Untersee. The humble, half timbered *Bauernhaus* which had been built during the Thirty Years' War and which now became their home, still stands in its cluster of old thatch-roofed cottages opposite a little red chapel. But for a modest sign, nothing suggests that peasants have not always lived there. Now, just as fifty years ago, animals are stabled in one half of the house's lower level, and chickens continue to scurry about the yard. The interior, too, has suffered little change. The rude staircase which once led to Hesse's study is as perilous as it ever was, and the study's raised threshold, over which young Stefan Zweig once bounded to greet his host, only to be struck down by the low door frame, continues its threat.

Hesse spent three boisterously happy years in this *Bauernhaus* before he decided to build his home more in keeping with his means and his calling, and more adequate for his growing family.[2] His second house, replete with plumbing which never functioned quite properly and with an elegant but temperamental tile stove, still stands on its knoll overlooking the lake. Time, however, has reduced to a shoddy boarding house what once was Gaienhofen's only villa. No placard recalls its celebrated builder, who had intended to spend the rest of his days there.

Hesse had hoped to establish himself in Gaienhofen, and to

become a responsible and respected member of society. This hope was never realized. Except for the first few years, his marriage did not alleviate his loneliness, nor could his idyllic retreat long contain his inherent restlessness. By 1912, Gaienhofen had lost all its meaning.

Despite their strong undercurrent of discord, these years from 1904 to 1912 were most prolific. A study of Boccaccio, as well as one of St. Francis of Assissi were published in 1904. With *Unterm Rad* (1906), Hesse paid his respects to the tendentious school-novel fashionable at the turn of the century, and with *Gertrud* (1910), he published his second *Künstlerroman*. Three volumes of *Novellen* were published in rapid succession, *Diesseits* (1907), *Nachbarn* (1908), *Umwege* (1912) ; and a third volume of poetry, *Unterwegs*, appeared in 1911. Although not published until 1913, *Aus Indien*, memoirs of Hesse's trip to the Orient in the second half of 1911, belongs to this period, also *Schön ist die Jugend*, which did not appear until 1916, and *Haus zum Frieden* (1947), which dates back to 1910. The novel *Berthold* (1944) was left a fragment in 1908, and the first part of *Knulp* (1915) was published in 1908. Five of the nine episodes of *Am Weg* (1915), more than half of the items of *Bilderbuch* (1926), and all but three of the twenty-three tales of *Fabulierbuch* (1935) were written from 1904 to 1912. Hesse also found time to help edit the periodical *März* (1907-1912), and to contribute to it, as well as to the *Neue Rundschau, Simplicissimus, Die Rheinlande,* and other journals, a steady stream of reviews, articles, and short stories.

Eventually Hesse found it unendurable to continue his established mode of existence in Gaienhofen. Recognizing the impossibility of his efforts to be both a *Phantasiemensch* and a *Bürger,* he fled to the East in the summer of 1911. In Ceylon, Malaya, and Sumatra, he sought in vain the perspective and the respite of distance. In 1912, about four or five months after his return to Europe, he left Gaienhofen with his family and moved into the home of his recently deceased friend, the Swiss painter, Albert Welti. It was in this spacious and elegant country home dating back to the seventeenth century, and still to be seen on Melchenbühlweg near Schloss Wittigkofen on the outskirts of Bern, that Hesse remained until the spring of 1919. These were grim years. Hesse's youngest son was seriously ill for more than a year. The war brought with it endless mental agony and even privation. An outspoken pacifist, Hesse eventually fell into serious disrepute. The death of his father proved a severe shock. His wife became deranged and began to spend most of her time in asylums. And Hesse himself was compelled to seek relief in psychoanalysis.[3]

Although Hesse was harassed incessantly, his prolificacy continued undiminished in Bern. His third *Künstlerroman*, *Rosshalde* (1914), foreshadowed the approaching impasse of his marriage, and *Demian* (1919), for which he received the *Fontanepreis*,[4] marked a turning point in his life. In 1915, *Unterwegs* was supplemented, and in 1916, *Musik des Einsamen*, a new volume of verse, was published. *Knulp* and *Am Weg* appeared in 1915, *Der Zyklon* in 1916, the stray items of *Kleiner Garten* and the *Märchen* in 1919. Although not published until 1920, *Heimkehr*, the first act of Hesse's only drama, his prose fragment, *Das Haus der Träume*, and *Im Pressel'schen Gartenhaus* were all written in Bern, as were all but two of the twelve items of *Sinclairs Notizbuch* (1923), and almost half of those in *Betrachtungen* (1928). *Kinderseele* and *Zarathustras Wiederkehr* were both finished in January, 1919. And during these same years, Hesse managed to help edit the *Deutsche Internierten-Zeitung* (July 1916 to December 1917), assisted in the preparation of its Sunday supplement, the *Sonntagsboten für die deutschen Kriegsgefangenen*, and continued to contribute reviews and shorter articles to many newspapers and periodicals.

Hesse left Bern in the spring of 1919 and wandered southward, "ein abgebrannter Literat," in quest of the solitude necessary to help reëstablish his bankrupt life. His wife remained in an asylum,[5] and his three sons were placed in the care of close friends. After a few weeks in Sorengo, he found the retreat he sought in the remote village of Montagnola. Here, in Casa Camuzzi, an ornate baroque edifice, he began painfully to take stock of himself, and to devote himself assiduously to his art. For almost four poverty stricken years Hesse lived like a hermit, and even thereafter, except for regular winter visits to Zürich, and for intermittent cures in Baden, he rarely left his new abode for any length of time. A brief interruption in this pattern of life, his marriage in December, 1923, to Ruth Wenger, daughter of the Swiss writer Lisa Wenger, was dissolved after a few months.

Casa Camuzzi, Hesse's home from May, 1919, to August, 1931,

has changed very little in the passing years. The four-room second-floor apartment in which he lived continues to be rented out by the Camuzzi family, and still contains some of Hesse's old furniture. Its lofty, turreted balcony still commands a sweeping view of nearby San Salvatore, the valley and Lake Lugano below, and of Mount Generoso in the distance.

In the *Weg nach Innen,* which is characteristic of this period, Hesse's art received a fresh impetus and assumed a new direction. The most productive years of his life ensued. The summer of 1919 was one of frenzied activity. *Klein und Wagner, Klingsors letzter Sommer,* and *Blick ins Chaos* followed one another in quick succession, and, as a diversion, he painted hundreds of water colors. *Siddhartha,* part one of which had been written in the closing months of 1919, was finally finished and published in 1922. *Kurgast,* recalling Hesse's two visits to Baden in 1923, appeared the following year, and *Nürnberger Reise,* the tart memoirs of a lecture tour through southern Germany in the autumn of 1925, was published in 1927. *Steppenwolf,* the most startling and controversial of Hesse's novels, appeared that same year. This was followed in 1930 by *Narziss und Goldmund,* the novel posterity may consider his best; and in 1932 (though completed in 1931) the fantasy, *Morgenlandfahrt,* appeared. A steady stream of verse accompanied this prose: *Gedichte des Malers* (1920), *Ausgewählte Gedichte* (1921), *Italien* (1923), *Verse im Krankenbett* (1927), the notorious *Krisis* (1928), and *Trost der Nacht* (1929). In addition, there were numerous very personal prose episodes and literary studies: *Wanderung* (1920), eleven of the many items in *Bilderbuch* (1926), a considerable portion of the *Betrachtungen* (1928), two-thirds of the *Traumfährte* (1945), and *Eine Bibliothek der Weltliteratur* (1929), a very intimate perusal of world literature. *Zum Gedächtnis unseres Vaters* (1930), *Diesseits* (1930), and *Weg nach Innen* (1931) were merely new collections of old material. In the midst of all this productivity Hesse managed to edit some twenty new books and to serve as co-editor of *Vivos Voco* (October 1919 to December 1921). He also contributed reviews regularly not only to this periodical (until 1923), but to the *Neue Rundschau,* the *Berliner Tageblatt,* the *Frankfurter Zeitung,* and the *Neue Züricher Zeitung.*

Thanks to the generosity of his close friend and patron, Hans C. Bodmer, Hesse was able to quit his Casa Camuzzi retreat in the summer of 1931, once more to have a home and a garden he could call his own. To Casa Bodmer, new-built, situated on a wooded hill within sight of Casa Camuzzi, Hesse brought his third and present wife, Ninon Ausländer, in November of that same year.

With the rise of Hitler's régime, Hesse's popularity in Germany again began to wane. During the First World War he had been branded a *Gesinnungslump* and *Vaterlandsfeind*. Now he became a *Judenfreund* and a *Volksverräter*. He was tolerated for a long while largely because he refrained from any public pronouncement of his antipathy toward the Third Reich. Finally, however, in 1943, his name was added to the official blacklist. Since 1945, Hesse has again become one of the most widely read and respected authors in Germany.

After the intense activity which began with *Klein und Wagner* and ended with *Morgenlandfahrt*, Hesse seemed almost to have exhausted his creative imagination. His later years have been marked more by effort than by spontaneity, more by persistence than by passion, and more by recollection than by new horizons. More than a decade was necesary to write the enigmatic and monumental *Glasperlenspiel* (1943), the only novel of this period. The major volume of verse published since 1931 is *Die Gedichte* (1942), Hesse's collected poems, which have been supplemented several times in more recent years. *Vom Baum des Lebens* (1934), *Neue Gedichte* (1937), *Der Blütenzweig* (1945), and *Jugendgedichte* (1950) are only minor collections of selected poems. The idyl, *Stunden im Garten* (1936), and the poetic episode, *Der lahme Knabe* (1937), both written in Greek hexameters, are the only verse publications which belong entirely to this period. These were published again as *Zwei Idyllen* in 1952.

Most of the many new collections of short stories, brief recollections, and articles are only re-publications of old material. Hesse's earliest works are represented in *Mahnung* (1933), *Kleine Welt* (1933), *Frühe Prosa* (1948), *Gerbersau* (1949), and *Die Verlobung und andere Erzählungen* (1951). *Wege zu Hermann Hesse* (1947), *Aus vielen Jahren* (1949), *Alle Bücher dieser Welt* (1950), *Lektüre für Minuten* (1949), *Glück* (1952), and *Hermann Hesse. Eine Auswahl* (1953), all afford sparse cross-sections of Hesse's lifetime work. The six volumes of *Gesammelte Dichtungen* (1952) represent the best, although still very incomplete publication of Hesse's collected works. *Haus zum Frieden. Aufzeichnungen eines Herrn im Sanatorium* (1947) was actually written in 1910, and the story *Freunde* (1949) was finished in 1909. Only eleven of the articles in *Krieg und Frieden*, published in 1946 and supplemented in 1949, belong to the Thirties and Forties. Two of the four items of *Dank an Goethe* (1946) were first published in the Twenties, and *Feuerwerk* (1946) was written in 1930. *Fabulierbuch* (1935) returns to the earliest period of Hesse's career. Most of the *Kleine Betrachtungen* (1941) were written almost as early. Ten of the seventeen recollections of *Gedenkblätter* (1937; supplemented in 1947), two of the five tales in *Der Pfirsichbaum und andere Erzählungen* (1945), and both landscape studies of *Berg und See* (1948), and *Erinnerung an André Gide* (1951) belong to the years since 1931. *Späte Prosa* (1951) and *Beschwörungen* (1955), diary-like miscellanies written from 1944 to 1950 and from 1947 to 1955 respectively, represent the major activity of Hesse's most recent years.

Recently, Hesse has also begun to publish some of his voluminous correspondence. *Briefe* (1951) includes a broad and fascinating selection of his letters from 1927 to 1950. *Eine Handvoll Briefe*, published the same year, is merely a briefer choice from this same period. And *Hermann Hesse/Romain Rolland. Briefe* (1954) presents a revealing interchange between these two kindred spirits from 1915 to 1940.

Hesse's fringe activities of the past twenty-five years reveal this same tapering-off. He continued to contribute reviews to the *Neue Rundschau* until 1936. His brief series of literary studies in *Bonniers Litterära Magasin* terminated that same year (1935-1936). However, occasional articles and reviews have continued to appear in the *Neue Züricher Zeitung*, and, since 1944, new poems and articles have been published quite regularly in the *Neue Schweizer Rundschau*. He has edited only about fifteen new books since 1931, and since 1945 this activity has ceased almost entirely.

Hesse's career has not been without its rewards. In 1936, Zürich honored him with the *Gottfried-Keller-Preis*. Frankfurt awarded him the *Goethepreis* in 1946, and that same year he received the Nobel Prize. In 1947, the University of Bern granted him an *Ehrendoktor*, and Calw made him its most illustrious *Ehrenbürger*. Braunschweig selected him for its *Wilhelm-Raabe-*

Preis in 1950, and in 1955, Hesse accepted his latest award, the *Friedenspreis des Deutschen Buchhandels.*

Despite this widespread and growing acclaim, Hesse has continued his humble way of life in remote Montagnola, still devoted to his art and patiently tending to his garden. When I paid him a brief visit in the summer of 1954, I found an elderly person, slight of figure, erect in his bearing, and slow but sure in his movements. A light summer suit and an open collar gave him a boyish appearance. The frank gaze of his blue eyes, the firm grasp of his hand, his slow smile, and the soft Swabian quality of his German, immediately put me at ease. As we talked, I was constantly reminded of Knecht's benign old *Musikmeister.*

HESSE AND HIS ART

I

A review of Hesse's prose and poetry reveals three distinct periods. Each represents a different stage in the course of the author's struggle with himself and with life as a whole, and each reflects a correspondingly different phase in his style. The first of these three periods, the two decades preceding *Demian* (finished in 1917), is one of uncertainty and vague presentiment. These are the early years of a sensitive outsider who cannot cope directly with his particular problem of existence. He resorts instead to fantasy and withdraws into the realm of beauty, there to indulge in the extremes of late nineteenth-century aestheticism. The first prose of these years (*Eine Stunde hinter Mitternacht*, 1899, *Hermann Lauscher*, 1901)[1] is enveloped in a perfumed melancholy. It is characterized by exclamatory remarks and rhetorical questions, by sensuous adjectives and adverbs in languid cadence. The form is loose, a random succession of vignettes and dramatic monologues held together primarily by their common spirit of decadent romanticism. *Eine Stunde hinter Mitternacht* is notable for its affected heroic pose, its pathos, profuse colors, and its muted sounds. *Hermann Lauscher,* a Hoffmannesque fusion of fantasy and reality, is both cynical and morbidly intimate. This is the work of a talented beginner whose world of experience is still too limited, and whose imagination is entranced by the facile flow of beautiful language. In the absence of discipline and restraint, the whole is sacrificed to the part, and what was meant to be art fails to become more than picturesque patter. It was not long before Hesse himself termed this mode of writing the *Theaterspielerei* of *Nervenkünstler,* and discounted it as:

> . . . krank, unverständlich und todeselend . . . alles klang wie ein spukhaft idiotisches Gewinsel, dessen Sinn nur besonderen Eingeweihten zugänglich war. Es tönte darin von Tempeln, Einsamkeiten, wüsten Meeren, Zypressenhainen, welche stets von einem zagen Jüngling unter schwerem Seufzen besucht wurden. Man begriff wohl, dass es symbolisch gemeint war, aber damit wenig gewonnen ("Karl Eugen Eiselein," *Nachbarn,* 1st. ed. [Berlin, 1908], p. 90).

Beginning with Hesse's determination to escape the isolation of the introverted aesthete, and with his consequent efforts in marriage to find a place for himself in the bourgeois world, this initial, emotionally intense romanticism yields abruptly to a hardier, more entertaining realism. *Peter Camenzind* (1904), *Gertrud* (1910), and to a lesser degree, *Rosshalde* (1914) continue the tradition of Keller's *Der Grüne Heinrich*. The many *Gerbersau Novellen*[2] (and even the more tragic school-novel, *Unterm Rad*, 1906), with their humorous and pleasantly ironic treatment of small-town life, are closely akin to the *Seldwyla* tales. The dream world of *Eine Stunde hinter Mitternacht* and *Hermann Lauscher* is succeeded by a more invigorating rustic reality. Hesse's characters become more human and less shadowy; inertia and desperation yield to movement and humor. His prose now achieves a more narrative style, and his language becomes more forceful, clearer, and crisper.

Of this first period from 1895 to 1916, the most representative poetic form is a three-quatrain poem, folksong-like in the simplicity and in the lyrical quality of its expression, *e.g.*:

Es nachtet schon, die Strasse ruht,
Seitab treibt mit verschlafenen Schlägen
Der Strom mit seiner trägen Flut
Der stummen Finsternis entgegen.

Er rauscht in seinem tiefen Bett
So wegverdrossen, rauh und schwer,
Als ob er Lust zu ruhen hätt',
Und ich bin wohl so müd wie er.

Das ist durch Nacht und fremdes Land
Ein traurig Miteinanderziehen,
Ein Wandern stumm und unverwandt
Zu zwei'n, und keiner weiss wohin.

("Nachtgang," *Die Gedichte* [Zürich, 1947] p. 133)

Decided preference is given to iambic tetrameter, and of diverse rhyme schemes, the alternate prevails. Imagery is as unsophisticated as form, syntax, and vocabulary. In the tradition of Romanticism, Hesse uses nature as a mirror for his moods and as a setting for his reflections. Late summer with its gentle, tired breezes, its wilted gardens, and slowly wandering clouds, is nearly spent. Autumn spreads its pall over mountain, valley, and forest. Lonely roads lead to remote and unfamiliar villages. A spirit of fatigue and melancholy pervades the atmosphere, and the prevailing silence is broken only by the murmur of a little stream, the sobs of a child, or the faint thud of falling fruit.

The nature-setting is usually presented in the first, sometimes in the first and second stanzas of a poem. Tersely sketched and faint, these descriptions are much less pictorial than evocative. The nostalgic, gloomy mood evoked is heightened by the use of faint and shadowy colors (*hell, bleich, blass, silbern, weiss, trüb, grau, dunkel, blau, schwarz*) languid adjectives (*allein, traurig, träg, schwer, müde, leise, fern, spät, fremd, schwül*), emotionally suggestive verbs (*wandern, erinnern, leiden, trauern, weinen, ruhen, neigen, klagen, schlafen, träumen*), and allusions to *Jugend, Heimweh, Sehnsucht, Einsamkeit, Schmerz, Welken, Ruhe, Tod, Nacht*, and *Grab*. The prevalence of long vowels in these adjectives, verbs, and nouns, Hesse's preference for verbs of description rather than of action, and his very frequent use of the verb *to be*, tend to retard the flow of the verse and to leave its rhythm slow and solemn, its tone modulated in accord with the mood of the setting.

Before the second stanza has concluded, Hesse himself appears upon the scene as a weary wanderer, a wistful observer, or a lonely dreamer. His element is the twilight and the night ("Nachtgang," p. 133). He moves across the dim landscape like the leaves before the wind ("Das treibende Blatt," p. 69). Few are the people he encounters and dark their dwellings ("Auf einer Nachtwanderung," p. 142). His friends are outcasts like himself ("Einsame Nacht," p. 122). Like theirs, his wandering is an endless quest for *Heimat* ("Abends auf der Brücke," p. 145). To the innocence and harmony of childhood, there is no return ("Wende," p. 83); and with love ("Der schwarze Ritter," p. 72) and close friendship denied him, life becomes little more than memory ("Schalflosigkeit," p. 203) and faint hope ("Über die Felder," p. 62). It is in this state of agitation that Hesse acknowledges the ultimate loneliness of the individual ("Im Nebel," p. 151), and that he becomes painfully aware of flux ("Kind im Frühling," p. 161). He begins to feel that life has now almost passed him by ("Wie kommt es," p. 60), and his thoughts linger over death. Perhaps only death can afford the *Heimat* denied by life ("Abends auf der Brücke," p. 145).

Such are the reflective notes upon which the poems characteristic of the years preceding 1917 end. Unfortunately, the transition from description to reflection is often unexpectedly abrupt, and the reflection itself is not always of a very poetic nature. Hesse frequently permits himself a too commonplace analogy with a concluding remark that may verge upon banality ("Sommerwanderung," p. 174). In most of these instances it would have been to greater advantage, poetically, simply to have omitted the last stanza. As it is, there are only a half-dozen or so purely descriptive two-quatrain poems (*e.g.*, "August," p. 56). These are among the finest of this early period, and the only poems in which Hesse does not immediately allude to himself.

Obviously, not all Hesse's earlier poetry falls within the general pattern just outlined. His very first poems (*Romantische Lieder*, 1899) lie only on its fringes. While the characteristic three-quatrain poem, iambic tetrameter and alternate rhyme are well represented, longer poems, many with irregular stanzas, mixed meters, and more complicated and irregular rhyme schemes are somewhat more common ("Grand Valse," pp. 12-13). The world of this poetry is no less removed from the beaten path than is its form. Neither knows much restraint. Not autumnal nature, sleepy hamlets and the weary wanderer are depicted, but a very romantic retreat of stormy seas and battle-fields, of temples and castles, of suffering kings and pale queens. This poetry of brilliant colors (*rotes Schloss, goldener Apfel, grüner Hungerblick, purpure Küsse, blaue Bäume*) and of exotic blooms (*Oleanderblüte, Hyazinth, Syringen, Astern, Feuernelken, Reseden, Akazien*) abounds with exclamation marks and restive dashes. It is most reminiscent of the art of *Eine Stunde hinter Mitternacht*. To this melodramatic fantasy a *heimatloses Königskind* retires from a world in which he finds himself an unhappy outsider ("Königskind," p. 35). Yet, despite all the pomp and ceremony of this earliest poetry, Hesse can only lament. It cannot be otherwise, for art is to him "Das Land der Heimatlosen,/ Das sonnenrote Reich der Kunst" ("Sarasate," p. 22). Although still young, he already appears exhausted in spirit ("Schauspiel," p. 14). Already he considers his life to be barren ("Geständnis," p. 18). Childhood has become a hypnotic memory and death a sentimental obsession ("Eine andre Welt," p. 46). It almost seems that Hesse had never, even as a youth, experienced a single surge of joy, which was not immediately dampened by dour reflection.

Hesse's occasional verse, the poems which owe their inspiration to Italy, those recalling his trip to the East (1911), and those which allude to the First World War, conforms even less to the characteristic three-quatrain pattern than the *Romantische Lieder*. Of the three dozen or so Italian poems, most of which were written from 1899 to 1902, the larger portion comprises longer poems, either with quite extended, irregular stanzas or with no stanza division at all. Iambic pentameter and rhymed couplets prevail. In these poems are recorded the highlights of the author's frequent trips to his favorite southern refuge. In a sauntering, conversational tone, unexpectedly playful upon occasion ("Venezianische Gondelgespräche," pp. 93-94), Hesse recalls the narrow streets and gables of Padua, the churches and ruins of Ravenna, the lacemakers of Burano, the harbor of Livorno, a storm in Spezia, Florence and her Lorenzo Medici, Chioggia's dead past, and a love affair amidst the beauties of Venice. He delights in the childlike nature, the carefree revelry of the Italians, and is reminded of his own happier childhood years, only to be made doubly aware of the problematic lot which has now become his. Only for brief moments can Italy quiet his yearning and alleviate his inner torment ("Piazzetta," p. 108). The *Heimat* Hesse seeks is no more to be found in the south than in the north ("Alpenpass," p. 224).

The East does not afford that sanctuary either ("Kein Trost," p. 195). While Hesse basks, or at least tries to bask, in the congenial atmosphere of Italy, he stands in awe of Asia with its turmoil of peoples, its stifling climate, and its primeval wilderness. In a casual diary-like manner, and principally in free verse (eight of fourteen poems), he traces the course of his trip from the coast of Africa and the oppressive desert terrain of the Red Sea to Ceylon, Singapore, Sumatra, and Colombo. He recounts such incidents as the pleasant relief in Ceylon after an endless ocean voyage; the monotonous throbbing of the ship's engines, sleepless nights; an ageless jungle river and the mournful evening chant of the frightened natives; a sedate oriental feast, a beautiful Chinese singer, and a twilight arrival in Colombo. As usual, however, the outside world and description are incidental to the inner world. The new background was but another change of setting for the continued drama of Hesse's *Ich.*

Like Goethe, a century before him, Hesse would not succumb to martial fervor. In 1914, as again in 1939, the fate of the German nation meant much to him, but the lot of humanity and a poet's supranational responsibility meant more. For the poet publicly to implore or to protest could only be futile. For him to acclaim, to foster the spread of misunderstanding and of hatred, was conveniently and unforgivably to capitulate to circumstances. He chose to remove himself from the fray, nurture his humane ideals, and patiently allow the maelstrom to exhaust itself. Except for a handful of articles and about two dozen poems, Hesse has never done otherwise. Although they deal with the war, these poems are not entirely out of keeping with the author's attitude. Most of the seventeen poems written during the First World War (fifteen in the autumn and spring of 1914-15) are expressions of anxiety rather than of protest. Thoughts linger with a friend in battle ("Denken an den Freund bei Nacht," p. 243). The tortures of war ("Herbsttag," p. 246) and even death are experienced empathically ("Tod im Felde," p. 248). He recalls a fallen comrade ("Einem im Felde gefallenen Freunde," p. 251). Some poems merely allude to the war ("Frühlingsmittag," p. 253) and others are ardent hopes for peace ("Friede," p. 245). Only once does anger break through the prevailing subdued and serious tone ("Am Ende eines Urlaubs," p. 264) ; and while five poems reflect a peculiarly enigmatic attitude toward the war, an ambiguity of mild abhorrence and hesitant acclaim ("Das Erlebnis," p. 243, "Bhagavad Gita," p. 245, "Herbstabend," p. 246, "Der Dichter," p. 248, "Kindern," p. 249), only two exhibit some of the patriotic bravado of the traditional *Kriegslied.*[3]

Although the half-dozen or more poems which recall the Second World War continue in this very personal vein, their thoughts and mood are far less contained. Older and more irritable, Hesse cynically deplores this repeated folly ("Der alte Mann," p. 411), disparages modern civilization ("Müssige Gedanken," p. 416), and is quite prepared to quit this life ("Leb wohl, Frau Welt," p. 425). Yet, notwithstanding this general disillusionment ("Oktober 1944," p. 427), Hesse never lost his faith in the wonders of reason and love, and never ceased to hope ("Dem Frieden entgegen," p. 431).

In terms of form, this small group of *Kriegslieder* is characterized by variety rather than by any one dominant pattern. Longer poems with irregular stanzas, others with six, five, or even two-line stanzas, and some with no stanza division at all, are intermingled with free verse and with poems consisting of four or five quatrains. Alternate rhyme is most prevalent, though couplets and mixed rhyme schemes are very common. While the iamb, with no marked preference for trimeter, tetrameter or pentameter, prevails in the poems of 1914-18, the trochaic tetrameter becomes the dominant meter of the poems of the Second World War.

It is significant to notice that in each of the four instances of deviation from the characteristic form (the early, romantic poems, the Italian poems, those of the Orient, and the war poems), there is a corresponding deviation of substance, which in turn reflects a brief divergence in the course of Hesse's life.

II

It was in this vein of poetic realism and plaintive lyricism that Hesse continued until his crisis of 1916-17. The decade to follow, the second of the three periods, marked the most dramatic and most critical years of his life. The war, and the tragic events in his family had brought with them an overwhelming accumulation of tensions. Hesse was now compelled to realize that in his desire to make existence less painful he had been avoiding a close look at the true nature of his inner discord, and had blinded himself to the morally and spiritually impoverished world around him. Like Veraguth (*Rosshalde*), Hesse left the comfortable fold of the bourgeois world, which had never afforded him the security, the "Stück Welt und Wirklichkeit" ("Geleitwort," *Eine Stunde hinter Mitternacht* [1941], p. 11) he had hoped it might, and accepted the more difficult existence of an outsider. In a desperate and determined attempt to find himself, he began systematically to diagnose his inner conflict, and to go his long-shunned *Weg nach Innen*. Only now did he finally come to grips with the intrinsic problems of human existence.

In Montagnola escape became quest, and in quest Hesse's inner problems resolved themselves into the basic *malaise humain*, into the tension between *Geist* and *Natur*. For years he had vacillated between these poles, acclaiming first one, then the other, then neither. Always he hoped for a harmonious accord, though well aware that for him this was impossible. In *Demian* (1919) he acclaimed the principle of *Geist*, with its *Selbsterkenntnis* and *Selbstverwirklichung*, and a Nietzschean emphasis upon the *Eigensinn* of the superior being. This was to culminate in the *Amor fati, Wille zum Leiden und Einsamkeit* of *Zarathustras*

Wiederkehr (1919). But *Geist* as a guiding principle of life could only mean greater individuation and more painful isolation; and as yet, Hesse lacked the firm conviction and the inner fortitude necessary to endure such consequences. The immediate reaction was as extreme as the initial impulse. The assertive Nietzschean activism yielded suddenly to a Schopenhauer-like passivity, a restless quest to a quietistic acceptance, and self-realization to a yearning for self-obliteration. *Natur* with its *Erleben* was as demanding and as impossible for Klein (*Klein und Wagner*, 1920) as was *Geist*, and respite was to be found only in the nirvana of a will-less *Sichfallenlassen*.

Hesse, however, was as ill-prepared to accept Klein's resolution as he had been to follow the path of Demian. Envisaging more possibilities and giving precedence neither to *Geist* nor to *Natur*, he proceeded with Klingsor (*Klingsors letzter Sommer*, 1920) to revel in the intoxication of both. Acknowledging the reality, the goodness and the necessity of both realms of experience, in *Siddhartha* (1922) he advanced yet another stage. Whereas Klingsor fails to emerge from his revelry, Siddhartha, exhausting and transcending both *das zufällige Ich der Gedanken* and *das zufällige Ich der Sinne*, achieves a *Seelenzustand* which knows only unity, affirmation, and humble service. *Kurgast* (1924), however, was a reminder that resolutions are more easily visualized than experienced. In a sober tone of acceptance, Hesse realized that despite all efforts to the contrary, his existence would probably continue as a restless tension, a constant vacillation between life's opposing poles. It is the most acute stage of this continued tension that is recorded in *Steppenwolf* (1927). In his own words, Hesse had reached another of those "Etappen des Lebens, wo der Geist seiner selbst müde wird, sich selbst entthront und der Natur, dem Chaos, dem Animalischen das Feld räumt" ("Nachwort," *Krisis*, p. 81). With his recuperation from this embittered and desperate state of mental exhaustion, this trying period of quest and indecision ended. A tired and wiser man, fully aware of the value and the necessity of humor, Hesse was at last prepared to accept *Geist*, that part of human nature so repeatedly deemed the very bane of existence during the difficult years immediately following *Demian*,[4] as his guiding principle.

The new, more vigorous approach to life of this second period, brought with it a new, more vigorous stage in Hesse's creative activity. The years from *Demian* to *Steppenwolf* were recklessly prolific. An abrupt change in both the substance and the style of his prose extended Hesse's literary horizons far beyond their previous conventional range. The course of this new, more dramatic phase of his writing became very unpredicatable, since it was characterized by spasmodic transition rather than by gradual progression.

With *Demian*, the once rather innocent *Unterhaltungs-schriftsteller* (*Traumfährte*, p. 108) suddenly became a disconcerting, problematic seeker whose complex expressionistic art all but defies satisfactory interpretation. The simplicity of language and clarity of thought which had become characteristic of Hesse's writings were now obscured in an atmosphere of Freudian symbolism. Hesse became so engrossed in his psychological self that his work tended more to suggest the effort of an analytic talent than that of a creative artist. *Demian* and the novella *Klein und Wagner* would almost prompt one to think of clinical reports. On the other hand, although obviously still under the influence of *Demian* and its symbolism, Hesse, in *Klingsors letzter Sommer,* returns to a decadent romanticism which suggests *Eine Stunde hinter Mitternacht*. The atmosphere is again scented, the scene removed and feverish; and although more vibrant and cohesive, the whole once more becomes a maze of melodramatic vignettes.

The unpredictable course of Hesse's art during this period is even more evident in the sudden transition from *Klingsors letzter Sommer* to *Siddhartha*. Intoxication and random spontaneity changes to contemplation and severe artistry. *Siddhartha* is classical in the symmetry of its form, in the stylized pattern of its expression, and in the lofty simplicity of its language. This is followed by an equally abrupt transition to the diary-like intimacy, the capricious, comic realism, and the acrid *leitmotif* technique of *Kurgast*. Even more startling are the extremes of *Steppenwolf*. Here Hesse's *Weg zu sich selber hin* reaches a climax in a fascinating confusion of symbol and irony, fantasy and realism.

While mood and sentiment had found ready expression in fixed stanzas, metrical patterns and rhyme schemes, intellectual experience and emotional distress were not to be contained by any traditional poetic restraints. The folksong-like poem, which was characteristic of the years preceding 1916, now yields to a restive prose verse, and dramatic situation replaces lyrical description. Accordingly, of the roughly one hundred and twenty-five poems written in the course of the subsequent decade, more than one-third are free verse, *e.g.*:

> . . . .
> Kinder sind wir, rasch macht die Sonne uns müd,
> Die uns doch Ziel und heilige Zukunft ist,
> Und aufs neue an jedem Abend
> Fallen wir klein in der Mutter Schoss,
> Lallen Namen der Kindheit,
> Tasten den Weg zu den Quellen zurück.
> Auch der einsame Sucher,
> Der den Flug zur Sonne sich vorgesetzt,
> Taumelt, auch er, um die Mitternacht
> Rückwärts seiner fernen Herkunft entgegen.
> Und der Schläfer, wenn ihn ein Angsttraum weckt,
> Ahnt im Dunkeln mit irrer Seele
> Zögernde Wahrheit:
> Jeder Lauf, ob zur Sonne oder zur Nacht,
> Führt zum Tode, führt zu neuer Geburt,
> Deren Schmerzen die Seele scheut.
> Aber alle gehen den Weg,
> Alle sterben, alle werden geboren,
> Denn die ewige Mutter
> Gibt sie ewig dem Tag zurück ("Die Nacht," pp. 266-267)

In general, this new form tends to be at least twice as long as the old with its three quatrains. Stanza division, when retained, is very irregular. Rhyme is continued, although quite without pattern. The syntax becomes more involved, and the vocabulary less evocative, more sober, and eventually quite common (*Trieb, Chaos, Fleisch, Luderleben, Maschinen, Geld, Fabriken; gierig, dreckig, neidisch, verflucht, verrückt, lasterhaft, teuflisch; hassen, lecken, brüllen, krepieren, saufen, stinken, speien*). Background imagery reveals just as decided a change. Nature is no longer a picturesque setting for a brief afterthought, but a casual reference point for more prolonged reflection ("Auch die Blumen," p. 270). In accord with this shift of emphasis from description and feeling to a more dramatic thought process, allusions to nature are now apt to be metaphorical or symbolical. As leaf upon leaf falls from Hesse's tree of life ("Vergänglichkeit," p. 284), he longs to experience all aspects of being; to die the death of a tree, a mountain, of sand and of grass; to be reborn a flower, a fish ("Alle Tode," p. 289). The moon and night, with its dreams of a lost childhood-*Heimat*, are associated with the sympathetic mother-principle. They become symbols of *Natur* ("Herbstabend

1918," p. 281). Day represents the stern father-principle, and the sun is *Geist* ("Die Nacht," p. 266).

During the first period of his career, Hesse was rarely given to metaphysical speculation. The painful facts of life (loneliness, flux, death) impressed themselves upon his soul, but little effort was made to delve into the nature of *being* and into the ultimate causes of suffering. He began to reflect seriously upon this problem in 1917. In the ensuing free verse, the *malaise humain* is attributed to the dichotomy of human existence and to the inherent flux of *being*. Immediately, Hesse acknowledges and accepts both the benign mother-principle (*Natur*), and the severe father-principle (*Geist*). Man essays the challenging, conscious heights of the latter, only to return to the enticing, oblivious repose of the former like a fatigued child to its mother ("Die Nacht," p. 266). During moments of greater despondency, however, when the natural inclination to seek refuge from the pain of awareness overwhelms Hesse, all woes are ascribed by him to the father-principle of law, perception, and individuation, and it is caustically repudiated ("Rückkehr," p. 278).

Just as distressing for Hesse as this suspension between life's two forces, is the incessant *becoming* of life ("Die Nacht," p. 266). To him existence is a painful experiencing of endless deaths and rebirths. While this flux is not to be stayed, the pain may be alleviated by a philosophical acceptance of the nature of things ("Auch die Blumen," p. 270), or by the realization that it is necessary to experience life in all its flux if one wishes to bring its poles closer together into a more bearable, harmonious interplay ("Alle Tode," p. 289). However, yet another and more enticing resolution presents itself. Indulging in the Sankhya system of Hindu philosophy, Hesse envisages a new *Heimat*, the soul-nirvana transcending both the realms of *Geist* and *Natur*, and all life's flux ("Media in Vita," p. 311). One had only to retire to one's innermost self. But Hesse was no Oriental.

A thoughtful, serious mood is evident even in Hesse's less philosophical free verse. Several poems are prayers and hopes in despair ("Gebet," p. 310) ; some are pleas and fantasies in fear and pain ("Krankheit," p. 309) ; others are scathing outbursts of anger ("Die Maschinenschlacht," p. 316), or serious thoughts of love ("Traum von dir," p. 314). A few are as conversational and diary-like as the free verse recording Hesse's trip to the Orient ("Heimkehr," p. 305). It can not be mere coincidence that most of the free verse written before 1916 (some thirty poems) is just as reflective in nature and as serious in mood ("Im Grase liegend," p. 216). Even then, intellectual experience and strong emotions chafed at the restraints of form.

In this relatively contained manner, Hesse continued for a number of years to ponder the lot of humanity and to reflect upon his personal problems. In his ascetic retreat at Casa Camuzzi, he seemed successfully to have reëstablished himself in life. However, it was only a matter of time before these very circumstances were to occasion a new crisis, before the metaphysical issues of the *Geist* and *Natur* dichotomy were to become a critical psychological fact. By 1926, seclusion had become stifling and sublimation was beginning to fail. *Geist* was dethroned. *Natur*, too long repressed, engulfed Hesse in a vengeful sensuality for almost an entire year. It is to this frantic interval that the poems of *Krisis* bear witness.

This unique collection consists mainly of free verse, embarrassing in its uninhibited intimacy. It is obviously the outburst of an imagination inflamed by frustration and obsessed by feelings of inadequacy and fear. Hesse flounders about feverishly in a mad vortex of dance halls, bars, and sex. He envies, and would be, a naïve *Naturkind*. He would play hot jazz and dance the shimmy ("Neid," *Krisis*, p. 28). He would be a rakish young man about town ("Bei der Toilette," p. 40), and experience sensual life in satiation ("Schweinerei," p. 58). Possessed by these impossible desires and tormented by his conscience ("Ahnungen," p. 67), Hesse becomes sardonic and despondent. The stench of life is unbearable ("Weinerlich," p. 64). He spares the smug bourgeois world no invective ("Missglückter Abend," p. 15). His self-disdain and self-disparagement know no bounds. In this bitter frame of mind, Hesse's ultimate recourse is cynical laughter ("Sterbelied des Dichters," p. 10) ; and his only hope for release is death ("Fieber," p. 53). However, the storm abates; he regains his equilibrium; *Geist* again prevails. And now, reconciling himself to this fitful vacillation between life's two poles, to being alternately saint and sinner, and convinced that even the most dissolute ordeals of *Natur* are also God's design, Hesse is prepared to experience and to exhaust whatever destiny may yet hold in store ("An den indischen Dichter Bhartrihari," p. 76).

Krisis is not a collection of pleasant verse, nor is it poetically of much significance. The subject matter is crude, the language

common, the emotions turbulent, and the thoughts undistilled.
It tries the very limits of poetry. However, much more vital to
Hesse than either poetic propriety, or his reception by the public,
was hope of his own rehabilitation through self-knowledge and
sincerity. *Krisis* was primarily meant to be therapeutic in
function. As such, it fulfills what Hesse himself has maintained to
be the first and most important function of all poetry:

> Ein Gedicht ist in seinem Entstehen etwas ganz Eindeutiges. Es
> ist eine Entladung, ein Ruf, ein Schrei, ein Seufzer, eine Gebärde,
> mit welcher die Seele sich einer Wallung zu erwehren oder sich
> ihrer bewusst zu werden sucht. In dieser ersten, ursprüng-
> lichsten, wichtigsten Funktion ist überhaupt kein Gedicht beurteil-
> bar. Es spricht ja zunächst lediglich zum Dichter selbst . . ."
> ("Schlechte Gedichte," *Betrachtungen*, p. 97).

At this time of personal crisis, Hesse could not continue to write
the *schöne Gedichte* expected by his public; he would not reduce
his poetry to palatable bonbons.

The period from 1916 to 1926 is not entirely one of severe
mental-emotional agitation and free verse. Moments of relative
equanimity, with their more conventional verse form, occur. At
such times, Hesse reverts to the romantic wanderer whose element is the night, the open road, and unfamiliar places ("Gang
am Abend," p. 268), who continues to be disturbed by the flux
of life ("Regenzeit," p. 274), and who is still very much concerned
with death ("Bruder Tod," p. 279). But *Heimat*, or release from
himself and his painful lot, is no longer Hesse's prime concern.
Only occasionally does he now yearn for the innocence and
harmony of childhood ("Verlorenheit," p. 270) or for the oblivion
of death ("Bruder Tod," p. 279), and never for the solace of belonging to the group. Indifferent to consequences, Hesse will
henceforth seek "mein eigen Glück, mein eigen Weh" ("Konzert,"
p. 272) rather than continue as a discontented observer, vainly
longing for "ein volles Glück" ("Geständnis," p. 18) not meant
for him.

Hesse has become aware of a greater significance for the
individual within the framework of reality. He no longer considers man as an unrelated unit in the scheme of things, but as an
integral part of the whole, a part, even, of its very creative force.
Not only is *das Ewige, das Wesen* ("Bekenntnis," p. 273) inherent in his being, but the world itself is his creation ("Die
Welt unser Traum," p. 280). Hesse's sole concern now is to heed

himself and to live his own life ("Gang im Spätherbst," p. 288);
and love alone will help him to find his place in reality and experience its oneness ("Nächtlicher Weg," p. 303).

The occasional poem written during the second period may
recall the background imagery ("Gang am Abend," p. 268), the
simplicity of expression, and the lyricism of some of Hesse's
earlier verse. However, more often than not, there is a definite
change in form, as one would expect from his continued emphasis
upon reflection. Mood had formerly found expression in three
quatrains; thought now usually requires four. Hesse continues
to use alternate rhyme but often replaces the iamb with a more
emphatic and forceful trochee and shows a slight preference
for pentameter rather than tetrameter ("Regenzeit," p. 274).
Finally, just as in the free verse of these years, a prose quality
detracts from the lyrical nature of the poetry ("Bekenntnis," p.
273), and nature is used as a mere reference point or dispensed
with entirely ("Bruder Tod," p. 279).

III

The excruciating catharsis of *Steppenwolf* and *Krisis* brought
to an end Hesse's period of distress and quest. He had come to
terms with himself; he was now to come to terms with life at
large. Quitting his hermitage, he remarried, and, in a more
philosophical spirit, allowed the third and last phase of his life
to take its more even course.

Hesse now approached the turning point beyond which *Werden*
becomes *Entwerden*. The self is slowly transcended and unity is
ultimately experienced:

> . . . so bedarf es für das Erlebnis, das ich meine, doch eben des
> hohen Alters, es bedarf einer unendlichen Sum.ne von Gesehenem,
> Erfahrenem, Gedachtem, Empfundenem, Erlittenem, es bedarf einer
> gewissen Verdünnung der Lebenstriebe, einer gewissen Hinfällig-
> keit und Todesnähe, um in einer kleinen Offenbarung der Natur
> den Gott, den Geist, das Geheimnis wahrzunehmen, den Zusam-
> menfall der Gegensätze, das grosse Eine" ("Aprilbrief," *Neue
> Züricher Ztg.*, April 29, 1952).

In quiet retirement and ever closer communion with nature,
struggle with himself and with the circumstances of life gradually subsides. Emotions are subdued, and thought yields to
contemplation. The schizophrenic *Steppenwolf*, with his somber
seriousness and his desperate gospel of humor, becomes a serene

Glasperlenspieler who knows the value of playful observation ("Entgegenkommen," p. 381) and for whom acceptance is that of faith and love. It is only now that Hesse at last finds the peace of sincere *Selbstbejahung* and *Lebensbejahung*.

A corresponding change can be detected in Hesse's prose of these latter years. While the *Geist* and *Natur* dichotomy continues to be the vital issue in his world of thought, it is no longer the acutely personal problem it once was. It is in the milder, the more detached manner of recollection, rather than in further quest, that the question is reconsidered in *Narziss und Goldmund* (1930). Both poles of life are again acknowledged and affirmed by Hesse, but his previous attitude of resignation to a life drawn from one extreme to the other, is supplanted by a new, more determined adjustment to life. Despite distractions, the individual must obey the prevailing impulse of his being. He must take that path which the predominant aspect of his nature impels him to choose. Neither the *Naturkind* nor the *Geistesmensch* can change his basic nature. Each must be prepared to suffer the lot of his kind, and for either to attempt, in curiosity or desperation, to do otherwise, is to foster a perpetual *Steppenwolf*-like dissension. Determined as he was to suffer this inner discord no longer, Hesse's future road was obvious to him; it could only be that of all *Morgenlandfahrer* (1932), the way of *Geist*.

Glasperlenspiel (1943) represents the final stage on this road. *Geist*, formerly stressed primarily in terms of the individual and of self-expression, is now finally viewed in terms of humanity and of self-justification. Cultivated for its own sake in a Castalia-like isolation from reality, *Geist* must remain sterile. Only when it becomes a vital factor in human existence, mellowed by a spirit of love, service, and sacrifice (as exemplified in Knecht's way of life), can *Geist* serve its true purpose.

In keeping with this new adjustment to life and more dispassionate attitude toward what he regards as its basic problem, Hesse's once explosive inspiration became more disciplined and his creative activity less impulsive and also less prolific. His writing reflects the slower and more orderly tempo of his life. It is now less dramatic in its tensions and much more narrative in its new, expansive nature. The atmosphere is less charged, the language is less constrained, the vocabulary is marked more than ever by poetic simplicity, while syntax becomes more playfully involved and symbolism even more prevalent and profoundly enigmatic. In all three of the remaining tales, a romantic spirit again prevails. But, purged of its decadence, it is now mature, mellow, wider in its scope, and deeper in its thought. Hesse is now less conscious of himself, and more conscious of his art. *Narziss und Goldmund,* while very modern in its psychological depth, belongs to German Romanticism's best tradition of story-telling, that of *Franz Sternbalds Wanderungen* and *Ahnung und Gegenwart. Morgenlandfahrt,* reverting briefly to the episodic-tale form most characteristic of the second period, is a playful fantasia which could have been written by Novalis and would have been acclaimed by Tieck. *Glasperlenspiel* immediately recalls Goethe's *Wilhelm Meister,* both in substance and in its structure and baroque proportions. A life-time's variety of artistic expression is culminated in this variegated work of art. It is romantic in its loose composition, in its fragmentary nature, in the naïveté of its idyllic setting, and in its efforts to give symbolic expression to the otherwise inexpressible. It is romantic in its dream, the glass-bead game with its idea of universal harmony.

While Hesse's prose passes through the three phases just outlined, the center about which his creative activity revolves remains constant. This center is the individual, opposed to society, its mores, and its institutions. The individual is, of course, Hesse himself. He recalls, nostalgically, the simpler years of childhood. He reëxperiences youth with its excruciating years of awakening. He portrays modern man, the intellectual and the artist in particular, within the framework of a declining culture. He shows the predicament of human nature in a disjointed age. For his subject he provides an ever-changing setting. The Occident yields to the Orient, commonplace reality to the magic realm of nowhere; and the Middle Ages and the distant future are as immediate and vital as the present. This fluid, diversified, and yet continuous whole represents the Odyssey of Hesse's *wandelndes Ich.* It is in this, its intimately egocentric nature, that his art bears the stamp of its age, an age of cultural decline, of spiritual and moral distress, and of extreme loneliness.

Like many of his fellow individualists, idealists, and humanitarians, Hesse was unwilling and unable to live in accord with the soulless mass civilization which seemed to be emerging from the decline. Between the age and its most sensitive spirits, there developed an antipathy which was to change the course of art.

The inner and outer tensions and the loneliness which are nor-
mally a part of the artist's lot became acute. Normal introversion
became impassioned introspection, and art began to lose that
balance between the *Ich* and the world which it needs in order
to reach its highest fulfillment. To such an extent was Hesse himself caught up in this trend, that *Bekennen* and *Aufrichtigkeit*,
not beauty, became the motivating factors in his creative activity.
His art became confessional in form and therapeutic in function,[7]
his contribution to what he himself has termed the *Übergangs-
literatur* of an *Übergangsperiode* (*Die Nürnberger Reise*, [1927],
p. 77).

While time alone will ultimately confirm or disprove Hesse's
severe, though perhaps ironic, criticism of his own art, the
inordinately egocentric nature of this art is an immediate and in-
escapable fact. Like a hall of mirrors, the author's works never
cease to reflect his own image. His pre-1917 heroes are made
of soft stuff. They are predominantly aesthetes who live only in
dreams, hopes, and anticipation, and who shrink before realization. Self-preoccupied, temperamental artists, they are paralyzed
by chronic indecision and indulge in romantic morbidity. They are
outsiders consumed by their own loneliness, misfits to whom the
ars vivendi and the *ars amandi* are foreign, timid souls who ask
too little of life, expect too much of it, and, hence, live in perpetual
frustration and disillusionment. Such is the nature and fate of
the sentimental cynic Lauscher, of the would-be *Naturkind*
Camenzind, of the timorous composer Kuhn (*Gertrud*), even
of the more resolute painter Veraguth (*Rosshalde*), and of the
more stoical wanderer Knulp. Such, too, was Hesse.

While Hesse's figure looms behind the person and fate of each
of his pre-*Demian* heroes, in the decade to follow, author and
hero gradually merge in a poetic, autobiographical fusion.
Wayward Klein, frenzied Klingsor, and, in particular, the
rheumatic *Kurgast* and the desperate *Steppenwolf* are almost
flesh of Hesse's person and spirit of his being. Now, like Hesse,
in serious quest of self-knowledge and of self-actualization, these
new heroes shed their lethargy and take fate by the forelock. The
outside world has more than ever become a mere setting for the
prolonged drama of Hesse's *Ich*.

It is only in *Siddhartha* and in his last novels, *Narziss und
Goldmund* and *Glasperlenspiel*, that Hesse seems to have managed
to extricate himself sufficiently from this engrossment with his

own immediate, personal problems to enable him to mold his art
with that care necessary to insure it, beyond all doubt, against the
wear of time and to give it some of the more universal implications inherent in all truly great art.

A new way of life and a different attitude toward its problems
again brought with them corresponding changes in the general
nature of Hesse's poetry. Turbulent intellectual-emotional experience had found its most ready expression in dramatic free
verse.[8] Quiet contemplation was to find its most characteristic
poetic form in reflective-narrative verse. These longer poems
average about thirty lines,[9] although they occasionally extend to
more than a hundred. They generally consist of long, irregular
stanzas or dispense with stanza division entirely, and are usually
in iambic pentameter, with mixed rhyme patterns, e.g.:

> Wie jede Blüte welkt und jede Jugend
> Dem Alter weicht, blüht jede Lebensstufe,
> Blüht jede Weisheit auch und jede Tugend
> Zu ihrer Zeit und darf nicht ewig dauern.
> Es muss das Herz bei jedem Lebensrufe
> Bereit zum Abschied sein und Neubeginne,
> Um sich in Tapferkeit und ohne Trauern
> In andre, neue Bindungen zu geben.
> Und jedem Anfang wohnt ein Zauber inne,
> Der uns beschützt und der uns hilft, zu leben.
>
> Wir wollen heiter Raum um Raum durchschreiten,
> An keinem wie an einer Heimat hängen,
> Der Weltgeist will nicht fesseln uns und engen,
> Er will uns Stuf' um Stufe heben, weiten.
> Kaum sind wir heimisch einem Lebenskreise
> Und traulich eingewohnt, so droht Erschlaffen;
> Nur wer bereit zu Aufbruch ist und Reise,
> Mag lähmender Gewöhnung sich entraffen.
>
> Es wird vielleicht auch noch die Todesstunde
> Uns neuen Räumen jung entgegen senden,
> Des Lebens Ruf an uns wird niemals enden . . .
> Wohlan denn, Herz, nimm Abschied und gesunde!
> ("Stufen," p. 419.)

Nature, although represented in sharper outline and greater
detail than before ("Durchblick ins Seetal," p. 403) now appears
less frequently. Dispassionate reflection with its more complex
syntax, deliberate vocabulary, and halting rhythm, becomes more
common ("Buchstaben," p. 382). At the height of Hesse's detachment, his thoughts soar to visions of the world's creation and of

the decline of the spirit which had found its ultimate expression in the Gothic cathedral and in the music of Bach. His poetry then becomes almost transfigured: lofty narrative in studied simplicity ("Orgelspiel," p. 395), or a play of symbols in a slow impelling sweep of sound and suggestion ("Zu einer Toccata von Bach," p. 383).

The more conventional quatrains of the last period follow this same trend. Except for the characteristic change from iambic tetrameter to the slower rhythm of iambic pentameter, the three-quatrain poem and the alternate rhyme of the first period again prevail. Autumn, wilted gardens, empty fields, winds, and rain continue to fascinate Hesse; but the once melancholy wanderer, to whom nature had been little more than a mirror for mood, is now an impassive observer, has himself become but a mirror ("Gedenken an den Sommer Klingsors," p. 352); and vague landscapes and silhouettes gradually give way to the more detailed descriptions of particular moments and situations ("Augenblick vor dem Gewitter," p. 371). Just as detached observation reaches a climax in dispassionate, purely descriptive, lyrical poetry, so does Hesse's detached review of life's basic problems culminate in dispassionate, purely reflective lyrical poetry ("Klage," p. 380); and as his thoughts again rise to visions, only symbol remains to give them expression ("Das Glasperlenspiel," p. 391).

Following *Krisis*, Hesse's continued preoccupation with the flux of *being* and the dichotomy of existence reverted to its earlier metaphysical plane. Man is again a child of nature whose destiny is the realm of *Geist* ("Besinnung," p. 376), a discordant composite ("Doch heimlich dürsten wir," p. 381) prey to life's relentless flux ("Klage," p. 380). However, Hesse no longer felt that he must try, through philosophical speculation, to make these circumstances of life more tolerable. The acceptance of life for which he had so long and vainly sought, he now found in religious experience, namely, faith in the ultimate meaningfulness of life. This faith now made possible that love which can bring order into chaos, alleviate anxiety and loneliness, reconcile *Geist* and *Natur* ("Nachtgedanken," p. 408), and through which life's flux can be acclaimed ("Stufen," 419).

In memory and dream, Hesse had long clung to the *Heimat* which he had lost with his childhood. He had hoped to find this *Heimat* again in the worship of beauty and of nature, and long anticipated it in death, and had sought it in philosophical speculation. At the end of his quest, he found, not the oblivious harmony so long pursued, but the conscious harmony of man's second stage of innocence and grace.[10] Life itself had become his refuge.

In Hesse's first period, as we have seen, evasive groping characterized his adjustment to life, and vague presentiment distinguished his insight into his inner discord. His creative mood was languid and sentimental. The prose of these years was traditional, even imitative, with a distinctly lyrical quality. His most characteristic poetic expression was a lyrical, unsophisticated three-quatrain poem in which, against an evocative, autumnal background, he reflected briefly upon loneliness, flux and death. The second period, 1916 to 1926, was one of self-imposed isolation. Through exhaustive self-analysis, Hesse resolved his inner discords and came to terms with himself. He now worked in a tense and serious mood. His prose became more original, modern, and decidedly dramatic. His intellectual experience and violent emotional distress found their most ready expression in dramatic free verse where syntax was more complex, vocabulary less romantically evocative, and nature but a reference point for prolonged reflection. In his last period, quiet years of final adjustment, Hesse learned to accept and to affirm both himself and life. He became less concerned with himself and more concerned with humanity and with the individual's obligations to humanity. His creative mood became sober and tranquil. In its new expansiveness and measured tread, his prose assumed a truly epic quality. And in the more dispassionate detachment of these years, his verse took on a longer, reflective-narrative form, language was freed of all sentimental and dramatic dross, and he achieved a classical lucidity. One of Hesse's greatest consistencies was the life-long, immediate correspondence between his personal and his artistic development.

HESSE AND HIS AGE

Den ewigen Bildern treu, standhaft im Schauen
Stehst du zu Tat und Opferdienst bereit.
Doch fehlt in einer ehrfurchtlosen Zeit
Dir Amt und Kanzel, Würde und Vertrauen.

Dir muss genügen, auf verlorenem Posten,
Der Welt zum Spott, nur deines Rufs bewusst,
Auf Glanz verzichtend und auf Tageslust,
Zu hüten jene Schätze, die nicht rosten.

Der Spott der Märkte mag dich kaum gefährden,
Solang dir nur die heilige Stimme tönt;
Wenn sie in Zweifeln stirbt, stehst du verhöhnt
Vom eigenen Herzen als ein Narr auf Erden.

Doch ist es besser, künftiger Vollendung
Leidvoll zu dienen, Opfer ohne Tat,
Als gross und König werden durch Verrat
Am Sinne deines Leids: an deiner Sendung.
("Der Dichter und seine Zeit," *Gedichte* [1947], p. 352)

Hesse's general attitude toward his age, namely his judgment of modern Western civilization, his conception of the predominantly bourgeois society of our era, his digression as a humanitarian into the field of politics, and his crusade as a pacifist against the folly of warfare, reminds one of Schiller's familiar admonition: "Lebe mit deinem Jahrhundert, aber sei nicht sein Geschöpf, leiste deinen Zeitgenossen aber, was sie bedürfen, nicht was sie loben."[1] This doctrine might be termed the guiding principle of Hesse's persistent denial of our modern cultureless civilization, of his castigation of its bourgeois nucleus, and of his adamant adherence to his own ideals and way of life. That such an attitude would court the disapproval of his age, and that he might be repudiated and ignored by his fellow men, could not deter Hesse from his determination to give uncompromising expression to his convictions.

> Unser Verhalten gegen alle wirklichen Werte des Menschen ist von einer Barbarei und Roheit, wie sie die Welt seit Jahrhunderten nicht mehr gesehen hat. Dies zeigt sich in unserm Verhalten zur Religion, in unserm Verhalten zur Kunst, in unserer Kunst selbst. Denn die beliebte Meinung, dass die Kunst des modernen Europa auf einer ungeheuer hohen Stufe stehe, ist ebenso ein Irrtum der Bildungsphilister wie die Meinung vom

Vorhandensein einer hochstehenden und Respekt verdienenden *Kultur* unserer Zeit ("Weihnacht," 1917, *Krieg und Frieden* [1949], pp. 41-42).

This fervor and absolute conviction characterize Hesse's conception of our modern world. For him, just as for the romanticist who lives only in the glorious past and the ideal future, the present appears spiritually and culturally hopeless. Our era is one of moral depravity and intellectual mediocrity, of surface glitter, smug comfort, sham conventionality, and foolish optimism. It is a materialistic age where science has become a religion and the ultimate criterion of value is function. Man has lost his soul in this world of money, machines, and distrust. He has exchanged his spiritual peace for physical comfort. Like a will-less automaton, he is swept along by the scientific forces which he has set loose. He has become a mere "Frommer des Fortschritts" (*Bilderbuch*, p. 224), a worshipper of the slide rule. With his imagination stinted and his feelings stifled, he no longer appreciates beauty, nor is he capable of artistic creation. All vital rapport with God and with nature has been lost, reason has supplanted faith, and society has forgotten that "jedes Menschen Geschichte ist wichtig, ewig, göttlich. . . .In jedem ist der Geist Gestalt geworden . . ." (*Demian* [1919], p. 10). Hesse would attribute these deplorable circumstances of Western civilization to two prevailing aberrations: "dem Grössenwahn der Technik und dem Grössenwahn des Nationalismus" (*Krieg und Frieden* [1949], p. 211).

In this best of all worlds, the anaemic European represents our finest specimen. Our age has left its unmistakable imprint upon his soul: "Seine Augen sind blass und schwächlich, sein Gesicht blickt böse und traurig, kein heller Klang geht von ihm aus: Gewiss, es ist nicht richtig mit ihm—" (*Krieg und Frieden*, p. 65). However, to Hesse's even greater chagrin, the most prevalent and most acclaimed type of modern humanity is the bourgeois. A stalwart and stodgy nonentity, he is governed in all his ideals and pursuits solely by the impulse of self-preservation. He fears individuation, and deliberately sacrifices the precarious but precious intensities of life for comfort and security: "statt Gottbesessenheit erntet er Gewissensruhe, statt Lust Behagen, statt Freiheit Bequemlichkeit, statt tödlicher Glut eine angenehme Temperatur" ("Tractat vom Steppenwolf," *Steppenwolf* [1931], p. 16). The middle-class core of our civilization has always been the butt of Hesse's ire. The bourgeois represents all that is negative. He is the characterless Philistine who epitomizes mediocrity, cowardice, compromise, irresponsibility, and servility. He is the strapping, insensitive physical specimen who exudes health and wealth but lacks all culture. He has a sound appetite but no taste, a great deal of confidence but no ideals. He possesses a surfeit of zeal and diligence but has no lofty aspirations or worthy goals. It is to him that the world belongs, while the sensitive worshipers of beauty (Hermann Lauscher), the children of nature (Knulp, Peter Camenzind), and the earnest seekers after truth and the meaning of life (Demian, Harry Haller, Josef Knecht) are outcasts and lonely wanderers. At times, Hesse is so exasperated by this bourgeois fellow that he would contest his very reality. More frequently, however, his pique is vented in witty characterizations which are tinged with a Keller-like irony and faint malice. Nevertheless, Hesse's attitude toward the bourgeois is no less ambiguous than Thomas Mann's. He is attracted almost as much as he is repelled. In his berating there is much self-criticism, and his animosity is not without envy.

Our world is as unsatisfactory for the protagonists of Hesse's stories as it was for himself. Restless Peter Camenzind, robust in body but hypersensitive in spirit, tosses about on the sea of life like a ship without a rudder. Modern society is shallow and hypocritical. Its pursuits are frantic and futile, and its intellectuals and artists have become irresponsible dilettantes. A stranger in this cultural vacuum, Camenzind turns for sustenance to a gospel of nature and love, only to withdraw soon thereafter to the complete seclusion of his mountain birthplace. Like Camenzind, Kuhn (*Gertrud*) and Veraguth (*Rosshalde*) exist only on the fringes of modern society. They, too, are bewildered and disillusioned *Zaungäste* who grope about helplessly with only their souls to guide them in a soulless world. Knulp, the vagabond wanderer, is the romantic *Taugenichts* who refuses to sell himself to constraining bourgeois society; and Sinclair (*Demian*) is determined to free himself from its traditional religious and moral shackles. Klein is a traitor to the bourgeois cause; and mad Klingsor, completely emancipated, lives as he wills in a fantastic world of his own creation. The world of the *Kindermenschen* holds only a brief attraction for protean Siddhartha, and the testy *Kurgast* sits at its edges, scoffing at its idols.

In his delineation of Harry Haller's fate, we see Hesse's most acrid indictment of the modern era. Western civilization with its "verlogenen und gemeinen blechernen Jahrmarktglanz" (*Steppenwolf*, p. 42) is a sham world where music has become a "Schweinerei" (p. 60) and where existence is possible only for "Politiker, Schieber, Kellner und Lebensmänner" (p. 192). Modern culture is nothing but a cemetery of lifeless values and ideals: "Ein Friedhof war unsre Kulturwelt, hier waren Jesus Christus und Sokrates, hier waren Mozart und Haydn, waren Dante und Goethe bloss nur erblindete Namen auf rostenden Blechtafeln, umstanden von verlegenen und verlogenen Trauernden, die viel dafür gegeben hätten, wenn sie an die Blechtafeln noch hätten glauben können, die ihnen einst heilig gewesen waren . . ." (pp. 81-82).

Like Knulp, Goldmund cannot long tolerate the stifling atmosphere of the bourgeois world, and his biting appraisal of the *Sesshaften* echoes Haller's sentiment at its worst: "Alle waren sie vergnügt oder beschäftigt, hatten es wichtig, hatten es eilig, schrien, lachten und rülpsten einander an, machten Lärm, machten Witze, zeterten wegen zwei Pfennigen, und allen war es wohl, sie waren alle in Ordnung und höchlich mit sich und der Welt zufrieden. Schweine waren sie, ach, viel schlimmer und wüster als Schweine" (*Narziss und Goldmund* [1931], p. 237). The fantastic flight through time and space of H. H. and his fellow *Morgenlandfahrer*, and the withdrawal of the *Glasperlenspieler* into their ideal Castalia, are only more subtle, but no less resolute rejections of our bourgeois age.

Glasperlenspiel represents Hesse's final, most detailed, and most mature scrutiny of our period. Looking back from a distant future, he notes that our civilization had run its course and was fast approaching cultural bankruptcy. The bourgeois age had long made a fetish of individualism, had long basked self-satisfied in its mediocrity, and was still given to materialism and utilitarianism; but it could no longer find comfort in its concept of progress. Its old-time optimism, despite continued prosperity, began to yield to disillusionment and pessimism. An *Untergangsstimmung* beset the age, and a desperate futility was reflected in all its pursuits. Most characteristic of the cultural climate was the ceaseless flow of inferior newspapers, magazines, and pamphlets, featuring the most sensational trivia and catering to an escapist reading public. Not journalists alone, but scholars and writers prostituted themselves to the ever-declining intellectual *niveau*. Writing anecdotes and publishing letters became their favorite pastime. Their intellectual prowess was wasted on such efforts as *Nietzsche und die Frauenmode um 1870* and *Die Rolle des Schosshundes im Leben grosser Kurtisanen* (*Glasperlenspiel* [1943], Vol. 1, 29). Incompetence and inefficiency were prevalent on all sides. While chemists and musicians propounded political theories, poets and actors devoted their interests to the merits of bachelorhood and the causes of financial crises. Institutions of learning had become mere means to questionable ends: "auf raschen und leichten Gelderwerb, auf Ruhm und Ehrungen in der Öffentlichkeit, auf das Lob der Zeitungen, auf Ehen mit den Töchtern der Bankiers und Fabrikanten, auf Verwöhnung und Luxus im materiellen Leben" (Vol. 1, 51). Religion and morality had fallen by the wayside. Meanwhile, the intelligentsia and the masses alike, with fear of death and pain lurking in their hearts, sought a childish oblivion in intricate card games, complicated cross-word puzzles, and frantic music. Cultural twilight was rapidly approaching. It was an era of general bewilderment, growing cynicism, and desperate escapism: "Es waren heftige und wilde Zeiten, chaotische und babylonische Zeiten, in welchen Völker und Parteien, Alt und Jung, Rot and Weiss einander nicht mehr verstanden" (Vol. 2, 121).

With the passing of years, Hesse was gradually compelled to realize that his early idea of a return to nature, to simplicity, and to the way of love and service exemplified by St. Francis of Assisi, was hardly a practical answer to the world's ills. Our culture was mortally sick. Remedial measures could only prolong its agony; they could never afford a cure. Death and rebirth were necessary and impending. After much warfare and anarchy our civilization would go the way of all civilizations, and from its ashes would rise a new and better tomorrow, a second Middle Ages, the *âge d'or* envisaged by Novalis: "Wenn nicht mehr Zahlen und Figuren/Sind Schlüssel aller Kreaturen."[2] It is such a world to which the *Morgenlandfahrer* aspire and which is ultimately realized in Castalia.

No great perspicacity is required to perceive the exaggerated severity of Hesse's attitude toward modern Western civilization and its bourgeois nucleus. Intensely disturbed by the crassness and the inhumanity of our age, and determined to discredit its golden calves, the machine and the practical sciences, Hesse simply would not, or could not contain his criticism. In his intemperate reaction to the existing tendency to equate immediate usefulness with ultimate value, he frequently gives expression to an attitude which is perhaps equally untenable: "Je unnützer eine Kunst, je weniger sie irgendwelchen Notdürften dient, je mehr sie den Charakter des Luxus, des Müssiggangs, der Kinderei an sich trägt, desto lieber ist sie mir" (*Feuerwerk*, p. 10). The innumerable generalizations which he permits himself are hardly more valid—"Wissenschaft hat noch niemand glücklich gemacht" (*Dürerbund Flugschrift* [1905], p. 7)—and are frequently more melodramatic than analytical:

> Hinter der Zivilization her ist die Erde voll Schlackenbergen und Abfallhaufen . . . folgen ihnen Heere von Bergwerksarbeitern mit blassen Gesichtern und Hungerlöhnen, es folgen ihnen Krankheiten und Verödung; und dass die Menschheit Dampfmaschinen und Turbinen hat, dafür zahlt sie mit unendlichen Zerstörungen im Bilde des Menschen, dafür zahlt sie mit Zügen im Gesicht des Arbeiters, mit Zügen im Gesicht des Unternehmers, mit Verkrümmungen der Seele, mit Streiken und Kriegen, mit lauter schlimmen und abscheulichen Dingen. Während dagegen dafür, dass der Mensch die Violine erfunden und dafür, dass jemand die Arien im *Figaro* geschrieben hat, keinerlei Preis bezahlt werden muss (*Feuerwerk*, p. 9).

Hesse's unconditional denial of modern science and his pungent arraignment of the bourgeois stratum of our civilization, like Nietzsche's repudiation of Christianity and disparagement of the *Herdenmensch*, cannot bear an examination as to detail. Neither writer, however, was intent upon a minute diagnosis, factual in all its particulars. The world was obviously out of joint. Bold poses and grand gestures might set it right, whereas point-by-point criticism would surely fall upon deaf ears. At any rate, exaggeration does not invalidate the cause, but only serves to emphasize it.

While his attitude toward the bourgeoisie and its civilization did little to endear Hesse to his German Philistines, his rôle in the First World War managed eventually to arouse the open hostility of his less humane and less international minded compatriots. At the outset of hostilities, while he was still a citizen of Germany although a resident of Switzerland, Hesse reported for service to the German consulate in Bern. Rejected because of his age, ill health, and family, he decided to help alleviate the wretched lot of the German prisoners of war in France. From July, 1916, to December, 1917, the very months during which his own physical and mental health was in jeopardy, he managed to serve as co-editor of the *Deutsche Internierten-Zeitung*, and even to collaborate in the preparation of its Sunday supplement, *Sonntagsboten für die deutschen Kriegsgefangenen*. From 1918 to 1919, with Richard Woltereck, Hesse spent much of his time editing the *Bücherei für deutsche Kriefsgefangene* (Vols. 1-22). Had his participation in the war been limited to these activities, he would certainly not have become suspect in Germany.

During the first year and a half of the war, Hesse's own literary work, though slightly more suspicious, gave the Germans just as little cause for offense. His few poems dealing with the war are, mainly, very personal expressions of anxiety, empathic experiences, and prayers for peace. Some manifest a peculiar ambiguity of mild acclaim and disclaim. Although war is generally disparaged, in no instance is Germany itself taken to task, and upon two occasions, the sentiment of the traditional German *Kriegslied* becomes unmistakable.[3] In "O Freunde, nicht diese Töne!" (*Neue Züricher Zeitung*, Nov. 3, 1914), the first of the nine so-called political essays written during the war years, Hesse again disparages warfare and espouses the ideal of peace on earth and good will among men. His main argument, however, is directed less against war itself than against those intellectuals and artists who have chosen to enter the fray in protest, and those who, yielding to expediency, are bent upon extending misunderstanding and hatred into the realms of thought and of art. Inasmuch as the more humane and international minded faction of society could hardly expect its supplications to end the war, it might be wiser for its members to think about the future betterment of international relations. And this, in Hesse's opinion, was very much contingent upon the strict neutrality of those who hoped to see this betterment come about. Nevertheless, Hesse is very careful to assure the Germans: "Ich bin Deutscher, und meine Sympathien und Wünsche gehören Deutschland . . . Ich bin der letzte, der in dieser Zeit sein Vaterland verleugnen möchte . . ." (*Krieg und Frieden* [1949], pp. 13-16). Those Germans who had nevertheless begun to suspect his loyalty to their cause must have been pleasantly surprised by his unusually warm review of Max Scheler's nationalistic *Der Genius des Krieges und der deutsche Krieg* (Leipzig, 1915),[4] and Hesse's quarrel with the pacifist movement ("Die Pazifisten," *Die Zeit*

[Wien], Nov. 7, 1915) could only make him even more pleasing in the eyes of his countrymen.

Goethe seems to have been Hesse's chief inspiration for the ideal of humane neutrality to which he aspired during the earlier months of the war. His defense of Goethe against those ultra-patriotic Germans who were inclined to look askance at the poet's withdrawal during the Wars of Liberation and disapprove of his refusal to indulge in invective and patriotic song, is no less a vindication of himself:

> Goethe war nie ein schlechter Patriot . . . Aber über die Freude am Deutschtum, das er kannte und liebte wie nur einer, ging ihm die Freude am Menschentum. Er war ein Bürger und Patriot in der internationalen Welt des Gedankens, der inneren Freiheit, des intellektuellen Gewissens, und er stand in den Augenblicken seines besten Denkens so hoch, dass ihm die Geschicke der Völker nicht mehr in ihrer Einzelwichtigkeit, sondern nur noch als untergeordnete Bewegungen des Ganzen erschienen ("O Freunde, nicht diese Töne!" *Krieg und Frieden*, pp. 17-18).

However, where Goethe's attitude was resolute and consistent, Hesse's was weak and wavering, and in this uncertainty, became strangely ambiguous. He could not maintain his neutrality, nor would he renounce his supranational ideals. With this in mind, the appropriateness of Romain Rolland's warm tribute to Hesse in April, 1915, becomes rather questionable: "Mais de tous les poètes allemands, celui qui a écrit les paroles les plus sereines, les plus hautes, le seul qui ait conservé dans cette guerre démoniaque une attitude vraiment goethéenne, est . . . Hermann Hesse."[5] While undoubtedly valid today, this analogy was decidedly premature at the time.

Hesse's subsequent year and a half of silence was a period of reconsideration, and the beginning of his *Erwachen*. Only now did he begin seriously to take stock of himself and the world situation. Of the eight remaining essays written during the war, four belong to the latter half of 1917 and the others to the first seven or eight months of 1918. Whereas Hesse had once been able flippantly to proclaim, "Da man jetzt einmal am Schiessen ist, soll geschossen werden-" ("O Freunde, nicht diese Töne!" p. 16), he now has but one passionate desire, the immediate and unqualified termination of the purposeless slaughter ("An einen Staatsminister," Aug., 1917). Once willing to acknowledge an ideological justification for the war, Hesse now recants. Indefinite continuation of hostilities can only bring

economic ruin to all participating nations and hasten the advent
of a morally and intellectually bankrupt political-military state,
where the individual, stripped of all human dignity, cannot live
without his *Existenzbewilligung* nor die without his *Sterbekarte*
("Wenn der Krieg noch zwei Jahre dauert," late 1917). In
1914, Hesse had simply been exceedingly troubled by the hypoc-
risy of the fair-weather friends of internationalism, and very
disturbed by the prevalent boycotting of foreign art. By 1917,
he was prepared not only to remind the German intelligentsia of
its shameful neglect of its own humanizing art ("An einen
Staatsminister") and to confront it with the more serious hypoc-
risy of its sentimental lip service to Christianity ("Weihnacht,"
Dec., 1917), but also to condemn statesmen and generals alike
for their "gelogene idealistische Phrasen" ("Soll Friede werden?" Dec., 1917, p. 49). Well-meaning intellectuals once be-
rated for their vain intercession—"Als ob ein Künstler oder
Literat, und sei er der beste und berühmteste, in den Dingen des
Krieges irgend etwas zu sagen hätte." ("O Freunde, nicht diese
Töne!" p. 15)—are now exhorted to action: "Rühren wir uns
also! Bekunden wir doch unsere Friedensbereitschaft auf jede
Weise!" ("Soll Friede werden?" p. 49).

Hesse's last four wartime essays are much more contained,
less acrid in tone, and far less aggressive in nature. Looking
into the future, he sees dark things to come. In the completely
militarized state of 1925, the relatively cultured and humane
Vorkriegsmensch will have become a relic of the past, and all
those who are no longer of any use to the cause will simply be
liquidated ("Wenn der Krieg noch fünf Jahre dauert," Aug.,
1918). Looking into the more distant future, he envisages the
final, foolishly heroic days of warfare, God's ultimate disgust,
a second Deluge, and the beginning of a new age in which the
tragically comic European with his destructive intellect will no
longer be a threat, but will serve only as a warning from the dim
past ("Der Europäer," Jan., 1918). In his "Traum am Feier-
abend" (March, 1918), Hesse merely indulges in pleasant reverie,
and "Krieg und Frieden" (Summer, 1918) represents an exegesis
of the Sixth Commandment.

In the immediate postwar period, Hesse continued this mod-
erate berating and exhorting. In "Weltgeschichte" (Nov., 1918),
he cautions against the traditional tendency to overestimate the
significance of the external world of newspapers, politics, and
wars, and to remain oblivious to the greater reality of the inner

world, and against the irresponsible shifting of allegiance from old to new political ideologies without the necessary, prior and corresponding inner changes. In "Das Reich" (Dec., 1918), he reminds Germany of the cultural heritage she thoughtlessly forsook for machines, material wealth, political power, and for ultimate war, and advises her to begin her regeneration by a sincere self-analysis and self-acceptance. It is upon this theme of acceptance that Hesse continues to dwell in "Der Weg der Liebe" (Dec., 1918). Germans are admonished to put aside all their self-righteous indignation, their hatred, end their smoldering thoughts of revenge, to cease their theatrical worship of heroism, and to counter their adversity with love and a religious acceptance of fate; for only in this manner is the trust and good will of the rest of the world to be regained. And while, in its necessary reassessment of values, the nation as a whole will have to learn about the powers of love, the individual will have to begin, paradoxically, to recognize the importance of much misunderstood self-love ("Eigensinn," 1919).

This gradual shift of attention from the international and national plane to the level of the individual, and from the outer to the inner world, culminates in "Zarathustras Wiederkehr" (1919), Hesse's most impassioned and direct appeal to German youth. Published anonymously, for fear that it might otherwise be ignored, and put in a Nietzschean guise to make it immediately attractive, this manifesto represented a bold and unequivocal challenge. Youth is enjoined to discontinue all traditional escapist activities, to cease its childish wailing and gnashing of teeth, its concern for, and identification with its Fatherland, and its promotion of *Weltverbesserung*. Each person should henceforth concentrate solely upon himself, learn to know and to accept himself, and thereby to know and to accept his fate. For each is his own fate. Each person must learn to suffer, and thereby to live, for to live is to suffer. Only in loneliness can one expect to find one's own fate, live one's own life, and die one's own death. A nation of children is exhorted to become a nation of men.

After "Zarathustras Wiederkehr," Hesse's renewed appeal to Germany's youth to go its *Weg nach Innen* ("Brief an einen jungen Deutschen," 1919) is quite anti-climactic, as, too, is his continued censure of our Western world's persistent disregard for the Sixth Commandment ("Du sollst nicht töten," 1919), and his reiteration of "Lernet euer Leben zu leben! Lernet euer

Schicksal erkennen!" ("Chinesische Betrachtung," 1921). Except for the faintest of allusions to politics and war in "Weltkrise und Bücher" (1937), and in "Blatt aus dem Notizbuch" (1940), Hesse now lapsed into silence and did not begin again to address himself publicly to Germany until after the Second World War.

Until 1914, Hesse was decidedly less conscious of the political and social world about him than of art and the immediate circumstances of his own existence. Although he had helped to found the periodical, *März* (Leipzig), in 1907, together with Ludwig Thoma, Albert Langen, and Kurt Aram, and had continued as a co-editor until 1912, he had devoted himself exclusively to literary matters and had never actively associated himself with the periodical's vigorous crusade against the despotism of Wilhelm II, the militarism of the Empire, and the reactionary *Junkertum* of Prussia. His long association with the politically very active *Simplicissimus* was just as unpolemic in nature.[6] Like many other German intellectuals of the day, Hesse had preferred to leave politics to the politicians and the world to itself. It required the "sogenannte grosse Zeit" (*Traumfährte*, p. 103) to startle him from his retreat, to make him acutely conscious of the plight of our Western world, and to persuade him finally to examine the political field. His subsequent expostulations were not those of a zealous reformer of political and social institutions, but those of a contrite humanitarian. They were moral appeals to the individual. This emphasis upon the individual reflects Hesse's incipient determination to deal with causes and not to linger over symptoms, and gives evidence of his growing faith in the intrinsic goodness of man. It was this determination and faith which conditioned his approach to war and politics, which persuaded him against *Weltverbesserung*, and which permitted him to advocate both *Selbstverbesserung* and *Eigensinn*. Hesse championed a spiritual reform, and the individual was his starting point. All else would follow of its own accord. To the sceptics who were prone to ridicule such an approach to the world's ills, Hesse could only reply: "Wer will, kann auch darüber lachen und es 'Verinnerlichungsrummel' heissen. Wer es erlebt, dem wird der Feind zum Bruder, der Tod zur Geburt, die Schmach zur Ehre, Unglück zu Schicksal" ("Krieg und Frieden," p. 77).

Hesse's convictions fell upon deaf ears and his remonstrations only managed to arouse animosity. In many quarters his words were dismissed forthwith as *Humanitätsduselei*, the idle chatter of a naïve idealist. Professors reprimanded him, fellow artists repudiated him, newspapers denounced him, and bookdealers complacently informed him "dass ein Autor von so verwerflichen Gesinnungen für sie nicht mehr existiere" (*Traumfährte*, p. 106). Even Hesse's supposed friends, revelling in their new-found patriotism, turned their backs upon him, proclaiming "dass sie eine Schlange an ihrem Busen genährt hätten, und dass dieser Busen künftig nur noch für Kaiser und Reich, nicht aber mehr für mich Entarteten [Hesse] schlage" (*Traumfährte*, p. 106). That Hesse chided Germany as severely as he did only because he loved her dearly, expected nobler things of her, and had great faith in her future, did little to mitigate this wave of resentful indignation. He was obviously a traitor to the cause, and as such, was unceremoniously relegated to the black list of undesirables, the "Vaterlandsfeinde, Defaitisten und Mies-macher" ("Weltgeschichte," p. 81).

Undismayed by this invective, and with his faith in Germany reaffirmed by German youth's wild acceptance of *Demian* (1919), Hesse persisted doggedly in his campaign for a more humane future. The periodical, *Vivos Voco* (Leipzig), established in October, 1919, by himself and Richard Woltereck, was to herald and to help prepare the way for this better tomorrow. Although Hesse again limited himself to literary discussions, refraining from active participation in political and social matters, *Vivos Voco*, unlike *März*, did reflect ideals and aims very akin to his own. Its appeal to youth was undoubtedly more effusive than his own, and the reforms it promoted were more concrete (*e.g.* educational reforms). However, its bywords (*Internationalis-mus, das Menschliche, Klassenversöhnung, Völkerversöhnung, angewandter Pazifismus*) certainly represented Hesse's own aspirations; and he himself was just as anxious to help be-wildered postwar youth to divorce itself from the materialistic tradition of its fathers, to prevent it from falling prey to a re-surgent nationalism and a spreading Communism, and to assist it in its quest for higher spiritual values and more worthy in-tellectual and physical pursuits. Unfortunately, energy and time were expended to little avail, and anticipations soon proved most untimely. Idealistic youth movements degenerated rapidly into radical, political rabble. Perceiving the dangers inherent in this trend, which was to culminate in the *Hitler Jugend*, Hesse terminated his editorship of *Vivos Voco* in December,

1921. This was to be his last organized attempt to help reform society.

Until the First World War, Hesse's reputation was untarnished. His work pleased both young and old. The *Gerbersau Novellen* were enough like the *Seldwyla* tales to attract the older generation which was still immersed in the Keller tradition. The more romantic natures found a kindred spirit in his melancholy lyrics and a second *Taugenichts* in his errant Knulp. Youth saw itself and its trials warmly mirrored in *Unterm Rad* and *Peter Camenzind*. After 1914, however, the ebb and flow of Hesse's fortunes became quite erratic. Hardly had official Germany branded him a traitor when *Demian* raised him to an unprecedented eminence. He was enthusiastically received by postwar youth as their spokesman.[7] Hesse's own generation, however, was far less prone to forgive and forget, and while youth extolled him, older die-hard nationalists continued to feel the sting of his wartime essays and to nurture their enmity. Nor was youth's espousal of his views more than an interlude; only a few years were to elapse before other ideals began to fire its imagination, and in the course of the Twenties, Hesse's popularity waned rapidly and steadily.

Even while Klabund and others were still praising *Demian*,[8] Hesse had already become a common target for abuse. His internationalism and pacifism had already become anathema to the rapidly increasing number of university students who were falling prey to a resurgent activistic nationalism. In the more reactionary academic circles his art was already being discounted, and he himself was again being branded a traitor to his German heritage. The decline, by 1921, of Zarathustra's challenging ideals and the rise of the very escapist heroics against which Hesse had so earnestly cautioned are clearly evidenced in the following extract taken from one of the many similar letters sent to Hesse by indignant students:

Ihre Kunst ist ein neurasthenisch-wollüstiges Wühlen in Schönheit, ist lockende Sirene über dampfenden deutschen Gräbern, die sich noch nicht geschlossen haben. Wir hassen diese Dichter, und mögen sie zehnmal reife Kunst bieten, die aus Männern Weiber machen wollen, die uns verflachen und internationalisieren und pazifisieren wollen. Wir sind Deutsche und wollen es ewig bleiben! Wir sind Jünger eines Schiller und Fichte und Kant und Beethoven und Richard Wagner, dessen schmetternde Inbrunst wir in alle Ewigkeiten lieben werden. Wir haben ein Recht zu fordern, dass unsre deutschen Dichter (sind sie verwelscht, dann mögen sie uns gestohlen bleiben!) unser schlummerndes Volk aufrütteln, dass sie es wieder führen zu den heiligen Gärten des deutschen Idealismus, des deutschen Glaubens und der deutschen Treue! . . . Sie [Hesse] sind tot für uns, wir lachen über Sie ("Hassbriefe," *Vivos Voco*, 2 [July 1921], 235-236).

Hesse did not hesitate to remind these students that this blatant national conceit was the traditional refuge of the "Durchschnittsgebildeten," and that it was this very "deutscher Geist" which had fostered the wars of 1870 and 1914. Perceived historically, theirs was but the "bequeme unselbstständige, streng autoritative und vor jedem kollektiven Ideal sich verneigende Bürgerglaube, gegen den Goethe so oft gekämpft und protestiert hat, an dem Hölderlin gebrochen ist, den Jean-Paul ironisiert und Nietzsche so wütend denunziert und an den Pranger gestellt hat" (*Vivos Voco*, p. 238). This irresponsible swaggering spirit was only the bravado of cowards, "der Geist, der Angst vor sich selber hat und jede Verlockung von der gewohnten Fahne weg gleich als satanisch empfindet, der aber diese innere Feigheit hinter lärmendem Säbelrasseln verbirgt" (p. 238).

Hesse's rebuke only managed to draw more invective. *Siddhartha*, termed "ein klassisch geformtes Gedicht"[9] in more recent years, was flippantly dismissed by these same young nationalists as "blass, geschwätzig, sehr eitel, mit einem Wort sehr schlecht," and Hesse himself was again subjected to familiar indignities: "Aber wenn er ein Dichter und nicht ein Ästhet, nicht nur ein armer Literat wäre, so müsste irgend etwas von dem Schrei der Zeit, dem Stöhnen seines Volkes in ihm nachklingen, irgend ein Zug von Grösse, Tiefe, von letztem menschlichem Mitgefühl sichtbar werden."[10]

By 1926, this antipathy had even begun to infect the cultural circles of Hesse's native Württemberg. Invited to take part in the annual celebration of the *Schwäbischer Schillerverein* in Stuttgart, he found the wisdom of the committee's choice seriously questioned by the local press, and himself termed a weak undesirable. By 1928, Germany as a whole was already very much inclined to repudiate him a second time. The publication of *Betrachtungen* with its collection of wartime essays managed only to stir bitter memories and to invite more calumny: "aber er hat ihr (der neuen Gottheit) nicht mit befreitem Herzen in Freude gedient, sondern er hat es mit gedrücktem Herzen, fanatisch und in Finsternis getan, mit dem überanstrengten Willen des Unbefriedigten, mit den krankhaften Übertreibungen des sich verdammt Fühlenden. In dieser Verfassung schrieb der unselige Mann eine Menge von anti-deutschen Streitschriften, Pamphlete voll Bosheit und auch Rohheit, die zum Glück längst vergessen sind."[11] Few cared to oppose this sentiment.

Very much disturbed by this growing animosity, and painfully disillusioned by the postwar political developments in Germany, Hesse became progressively more inclined to divorce himself from all that was German.[12] His faith in the Germans had obviously been misplaced. They had refused to acknowledge their war guilt, had suffered little remorse, and had experienced no moral regeneration. They had botched the revolution of 1918, and their political life had continued its corrupt and infantile course. The rift between Hesse and Germany was beyond repair long before 1933. For Hesse, Germany had become "eine verlogene Republik, an der wir keineswegs weiter herumzuflicken brauchen" (Briefe, p. 91) and for Germany, Hesse had remained "ein Besudler des deutschen Namens."[13]

Except for his allusion to politics and war in "Chinesische Betrachtung" (1921), and for his renewed attack upon Germany's intellectuals in Steppenwolf—an acrid disparagement of their inane ivory-tower pursuits, of their indiscriminating patriotism, their social irresponsibility, poltical immaturity, childish anti-Semitism, and hatred of Communists—Hesse ceased in the Twenties to dwell publicly upon current events. In the Thirties, but for his brief altercation with Will Vesper, his silence became complete.

In 1932, the editorial board of the newly established Swedish periodical, Bonniers Litterära Magasin, invited Will Vesper to become a regular contributor of Literaturbriefe dealing with contemporary German literature. The board was quite unaware that Vesper was a rabid adherent of the new ideology sweeping through Germany and that he represented the vanguard of Nazi literary critics. Vesper, however, was given no opportunity to carry his polemics abroad, for his very first article was declined, and his contract promptly terminated. Arthur Eloesser succeeded Vesper, and was, in turn, replaced by Hesse in the early part of 1935. Hardly had Hesse assumed this position before he incurred the wrath of Vesper. Insisting vehemently that a grossly distorted picture of modern German literature was being fostered abroad, that good Aryan writers were being belittled or totally neglected while such infamous Jews as Franz Kafka,

Alfred Polgar, Ernst Bloch, and Stefan Zweig were being extolled, Vesper unhesitatingly branded Hesse a rank Jew-lover whose probity was to be questioned and whose treachery was to be denounced:

> Er [Hesse] beschimpft die ganze neue deutsche Dichtung und verdächtigt die deutschen Dichter, auch die Dichter, die lange vor der Wende Deutsch schrieben und schufen, der Konjunkturmache. Mehr noch, er verschweigt sie alle, die jungen wie die alten. Er tut als habe Deutschland, das neue Deutschland, keine Dichter, als wäre das neue deutsche Schrifttum nur von Konjunkturschmierern geschrieben. Er verrät die deutsche Dichtung der Gegenwart an die Feinde Deutschlands und an das Judentum. Hier sieht man, wohin einer sinkt, wenn er sich daran gewöhnt hat, an den Tischen der Juden zu sitzen und ihr Brot zu essen. Der deutsche Dichter Hermann Hesse übernimmt die volksverräterische Rolle der jüdischen Kritik von gestern. Den Juden und Kulturbolschewiken zuliebe hilft er im Auslande falsche, sein Vaterland schädigende Vorstellungen verbreiten (*Neue Literatur* 36 [1935], 686).

Hesse refused to grace these absurd allegations and this tasteless slander with more than a token protest. That he might himself be interested in helping the cause of German letters abroad was dismissed by Vesper as absurd. That he had not lived in Germany for twenty-three years, and that he had become a Swiss citizen in 1923, was brushed aside as of no import. Born a German, he would remain a German. His new allegiance was nothing less than "eine Fahnenflucht," and his literary criticism betrayed "ein Verräter an unserem Volkstum" (*Neue Literatur* 37 [1936], 239-240). Furthermore, this aberration exemplified the maleficent influence of Jewry: "Hermann Hesse ist als Schriftsteller in tiefe Abhängigkeit von der Psychoanalyse des Wiener Juden Freud geraten . . . Das sollte einmal öffentlich gesagt werden, dass Hesse ein Schulbeispiel dafür ist, wie der Jude die deutsche Volksseele zu vergiften vermag" (p. 242).

Hesse's resolute silence throughout the Nazi régime was not that of indifference to current events, but that of resignation. Germany had not heeded him in the confusion and despair of defeat. That she should now, in the intoxication of a new ideology and in the anticipation of new power, be more receptive, was most unlikely. What better could Hesse do than devote himself solely to his art and hope that this political maelstrom would soon exhaust itself? It was only this withdrawal that persuaded Goebbels' *Reichskulturkammer* not to enforce an immediate boycott. Hesse's books and articles were published freely until 1938, when they were tacitly banned. Publishing houses immediately ceased to print them and bookdealers to display them. Hesse's works became unavailable long before he actually was put on the *Schwarze Liste* in 1943.

Literary critics conformed to the desires of the *Kulturkammer* just as readily as publishers and bookdealers, and gradually ceased to be aware of Hesse. By 1937 their silent treatment was complete. Only a handful of literary historians continued to perpetuate his memory. Hans Naumann is very casual in his reference to Hesse (*Die deutsche Dichtung der Gegenwart* [1933], pp. 219-220); Guido K. Brand's is a good noncommittal description (*Werden und Wandlung* [1933], pp. 335-337); Johannes Mumbauer presents an excellent, detailed survey (*Die deutsche Dichtung der neuesten Zeit* [1936], pp. 573-587); while Johannes Beer (*Deutsche Dichtung seit hundert Jahren* [1937], pp. 197-198) and Walter Linden (*Geschichte der deutschen Literatur* [1942], pp. 421-422) are grudgingly brief. Although Franz Koch is annoyed by Hesse's extreme individualism ("seinem Volkstum entfremdet"), he does concede that he is a writer of merit (*Geschichte deutscher Dichtung* [1937], p. 281); Josef Nadler's short appraisal is not unfavorable (*Literaturgeschichte des deutschen Volkes* [1938], Vol. 3, 696-697); Christian Jenssen reluctantly acknowledges that Hesse has had considerable influence upon German youth (*Deutsche Dichtung der Gegenwart* [1936], pp. 62-63); and even anti-Semitic Adolf Bartels, who had long suspected Hesse's ancestry,[14] is surprisingly civil (*Geschichte der deutschen Literatur* [1943], p. 601). While neither Franz Lennartz (*Die Dichter unserer Zeit* [1941], pp. 173-176) nor Willi Duwe (*Deutsche Dichtung des zwangzigsten Jahrhunderts* [1936], pp. 275-280) deign to make mention of Thomas Mann, their treatment of Hesse is both informative and just. Such thorough Nazis as Theodor Langenmaier (*Deutsches Schrifttum unserer Zeit* [1935], Helmut Langenbucher (*Volkhafte Dichtung der Zeit* [1937], Hermann Gerstner and Karl Schworm (*Deutsche Dichtung unserer Zeit* [1939] venture to ignore Hesse completely.

With the termination of the Second World War, history began to repeat itself in an uncanny manner. Twice denied, Hesse now found himself abruptly reacclaimed. Suddenly books which had been banned could not be published in numbers adequate to meet the demand. Critics who had long ignored him seemed frantically eager to atone for their neglect. Academies eagerly extended their invitations. Intellectuals who had branded him an alien and dangerous element in German society now looked forward to his participation in Germany's regeneration. German youth seemed again to have found in him a spiritual guide. With the *Goethepreis* of 1946, Hesse's acceptance received its official recognition. Bitter experience, however, had left him far more skeptical than he had been in the years immediately following 1918. The renewed plaudits of his former countrymen were accepted with considerable reservation. Nor did the sudden flood of lettters which swept into Montagnola help to dispel his suspicions. With rare exception, German prisoners of war complained about their fate. Some requested impossible aid, and others had already begun to harbor thoughts of revenge. Many former acquaintances now brazenly affirmed their unbroken friendship and good will. Some explained that they had joined the Nazi party merely to help temper its methods. Others, carefully avoiding any mention of the Nazi interlude, dwelt only upon their own hardships and the blunders of the occupational forces. Most would have denounced Hitler long ago but for compelling circumstances, and none had actually ever been a Nazi or even a real sympathizer. And die-hard nationalists began again to write their *Schmähbriefe*.

There was very little reason to believe that Germany would now be any more inclined to bear its cross than it had been after the First World War. Nevertheless, Hesse felt impelled to break his silence, once more to admonish and to exhort. With little faith in the efficacy of his pleas, and with less spirit than thirty years before, he again reminds the Germans that defeat can be a new beginning, an opportune moment for a moral regeneration ("Schluss des Rigi-Tagebuches," August, 1945, *Krieg und Frieden*), again pleads for patient acceptance of life and the brotherhood of man ("Ansprache in der ersten Stunde des Jahres 1946"), and again cautions against the two scourges of our age: "der Grössenwahn der Technik und der Grössenwahn des Nationalismus" ("Danksagung und moralisierende Betrachtung," 1946, p. 211). The silence which greeted Hesse's *Krieg und Frieden* did little to allay his fears.

Nor has German youth of more recent years been inclined to have any greater patience with Hesse than the Activist youth of the Twenties. *Glasperlenspiel's* Castalia is just as removed from the social and political reality of postwar Germany as *Siddhar-*

tha's world had been, and Hesse has again been rejected by those seeking ready answers to life's immediate problems. Like Jörn Oven in 1923, H. G. Thurm is convinced in 1947 that Hesse has become too alien to the German world to be of any consequence whatsoever in the so-called "Neuformung des deutschen geistigen Menschen";[15] and Wolfgang von Schöfer, typical of those obviously in quest of a new, practical *Führer* with a dynamic program, repudiates him in a manner no less blatantly derisive than any of the *Hassbriefe* of the Twenties.[16] Critics such as Thurm and von Schöfer have failed to realize that Hesse's concern has never been the "Neuformung des deutschen geistigen Menschen," but the more basic humanizing of the individual, and that he has never proposed a rectifying ideology for the many, but a moral challenge for the few. His critics need only have recalled Zarathustra's words: "Von mir, ihr Freunde, könnt ihr nicht lernen, wie man Völker regiert und Niederlagen wieder gutmacht. Ich weiss euch nicht zu lehren, wie man Herden befehligt und wie man Hungernde beschwichtigt. Das sind nicht Zarathustras Künste. Das sind nicht Zarathustras Sorgen" (*Krieg und Frieden*, p. 111). Hesse has never desired or purported to be *ein Führer*; the very concept is contrary to his demands upon, and his fundamental faith in the individual. Rather than continue to censure Hesse for not being what he cannot be, and for not affording what he cannot afford, German youth might better begin to accept and to judge him for what he actually is: "ein Ahnender und Mitleidender, ein älterer Bruder . . . Ich bin ein Leidender unter der Not unserer Zeit, nicht aber ein Führer aus ihr heraus . . ." (*Briefe*, pp. 80-89).

Unlike his long-time friend Romain Rolland, who was a militant humanitarian ever ready to organize his fellow liberal spirits against war, social injustices, and political corruption, Hesse has always carefully avoided the public arena with its collective programs and causes. It is not that the world no longer needs or is capable of improvement, but that the reform of society is contingent upon the more fundamental reform of the individual, who, in turn, should neither be led nor taught, but is best encouraged by example. For an artist or intellectual to allow himself to be harnessed to any cause, just though it might be, is only to sanction a gross misuse of his talents and office, and to avail little beyond the incurring of disrepute. Except for embittered Harry Haller's brief disparagement of the German intellectual's pitiful rôle in his country's political history, Hesse has never deviated from this conviction. Artists and intellectuals are not meant to govern or to reform, but to be the conscience of their age, to treasure lofty ideals, and to foster a love of knowledge and of truth: "Wir sind Fachleute des Untersuchens, Zerlegens und Messens, wir sind die Erhalter und beständigen Nachprüfer aller Alphabete, Einmaleinse und Methoden, wir sind die Eichmeister der geistigen Masse und Gewichte ... unsere erste und wichtigste Funktion aber, deren wegen das Volk unser bedarf und uns erhält, ist jene der Sauberhaltung aller Wissensquellen" (*Glasperlenspiel*, Vol. 2, 127).

It was for these reasons, and at the constant risk of being dismissed as a dreamy-eyed, irresponsible aesthete, that Hesse never joined the organized ranks of the pacifists during the First World War, that he was hesitant in accepting Romain Rolland's invitation to take part in the International Conference of liberal intellectuals in Lugano, in 1922, that he carefully refrained from becoming involved with political Germany in the Thirties, and that he has refused to lend his name to any of the organizations which have appealed to him since 1945. Hesse's answer to Max Brod's request in 1948, that he raise his voice on behalf of the new Jewish state threatened by the Arabs, should be taken to heart by his Activist critics:

Nein, so schön und edel Ihre Absicht ist, ich kann Ihre Auffassung nicht teilen. Ich halte im Gegenteil jede geistige Scheinaktion, jedes Mahnen, Bitten, Predigen oder gar Drohen der Intellektuellen den Herren der Erde gegenüber für falsch, für eine weitere Schädigung und Herabwürdigung des Geistes, für etwas, was unbedingt und in jedem Fall unterbleiben sollte. . . . Die Minister und anderen Politikmacher gründen ihre kurzfristige Macht nicht auf Herz und Kopf, sondern auf die Masse derer, deren Exponenten sie sind. Sie operieren mit dem, womit wir nicht operieren können noch dürfen, mit der Zahl, mit der Quantität, und wir müssen ihnen dieses Feld überlassen. . .ich habe versucht als Dichter und Literat meinen Lesern immer wieder die Mahnung an die heiligen Grundgebote der Menschlichkeit zuzurufen, niemals aber habe ich selbst versucht, die Politik zu beeinflussen, wie es in den Hunderten von Aufrufen, Protesten und Mahnungen der Intellektuellen immer und immer wieder feierlich, aber nutzlos und zum Schaden des Ansehens der Humanität geschah und geschieht.[17]

That Hesse has persistently resisted embroilment in political and social causes certainly does not mean that he has never troubled to keep in touch with current events, or to acquaint

himself with the major political ideologies of his age, and to
arrive at fixed notions of his own. Though feeble, his opposition
to *Wilhelminismus* does represent an attitude. He hailed and
expected much of the German revolution of 1918 (*Briefe*, p. 57),
had faith in the Weimar Republic until it became obvious that
the Germans themselves were determined to sabotage it (*Briefe*,
p. 238), and repudiated, in no uncertain terms, the infamy which
followed.

Hesse's letters reveal just as unequivocal an attitude toward
our current World Powers and their conflicting ideologies.
America is a paradoxical colossus. It is an exponent of democracy, yet not averse to supporting the Spanish dictatorship
(*Briefe*, p. 326). It is the stronghold of capitalism, yet is itself
"eine gut erzogene Kollektivwelt" (*Briefe*, p. 359). For Hesse,
just as for most Europeans, America suggests youth, vigor,
technical skill, naïveté, and a cultural vacuum. He anticipated
the so-called Americanization of Europe as early as 1912—"Die
Amerikaner sind ein Volk, von dem wir später gefressen werden
sollen, und so ist es gut, den Feind vorher kennen zu lernen.
Dazu kann dies Buch dienlich sein; es zeigt den Amerikaner in
ş̧einer schlechthin imponierenden Smartheit ebenso wie in
seiner geistig-kulturellen Inferiorität" (*Der Bücherwurm*, 2
[1912], 250)—and he continues to deplore it.

While Hesse's repudiation of German Fascism was sharp and
absolute, he has carefully qualified his rejection of Russian Communism. Stalin's methods were undoubtedly comparable in
their cruelty to Hitler's, but his policies were at least nobly
motivated. In contrast to base and reactionary Fascism, Communism looks to the future, to a more just distribution of worldly goods, and to a more harmoniously integrated society (*Briefe*,
pp. 327, 397). That Communism has resolved itself into an
inane and inhumane dictatorship of the proletariat is a deplorable deviation; nevertheless, it does represent an attempt which
had to be made and which will probably have to be repeated any
number of times before Communism will finally begin to realize
its aspirations (*Briefe*, p. 327).

Neither America nor Russia has inspired much faith or confidence in Hesse. Both have shown themselves to be far too
militant, too impatient, unimaginative, and uncreative (*Briefe*,
p. 398). Neither seems yet to have realized that power politics
and stock-piled atom bombs can only prepare the way for another and more devastating holocaust (*Briefe*, p. 393). Indeed,

Gandhi was a greater blessing to the world than all the American Presidents of the twentieth century combined with all the leaders of Communism from Marx to Stalin (*Briefe*, p. 398).

Although the Western world in decline has been Hesse's most persistent background theme, it was not until the years immediately following the First World War that he began to dwell intently upon this phenomenon. In those years, under the influence particularly of Dostoyevsky's *The Brothers Karamazov*, he evolved a loose-knit morphology of history akin in its broader implications to that of Oswald Spengler.[18] Reflecting both Dostoyevsky's novel and the disastrous trend of modern European history, Hesse concludes that *Untergang* is an imminent fact and an organic inevitability. Every culture, just as every social structure, rests upon a particular moral-religious myth which accepts certain of man's primal urges while others are curbed. Out of any cultural context, these *Urkräfte* are beyond the dichotomy of good and evil; none can ever be extirpated nor forever suppressed or sublimated. Periodically, whenever an age begins to lose faith in the myth about which its culture has crystallized, all the drives long denied and pent-up begin again to assert themselves, absolutes fall by the wayside, and another civilization has almost spent itself (*Blick ins Chaos*, pp. 10-12).

Hesse was not only convinced that Europe was fast approaching this stage of cultural dissolution, but that this impending *Untergang* was mirrored in Dostoyevsky's novels. The Karamazovs are the children of tomorrow's anarchy. They are hysterical, unfathomable creatures, irresponsible egoists, dangerous criminals, potential saints, sensitive dreamers, childlike innocents, and uncouth drunkards. Their Asiatic ideal is tomorrow's "Abkehr von jeder festgelegten Ethik und Moral zugunsten eines Allesverstehens, Allesgeltenlassens, einer neuen, gefährlichen, grausigen Heiligkeit" (*Blick ins Chaos*, p. 2). However, this relapse into chaos is actually a return to Asia, to *mother*, to the beginning of things. As such, it not only marks the death of one culture, but anticipates the birth of another, whereupon the cultural cycle begins anew.

That Hesse was directly or even indirectly influenced by Spengler is exceedingly doubtful. Spengler's philosophy of history did impress him very favorably, but "Die Brüder Karamasoff oder der Untergang Europas" and "Gedanken zu Dostojewskis Idiot" (summer 1919) were written before his first reading of *Untergang des Abendlandes* (end of 1919), and many of

Hesse's own notions of cultural decline actually predate the publication of Spengler's work (1918). Much is already evident in *Demian* (written 1917). Ambivalent Abraxas is none other than the Demiurge of the Karamazovs, "der Gott, der zugleich Teufel ist" (*Blick ins Chaos*, p. 5). Like the Karamazovs, Demian and his kindred souls live beyond the pale of good and evil. And Hesse's future theory of decline is clearly anticipated in Demian's concluding premonition: "Die Welt will sich erneuern. Es riecht nach Tod. Nichts Neues kommt ohne Tod." This trend of thought continues in *Klein und Wagner* and *Klingsors letzter Sommer*, the immediate stepping stones to *Blick ins Chaos*. Klein's *Sichfallenlassen* is nothing else than the *Allesgeltenlassen* of the Karamazovs, and the God he envisages in his dying moments is again an anarchic Demiurge. Klingsor revels in the intoxication of his conviction that the end is at hand: "Ich glaube nur an Eines: an den Untergang... Wir stehen im Untergang, wir alle, wir müssen sterben, wir müssen wieder geboren werden, die grosse Wende ist für uns gekommen.... Bei uns im alten Europa ist alles das gestorben, was bei uns gut und unser eigen war; unsre schöne Vernunft ist Irrsinn geworden, unser Geld ist Papier, unsre Maschinen können bloss noch schiessen und explodieren, unsre Kunst ist Selbstmord" (*Weg nach Innen*, p. 401). Klein and Klingsor are *Untergangsmenschen*, the Karamazovs of Western civilization in decline and the raw material of a culture yet to come.

Since *Steppenwolf*, Hesse's attitude toward the decline of the West seems to have experienced considerable modification. In *Glasperlenspiel* he is no longer impatiently eager to leave our spent Christian-bourgeois age behind him, nor inclined to believe that the subsequent cultural vacuum may only be of brief duration, and that the reëvaluation of values may take place in the souls of one generation. Knecht is not a Karamazov, nor is he the man of tomorrow who will eventually emerge from our *Untergang*; and the world which surrounds Castalia in 2200 is still our tottering, Western, Christian civilization. Hesse is now decidedly less interested in the culture to come and its precursors than in the salvage of our own. Castalia is a repository of all that is best in our culture, and its inhabitants are the guardians and disseminators of this tradition.

Part Two

HESSE AND HIS CRITICS

I

BOOKS

Hugo Ball

Hermann Hesse, sein Leben und sein Werk (1927, 243 pp.) was undertaken at the request of Hesse's publisher, S. Fischer. It was written in the course of a few weeks and published upon the occasion of Hesse's fiftieth birthday. Ball was not intent upon writing a systematically-presented scholarly work. Having learned to know and to appreciate Hesse, he simply wanted to share his experience with others.

Ball follows Hesse leisurely from childhood to his fiftieth birthday. He describes the little boy listening eagerly to his mother's stories, the distraught student fleeing from Maulbronn, the apprentice mechanic in Calw, and the young bookdealer in Tübingen. Hesse's marriage and his futile attempt to establish himself on the Bodensee are related in considerable detail. The difficult war years on the outskirts of Bern are touched upon, and Hesse's psychoanalytical treatment, the break-up of his family, and his eventual retirement to Montagnola are discussed quite candidly.

Fully aware, however, that Hesse was deeply rooted in a strong family tradition, and that his sensitive nature was very susceptible to the influence of environment, Ball does not restrict himself to just these biographical facts. Swabia, Estonia, and India, the world of his forebears, and Calw and Basel, the world of his childhood, are constantly in the background. A multitude of stray but interesting details concerning various members of the Gundert and Hesse families are appropriately introduced. Mention is made of Grandfather Gundert's scholarly work and of his library, where young Hesse steeped himself in the German authors of the eighteenth century. Grandfather Hesse and life in Russian Weissenstein are described. Hesse's difficulties in Maulbronn recall Uncle Paul Gundert's escapades in that same institution. Life in the Hesse home in Calw is pictured in considerable detail, and the literary activities of both father and mother are remarked upon. The Pietism of Swabia and the particular form this Pietism assumed in the Hesse household are discussed at length.[1] Even the Swabian school system is carefully examined. Mention is also made of the various circles in which Hesse moved at different times, and of his closest friends: the Laroches and the Wackernagels in Basel, Ludwig Finckh in Gaienhofen, the psychoanalyst Dr. Lang, the painter Louis Moilliet, and many others.

Ball's treatment of Hesse's art is just as informal as his presentation of the facts of Hesse's life. At the appropriate time, each major work is loosely woven into the fabric of the biography. The genesis is remarked upon, the contents are recalled, and attention is generally drawn to the major autobiographical aspects. At no time, however, does Ball venture a critical analysis of the subject matter, and his treatment of form remains on the plane of generalities (aestheticism, realism, romanticism).

Despite the haste with which Ball's book was written, the number of factual errors is negligible. Referring to the futile attempt of Blumhardt *Sohn* to drive the devil out of young Hesse, Ball implies that Johann Christoph Blumhardt, the deceased father, was also present. Ball also states that Hesse began to edit the periodical, *März*, in 1905 with Ludwig Thoma and Conrad Haussmann; actually this was not until 1907, and with Thoma, Albert Langen, and Kurt Aram. Furthermore, Hesse's grandmother on his father's side was not Adele von Berg but Jeanette Agnes Lass (see Ludwig Finckh, *Schwäbische Vettern* [1948], p. 6). More regrettable than these slips is Ball's failure to give adequate references for his many quotations. Haste was perhaps also responsible for Ball's occasional lapse into a confusingly random association of thoughts.

Since 1927, three different supplemented editions of Ball's biography have been published. In 1933 it was brought up to date by Anni Rebenwurzel's concluding chapter, "Vom *Steppenwolf* zur *Morgenlandfahrt*," pp. 237-258. It was enlarged again in 1947 by Anni (Rebenwurzel) Carlsson's "Hermann Hesses *Glasperlenspiel* in seinen Wesensgesetzen" (an essay which had appeared in *Trivium*, 4 [1946]). The edition of 1933 was supplemented a second time in 1947 by the addition of Otto Basler's "Der Weg zum *Glasperlenspiel*," pp. 272-340. Ball's text was left unaltered in every instance, and with the exception of the publication of 1947 supplemented by Anni Carlsson alone, all the editions are copiously supplied with family portraits.

The appendages of both Basler and Carlsson ("Vom *Steppenwolf* zur *Morgenlandfahrt*") pattern themselves rather closely after Ball in their mode of presentation, lacking only the latter's tone of intimacy. In both instances description prevails over interpretation and evaluation. Carlsson extends the biography from *Steppenwolf* through *Narziss und Goldmund* to *Morgenlandfahrt*, and Basler focusses attention upon the period 1932-1945. The latter's survey, particularly, is very cursory. Of much greater value and interest than his listing of Hesse's publications during these years and his stray remarks about them, are the few rays of light he sheds upon Hesse's life during the Nazi period, a phase about which little is as yet known.

Although Ball's book leaves much to be desired, it is still the only real biography of Hesse and therefore continues to be an indispensable reference work.[2]

Heinrich Geffert

In view of Hesse's great interest in youth's problems of physical and mental development and the attendant family, social, and educational conflicts, it is not unusual that one of the earliest, major, scholarly works about him (Heinrich Geffert, *Das Bildungsideal im Werk Hermann Hesses* [1927], 107 pp.) should concern itself with his *Bildungsideal*.

In his efforts to determine the nature and significance of Hesse's educational ideal, Geffert first dwells upon those factors in the author's life which would help to condition this ideal. He draws attention to Hesse's mystical attachment to nature, to his repudiation of today's practical bourgeois civilization, and to his hostile attitude toward intellectualism. He mentions Hesse's unorthodox moral and religious views, his emphasis upon the soul, fantasy, and contemplation, rather than upon the mind, reason, and activity. He points out Hesse's attachment to childhood, his acclaim of the childlike nature, and finally his firm belief in the inherent unity of both the inner world of *Geist* and *Natur* and the outer world of material reality and flux.

In his second chapter Geffert undertakes to show how Hesse's *Bildungsideal*, with its emphasis upon the whole and harmonious development of the individual, finds expression in *Hermann Lauscher, Peter Camenzind, Unterm Rad, Freunde, Weltverbesserer, Gertrud, Rosshalde, Knulp, Demian*, and *Siddhartha*. While the first chapter is informative and suggestive, the second is hardly more than a detailed, pedestrian recall of the lives of Hesse's heroes, a recounting in which Geffert loses sight of the ideal itself. Geffert's casual association of Hesse with the nineteenth-century Romanticists is a purposeless digressive.

In his brief concluding chapter, Geffert does manage to show quite convincingly that Hesse's educational ideal was typical of the times, that he was only voicing the prevalent pedagogical trends, which endeavored to free the individual from the mass complex of an overly rational machine age. He notes, too, that Hesse's appeal for a return to nature was quite in accord with the growing popularity of such writers as Whitman, Emerson, and Thoreau. Nor was *Unterm Rad* and its diatribe against existing educational institutions an exception; while *Demian*, with its *Weg nach Innen,* reflected the widespread interest in Freud which followed the First World War. Geffert remarks, quite correctly, that while German youth of the early Twenties, in its quest for a new meaning of life and a new adjustment to it, had made a motto of Hesse's "das Leben jedes Menschen ist ein Weg zu sich selber hin" (*Demian*), it could not accept the implied isolation and passivity of the individual. Geffert might have added that this same generation was soon to forget its motto in a new enthusiasm, and that within a few years, Hesse was to be listed·among those writers of whom was written: "Wir hassen diese Dichter . . . die aus Männern Weiber machen wollen, die uns verflachen und internationalisieren und pazifisieren wollen" ("Hassbriefe," *Vivos Voco*, 2 [July 1921], 235-236).

Geffert's is an informative study which breaks ground and offers a promising approach. Hesse's *Bildungsideal* itself, however, remains ill-defined, and its philosophical and religious implications as well as its social significance receive only token consideration.

Clarence Boersma

It was not until twenty years later that Hesse's *Bildungsideal* was again to receive detailed consideration, and then by a student apparently quite unaware of Geffert's earlier work. Although, under the circumstances, much repetition was inevitable, Clarence Boersma ("The Educational Ideal in the Major Works of Hermann Hesse" [Diss., University of Michigan, 1948], 308 pp.; available on microfilm) presents a much clearer picture of Hesse's educational ideal than Geffert; and with more recent material upon which to draw, he provides a fuller and more up-to-date study.

Like his predecessor, Boersma is convinced that to understand Hesse's *Bildungsideal,* his *Weltanschauung* must first be understood, and that to throw more light upon both, attention ought to be drawn to relevant biographical details and to the major influences in the author's thought. With this in mind, Boersma proceeds to present a sketch of Hesse's life, to comb his writings for all direct and indirect criticism of contemporary educational institutions, to discuss his *Bildungsideal* in terms of his *Weltanschauung,* to consider its nature and its attainment, and finally to draw brief attention to the significance in Hesse's life of the Orient, of Goethe, Nietzsche, Jakob Burckhardt, Dostoyevsky, and Novalis.

In Hesse's criticism of education, Boersma notes a gradual evolution from the subjective, literary propagandist of *Unterm Rad,* to the more profound, objective prophet of *Glasperlenspiel,* who shows greater concern for humanity itself. He notes, too, that although Hesse has always championed the natural right of children and has never ceased to denounce intellectualism, his immediate object of criticism has repeatedly shifted. Hesse turns from the school itself (*Unterm Rad*), to the home, church, and school (*Demian*), then to the modern intellectual's lack of harmonious and balanced growth (*Steppenwolf*), and, finally, to the whole Western world of today in its disorganized diversity and its concern for trite details and fragmentary, unrelated knowledge (*Glasperlenspiel*).

It is in this, our atomized "feuilletonistisches Zeitalter," that Hesse's heroes, themselves children of the age, strive incessantly to attain to a *Weltanschauung* which knows of a cosmic unity behind all diversity. While creative fantasy or music affords Sinclair, Haller, and Goldmund brief glimpses of the primal oneness of reality (*Mutter Eva*), Siddhartha and the *Magister Musicae* realize the ideal through meditation and humor. It is upon the attainment of this faith in the inherent unity and harmony of the world, that Hesse's *Bildungsideal,* the development of a harmonious, unified inner world, is contingent. Realization of this *Bildungsideal* requires an uncompromising individualism which is prepared, in its pursuit of self-knowledge and in its implicit obedience to the inner voice, to break through the barriers of the conventional world and to suffer the consequent agonies of isolation and loneliness. The individual will then eventually emerge in a *Vollendung* which has transcended the painful *principium individuationis* besetting modern man, and which confirms life and knows only unity and harmony.

Boersma manages very ably to reduce Hesse's *Bildungsideal* to its essentials. His treatment of the theme is laudable in its scope and generally sound in its conclusions. Unfortunately, his repeated chronological examination of Hesse's works in the course of the various chapters results in a tedious amount of distracting repetition. Frequently too, forgetting his subject, Boersma lingers far too long over extraneous plot material. Of greater import than these lapses is the occasional unguarded statement which does not bear close examination, *e.g.*, Boersma's remark that the theme of service does not become prominent until late in Hesse's career. On the contrary, the theme begins in *Peter Camenzind* and *Franz von Assisi* and remains an almost constant refrain thereafter. Other casual remarks reflect questionable interpretations, *e.g,* the association of Demian and his mother with the "russische Menschen" of Dostoyevsky. Boersma recognizes that power is foreign to the aim of the Karamazovs, but is this true of Demian and his *Herrenmensch* principle? It is quite apparent that Sinclair outgrows the principles of middle-class society, but does he, as Boersma would maintain (p. 281), develop in the direction of the Karamazov ideal? Is the relativity of the Demian ideal of the same fiber as that of the Russian ideal? Does the latter not mark a return to the beginning of things (the *Sichfallenlassen* of Klein), characterized by a Schopenhauer-like passivity, mysticism, and nihilism; while the former, in its intellectual activism strives for greater individual responsibility, for a superior morality with its onus directly upon the individual himself ("ein Orden des Gedankens und der Persönlichkeit," *Demian* [1919], p. 102)? Like many other students of Hesse, Boersma fails to perceive the significance of Hesse's swing from Nietzsche to Schopenhauer.

One might argue, too, that though the facts of Hesse's life are unquestionably pertinent to such a study, Boersma's forty-four pages of biographical details are disproportionately numerous, and that his concluding chapter, a haphazard compilation of the so-called major influences in Hesse's life with no effort made to show their bearing upon the theme, remains little more than an irrelevant appendage. A final and more regrettable shortcoming of Boersma's otherwise very respectable dissertation, is its noncommittal approach, the absence of evaluation. In his extremely short conclusion, he can do no more than regret the extreme lack of faith in the sciences which is reflected in Hesse's educational ideal. This ideal itself is not brought into relationship with the world of today, nor does Boersma consider whether it might be practical or whether it is only the idle fancy of a dreamer; and no effort is made to weigh the merits of Hesse's cult of the *Ich* with its doctrine of *Eigensinn* and its belief in the inherent goodness of man. Since these and related questions are left unanswered, the full significance of Hesse's *Bildungsideal* is not brought out.

Only eight other scholars have concerned themselves specifically with this *Bildungsproblem*. In the winter of 1947-48, Professor J. Boyer of the University of Toulouse read a paper entitled "Le Problème de l'éducation dans l'oeuvre de Hermann Hesse," a work which was unfortunately never published. After considering the course of Hesse's own education in considerable detail, P. Hedinger-Henrici ("Hermann Hesse als Erzieher," *Schweizerisches Evangelisches Schulblatt*, 83 [1948], 329-334) regrets his endeavor to bring good and evil together in a higher unity, condemns his heathen acclaim of Abraxas, and finally rejects Hesse as an educator in a Christian community. Edith Braemer's rejection of Castalia as a pedagogical province is just as unequivocal ("Kastalien als pädagogische Provinz," *Die Neue Schule*, 3 [1948], 251-253). A world of abstractions where only a partial development of the individual receives emphasis and where little concern is shown for society, Castalia, when compared with Goethe's province, can only be considered an inconsequential "Verfallserscheinung, ein Rückschritt." On the other hand, although she regrets the absence of God in Castalia, and in the absence of women perceives an impractical utopian educational ideal, Amalie Bonitz is convinced that the virtues of Hesse's *Bildungsideal* exceed its weaknesses and dangers ("Der Erziehungsgedanke in Hermann Hesses *Glasperlenspiel*," *Schola*, 3 [1948], 803-815).

G. C. Cast ("Hermann Hesse als Erizieher," *Monatshefte*, 43 [1951], 207-220) notes astutely that Hesse's *Erziehungsideal*, with its inherent individualism, has in fact two aims: while the individual and the development of all his potentialities (brief references are made to *Peter Camenzind*, *Unterm Rad*, and to *Demian*) is of most immediate concern, the ultimate purpose is service rendered to humanity and to *Geist* (evidenced in Hesse's late works, in *Narziss und Goldmund, Morgenlandfahrt,* and particularly in *Glasperlenspiel,* to which Cast gives his most detailed attention). Like Boersma, of whose work he seems to have been unaware, Cast is very conscious of the rôle played by family tradition and home in the development of Hesse's attitude towards the problem of education and in the molding of his *Erziehungsideal.*

Proceeding one step beyond Cast, Friederich Lieser ("Die Frage der Menschenbildung bei Hermann Hesse," *Bildung und Erziehung,* 8 [1955], 625-641) ventures to weigh the practicality of Hesse's educational ideal. Hesse's fervent acclaim of the individual, his gospel of self-knowledge and self-realization before all else, and his ultimate aspiration to the pious wisdom of a Siddhartha are most laudable; but actually they constitute an ideal which is feasible only for the exceptional person. Lieser's reservations are obviously those of the professional educator, whose concern is primarily for the many and not for the few, and who is convinced that youth as a whole fares best in common striving for a common cause.

Hermann Lorenzen's "Kastalien—eine moderne pädagogische Provinz im *Glasperlenspiel* Hermann Hesses" (*Pädagogische Rundschau,* 9 [1954-55], 264-268) is probably an excerpt from his pamphlet. And Gisela Wagner's "Kastalien und die Schulen auf dem Lande" (*Pädagogische Provinz,* 10, No. 2 [1956], 57-64) was not available for examination.

Hans R. Schmid

From the very beginning, Hesse's works have given clear and ample evidence of a highly problematic personality. He has, himself, upon numerous occasions and almost always with a slight touch of defiance, acknowledged himself to be "ein Neurotiker und Psychopath" (*e.g., Kurgast*) ; and his own psychoanalytical treatment (1916-17) has been common knowledge since Ball's biography. Hesse admits quite candidly that his art is primarily autobiographical (*Betrachtungen,* p. 174), confessional in form, and therapeutic in function ("Aus einem Tagebuch. . ." *Corona,* 3[1932], 197). That his art is pregnant with Freudian symbols, and that it mirrors well-categorized psychic complexes, is obvious even to the layman's eye. Nor have literary historians failed to allude to the strong psychoanalytical tendency in Hesse's writings. However, most of the major works about Hesse have very carefully avoided any approach which might introduce psychoanalysis. Hans R. Schmid (*Hermann Hesse* [1928], 218 pp.), Hugo Mauerhofer (*Die Introversion, mit spezieller Berück-sichtigung des Hermann Hesse* [1929], 61 pp.), and Ingeborg Heiting (*Der Muttergedanke als Zeitausdruck in neuerer Litera-tur* [1938], pp. 31-41) are the exceptions.[3] Heiting's references to Hesse are inconsequential in their brevity and superficialty, Mauerhofen's short work is well documented and demanding in its depth of analysis, though somewhat taxing in its technical jargon. Schmid's study, the widest in scope of the three, is re-freshing in its bold approach (whether one is inclined to approve or not), challenging in its arguments, and like Mauerhofer's, rather provocative in its bias and its unreserved conclusions.

Schmid's book reflects a general interest in the intimate nature of twentieth-century German literature, and an intense, specific interest in the problem of the artist and society, a prob-lem, once ethical, which has become acutely psychological. Modern literature is viewed in terms of a reawakened Romanticism which has become decadent, and it is this decadence that Schmid wishes to analyze. The decadent personality is to be studied in its mode of thought, its emotional experience, its psychic complexes, its way of life, and its *Weltanschauung*. Selecting Hesse as his subject, Schmid proceeds to analyze the latter's works according to theme, interpreting their salient characteristics in terms of psychic experience. The thematic arrangement is of such a nature that the analysis is at the same time a chronological one. Except for two instances in which his discussion is of a very general nature ("Künstlertum und Dekadenz"; "Das Mutterproblem"), each chapter presents a specific problem which is thrashed out in a detailed study of one or two pertinent works, concluding with references, by way of elaboration and confirmation, to various other writings. In contrast to Ball's study, Schmid's presents biographical details only in corroboration of views based upon Hesse's art.

In the introductory chapter, modern art, including Hesse's, is briefly characterized as confessional and therapeutic, as com-pensatory in nature, and as the work of autopsychographic talent ("Künstlertum und Dekadenz" treats this theme in greater detail). Attention is then drawn to the predominantly romantic

traits in Hesse's personality and to his attitude towards life: an
extreme individualism for which the world exists only in terms
of the ego; the inherent dualism of his nature; his greater concern for the past than for the present, for anticipation than for
realization; his life of memory and longing, full of contradictions
and suffering; and his painful individuation with its yearning
for self-obliteration. There is a concluding biographical sketch
based largely on Ball's book and Hesse's own "Kurzgefasster
Lebenslauf" (*Traumfährte*).

In the ensuing chapters, assuming that the personality of the
artist, in all its complexities and most intimate experience, finds
expression in his art, Schmid seeks out the ascendant features of
Hesse's writings and then undertakes a psychoanalytical interpretation of these. An examination of the first three publications
(*Eine Stunde hinter Mitternacht, Romantische Lieder, Hermann
Lauscher*) suffices to disclose the general nature and the problems
of Hesse's work as a whole. It is an intimate art reflecting an
intensely emotional world, shrouded in melancholy, heavy with
loneliness, permeated by a longing for beauty and for love, limp
with fatigue and torn by doubt and self-torment. It is an art
centered about a sentimental, introspective outsider suffering in
the lonelines of his extreme individuation, and though but a mere
youth, already looking back with nostalgia to his lost childhood,
and yearning for a vague type of love that desires no fulfillment.
In the remaining chapters, these characteristics of Hesse's art are
studied in greater detail and in the light of subsequent works.
Peter Camenzind is analyzed in terms of the outsider and his
nature worship, and *Unterm Rad,* in terms of *Jugendsehnsucht.*
In Hesse's conception of childhood, Schmid perceives more
longing and retrospective conjecture, conditioned by later circumstances in life, than actual memory. In Hesse's picture of nature,
there is less reality than projection of the self; and in his praise
of childhood and nature, Schmid detects both a desire to com-
pensate for an isolated existence and an escape motive fostered
by an obsession of inadequacy in the face of life. Both preoccupa-
tions reflect a desire to return to the womb, where the dichotomy
and discord of life are yet unknown. *Gertrud* and *Rosshalde* are
viewed in terms of *Einsamkeit*, of the island existence to which
so many modern artists and intellectuals feel themselves con-
demned. This isolation is attributed to an extreme individualism
combining within it elements of social inadequacy and narcissism

and incapable of any lasting intimacy with fellow humans. The work of artists plagued in this manner is largely an effort to seek recompense for a bankrupt existence. Demian is seen in terms of cathartic self-exposure, the tale of a neurotic bent upon ridding himself of his complexes, the climax and end of Hesse's *Mutter-problem.* The longing for childhood and the worship of nature, which characterize Hesse's writings before *Demian,* are for Schmid manifestations of a severe mother complex. This complex is also reflected in the strength of Hesse's heroines and in the contrasting effeminacy of his heroes, whose quests are for mothers and not mates. Following *Demian,* Hesse and his heroes are no longer beset by this mother complex; his libido has now become attached to the feminine counterpart within himself.

Adding sadism, fear, and guilt (all very evident in each of Hesse's many tales recalling childhood) to his enumeration of psychological traits, Schmid scrutinizes all of these tendencies in his chapter entitled "Psychoanalyse." Relying upon the authority of Freud, Jung, and Adler, he attributes all of these disturbances to a strong Oedipus complex. Hesse's abnormal preoccupation with nature and with childhood are considered manifestations of a mother fixation which is rooted in an Oedipus complex and is commonly accompanied by an obsession of guilt. Sadism and autoerotic tendencies attending an Oedipus complex, as in the author's case, frequently resolve themselves into a sentimental auto-sadism and self-sympathy. Hesse's anxiety neurosis, in turn, can be considered a by-product of an attempt to sublimate his Oedipus complex.

Schmid obviously allows himself to be swept away by his enthusiasm for a theory, yet his conclusions are reasonably well-substantiated by Hesse's art. The period of *Demian* was, in fact, one of purgation for Hesse. Having resolved or ameliorated his inner discord (for Schmid, an Oedipus complex) he does cease to cling passionately to nature and childhood; and *Klingsors letzter Sommer* reflects the last traces of severe anxiety neurosis. The mother-figure in Hesse's works ceases to be of exclusive concern, gradually becomes little more than a principle, and the father-figure finally comes into its own.

While the literary critic is very apt to sin in the naïveté of his psychological insight and in his irresponsible use of highly technical terminology, medical men well-versed in psychoanalysis,

venturing into the study of literature, generally reflect a dearth
of aesthetic understanding and appreciation. Schmid's study reflects neither the extreme sins nor the highest virtues of either
group. As a student of literature, he does not forget that in the
final analysis he is concerned with works of art and not merely
with clinical reports; he does, therefore, make an effort to see
a relationship between Hesse's psychic life and the form and
substance of his art. However, in his disparaging evaluation of
Hesse's art, Schmid has not only allowed his antipathy toward
what he terms a decadent personality to mar his judgment, but
has erroneously applied the criteria of good classical literature to
art which is decidedly romantic. As a student of psychoanalysis,
Schmid presents excellent interpretations of the enigmatic
symbols and dreams prevalent in Hesse's writings and particularly so in *Demian*. However, while he refuses to accept the divine
mystery of art and its inspiration, his own attempts to diagnose
this inspiration, to determine the psychic factors involved, go
little beyond an amateurish application of general theories.

Schmid concludes his monograph by focussing his attention
upon Hesse's ethical system, with which he himself is so much at
variance that he can hardly restrain himself from scoffing. He
perceives only an extreme individualism which recognizes no
responsibility to society and which is incapable of any genuine
feeling for or communion with fellow humans. This individualism
is a confusion of skepticism, mysticism, and deliberate escape
into illusions. In its flight into a relativity which ends in ethical
nihilism, it sacrifices not only morality, but the very principle of
truth.

In view of the sentiment of Hesse's writings since *Steppenwolf*—the *Eigensinn* of the *Demian* period slowly supplanted by
a social consciousness culminating in the *Liebe* and *Dienst* of
Glasperlenspiel; the gradual disappearance of the somewhat
anarchistic relativity of *Klingsor* and *Blick ins Chaos;* and the
Steppenwolf's acrid skepticism transformed into the *Heiterkeit*
and the *Bejahung* of Josef Knecht—Schmid might today ameliorate his severe appraisal. On the other hand, he might be tempted
to discount the altruism and more humanitarian spirit of Hesse's
later works as psychological necessities rather than ethical convictions.

Hugo Mauerhofer

While it is principally the psychology of the modern decadent
artist that interests H. R. Schmid, it is the problem of introversion and art that attracts Mauerhofer (*Die Introversion, mit
spezieller Berücksichtigung des Dichters Hermann Hesse* [1929],
61 pp.). In each instance, however, it is the psychology of the
artist and not his art which is given prime attention.

It is only after he has expounded at length upon introversion,
drawing heavily upon Freud, Kretschmer, and Bleuler, and quot-
ing liberally from Jung, that Mauerhofer proceeds to determine
the significance of this psychological phenomenon in the life
and the art of Hesse. A psychography of Hesse (based upon
Ball's book and Hesse's own writings, and drawing attention to
personality characteristics, to narcissistic and neurotic tendencies, to conflicts in the home, in school, and in society, and to
the psychoautographical nature of Hesse's art) marks him as a
decided introvert, an asocial, narcissistic personality, who is
preoccupied with the inner rather than the outer world, and
who seeks isolation as a protection against unpleasant experience
and the overpowering influence of reality about him. Such a
person is at home in abstract thought, is capable of great emotional restraint, yet is periodically prone to depression and self-
castigation. His *Weltanschauung* is characterized by an aesthetic intellectualism, solipsism, and resignation.

Having pedantically ascertained Hesse's introversion, Mauerhofer examines his art in terms of this introversion and arrives
at two innocent observations and one questionable conclusion.
That Hesse's art teems with characteristics commonly associated
with introversion, is almost too obvious to be remarked upon,
let alone to be lingered over. That Hesse's style experiences a
gradual change (ever diminishing action, growing introspection,
a progressively heightened subjectivity with the ultimate exclusion of everything not within the orb of the *Ich*) which ac-
cords with the gradual intensification of his introversion, is
hardly to be refuted. However, the thesis which Mauerhofer is
bent upon establishing, that introversion is unequivocally the
causative factor in Hesse's art ("Die Introversion war sowohl
Ursacher seines schmerzlichen Lebenskampfes als auch seines
Werkes. . ." p. 43), is indeed a doubtful contention.

To maintain that introversion and art stand in a cause and

effect relationship is hardly more tenable than Max Nordau's notorious association of disease and art (*Die Entartung*, 1892). Introversion is, more plausibly, only one of the many necessary conditions of creative work. In its extremes, like any other psychic tendency which has become predominant, it may act as another impulse which can condition art in both its substance and form, but can surely not cause it. The artist in Hesse, or any other writer, is not to be sought in one particularly strong psychic tendency, or in a school of complexes. Rather, he is to be sought in a complexity of conditions which would include, among others, a sensitive awareness, a capacity for deep emotional and intellectual experience, a creative imagination, and a cultured and disciplined mind.

Mauerhofer's study makes some contribution to a psychological understanding of Hesse, but in its oversimplification of the problem of art and its creation it can contribute very little to an understanding of the process by which art comes into being.

Ernst A. F. Lützkendorf

Hesse's kinship with German Romanticism has been obvious to most of his critics from the very outset. It was inevitable that this relationship would become a popular subject for doctoral dissertations. Lützkendorf's was the first of these ("Hermann Hesse als religiöser Mensch in seinen Beziehungen zur Romantik und zum Osten," Leipzig, 1931). Heta Baaten's followed a year later ("Der Romantiker Hermann Hesse," Münster, 1932). Almost two decades passed before Franz Baumer took up the theme ("Das magische Denken in der Dichtung Hermann Hesses," München, 1951). Five more dissertations were completed in rapid succession: Kurt Weibel, "Hermann Hesse und die deutsche Romantik," Bern, 1954; Hans Horst Lehner, "Nachwirkungen der deutschen Romantik auf die Prosadichtung Hermann Hesses," Würzburg, 1954; Loyal N. Gould, "Romantic Elements in the Characters of Hermann Hesse," University of North Carolina, 1955; Gerhard Mauer, "Hermann Hesse und die deutsche Romantik," Tübingen, 1955; Th. J. Ziolkowski, "Hermann Hesse und Novalis," Yale, 1956. Otto Langlo's "Hesse und die Romantik" (Kiel) is still in progress. Of these nine studies, only Lützkendorf's, a portion of Baaten's, and Weibel's have appeared in print.

Before turning to Hesse himself, Lützkendorf (1932, 95 pp.) dwells at length upon Germany's budding awarenes of the Orient; he considers the temperament of the Romantic School, focussing particular attention upon those of its members who fostered its *Drang nach Osten* (Friedrich Schlegel, Görres, and Novalis); and finally seeks out those aspects of the East which most attracted the West (cradle of mankind, birthplace of religion and poetry, home of the myth, the fairy tale, and of mystery). With this background constantly in mind, Lützkendorf then shows how Hesse was reared in a pietistic tradition similar to that of Novalis, was educated in the same Swabian institutions where Mörike and Hölderlin had suffered before him, was temperamentally akin to Wackenroder and Eichendorff, and, like them, was more concerned with the metaphyiscal than the physical world. He draws attention to Hesse's preoccupation with his predecessors, to his avid reading of their works, and to his many casual references to Novalis, Hölderlin, Jean Paul, Eichendorff, Brentano, and to Hoffmann. He mentions Hesse's essays about these authors, and the writings by them which Hesse has edited. Lützkendorf now shows briefly how this interest and kinship is reflected in Hesse's own art: the fragmentary *Künstlerroman*, the attraction of the *Novelle* and the *Märchen*, lyrical prose, melodious verse, attachment to nature, and melancholy atmosphere. Concluding this portion of his dissertation, Lützkendorf is very careful to caution against any inference that Hesse is an epigonus, a *Spätromantiker*, as Ball would term him. He would prefer to consider him just as original a Romanticist as either Novalis or Eichendorff. That they should have so much in common (extreme introspection, constant yearning, enervating doubt, playful irony, a similar conception of, and attitude toward woman, a passion for oblivious release from the dichotomous *Ich*, with its preoccupation with death and the mother symbol, and its attachment to childhood and to nature), is to be attributed to a common temperament, mode of thought, and attitude to reality, rather than to influence and imitation.

In the concluding chapter of his study, Lützkendorf first outlines the intimate contact with India experienced by Hesse's parents and grandparents on his mother's side, then proposes that it was not this family background nor Hesse's trip to the East in 1911 which eventually led him to his true understanding and appreciation of the Orient, but an inner crisis, occasioned to a great extent by the First World War and by the hopeless disillusionment of the immediate postwar years. Like many other intellectuals of the time, Hesse found himself in a spiritual vacuum and turned to the East for renewed hope. A religious rebirth ensued, marked by an Oriental affirmation of life and its suffering, and bringing with it a warm appreciation of the spirit of Dostoyevsky's Russia, and an acceptance of the decline of the West, with a faith in a cultural and spiritual rebirth to follow.

Lützkendorf's is a systematic, well-documented, and convincing analysis of two very difficult themes (Hesse himself speaks highly of the dissertation, *Briefe* [1951], p. 364). Only the second of these is open to serious criticism. No clear distinction is made between Hesse's attitude towards India and China. Lützkendorf fails to note his gradual antipathy for the "indische-asketische Weisheit," and his growing acclaim of the more balanced, the more mature wisdom of China's philosophers (*Eine Bibliothek der Weltliteratur* [1946], pp. 61-62). Furthermore, to speak of *Demian, Zarathustras Wiederkehr, Klein und Wagner, Blick ins Chaos,* and *Siddhartha* in one breath, and to associate them as a group with Hesse's religious rebirth, seems to be a decided oversimplification of the different trends of Hesse's thinking and inclinations during this critical period. Are not *Demian* and *Zarathustras Wiederkehr* born of a different spirit than the other mentioned works, of a Nietzschean spirit with its passionate desire for self-knowledge and self-realization? Does this Nietzschean activism not subsequently yield to a Schopenhauer-like, Oriental quietism with its quest for nirvana, characterized by the *Sichfallenlassen* of *Klein und Wagner,* and the *Allesgeltenlassen* of *Blick ins Chaos?* Might one not look upon the *Demian-Zarathustra* period as a brief and vain effort by Hesse to preserve himself from the pessimistic feeling prevalent among the intellectuals of the day, that a cultural chaos from the East would soon sweep away Western civilization? And does *Blick ins Chaos* not reflect an acceptance of the encroaching chaos and an adjustment to it? Lützkendorf seems to have been completely unaware of these implications.

Walter Plümacher

In the hope that it might lead to a deeper insight into the factors which determine style, and consequently to a better under-

standing and fairer evaluation of a work of art, it became common
in both literary and art circles soon after the first decade of the
twentieth century to resort to concepts embracing opposites
(*e.g.*, Heinrich Wölfflin, *Kunstgeschichtliche Grundbegriffe,*
1915; Fritz Strich, *Deutsche Klassik und Romantik,* 1928). It is
the validity of this new approach to literature which Walter
Plümacher is most determined to establish in his dissertation
(*Versuch einer metaphysischen Grundlegung literaturwissenschaftlicher Grundbegriffe aus Kants Antinomienlehre mit einer
Anwendung auf das Kunstwerk Hermann Hesses* [1936], 81 pp.).
His actual study of Hesse is little more than an appended
illustration.

Approaching his problem historically, Plümacher traces the
polar concept in art back to Schiller's *naiv und sentimental,* an
association which Nietzsche acknowledged in his *apollinisch und
dionysisch,* which Wölfflin saw in terms of *Klassik und Barock,*
and Strich in *Klassik und Romantik,* or *Vollendung und Unendlichkeit.* These formulations are then examined and compared,
and finally established as only varied nomenclature for identical
phenomena. Kant is now drawn into the argument to provide
the necessary metaphysical basis for these so-called *Grundbegriffe;* and with Kant, Plümacher bogs down in a confused and
confusing metaphysics of art. Painfully winding his way through
Kant's conception of genius and art, and delving into his belief
in the antinomy inherent in pure reason, he concludes that it was
Kant's unexpressed conviction that reason was the source of all
art, and by so surmising he manages, questionably, to link the
polar concepts with Kant and to find the desired metaphysical
confirmation for a new approach to literature.

Of much more immediate interest to the student of Hesse than
the theory underlying this approach to literature, is its application in Plümacher's concluding thirty pages. Examining the
Gehalt of Hesse's prose works briefly and chronologically,
Plümacher arrives at one basic and ever recurring theme, the
conflict between the inner and the outer worlds and the quest for
unity. He now proceeds to show how this basically romantic
substance can find expression only in a correspondingly romantic
form. Consequently, born of a particular attitude toward divinity,
man, and life, romantic art can be judged only in terms of its
own criterion (*Unendlichkeit*); and classical art, in turn, only in
terms of its particular criterion (*Vollendung*). Having estab-

lished Hesse's art as unquestionably romantic in its substance and form, Plümacher ends by analyzing Hesse's attitude to such aspects of life as religion, fate, love, music, the ego, the mother myth, reality and the dream world, and concludes convincingly that his *Weltanschauung* is essentially a romantic one. And so the circle is closed: *Weltanschauung* determines *Gehalt*, which in turn conditions *Gestalt*.

Confining a book-length theme to a single chapter will inevitably leave much to be desired. Plümacher is explicit in his purpose and very systematic in his approach and presentation. However, like so many other protagonists of this approach to literature, he cleverly pinpoints his way above the individual works of art rather than penetrates them. A casual remark or two is hardly enough to prove that substance violates form in *Hermann Lauscher*, that the substance is too personal in the novels of Gaienhofen with their *geschlossene Gestalt,* and that from *Demian* on, substance finally receives perfect expression in its form. Such generalizations have frequently and deservedly drawn the sharp criticism of opposing schools of scholarship. Nevertheless, Plümacher's study is demanding in its ideas and stimulating in its suggestions. His association of life, substance, and form merits a book-length reconsideration.

Johanna M. L. Kunze

One might logically assume that a work of art, considered by one scholar to be a *unicum,* "die östlichste Dichtung in der deutschen Sprache" (Lützkendorf, p. 71), by another to be Hesse's "einheitlichstes und tiefstes Werk" (H. R. Schmid, p. 175), and by a third to be "ein klassisch geformtes Gedicht in Prosa" (R. B. Matzig, *Hermann Hesse in Montagnola,* p. 48), would very soon become the center of considerable scholarly activity. Quite to the contrary, until 1946 *Siddhartha* was almost completely ignored. Ball is rather indifferent to the tale, H. R. Schmid alludes to it in superlatives but allots it no more than a cursory eight pages (pp. 170-177), Matzig even fewer (pp. 43-48) ; and although M. Schmid's treatment is more extensive (*Hermann Hesse. Weg und Wandlung,* pp. 59-72), the subject begs for a deeper analysis and less descriptive recall. And except for three inconsequential articles,[4] and a number of insignificant reviews written soon after *Siddhartha* was published,[5] nothing more has appeared in periodicals. Only the rather recent dissertation of Johanna M. L. Kunze (*"Lebensgestaltung und Weltanschauung in Hermann Hesses Siddhartha"* [1946], 84 pp.) affords an insight into the novel which is more than superficial.

To make possible a better understanding of the problem thrashed out in *Siddhartha*, Kunze introduces her study by surveying the literature which paved the way to this climactic novel, presenting a penetrating survey which goes far beyond mere listing and describing. She contends that from the very beginning of his career Hesse was in quest of *den Kern seines Wesens*, and that *Demian* marks a major turning point in this search. From *Hermann Lauscher* to *Demian*, his road is one of *Vergeistigung* (p. 4.). In *Lauscher* it is the way of aestheticism, in *Peter Camenzind* and *Unterm Rad* the way of learning, and in *Gertrud* and *Rosshalde* it is the the way of art. With *Demian* a reaction sets in which leads Hesse through the world of the senses to the extremes of the *Sichfallenlassen* of *Klein und Wagner* and to the amoral relativity of Klingsor. In *Siddhartha*, these diverse roads of approach to the self are brought together for renewed perusal and reëvaluation.

Convincingly systematic and plausible though Johanna Kunze's theory is, it does not always fit. Quite contrary to her contention that Hesse first sought self-knowledge in aestheticism, the author himself clearly states that *Lauscher* was his first attempt to escape the dangers of aestheticism and to emerge from the beauty worship of *Eine Stunde hinter Mitternacht* with its sentimental depression and lonely isolation (*Eine Stunde hinter Mitternacht* [1941], p. 11). The novels which follow are repeated steps in this direction, reflecting Hesse's ceaseles efforts to adjust himself to the world, to gain for himself "ein Stück Welt und Wirklichkeit." Instead of marking the futility of knowledge, discipline, and will in his quest for the self, *Camenzind, Gertrud,* and *Rosshalde* reflect Hesse's inability to escape from himself in his attempted reconciliation with life at large. Camenzind seeks escape from aestheticism and isolation in St. Francis of Assisi's way of love and service; Kuhn and Veraguth seek escape in rigid discipline and ascetic devotion to their compensatory art. Kunze fails to note that each of these heroes is a reincarnated Lauscher, "ein Aesthet und Sonderling" (*Hermann Lauscher* [1920], p. 16), a hypersensitive, introspective personality to which the *ars amandi* and the *ars vivendi* are quite foreign, a personality which nevertheless makes repeated and determined efforts to find for itself a place in life. Escape from, rather than quest for the self characterizes this struggle. With *Demian* (and already foreshadowed in *Rosshalde* and *Knulp*) Hesse finally realizes that a real adjustment to life is absolutely contingent upon self-knowledge, and only now does his *Weg nach Innen* begin.

Elaborating further upon the background necessary for a better understanding of *Siddhartha*, Kunze presents a clear and concise outline of Brahmanism, Buddhism, and of Hinduism, drawing particular attention to their most characteristic traits. She does not fail to perceive that this Eastern world is but a new setting for an old problem, that Hesse's new hero is still a Western, Faustian spirit eagerly seeking the meaning of life and an adjustment to it despite the exotic Eastern setting of the sixth century B.C. with its Buddha, its Brahmans, and its Samanas.

In the second portion of her study, concerned exclusively with *Siddhartha*, Kunze first retells the story itself, interspersing a running, interpretive commentary. The Brahman stage of knowledge, of stereotyped ritual, and the asceticism of the Samanas, are seen in terms of *Camenzind*, *Gertrud*, and of *Rosshalde*, in terms of *Wissenserlebnis* and of *Willenserlebnis*. The Kamaswami-Kamala period of substance and flesh is seen in terms of the *Demian*-reaction, of *Sansaraerlebnis*. The Vasudeva-culmination of quiet observation, acceptance, and of affirmation is seen in terms of a *Vollendung* where abstract thought and deed have yielded to a *Sinnesempfindung*.

Kunze now ventures to extract a systematic *Weltanschauung* from *Siddhartha*, and she does so by perceiving in it an analogy to the philosophy of Heraclitus (p. 69). Like Heraclitus, Siddhartha accepts the principle of being in becoming, and like him, he embraces reality as a harmonious unity; but while *Logos* (*Geist*) is for Heraclitus the unifying principle which makes this attitude possible, for Siddhartha it is *Liebe*. Kunze believes that Hesse clearly implies that this love is born of both *Geist* and *Natur*, and in view of this implication and of Siddhartha's final denial of the world of thought and his acceptance of a vegetative, instinctive sort of existence, she maintains that "ein Riss geht durch dieses Werk" (pp. 76-77). Oddly enough, another scholar, employing a similar figure of speech, censures

Hesse for the very opposite reason, for a predilection for *Geist*, evident in the very thought process of Siddhartha's response to Govinda's desire for enlightenment (M. Schmid, p. 71). Neither criticism seems warranted and each may be attributed to a misinterpretation of the final stage of Siddhartha's life. Siddhartha recognizes the futility of both *das zufällige Ich der Gedanken* and *das zufällige Ich der Sinne* as ends in themselves. Neither can of itself be an avenue to the much desired *Einheit*. Though he denies each, yet he affirms both, for they are the very stuff of life. After exhausting both attitudes, he achieves an affirmation which can accept existence in its totality. It is this state of *Vollkommenheit* to which Siddhartha attains. It is a *Seelenzustand* which has transcended both *Geist* and *Natur*, an end result of both, but not a synthesis. Having termed the world of the mind *Wissenserlebnis*, the world of the senses *Sansaraerlebnis*, Siddhartha's culminating world of experience might appropriately be termed a *Seelenerlebnis*.

It is indicative of the common trend in Hesse scholarship that even *Siddhartha*, which more than any other of Hesse's novels invites analysis as a work of art, is viewed only in terms of its substance. Hesse's careful simplicity of language; his extended, stylized sentences with their intricately interwoven parallel phrases and clauses; the archaic, ornate, and highly formalized presentation of his thought; the resultant polite, impersonal air which pervades the tale; the rhythm of the prose, a religious chant-like succession of movements each of which trails two refrains in variation, like three-stress melodies recreating the monotonous beat of the music of India—all of this remains unnoticed by Kunze.

Otto Engel

Otto Engel's work (*Hermann Hesse. Dichtung und Gedanke* [1947], 95 pp.) consists of two basically independent units. The first of these (pp. 7-24) is a reprint of a speech given in 1945, and itself falls into two parts. In the first part, Engel characterizes Hesse's poetry briefly and well, noting the extreme subjectivity, the sentimental, melancholy atmosphere, the fatigue, and the pure musicality of the early poems, and the greater maturity, the objectivity, and the pictorial quality of the later poems. His attempt, however, in the second part, to prove that Hesse is a philosophical and religious thinker, that reason and faith are the formative forces in his art and the basis of his belief in the unity of reality, is feeble and confusing.

The main body of Engel's book is devoted entirely to *Glasperlenspiel.* From the title, and in view of the length of his treatment, one might have expected a thorough analysis of both form and substance, with attention given to such matters as language and symbol, philosophical, religious, and social implications. Engel presents, instead, a lengthy description of Castalia and of the bead game, and an elaborate resumé of Knecht's life. That *Glasperlenspiel* is a work of old age, heavy with thought, full of abstractions and digressions, with a playful love of details, graphic in its presentation of unforgettable situations, clear in the delineation of its figures, and written in a language which becomes epic in the slow tempo of its flow, is hardly adequate reason for deeming it superior to Goethe's *Wilhelm Meister* in both "Tiefe der Konzentration" and "innere Verdichtung" (p. 28). Knecht's ambiguous death is casually accepted as one of life's many chance incidents. Just as little heed is paid to Hesse's diagnosis of our age. Only the peculiar blending of philosophy and religion in Hesse's attitude toward life receives more than passing attention. It is the basic piety of Hesse's *Lebensanschauung* (not recognized by orthodoxy) that Engel is particularly anxious to establish. In response to those who have disparaged the worldliness of this *Lebensanschauung,* as evidenced in Castalia, he accepts *Glasperlenspiel* as a thoroughly religious book, religious in its belief in the unity of reality and in its emphasis upon meditation. It is quite obvious that this great variance of critical opinion is basically one of terms and meaning.

Engel's is the introductory study he intended it to be. It was not meant for scholars but for his fellow Germans who had not yet been able to read the novel itself. It served this purpose well.

Richard B. Matzig

Richard B. Matzig's view of art is a very balanced one. While form is the essence of art, substance cannot be ignored, and the artist is not to be forgotten. In his study of Hesse (*Hermann Hesse in Montagnola. Studien zu Werk und Innenwelt des Dichters* [1947], 119 pp.) he proposes to remain cognizant of all three factors.

Like so many of Hesse's more recent interpreters, Matzig chooses to by-pass everything preceding *Demian*. However, that *Demian* marks a new beginning, a sharp break in Hesse's life and art, a fact which might justify such an approach, is a point of contention. And though Hesse's later works may be more significant than those predating *Demian*, their full significance can be made apparent only in comparison and not in isolation.

Following a brief introduction in which he recalls a visit with Hesse in Montagnola, Matzig touches upon the prevalent themes and the general nature of Hesse's art, and then proceeds to give considerable attention to *Demian*, much less to *Kinderseele, Klein und Wagner, Klingsors letzter Sommer, Kurgast*, and *Nürnberger Reise* (all grouped in one chapter). *Steppenwolf* and *Narziss und Goldmund* fare well in their respective chapters, but *Morgenlandfahrt, Glasperlenspiel* and the *Gedichte* are quite inadequately treated in the concluding chapter. As he proceeds chronologically from work to work, he remains very mindful of substance and the author, but form fares badly. In each instance the story itself is recalled, the hero's lot is commented upon, the relevant circumstances of Hesse's own life are interwoven, and form is occasionally alluded to. Matzig dwells at length upon the internal stress that gave birth to *Demian* and upon the events in Hesse's life which occasioned this psychological crisis. He draws attention to Hesse's flight to Montagnola and to the ebullient spirit of release and freedom which finds its expression in *Klein und Wagner* and *Klingsor*. He discusses Hesse's interest in Oriental thought in connection with the new adjustment to life which he seems to find in *Siddhartha*, and details the simmering unrest recorded in *Kurgast* and *Nürnberger Reise*. He attempts to analyze its eventual eruption in *Krisis* and *Steppenwolf*, and traces the spiritual recuperation which leads ultimately to the more mature acceptance of life's dichotomy which finds reflection in *Narziss und Goldmund, Morgenlandfahrt*, and *Glasperlenspiel*.

So intent is Matzig upon accumulating all the biographical details relevant to each of these works, that the works proper are slighted. He recounts rather than analyzes, and proves to be more informative and interesting than stimulating or provocative. His study represents an excellent introduction to Hesse and his writings, but no more.

Max Schmid

H. R. Schmid, as has been noted, is primarily interested in the psychology of the modern decadent artist. He analyzes Hesse's works from *Eine Stunde hinter Mitternacht* to *Steppenwolf* in terms of psychic stresses, and relies for authority upon Freud, Jung, and Adler. Max Schmid (*Hermann Hesse. Weg und Wandlung* [1947], 288 pp.), skeptical of psychoanalysis, prefers to consider Hesse's problem as a metaphysical one. He analyzes all works from *Demian* to *Glasperlenspiel* on this basis, and looks to Ludwig Klages and his *Geist als Widersacher der Seele* for confirmation of his conclusions.

According to Klages (and quite contrary to the general thinking of the Western world), *Geist* is basically a foreign and hostile element in life, which in the course of time became a part of human nature, bringing to an end a natural nirvana-like coexistence of body and soul. *Geist* destroyed man's original state of harmony, making him aware of painful time, reducing life to a maze of conflicting principles, and leaving behind a ceaseless yearning and a perpetual quest for the *Welt der Bilder* that once was. With this argument Klages reduces the enigma of existence to the dichotomy of *Geist* and *Seele* (*Seele* is apparently understood to include the subsidiary body). With neophytic enthusiasm, Max Schmid undertakes to subject Hesse to this, Klages' way of thinking, and no less mercilessly than H. R. Schmid with his passion for psychoanalysis.

Until *Demian*, Hesse's life is an errant one, an uncertain groping about for his soul's lost *Bilderwelt*. With *Demian* comes the realization of the error of his past quest, and an awareness of the true nature of his inner conflict (*Geist* and *Seele*). Hesse now undertakes a long and calculated search for a second nirvana ("selbstlose Welt," p. 221). Both poles of existence can afford means of self-obliteration. The frigid realm of pure *Geist* (Fichte's absolute *Ich*) is timeless and consequently contains no self-awareness ("Jenseits im Sternenraum," p. 90). The realm of life (*Lebensstrom, Seelenstrom*), void of *Geist*, is equally unconscious of time and the *Ich* ("Jenseits im Diesseits," p. 90). In his desperate determination to resolve the struggle between *Geist* and *Seele*, and thereby to restore harmony and unity to life, Hesse leaves no possibilities untried. For a number of years he leans toward *Seele* in the *Sichfallenlassen* philosophy reflected in *Blick ins Chaos, Klein und Wagner,* and most clearly expressed in the *Entselbstung im Strom des Lebens* of *Siddhartha* ("An Stelle des Geistigen und des Triebhaften aufersteht der Beseelte." p. 64). However, modern Westerner that Hesse is, he was not to escape for long the curse of *Bewusstsein* as opposed to *Erleben*. The principle of *Geist*, briefly and unsuccessfully acclaimed in *Demian*, was soon to nullify Siddhartha's panacea. In *Steppenwolf*, Hesse embraces "den ausserraumzeitlichen Geist" (p. 221) ; and the cold, eternal land of the saints, the intellectuals, and such artists as Goethe and Mozart replaces the ideal of the oblivious soul and the warm stream of life. While *Narziss und Goldmund* reaffirms the *Steppenwolf* turn of mind, *Morgenlandfahrt* gives brief evidence of a third solution of the *Geist* and *Seele* dichotomy. These two conflicting elements are now brought into accord through a mysterious contemplation (*Versenkung*) ; and their harmony is characterized by a "lebenswarme Vernünftigkeit" (p. 147). This third ideal, however, is abandoned as quickly as it was proclaimed, and in *Glasperlenspiel*, *Geist* is left to rule supreme.

This is the gist of Max Schmid's argument, and he is convinced that his approach affords a deeper insight into Hesse and his art than a psychoanalytical investigation. It is rather difficult to understand how, of itself, Max Schmid's *Geist* and *Seele* terminology can be any more metaphysical, or for that matter, any less psychoanalytical than the *Geist* and *Natur* duality of H. R. Schmid, particularly since the former's concept of *Seele* embraces *Natur* and *Triebe*, and the latter's concept of *Natur* extends beyond mere *Triebe*. Whether Klages' myth of life furnishes the key to Hesse's problems, remains to be seen.

Hesse's early worship of nature, his nostalgia for childhood, and his efforts to adjust himself to a peaceful bourgeois way of life are expressions of his ceaseless quest for a *Heimat*. Viewed psychoanalytically this quest would suggest an Oedipus complex. Metaphysically, *Heimat* becomes a *Bilderwelt* upon which Klages expounds as follows:

> Aus der polaren Berührung von Innen und Aussen gebärt sich unablässig das selber beseelte Bild (unaufhörliche Ausgeburt). Das Aussen zeugt, das Innen empfängt, und aus der Umarmung ihrer beider bricht der Feuerstrom der Bilder des Alls, der tanzende Stern des zum Kosmos gegliederten Chaos (M. Schmid, p. 12).

While insight into the Oedipus complex affords no criteria of value in aesthetic appreciation, it can lead to a better understanding of the artist himself, may even be helpful in interpretation, and is certainly indispensable in the psychology of art. Max Schmid's poetically conceived *Bilderwelt*, on the other hand, can only mystify.

Philosophically, religiously, and morally, *Demian* marks the turning point in Hesse's attitude toward, and understanding of his inner conflict. Hesse's consequent struggle to find his *Weg nach Innen* is analyzed by Max Schmid solely in terms of a *Geist* and *Seele* conflict with a prevailing desire for self-obliteration in a restored *Seelenwelt*, or if necessary, in a *Geisteswelt* which will transcend the immediate reality of time, space, and the *Ich*. Refusing to acknowledge the psychoanalytical nature of Hesse's new search, Max Schmid remains totally unmindful of his constant and acute concern with *Natur* as sexual expression. Convinced that base *Triebe* can be of little moment in the metaphysical issue of *Geist* and *Seele*, Schmid simply chooses to ignore their appearance in Hesse's works. Proceeding with his analysis, Schmid maintains that *Demian* reflects an unsuccessful resolution of the duality of *Geist* and *Seele* in an impossible compromise ("Selbstentwicklung und Hingabe an Eva vertragen sich nicht." p. 35) ; that Klein escapes this painful dichotomy in death, a will-less surrender and return to the *Strom des Erlebens*; that Klingsor, as an artist who must give expression to the soul's pictures, is destined always to vacillate between these two tensions of existence; that Siddhartha finally attains in life what is Klein's only in death; that Haller's sojourn in Maria's world of the senses is but to allow his *Seelenwelt* to recuperate and thereby make possible the renewed struggle between *Geist* and *Seele* with its resultant preference for the former; that Narziss' world is the *Jenseits im Sternenraum* to which *Steppenwolf* is dedicated and which Hesse now accepts; that Goldmund cannot, except upon rare occasion, experience the *Bilderwelt* of the soul; and finally that with *Glasperlenspiel*, the metaphysical problem of *Geist* and *Seele* has resolved itself into an ethical issue, *vita activa* as opposed to *vita contemplativa*.

Though Max Schmid's approach is consistent and his argument clearly evolved, his interpretation is not entirely convincing. Many of his conclusions reflect the force of a theory rather than show a careful consideration of all factors involved. The impossible compromise of *Demian* hinges entirely upon a particular interpretation or misinterpretation of the symbol, *Mutter Eva*. Union with Eva need be no more productive of oblivion for Sinclair than it is for Demian. This union could be symbolic of an ideal realized, indicative of the attainment of absolute self-awareness and self-realization ("Ihr Blick war Erfüllung . . ." [1919], p. 217). The diagnosis of the Klein case is almost absurd in its oversimplification. His suicide following a brief period of agitated indulgence in sensual pleasures is explained as follows: "Das Leben aber lässt ihn das köstliche Land der Seele schauen, und die Sehnsucht, in ihm beheimatet zu sein, löscht er, indem er sich hingibt" (p. 50). Schmid does not seem to realize that, in this tale, the *Weg des Geistes* and the Nietzschean way of life approved of in *Demian* are being put to the test ("Lernet euer Leben zu leben! Lernet euer Schicksal erkennen!" "Zarathustras Wiederkehr," *Krieg und Frieden* [1949], p. 115), and that after the waning of initial enthusiasm, this ideal proves, as yet, to be too trying. Klein shows himself to be inadequate for the increasing loneliness and isolation demanded by greater self-awareness (*Geist*). Hoping for oblivious release from this painful self-awareness, he turns to a life of the senses (*Natur*), but physical experience can offer him neither solace nor escape from the self he had been so intent upon developing, and in sheer exhaustion, incapable of any further readjustment to life, he commits suicide.

Nor is it as much Haller's *Seelenwelt*, as his *Geist*, which recuperates in his association with Maria and Pablo. It is Harry Haller's *Geist* which has weakened and which quails before the next necessary readjustment to life, which is greater individuation with its greater isolation. Nor need one assert quite as strongly, that the *Geist* and *Seele* (or *Natur*) problem ends with *Narziss und Goldmund,* yielding to an ethical issue in *Glasperlenspiel.* Has the same old problem not merely been raised from a personal, psychological level to an ethical plane?

Furthermore, argue persistently though one may, that Hesse's problem is fundamentally a metaphysical and not a psychological one, the obvious fact remains that Hesse himself would more than suggest the contrary. To ignore this is to make a detailed interpretation of Hesse's works from *Demian* to *Narziss und Goldmund* almost impossible, and this is the chief weakness of Schmid's study. While he hovers above the individual works with his *Geist* and *Seele* generalities, enigmatic details remain untouched. The copious dreams of Sinclair, Klein, Siddhartha, Haller, and of Goldmund are brushed aside with little ado, the significant paintings of Sinclair and Klingsor are merely referred to, and the token attempt to delve into the meanings of such mysterious figures as *Mutter Eva*, Demian, Hermine, and Leo, is as inadequate as the predominantly descriptive report of Siddhartha's river and Pablo's magic theater. And because *Natur*, in its physical urges, is of little consequence in Klages' scheme of things, Schmid prefers to ignore its implications in Hesse's writings. Only once does he deign to acknowledge that sex, too, is a factor to be reckoned with (p. 121). That the *Erlebnis*, the *Traumwelt* of Klingsor may smack more of *Triebe* than *Seele*, and that the Klein-Teresina, Siddhartha-Kamala, and the Haller-Maria affairs may suggest a *Geist* and *Natur*, rather than his *Geist* and *Seele* dichotomy, does not at all disturb Schmid. In his determined adherence to Klages' *Geist als Widersacher der Seele*, he fails to note the very personal nature of Hesse's analysis of Hölderlin, "Er hat eine Geistigkeit in sich hochgezüchtet, welche seiner Natur Gewalt antat" ("Über Hölderlin," *Betrachtungen*, p. 206) ; and he completely ignores the revealing self-analysis of the "Nachwort an meine Freunde" (*Krisis*), in which Hesse points out that he has reached one of those "Etappen des Lebens, wo der Geist seiner selbst müde wird, sich selbst entthront und der Natur, dem Chaos, dem Animalischen das Feld räumt." However, in stubborn defense of Klages' theory, Schmid maintains that the *Geist* and *Natur* duality is but an illusion of the modern Western mind, which is no longer aware of the "einzig befruchtende, allverbindende Kraft der Seele" (p. 122).

Hesse's works proper advise us just as unequivocally against Schmid's metaphysical theory as his direct words. Of the scholar, in his brief tale "Der Mann mit den vielen Büchern," he writes:

> Er war betrogen, er war um alles betrogen! Er hatte gelesen, er hatte Seiten umgedreht, er hatte Papier gefressen—ach und dahinter, hinter der schändlichen Büchermauer, war das Leben gewesen, hatten Herzen gebrannt, Leidenschaften getobt, war Blut und Wein geflossen, war Liebe und Verbrechen geschehen. Und nichts von alledem hatte ihm gehört, nichts war sein gewesen, nichts hatte er in Händen gehabt, nichts als dünne, flache Schatten und Papier, in Büchern! (*Fabulierbuch*, p. 358).

Of the cultivation of Geist in the pursuit of art, Hesse has Louis der Grausame remark: "ein zu schwer bezahlter Ersatz für versäumtes Leben, versäumte Tierheit, versäumte Liebe (*Weg nach Innen*, p. 365). In *Kurgast*, which Schmid fails even to mention, life's two basic tensions are referred to in this manner:

Denn ebenso wie. ich zwischen Essen und Fasten . . . muss ich auch zwischen Natürlichkeit und Geistigkeit . . . hin und her pendeln. Dass ein Mensch sein Leben lang immer und immer den Geist verehren und die Natur verachten kann . . . scheint mir auch ebenso fatal . . . (1925, pp. 139-140).

And in *Steppenwolf*, man is described as the "gefährliche Brücke zwischen Geist und Natur" ("Tractat").

Schmid concedes that in the case of Thomas Mann and C. F. Meyer the basic problem is one of *Geist, Leben,* and Nietzsche; but that such may also be true of Hesse, is quite impossible, for, he maintains: "Hermann Hesse dagegen ist nicht so arm an Liebe und Leben. Viele Gedichte singen von Erfüllung. Klein, Klingsor, Siddhartha und auch Harry Haller trinken den dunklen feurigen Wein der Liebe" (p. 56). Schmid might be reminded that for every one of Hesse's poems which reflects love, life, and fulfillment, there are at least a dozen others which speak only of painful yearning, disillusionment, and of renunciation. And if many of Hesse's post-*Demian* heroes drink deeply of the cup of life, is it not in desperation, and does it not represent more wish than fact for Hesse himself?

Nor does Schmid's confusion of terminology aid his cause. *Bewusstsein* and *Erleben,* and *Geist* and *Seele* are treated as synonymous. *Erleben* is subdivided into *Seele* and *Triebe,* with the experience of the former termed *Bilderstrom* and *Seelenstrom,* of the latter, *Lebensstrom.* The so-called *Bilderwelt* is the product of the *schauende Seele* and of the *beschaute Wirklichkeit,* and upon this world the *Triebe* can leave no impression, despite Hesse's notion to the contrary in *Narziss und Goldmund* (that all of Goldmund's sexual experiences leave their mark upon his *Mutterbild,* is an impossibility according to Schmid's theory, and Hesse is taken to task for this alleged error, p. 115). To complicate matters, Schmid ventures occasionally to use the terms *Natur* and *Leben* as synonyms for *Erleben,* then *Leben* interchangeably with *Seele.* Notwithstanding, he continues to maintain that Hesse's problem is one of *Geist* and *Seele,* and not of *Geist* and *Natur.* This turbidity could easily have been avoided had Schmid restricted himself to the terms *Erleben* and *Bewusstsein,* and made no further effort to bring Klages into the picture.

That Hesse is a *Seelenmensch,* is not to be contested, and one must agree with Schmid when he asserts that Hesse's whole life reflects a quest for a *Heimat,* for a *Seelenzustand,* a world in which life's tensions are resolved. But that Hesse's inner discord is to be attributed to the *Geist* and *Seele* conflict conceived by Klages remains a very moot point. His actual problem is one of *Geist* and *Natur*, and this conflict remains on the personal, psychological level until *Steppenwolf* (Hesse's *Werden*), and then gradually rises to the impersonal, the ethical and religious plane of *Glasperlenspiel* (his *Entwerden*).

Though Schmid's study may be taken severely to task, it still remains one of the most stimulating and challenging analyses of Hesse and his art. The different approaches of Max Schmid and of H. R. Schmid have contributed much to Hesse scholarship; a synthesis of these extremes promises even more.

Helmut Bode

Helmut Bode represents a third and almost equally extreme approach to Hesse (*Hermann Hesse. Variationen über einen Lieblingsdichter* [1948], 169 pp.). His excessively prolonged introduction ("Uber die Notwendigkeit einen Lieblingsdichter zu besitzen," pp. 7-35), is nothing short of an apology for, and defense of this approach. At the same time it is a sharp polemic against bookish scholars and compilers of histories of literature, against their scientific, objective methods and their total lack of understanding of, and inability to appreciate a work of art. It is for dilettantes such as himself, and not for pedantic scholars, that Bode intends his book.

As could be expected in view of this introduction, Bode's consideration of Hesse the poet is largely an enthusiastic appreciation and not an analysis, a random hovering about in the fragrance and atmosphere of Hesse's poems. Too frequently, also, he is more concerned with himself and his own poetic experience than with his favorite author. Yet there is some system and order behind Bode's rambling. Attention is drawn to the autobiographical tendency of Hesse's poetry, to its early folksong-like simplicity, and to the frequently used themes of nature, loneliness, longing, beauty, and death. Bode is also one of the few writers who notes the change in spirit of Hesse's later poems, where fear, suffering, and loneliness yield to affirmation and quiet humor, feeling to contemplation, and Chopin to Bach.

For a theme which promises so much, Bode's third chapter yields very little ("Der Erzähler Hermann Hesse"). His own

words best characterize his treatment: "lückenhafte und frag-
mentarische Anmerkungen" (p. 110). The mode of presentation
is delightfully novel and very indirect, so indirect, indeed, as
to become quite obscure at times. To introduce a stranger to
the world of Hesse's prose, a fantastic dream is related, a dream
in which all of Hesse's heroes and heroines appear at a large ban-
quet. In a breath-taking flurry of names and casual references,
brief attention is then drawn to the geographical background of
Hesse's prose (Swabia), and to its predominant themes (childhood and youth, *Geist* and *Natur*). But for a few pages devoted
to *Glasperlenspiel*, no story or novel receives any specific attention.

In his ensuing chapter ("Der Essayist Hermann Hesse"),
Bode broaches a theme to which students of Hesse have paid little
or no attention. He allows the vast number of essays to fall into
four major categories (nature, literature, politics, and autobiog-
raphy), touches lightly upon these, and then loses himself in a
stream of stray references, irrelevant digressions, and excessively
long quotations. Though, as usual, Bode only skirts the field, his
survey is quite informative, and the thematic approach he suggests merits reconsideration.

Bode's final chapter ("Die Weisheit des Glasperlenspielers"),
is primarily concerned with Hesse's wisdom as reflected in his
adjustment to life. Attention is centered about Hesse's resolution
of the dichotomy of spirit and flesh, about his emphasis upon self-
knowledge and self-realization, upon love, service and respect,
and about his final acceptance of life, made possible in patience
and meditation.

If nothing else, Bode's book is certainly different from the
common run of monographs. It is an undeniably pleasant antidote
to the tedious detail and the pedantry of some scholars, but
whether it actually contributes much to Hesse scholarship, is
rather questionable. But then, Bode did not intend that it
should.

— Edmund Gnefkow

In the "Geleitwort" of *Krieg und Frieden*, Hesse admits to
three major influences in his life: the Christian, cosmopolitan
tradition of his family background, the writings of Jakob Burckhardt, and those of the great Chinese philosophers. Though not

unnoticed, except for family background these influences have received little attention. Until Edmund Gnefkow's book (*Hermann Hesse. Eine Biographie* [1952], 143 pp.), no serious study was made of Hesse and China; and the influence of Burckhardt continues to be ignored.

Assuming that unity has been the sole dogma of his *Weltanschauung,* and realization of this ideal his life's most ardent aspiration, Gnefkow pictures Hesse's development as a movement spiralling slowly upward through four distinct levels and culminating in an *Ich-Welt-Gott-Einheit.*

In an effort to determine why diversity and unity should so have concerned Hesse, Gnefkow first presents a study of his family background, of his personality, and of the influence of the times. The biographical details to which attention is drawn (north-south ancestry, child-like paternal grandfather and intellectual maternal grandfather, stern father and spirited mother, Western piety and Eastern wisdom: a world which had, in religion, found unity behind reality's apparent diversity) are not new and can be found more fully presented and discussed in both Ball and Baaten. However, Gnefkow's attempt to categorize Hesse's personality in terms of Ernst Kretschmer's typology (*Körperbau und Charakter*), is indeed novel. Examining Hesse's protagonists very briefly, he concludes cautiously and with no desire to be derogatory, that they are quite obviously inclined to be schizoid and probably reflect a similar propensity in their author. Conditioned by this background, so disposed in personality, and born into an age out of joint, Hesse seemed almost predestined to suffer inner and outer discord and to seek a resolution in some ideal of unity.

After this introduction, Gnefkow proceeds to analyze each of the four stages of Hesse's striving for unity, emphasizing in each instance the direction of the struggle, its general nature and major influences, and its results. The unity which Hesse sought until 1916 ("romantisch-dualistische Stufe des Ausgeliefertseins," p. 56) was the *Natur-Ich-Gott-Einheit* which is possible in a religious-aesthetic devotion to nature. This was the unity found by kindred spirits, the early nineteenth-century Romanticists, whose influence over him prevailed during this entire period. The unity actually realized, however, was at best an illusion which soon paled in the reality of marriage and died under the impact of the war.

Only after acquiring his first real conception of polarity, in the psychoanalytic theories of Jung, and with his first serious study of the philosophies of India, did Hesse give new and higher direction to his struggle for unity. From 1916 to 1926, his quest became primarily one for *Ich-Einheit* and was sought rationally, first in the self-knowledge and self-expression suggested by psychoanalysis, then in the willed nirvana of India ("die psychoanalytisch-meditative Stufe der Selbst-Erlösung aus der Ich-Polarität," p. 87). Again, however, Hesse's life was to come to an impasse. To follow the path of Demian could only lead to the more painful isolation of greater individuation and might well have ended, as did Klein's, in suicide; and the meditative way of Yoga could only lead to a unity which denied polarity. Siddhartha's Chinese unity of acceptance and affirmation was as yet only wishful anticipation, and Hesse's incessant attempts, until *Steppenwolf*, to realize a harmonious interplay of *Geist* and *Natur*, were always unsuccessful.

Not until he came under the influence of Chinese thought, was Hesse finally able to transcend himself and thereby to raise his struggle for unity to the higher level of dispassionate observation ("Spiegelstufe der Ich-Überwindung," p. 104; 1927-32). The *Ich* and the *Ich-Gott-Einheit* were now fully realized: not in actual experience, in the *Schau* of Tao, but in renunciation and withdrawal into the spiritual reality of *Morgenlandfahrt* (East-West synthesis).

Now that Hesse had come to terms with himself and his God, higher aspirations again gave a new direction to his search for unity ("Glasperlenspielstufe der Welt-Überwindung," p. 113). The *Ich-Welt-Einheit*, which alone had yet to be realized, was now made possible through Knecht's humanitarian ideal of service and sacrifice. Only on this ethical plane could the *Geistesmensch* justify his existence. The ultimate *Ich-Welt-Gott-Einheit*, which Hesse had spent a lifetime seeking, was finally fully realized.

As Gnefkow correctly maintains, Hesse's life has been a persistent pursuit of *Einheit*, or *Heimat*, as he himself often terms it; and the four stages through which Gnefkow would have this quest pass, are well founded. However, Hesse seems hardly to have striven as consciously for the *Natur-Ich-Gott-Einheit* as intimated, nor did he realize this unity only to have the

illusion shattered in his marriage (p. 53). There is no evidence
to prove that Hesse ever achieved any sort of harmony in his
early aestheticism, and the only illusion that was dispelled during
the Gaienhofen years, was the hope for security. Furthermore, in
his determination to show that Hesse rises above the psychoanalytical plane upon which Ball and Matzig keep him, Gnefkow is
tempted to discount the value of Hesse's *Weg nach Innen*. To
liken the period from *Demian* to *Steppenwolf* to the valley
Morbio Inferiore (pp. 75, 103), is almost to consider it a deviation
or a relapse, and not the necessary progresion that it actually
was. Nor is Gnefkow's work enhanced by his occasional far-
fetched interpretations, *e.g.*, that the Hermine episode represents
a brief, supreme unity of *Geist* and *Natur* (p. 97), or that Leo
is God and the transformation of the figurine symbolizes "die
sich vollendende Ich-Gott-Einheit" (p. 101). Also to be regretted
is the frequent sweeping assertion which can never really be
proved or disproved, *e.g.*, that Hesse owes his *Morgenlandfahrt*
to his acquaintance with China's wizards, and that the synthesis
of *Glasperlenspiel* would hardly have been possible without China
(p. 96). It would be better if page references had been given
for the many quotations. And that Hesse married Lisa Wenger, a
Swiss writer some twenty years older than he, from which certain
deductions are to be made, is an error which should not be
perpetuated (Hesse's second marriage, in the early Twenties, was
not to Lisa, but to her daughter Ruth, who was considerably
younger than he). And while the uncluttered clarity of a bird's-
eye view is very persuasive, the proof of detail, so wanting in
Gnefkow's almost casual references to individual works, would
undoubtedly be more appreciated.

All in all, however, Gnefkow's book, of which Hesse himself
has spoken very favorably, represents a well-argued thesis which
assumes that the reader has both insight and a thorough knowledge of Hesse. Nor is his perusal of the philosophies of India and
China, in terms of their influence upon Hesse, extended beyond
the pertinent. His study of I Ging, Lao-Tse, Dschuang Dsi, and of
the poets Li-Tai-Po and Thu-Fu breaks new ground and makes
possible a far better understanding of *Siddhartha* and its Chinese
influences, of the concept of time and space in *Morgenlandfahrt*,
and of the *älterer Bruder* and the *Chinesenhausspiel* in *Glasperlenspiel*.

Dank an Hesse (1952), 122 pp.

Hermann Hesse's seventy-fifth birthday brought with it a flood of acclaim almost comparable to that of 1947. In honor of the occasion, Suhrkamp published the *Gesammelte Dichtungen*, *Zwei Idyllen*, and Siegfried Unseld's *Brevier*; Reinhard Buchwald edited a school edition of selected items (*Eine Auswahl*, 138 pp.), and the *Neue Schweizer Rundschau* dedicated its July issue to Hesse (*Deutsche Beiträge* paid its respects similarly in 1947). While only one book-length study of Hesse (Gnefkow, see above), two pamphlets (Gerhard Kirchhoff, *Reine Gegenwart*, 28 pp.; *Hermann Hesse als Badener Kurgast*, 26 pp.), and two brief bibliographies (Martin Pfeifer, *Bibliographie der im Gebiet der DDR seit 1945 erschienenen Schriften von und über Hermann Hesse*, 15 pp.; Klaus W. Jonas, "Hermann Hesse in Amerika," *Monatshefte*, 44 [1952], 95-99) appeared in the course of 1952 as compared with the three books, the five pamphlets, and the extensive bibliographical work of Kliemann and Silomon which were published in 1947, newspaper notices, speeches, and periodical articles (some thirty-five) were almost equally numerous upon both occasions.

Dank an Hermann Hesse, again published by Suhrkamp, comprises a representative cross-section of these notices, speeches, and articles. As is to be expected, much of the material consists of innocuous generalities and praise which is often so uncontained that Oskar Maria Graf's aversion to *Glückwünsche* becomes a very apt characterization: "eine Art biderben Auf-die-Schulter-Klopfens, deren anrüchige Überheblichkeit dem Gefeierten auf die Nerven gehen muss" ("Hermann Hesse—75 Jahre," pp. 7-9).

The *Festreden* of Rudolf A. Schröder (in Stuttgart; pp. 15-28) and Karl Schmid (in Zürich; pp. 51-64) are both popular surveys with the usual brief characterizations, digressive allusions, and uncritical attitude. However, whereas Schmid indulges in a protracted eulogy with random references to Hesse's life and an inconsequential rambling about in his works, Schröder does attempt to see Hesse in terms of tradition, *i.e.*, his early realism and its kinship to that of Gottfried Keller; the inherently romantic nature of his art, in which "das romantisch-mythische Moment" is stressed and "das so primär dichterische Prinzip des Märchens"[6] prevails, as in German poetry of the Middle Ages and German literature of the seventeenth century. He broaches two vital themes which deserve closer study: the *Doppelgänger* motif (see also Walter Naumann, "The Individual and Society in the Work of Hermann Hesse," *Monatshefte,* 41 [1949], 37) and the actual art of *Glasperlenspiel.*

More interesting than either of these *Festreden* is the casual reminiscing of Theodor Heuss ("Dank an Hermann Hesse," pp. 28-36). Recalling an exchange of letters with Hesse in 1910, Heuss quotes Hesse's interesting answer to his suggestion that he now select "den grossen Stoff," for in his "künstlerischsprachliches Vermögen" there was promise of a German Flaubert:

> Das mit dem Flaubert wäre schön, und ich will als noch junger Mann nichts versprechen. Aber vor dem künstlerischen Risiko solcher Werke graut mir doch zu sehr. Daran sind grosse Könner wie Zola völlig gescheitert. Und mir steht, als heimlicher Lyriker, der Wunsch nach reiner Melodie vielleicht zuletzt doch höher als der nach Durchdringung grosser Stoffe, so sehr mich solche im Privatleben rein intellektuell fesseln können (p. 30).

Except for the appended congratulatory letter of Thomas Mann, a reiterated expression of friendship and appreciation, the remaining articles deal briefly with more specific themes. Walter Haussmann's dedicatory speech (in Calw, at the unveiling of the memorial plaque at Hesse's birthplace; pp. 37-50) is a panegyric in praise of Hesse and the greater glory of Swabia. Hesse's uncompromising courage and faith, his determined inner quest, his dedication to truth, humility, piety, his mystical vein, and his melancholy musical mode of expression are all considered part of his great Swabian heritage, characteristic of that glorious tradition to which Schiller, Hölderlin, and Mörike belong. Johannes Kepler, Friedrich Christoph Oetinger, and Johann Valentin Andreä become Knecht's antecedents, and Swabia their Castalia. Continuing this exaggerated *pro gloria Sueborum,* Ernst Müller ("Vom Schwäbischen in Hermann Hesses Werk," pp. 103-108) detects a decided Swabian element in Hesse's attachment to the East, considers his adroit use of the German language peculiarly Swabian, and perceives more Schelling than Nietzsche in Hesse's difficult years. When Müller remarks, "Hesse hat bei uns, soweit ich literarisch zurückdenken kann, stets als Edelstein und Krone des heutigen schwäbischen Dichtertums gegolten," his ability to remember is hardly commendable.

Ernst Penzoldt ("Die guten Werke," pp. 66-69) undertakes to celebrate Hesse's language but does little more than emphasize

Germany's indebtedness to him. L. E. Reindl ("Der Dichter in seinem Garten," pp. 97-102) manages only a rhapsodical paraphrase of *Stunden im Garten*. Josef Mühlenberger ("Die Morgenlandfahrer," pp. 70-75), sees the unifying motif of Hesse's art in his *Morgenlandfahrt*, his quest for the unity of reality and timeless, complete being; this Novalis-like *Immer nach Hause* is inherent in every line of his prose and poetry, and only finds its purest and most immediate expression in the tale, *Morgenlandfahrt*. And as though to supplement Mühlenberger, Fritz Martini ("Der Dichter und Erzieher, Hermann Hesse," 76-81) draws attention to the noble tradition which Hesse's works continue: "im Wort des Dichters den Menschen zu bilden"—in Hesse's instance, to help his fellow man find his real self and the unity behind his separateness.

Continuing this emphasis upon his service to mankind, Christian E. Lewalter ("Hermann Hesse und unsere geistige Situation," 82-89) lauds Hesse's analysis of Western civilization and his warning of things to come. Unlike those who would have artists become activists Lewalter asks only that, as in Hesse's case, their horizons be extended and that they help extend the horizons of their age. Beyond Hesse's services to the individual and to his age, Anni Carlsson ("Dichtung als Hieroglyphe des Zeitalters: Hermann Hesses *Morgenlandfahrt*," pp. 90-96) perceives yet another service, to the future. Recalling Novalis' conviction that "jede Geschichte ist Weltgeschichte," she proceeds briefly and rather laboriously to show how *Morgenlanfahrt*, with its emphasis upon the soul, and its poetically depicted reaction to, and rejection of our civilization of "Geld, Zahl und Zeit," is indeed a document of its age, and in a deeper sense and on a higher plane of *Seelengeschichte*, valid historical source material. Carlsson's argument is not to be denied, but might better, in a more conclusive study, have encompassed more than one tale; for surely, by the same token, the major portion of Hesse's writings acquires historical significance.

Unlike his fellow contributors, Hermann Goern ("Der Maler Hermann Hesse," pp. 108-118) broaches a virtually untouched theme.[7] It was in 1917, when writing had become distasteful to him (*Traumfährte*, p. 115), and music unbearable (*Gedenkblätter* [1947], pp. 148-149), that Hesse first turned to painting, finding there the diversion he was never to tire of. A modest be-

ginning in Bern soon became a passion in Montagnola. Hundreds
of water colors, "Tagebücher der Farbspiele" as Ball so aptly
terms them (1947, p. 218), were painted during the frenzied
summer of 1919 (*Corona*, 3 [1932], 204), and hundreds more in
the course of the next few years. Hesse became so fascinated by
his new pastime, that he even dreamed occasionally that he might
some day put aside writing in favor of painting (*Nürnberger
Reise* [1927], p. 33; *Betrachtungen*, p. 45).

Most of Hesse's paintings have been so dispersed that the
bibliographer is confronted with an impossible task.[8] Many became *Bildermanuskripte*, illustrated poems or tales individually
prepared by Hesse upon request;[9] others were sent to friends as
greetings; a few have appeared in pamphlet form;[10] some have
been used by Hesse to illustrate his own publications,[11] others to
illustrate the publications of his friends,[12] and many more have
been reproduced in periodicals.[13]

Many of Hesse's friends have been painters. On the Untersee
he associated with Max Bucherer, Otto Blümel, Ludwig Renner,
Karl Stirner, and Erich Scheurmann. It was with the painter
Hans Sturzenegger that he travelled to the Orient in 1911, and
it was into the home of Albert Welti that he moved when he
left Gaienhofen for Bern upon his return from the East. Hesse's
oldest son, Bruno, was reared by Cuno Amiet. Among his close
friends in Lugano were Giuseppi Folgia, Karl Hofer, and the
closest of all, who is still in Montagnola, Gunter Böhmer. Louis
(der Grausame) Moilliet is celebrated in *Klingsor*, and it is to
Ernst Morgenthaler that *Traumfährte* is dedicated. Hesse has
written appreciative introductions for publications of his painter
friends,[14] and many of his own works have in turn been illustrated or have had their covers designed by various painters. To
list but a few: Gunter Böhmer, Louis Moilliet, Niklaus Stoecklin,
Alfred Kubin, E. R. Weiss, Heinrich Vogeler, and Otto Eckmann.

Naturally, Hesse's prose reflects his interest in painting.
Erminia Aglietti (*Peter Camenzind*), Brahm ("Maler Brahm,"
Simplicissimus, 11 [1906], 628-629), Gustav Weizsäcker ("Ein
Wandertag vor hundert Jahren," 1910, *Fabulierbuch*), Veraguth
(*Rosshalde*), Albert ("Der Maler," *Kleiner Garten*), Klingsor
(*Klingsors letzter Sommer*), and the hero of "Märchen vom
Korbstuhl," 1918 (*Fabulierbuch*), are all painters; and even
Sinclair (*Demian*) daubs. Louis der Grausame and Klingsor re-

appear with Paul Klee in fabulous Bremgarten (*Morgenland-fahrt*). A collection of essays is suggestively entitled *Bilder-buch*. One article bears the title "Aquarell" (*Der Pfirsichbaum* [1945], pp. 24-31) ; another "Maler und Schriftsteller" (*Gedenk-blätter* [1947], pp. 309-317) ; another "Bilderschauen in Mün-chen" (*Bodenseebuch* [1930], pp. 19-21) ; another is entitled, *Bilderschmuck im Eisenbahnwagen* (*Einblattdruck* without place of publication or date) ; and yet another, "Ohne Krapplack" (*Die Brücke zur Welt*, Oct. 8, 1955). And that Hesse should choose ironically to paint himself out of his prison in his "Kurzgefasster Lebenslauf" (*Traumfährte*), is certainly significant.

Goern draws attention to only a few of these details before he proceeds to examine the water colors themselves. The paintings he finds, are primarily pastoral, reflecting the landscape of Tecino. Lyrical in quality, happy and carefree in mood (unlike Hesse's poetry), unsophisticated in their implications, they are very human expressions of praise and gratitude, effortlessly executed in pure, radiant colors, the work of a wise and experienced person at peace with himself and the world.[15] In his determination to prove that Hesse's paintings are not the inconsequential "freundliche aber dilettantische Aquarelle" that the *Künstlerlexikon* (Thieme-Becker [1923], Vol. 16, 591) considers them to be, Goern goes to the opposite extreme. Taking this pastime far more seriously than Hesse himself has ever done (*Briefe*, p. 299; *Pfirsichbaum*, p. 29), he pictures him as a genius tragically torn between two talents,[16] one of the few artists of Europe who has not succumbed to the confusion of modern non-objective painting, but has continued to maintain the balance between subject and object which is characteristic of all great art. Allowing his enthusiasm to carry him away, Goern resorts to useless exaggeration (*Wanderung* is termed one of the "köstlichsten und kostbarsten Bücher deutscher Dichter überhaupt," p. 111), and indulges in meaningless generalities ("jedes Ding steht mit Farbe und Form am rechten Platz," p. 114) and rhapsodic paradox ('Alles Einzelne, Vereinzelte ist nur stellvertretend für das Ganze und zieht den Kosmos hinter sich her, ist überbegrifflich greifbar geworden. . ." p. 112).

Christa M. Konheiser-Barwanietz

The figure of Goethe casts its obvious shadow upon Hesse's

world of thought. Direct references and allusions to Goethe are innumerable.[17] It is with Goethe himself that Hesse argues in *Steppenwolf*. His acute awareness of the dichotomy of life and desire for harmony and unity recall Goethe's concept of polarity. The kinship between *Glasperlenspiel* and *Wilhelm Meister* is unmistakable. Yet, despite this very intimate relationship, and in spite of Hesse's own candid acknowledgment of great indebtedness to Goethe ("Unter allen deutschen Dichtern ist Goethe derjenige, dem ich am meisten verdanke. . ." *Dank an Goethe*, p. 7), it was not until 1954 that the first and only really comparative study appeared in print (Christa M. Konheiser-Barwanietz, *Hermann Hesse und Goethe*, 98 pp.).

After carefully distinguishing between influence ("fördernde Befruchtung") and rank imitation, Barwanietz draws attention to Hesse's first acquaintance with Goethe in the summer of 1891 ("Meine Kindheit," *Hermann Lauscher*), to his avid reading of the eighteenth-century writers in the library of his grandfather Gundert, and to his passion for Goethe while in Tübingen. She remarks briefly upon Hesse's repeated return to Goethe throughout his life, and then proceeds, in separate chapters and in greater detail, to outline their spiritual kinship. She maintains that Hesse, in his progression from stage to stage of life and in the repeated reintegration of his personality, must have found a model and consolation in Goethe. She insists that Goethe's theory of polarity was the inspiration for Hesse's search for a synthesis of *Geist* and *Natur*. She expounds upon Hesse's Goethean humanity, marked by its concern for the individual and truth, not politics, its supranationalism, and its hatred of all violence. She compares *Wilhelm Meister* and *Glasperlenspiel* in terms of the influence of the one on the other; and finally proposes that Hesse's transition from the romanticism of a lifetime (*Unendlichkeit*) to the classical level of *Glasperlenspiel* (*Vollendung*) is again to be credited to Goethe's influence.

That Goethe has always represented an ideal to which Hesse has never ceased to aspire, cannot be questioned, nor are influences to be denied. However, that Goethe has been a major factor in Hesse's every significant thought and deed, as Barwanietz would imply, is to perceive influence where too frequently there may only be coincidence. To detect a relationship between the *Bund der Morgenlandfahrer* and the *Gesellschaft vom Turm*

(p. 44), to associate the magic theater with *Walpurgisnacht* (p. 43), to think of Demian and *Mutter Eva* in terms of the *Verbündeten vom Turme* (p. 37), and to liken Hesse's withdrawal to Montagnola to Goethe's trip to Italy (p. 38), is to strain for influences in the chance similarity of inconsequential details. That Demian's words to Sinclair, "Nur das Denken, das wir leben, hat einen Wert," should recall and be equated with Goethe's "Denken und Tun, Tun und Denken ist die Summe aller Weisheit" (p. 37), is only to consider words out of context and to understand the real significance of neither remark. To associate the "stirb gern" of *Klein und Wagner* with Goethe's "Stirb und werde" (p. 39) is again merely to juxtapose similar words regardless of implication (surely Klein's *Sichfallenlassen* is more suggestive of Schopenhauer's will-less surrender than Goethe's upward aspirations). Again, to intimate a Goethean influence in Hesse's interest in the East (p. 40) is to forget the more immediate influence of family background. To insist that Goethe was for Hesse "das grösste Beispiel für die Realisierbarkeit einer Synthese von Geist und Natur" (p. 47) is to underestimate the indisputable influence of China's philosophers. (*Eine Bibliothek der Weltliteratur* [1946], p. 61). To insist that Hesse's "Auffassung der humanen Würde, seine Stellung zu Staat und Politik steht unter dem Zeichen Goethes" (p. 66) is not only to equate similarity with influence but to disregard Hesse's own acknowledgment:

> Man soll sich zu dem bekennen, was einen erzogen, geprägt und gebildet hat, und so muss ich nach häufiger Überprüfung der Frage sagen: es waren drei starke und lebenslänglich nachwirkende Einflüsse, die diese Erziehung an mir vollbracht haben. Es war der christliche und nahezu völlig un-nationalistische Geist meines Elternhauses, es war die Lektüre der grossen Chinesen, und es war, nicht zuletzt, der Einfluss des einzigen Historikers, dem ich je mit Vertrauen, Ehrfurcht und dankbarer Jüngerschaft zugetan war: Jakob Burckhardt ("Geleitwort," *Krieg und Frieden* [1949], p. 12).

Nor, in her determination to establish the closest of ties between Hesse and Goethe, does Barwanietz hesitate to disregard the simple facts of Hesse's life. Forgetting that he has spent the last thirty-five years contemplating himself and life in his mountain retreat, she ventures to compare his road through life to that of Goethe: "kein Weg der Gedanken, der Kontemplation, sondern ein Weg der Tat" (p. 45).

While *Glasperlenspiel* and *Wilhelm Meister* have repeatedly been linked together in casual reference, Barwanietz' study is the first and only detailed comparison of the two. Focussing her attention primarily upon Castalia, where the influence of Goethe's pedagogical province is unmistakable, she delves into the nature, methods, and aims of each utopia. Each is a male institution where every youngster is given the opportunity to develop his native talents, where family influence is negligible, and where community living is stressed. *Tätigkeit* and *Entsagung* are law in each; and music plays a dominant rôle in fashioning their ideal man of culture with his fully developed, harmoniously integrated personality. Barwanietz does not fail to note that Hesse's pedagogical province is not entirely like Goethe's: students do not choose to enter, but are chosen by school authorities interested in "eine Elite der Geistigen" and not in "den praktisch Tätigen" (p. 79). However, that Castalia, in its somber atmosphere, its colorless landscape, and its lifelessness, is everything Goethe's province is not, and that Knecht and Meister are as different as their names would imply, is completely overlooked.

In her endeavor to add another chapter to the endless *Goethesche Wirkungsgeschichte*, Barwanietz errs where she herself cautions: "Auch darf man Wirkung und Einfluss nicht in der Ähnlichkeit oder Gleichheit einzelner Stellen bei zwei Dichtern suchen" (p. 9). To sift the works of such a prolific reader as Hesse for the influences which another writer, even a Goethe, may have had upon him, is a ticklish task which may only too easily result in a maze of insignificant associations and questionable assertions. Barwanietz might better have concentrated upon similarities and differences.

Kurt Weibel

In his *Hermann Hesse und die deutsche Romantik* (Bern, 1954, 146 pp.), Weibel is intent upon establishing that Hesse has been strongly influenced by romantic writers. His brief characterization of German Romanticism, and his attempt to outline Hesse's conception of the term romanticism are quite incidental. Weibel's approach is very direct. He sifts Hesse's major prose tales, in chronological order, for whatever elements they may have in common with any works of the Romanticists. Evaluating his plethora of similarities, he concludes that Hesse has been influenced directly by Novalis, E. T. A. Hoffmann, Jean Paul, Brentano, and Eichendorff; on the other hand, Hölderlin, Lenau, Schleiermacher, Zacharias Werner, Tieck, and Friedrich Schlegel are found to be no more than kindred spirits preoccupied with similar problems. This close relationship between Hesse and the Romanticists is attributed to a common "magische Auffassung des Lebens" (p. 11).

Weibel's treatment of the pre-*Demian* period, when Hesse undoubtedly was most susceptible to influences, is disappointingly cursory. *Eine Stunde hinter Mitternacht* points to Novalis in its substance, its "Hingabe an den Bilderreichtum der Seele" (p. 29). *Hermann Lauscher* is Hesse's "Grundproblem, das Problem der Romantik schlechthin" (p. 30). No effort, however, is made to develop these contentions. Camenzind is a romantic spirit trying to peer into the soul of things; his friendship with Richard recalls Walt and Vult of Jean Paul's *Flegeljahre;* he is just as enthusiastic about clouds as Novalis in his *Heinrich von Ofterdingen;* and the *Naturdichtung* he envisages is the dream of all Romanticists. The water motif in *Unterm Rad* suggests Novalis, and Giebenrath's watery death is akin to "das erotische und schöpferische Traumelement im *Heinrich von Ofterdingen*" (p. 35). Had Weibel not chosen to limit his discussion to seven pages and to overlook *Knulp, Berthold, Gertrud, Rosshalde, Der Novalis,* the earliest essays in *Bilderbuch,* and Hesse's poetry, legends, and *Märchen,* he could certainly have made many more interesting associations of this kind. But are these similarities necessarily indicative of influences?

Demian is treated in greater detail. Weibel finds that Abraxas is akin to Omar's god in Tieck's *Abdallah*. Despite his evil influence, Omar can be equated with Demian, and the problem of puberty underlies both tales. Hesse's conception of fate ("Schicksal und Gemüt sind Namen eines Begriffs"), however, is not Tieck's, but Novalis'. And the fate of such demigods as Demian is already depicted in Hölderlin's *Der Rhein*. Sinclair's path leads to "Mutter Eva" just as Godwi's leads to "das steinerne Bild der Mutter" (p. 43); and each is impelled by a romantic longing for submersion in the oneness of reality.

Weibel continues in this same manner from tale to tale. A few stray similarities are always sufficient to argue for a close relationship. *Klein und Wagner* and Jean Paul's *Siebenkäs* are linked together because the hero of each flees from an unhappy marriage and experiences some sort of rebirth. At the same time, however, Klein and Teresina recall Theodor and Teresina of Hoffmann's *Die Fermate*, and Teresina is also related to Friedrich Schlegel's Lucinde. Mystical and frenzied Klingsor is both Novalis and Hoffmann; but he is also Lenau's Faust and Don Juan, revelling in their dance of death. According to Weibel, Siddhartha is almost a disciple of Schleiermacher: his emphasis upon immediate experience in the learning process corresponds to Schleiermacher's faith in immediate, religious experience; his mode of meditation is similar to Schleiermacher's; and his ultimate experience of unity is the very phenomenon described by Schleiermacher in the first of his *Monologen*. And Novalis' influence is again unmistakable: Ofterdingen and Siddhartha travel similar courses of life; Kamaswami, Kamala, and Vasudeva serve the same function as the supernumeraries in *Ofterdingen;* Kamala's return to Siddhartha recalls Mathilde's return to Ofterdingen; furthermore, both tales are "märchenhaftig." It is difficult to understand how such trivial simliarities can reflect obvious influence.

Weibel notes that Hesse moves away from romanticism after *Siddhartha*. Nevertheless, he continues to link him as intimately as ever with the Romanticists. Haller epitomizes Brentano's inner discord; his conception of Goethe is similar to Brentano's conception of Christ, and his angry outburst in the home of his friend, the young professor, recalls a similar incident in Brentano's life. Jean Paul's *Vorschule zur Aesthetik* is Haller's guide to humor. The magic theater is Hoffmannesque. Hermine recalls Novalis' Mathilde, and Pablo is another Klingsor (*Ofterdingen*). Narziss and Goldmund are not only projections of Brentano the ascetic and Brentano the libertine, but they are also resurrections of Mörike and Waiblinger respectively, and variations of Jean Paul's Vult and Walt. Like Novalis, Goldmund is fascinated by death, and like Brentano, he is enchanted by water; he also has much in common with Medardus of Hoffmann's *Elixiere des Teufels*. *Morgenlandfahrt* recalls Hoffmann's *Ritter Gluck*. Leo is Jean Paul's spiritual son; he can whistle as skillfully as Walt, loves life just as intensively, and like Vult, he has a deep understanding of human nature. The glass-bead game is a romantic notion clearly anticipated in Novalis' *Fragmente*. Hesse's theory of education reflects the influence of Jean Paul's *Levana*. And Knecht's life and sacrifice are reminiscent of the fate of Hölderlin's Empedocles.

Weibel's book is the only comprehensive study of Hesse and the German Romanticists which has yet been published. As such, it merits close attention. It is most unfortunate that he chose to perceive more influence than kinship in the intimate relationship, established so ably in his work. Only a very few of his many similarities actually indicate real influence. Some may suggest an unconscious imitation. Most of them, however, for want of any evidence to the contrary, might best be attributed to a kinship of personalities and to a common philosophy of life, or even to coincidence. Weibel's chronological approach is even more regrettable. His confusion of brief associations leaves only splinter impressions. He might better have devoted a separate chapter to each of the Romanticists linked most closely with Hesse, or have extended the thematic approach of his concluding chapter, "Nacht, Traum und Märchen." Despite these major shortcomings, Weibel's book, like Lützkendorf's, represents a very suggestive beginning in the study of a major problem.

II

PAMPHLETS

The many pamphlets which have been written about Hesse are almost as significant as the books and printed dissertations. They fall into four loose categories: appreciative surveys of life and works, which generally repeat the already familiar; studies centered about single issues, usually those which have not received thorough treatment in any book; varied composites of tribute and gratitude; and important bibliographical supplements.

1

To the first of these categories belong the works of Alfred Kuhn, Otto Basler, Hella Fuchs, Walter Kolb, Albrecht Goes, Otto Engel, Gotthilf Hafner, Georg Richter, Hans Huber, Hans Levander, Joachim von Hecker, and Franz Baumer. Only the first three of these pamphlets were published before 1945.

The congratulatory surveys of Basler (*Hermann Hesse, 60 Jahre* [1937], 8 pp.), of Fuchs (*Hermann Hesse zu seinem sechzigsten Geburtstag* [1937], 14 pp.), and of Kolb (*Ansprache und Rede für Hermann Hesse* [1946], 16 pp.; upon awarding of the *Goethepreis* to Hesse), are quite inconsequential in their eulogy and in their brevity, and Goes' speech (*Rede auf Hermann Hesse* [1946], 38 pp.), made on a lecture tour through southern Germany shortly after Hesse received the *Goethepreis*, is little more than a free association of familiar generalities, a pleasant rambling through Hesse's life and career. Engel's pamphlet (*Hermann Hesse. Ein Vortrag* [1947], 31 pp.), a lecture presented in 1945, and also the first part of his book, has already been discussed in the preceding chapter.

Alfred Kuhn

Kuhn's *Hermann Hesse* (1907, 54 pp.) is the earliest major study of the author. A few biographical remarks are followed by a brief and pithy characterization of Hesse's art, then by a chronological and more specific treatment of the individual works up to and including *Unterm Rad*. Although his biographical remarks have long since been rendered of little value by Ball's monograph, Kuhn's delineation of Hesse's inner self and his general description of Hesse's art have stood the test of time. He depicts Hesse as an eternal wanderer in search of beauty, forever yearning for the lost home of his childhood. He describes Hesse's prose and poetry as born of longing, rooted in lyricism, wrapped in melancholy and marked by simplicity of expression and beauty of language.

Though Kuhn's rapid perusal of the individual works is rather superficial, it does mark the beginning of a systematic analysis. His nine-page study of *Peter Camenzind* is particularly noteworthy since the novel has been treated in a comparably thorough manner only upon three other occasions (A. Waldhausen, O. Hartwich, and H. R. Schmid). Nor does Kuhn merely eulogize his favorite author. He is fully aware that his prose still lacks continuity and a balance between description and action, and that his *personae* are too weakly delineated, felt rather than seen. Nevertheless, he has faith in Hesse's art and its future, "Denn seine Kunst ist echt und ehrlich. Für sie ist Hoffnung" (p. 54).

Gotthilf Hafner

Within the narrow limits of eighty-seven pages, Hafner does ample justice to an ambitious undertaking (*Hermann Hesse. Werk und Leben. Umrisse eines Dichterbildes* [1947]). In keeping with the title, Hesse's life is precisely outlined and his prose works and poetry are succinctly characterized. Adding interest and value to his pamphlet, Hafner recalls Hesse's public reading in Stuttgart of a chapter from his then unpublished *Narziss und Goldmund*, includes a bibliography of Hesse's major publications and of the books edited by him, and also mentions the periodicals with which he has been associated as editor. Hafner's is a warm appreciation of a favorite author, an uncritical, informative survey meant to correct "manches Unrichtige der Biographie und Bibliographie, das in Literaturgeschichten und Aufsätzen über Hesse steht" (p. 86).

With the addition of five new sections and only minor alterations in his original text, Hafner's pamphlet was published as a book in 1954 (175 pp.). In "Quellen der Herkunft" (pp. 34-46) he delves into Hesse's ancestry, drawing heavily upon Ball's biography, Ludwig Finckh's *Schwäbische Vettern* (1948), upon *Marie Hesse. Ein Lebensbild in Briefen und Tagebüchern* (1934), and *Dr. Hermann Gunderts Briefnachlass* (1900). In "Der Traum vom reinen Mensch" (pp. 106-112), he draws at-

tention to Hesse's constant concern with "ein gültiges Menschenbild" which finally assumed its highest expression in the figures
of Siddhartha and the *Musikmeister.* "Zeitgenossen oder die
Unsterblichkeit" (pp. 113-152), a protracted argument dealing
with critics, writers, and immortality, with only a few casual
references to Hesse, might best have been omitted entirely.
"Briefe," the concluding chapter, represents a good review of
the volume of Hesse's letters published in 1951. Of Hafner's
recent appendages the only enhancing one is his convenient index
of names and places.

Georg Richter

Richter's is another of the post-war pamphlets which shows
the relative obscurity into which Hesse was thrust during the
Hitler régime (*Hermann Hesse, der Dichter und Mensch* [1947],
48 pp.). Writing his brochure expressly for the younger reading public for which Hesse had become hardly more than a name,
Richter undertakes to introduce the man and to draw attention
to his world of thought, particularly to those aspects of his
Weltanschauung which might have meaning for those who, after
the war, found themselves disillusioned and bewildered. He
stresses Hesse's humanitarian spirit, his denunciation of war
and nationalism, his emphasis upon the sacredness of the individual, upon love and communion with nature. Apt quotations
are liberally interspersed, and the events of a visit to Montagnola
are recalled.

Hans Huber

Huber ably characterizes his own work (*Hermann Hesse*
[1948], 72 pp.) : "so ist es mir nicht um eine umfassende literarische Darstellung zu tun, sondern darum, das Bild des Dichters
so zu zeigen, wie es seinen Freunden erscheint. Ich bemühe
mich im Folgenden nach Möglichkeit den Dichter selbst sprechen
zu lassen" (p. 7). This, and no more, is done. Approximately
one half of the pamphlet consists of quotations, and the re-
mainder of random references to works from *Demian* to *Glasperlenspiel,* with particular emphasis upon such catchwords as:
*Antinomien, Bipolarität, Einheit, Weg nach Innen, Geist und
Natur, Bekenntnis,* and *Aufrichtigkeit.*

Hans Levander

Levander's review (*Hermann Hesse* [1949], 63 pp.), though a good deal more objective than Hafner's, and decidedly more discerning than either Richter's or Huber's, repeats the usual biographical details, and again presents a brief resumé of each major work. While each of these works represents a station along Hesse's road toward self-realization, Levander has this course of development fall into three major stages (*cf.* Gnefkow). The growing years from *Romantische Lieder* to *Knulp* are a period of *Weltschmerz* and of pose, of erotic pessimism, resignation, and nature worship, of lyrical realism and softly musical poetry. The years of crisis from *Demian* to *Steppenwolf*, are a period of chaos, of *Untergangsmusik*, of mother-quest and search for the self, of cultural pessimism and cynicism, of new possibilities in life and in art. The more serene years dedicated to the service of *Geist* and extending from *Narziss und Goldmund* to *Glasperlenspiel*, are the years of Hesse's maturest and most monumental work.

Levander is not averse to bold appraisals. He considers *Unterm Rad* to be the best of Hesse's pre-*Demian* prose, and *Knulp*—the transition from the more idyllic to the critical and confessional—the most charming of his early tales. That hale and hearty Peter Camenzind should be so inept and unfortunate in the art of love, is just as incredible, he says, as Kuhn's (*Gertrud*) hapless resignation to a life of frustration, and just as unconvincing as Veraguth's (*Rosshalde*) ultimate reconciliation with life. The essentially religious and sexual nature of Hesse's inner discord becomes obvious in *Demian*. *Kurgast* is Hesse's most intimate work, and *Steppenwolf* his most notorious; *Krisis* is no less than shocking. *Kinderseele, Klein und Wagner* and *Siddhartha* are deemed flawless works of art. *Narziss und Goldmund*, primarily a novel of ideas, reflects Hesse's growing tendency to become more metaphysical. *Morgenlandfahrt* is rather precious and arabesque; and the composite *Glasperlenspiel*, Hesse's *chef d'oeuvre*, is considered to be a blending of Goethe's *Bildungsideal*, Hegel and Burckhardt, Indian metaphysics and Chinese wisdom, Christianity and agnosticism, and psychoanalysis and occultism. All of these allegations are very interesting, most of them are quite plausible, but none is convincingly established.

Joachim F. von Hecker

Deploring the tone of disapproval and the lack of respect
which began to characterize a number of periodical articles in
the years immediately following 1945 (*e.g.*, von Schöfer), and
disturbed by this misunderstanding of Hesse even in serious religious circles (*e.g.*, Kohlschmid), Karl H. Silomon (publisher
and bibliographer) felt almost morally obliged to persuade a
young student to supplement and to submit to him for publication a study of Hesse he had made two years previously, while
still at the *Gymnasium.* Von Hecker's panegyric (*Hermann
Hesse* [1949], 64 pp.), his confession of faith in, and gratitude
to Hesse, was meant by Silomon to help stem this inimical trend,
and to show that even youth could properly appreciate and find
meaning in *Glasperlenspiel,* the wisdom of Hesse's old age.

Apart from the generalities of a prolonged and diffuse introduction, and a sketch of Hesse's life, von Hecker deals in some
detail only with four major works: with *Siddhartha* and *Steppenwolf,* the highlights of the period of *Schauen und Begreifen*
which began with the discord of *Demian* and ended with the
harmony of *Narziss und Goldmund,* with *Morgenlandfahrt,*
Hesse's most remarkable work, and with *Glasperlenspiel,* his
profoundest.

Convinced that *Siddhartha* is a great work of art, and as such,
beyond any definitive interpretation, and that *Steppenwolf* leaves
much that can only be felt and surmised, von Hecker contents
himself with little more than appreciative summaries of each.
Venturing briefly, nevertheless, into the general significance of
these works, he resolves astutely that each represents a flight
from the conditioned existence of the bourgeois into a life of un-
curtailed intensity, but concludes inadequately that *Siddhartha*
soars into *das geistlich-Unbedingte,* and that Haller descends into
das sinnlich-Unbedingte. A more incisive study of *Siddhartha*
might rather have disclosed that the hero restlessly exhausts
and transcends both *das geistlich-Unbedingte* and *das sinnlich-
Unbedingte.* Pursuing *Steppenwolf* a little further, von Hecker
might have concluded that the ideal, the romantic irony (an intellectual attitude) to which Haller finally aspires, marks a return to *das geistlich-Unbedingte.*

Von Hecker's appraisal of *Morgenlandfahrt* is just as provocative. Because the tale is a fragment and because it is particularly diary-like in its intimacy, it is judged "das merkwür-

digste aller seiner Schöpfungen" (p. 35). Perhaps a fragment may bear witness to the mystery and wonder of the creative process, but is the fragment not less exceptional than typical in Hesse's writings? And that one fragment should evidence the creative process any more or less vividly than another, can hardly be more than a purely subjective matter. The personal, private nature of Hesse's works is, again, characteristic rather than unusual; and to contend that *Morgenlandfahrt* reveals more of the author, of both the man and the seeker, than any other work, is very questionable. If anything, the fantasy and enigmatic symbolism of the tale would suggest a heightening of Hesse's *Versteck-Spiel,* rather than its end.

Of the four works treated by von Hecker, the most lengthy consideration is given to *Glasperlenspiel* (pp. 39-61). Substance, however, proves quite incommensurate with length. Far too much effort is lost in apologizing for his inability to do justice to the metaphysical profundities of the novel, in protracted, reverent eulogy, and in pompous, abstruse exposition of the obvious. Von Hecker is amazed by Hesse's ability, in his introductory chapter, to bring into poetic focus all the cultural values of the Western world. He marvels that he is able to give such lucid expression on so lofty a plane to those elusive intellectual trends which gradually distill all fields of knowledge and ultimately reduce them to their common denominator and establish the "Unio Mystica aller getrennten Glieder der Universitas Litterarum" (*Glasperlenspiel* [1943], Vol. 1, 56). And he takes great pains to explain, obscurely, that the *Glasperlenspiel* (the game) is less important in itself than as a symbol.

Turning his attention to Knecht, von Hecker resolves that his lot is a tragic one. He is both a *Kastalier* dedicated to his cause and a *Mensch* possessed by *Eigensinn* with its passion for self-growth, in short, an individual torn between two missions. With more subtle perception, one might maintain instead that the tragic (?) factor in Knecht's life is to be attributed far less to insoluble conflict than to lofty aspiration. Knecht has but one mission, and that is, *Mensch zu werden*: to give full expression to both *Geist* and *Natur*, achieving a balance between *Bewusstsein* and *Erleben*. It is to this passion that his ordeals are to be attributed. Nor does the term tragic best characterize Knecht's life. Cannot Knecht's departure from Castalia represent the beginning of a new and closer rapport between the world of the spirit and that of the flesh (*vita contemplativa* and

vita activa), just as his death may only symbolize the service
and sacrifice necessary to attain the more ideal interplay of
Geist and *Natur* which is promised in Tito? While both his departure and death may seem like failure, yet each is a hope and
a promise, and as such, hardly tragic.

Unlike most critics who have hardly cared to go beyond brief
superlatives in their passing reference to the three *Lebensläufe*,
von Hecker at least makes a token effort to meet the challenge
they pose. In terms of art he would have the three tales represent the poetic highpoint of *Glasperlenspiel*. However, by way
of explanation, he can only resort to an ineffectual, though picturesque, analogy; he compares the body of the book to "einen
vom rein Geistigen oder zumindest mehr Gedanklichen her er-
richteten gewaltigen Bau," and the *Lebensläufe* to the surround-
ing "in Unschuld und reiner, naiver Freude und Hingebung
blühender Garten" (p. 56). Why von Hecker should then proceed to term these stories an elevated *Nachzeichnung* of Knecht's
life proper, rather than a *Vorzeichnung*, is difficult to understand, particularly when it is recalled that these tales were not
only written before the main body of the book, but were also
credited to a period in Knecht's life when all was yet to come.

Aware that the *Lebensläufe* are of more than chance significance to the story proper, von Hecker concludes, astutely, that
together they serve as both explanation and augury. They are
an *Ausdeutung* for Knecht's way of life, because they are an
exposition of that piety which stands in awe and reverence before the mysteries of existence, desires growth, knows sacrifice,
and is the very essence of Knecht's being. They are a *Vor-
deutung* of Knecht's departure from Castalia and ultimate death,
because their heroes also experience the same implied *Erwachen*.
There is no question but that the *Lebensläufe* are augury. Von
Hecker, however, fails to perceive their full subtlety. One might
more shrewdly and perhaps more correctly conclude that each
tale has its own augury, that each envisages one of Knecht's
final three stages of life. As the austere rainmaker in a primitive, matriarchal society, Knecht visualizes himself as aspiring
to the heights of self-development, and conscientiously attending to his duties and remaining faithful to his office to an extreme of self-sacrifice. This augury is realized when Knecht
becomes a *Glasperlenspieler*. Like the rainmaker, he is determined to develop to that focal point of potentiality where all
knowledge streams together and nothing is any longer impos-

sible; and, like the rainmaker, as long as he has faith in Castalia and in the purposefulness of his office, Knecht remains irreproachably loyal to the cause. The story of Josephus Famulus, the early Christian hermit of Palestine, augurs the second stage in Knecht's life, the period of doubt and dissatisfaction which culminates in departure from Castalia. Like Famulus when he loses his faith in his adjustment to life, in his *Amt und Mission* as confessor, Knecht, despairing of his office and of Castalia, does not hesitate, in flight and quest, to begin anew. The final stage of Knecht's life, his departure from Castalia to become a simple tutor, is foreseen in the last of the three *Lebensläufe*. Like Dasa, Knecht finally acknowledges the greatest of all virtues and the ultimate answer to the problem of life: service to, and sacrifice for humanity.

Silomon meant well and von Hecker tried hard, but more than the effusions of a *Gymnasiast* would have been necessary to counter the sharp criticism of von Schöfer and Kohlschmid.

Franz Baumer

Baumer's *Hermann Hesse. Der Dichter und sein Lebenswerk* (1955, 32 pp.), the most recent of these popular pamphlet surveys, actually presents nothing that has not already been said many times before. Voluminous undocumented quotations, pertinent though they are, and frequent, minor, factual errors hardly help to enhance the value of this otherwise exceedingly readable study. Hesse did not take the *Landexamen* or go off to Maulbronn at the age of twelve, but two years later (p. 4). Mörike attended Urach and not Maulbronn (p. 4). Oswald Spengler's *Der Untergang des Abendlandes* first appeared in 1918, not in 1919 (p. 20). Nor was *Peter Camenzind* written in Gaienhofen, but completed and published before Hesse left Bern (p. 11).

2

To the second and more significant category of pamphlets belong the studies of K. H. Bühner, Heta Baaten, Anni Carlsson, R. B. Matzig, H. L. Wüstenberg, Wilhelm Schwinn, Walter Kramer, Karl Schmid, J. F. Angelloz, Rudolf Adolph, Gerhard Kirchhoff, and of Hermann Lorenzen. Only the first four of this group were published before 1945.

Karl H. Bühner

Though once most widely read and still generally acclaimed, the Gaienhofen *Novellen* (*Diesseits*, 1907; *Nachbarn*, 1908; *Umwege*, 1912) have remained the major phase of Hesse's work most neglected by scholars. Not a single, separate, detailed study of these tales has yet been made. And only rarely has their customary association with Keller's *Seldwyla* stories received more than token consideration.

Bühner undertook his *Hermann Hesse und Gottfried Keller* (1927, 59 pp.) in response to an essay contest sponsored by the *Technische Hochschule* of Stuttgart in 1925-26. His study is restricted to the influence of Keller upon *Diesseits* and *Nachbarn* ("Hesse schuf Dichtung aus Kellers Dichtung, er hat Art von Keller's Art," p. 19). The general remarks made in the introductory pages promise a meritorious analysis. Attention is drawn to the common racial, geographical, political, and cultural background of the two authors, to the similarities in their natures and *Weltanschauung* as reflected in the themes and characters of their writings, and to their common motifs (*e.g.*, *Romeo und Julia auf dem Dorfe—Marmorsäge; Die drei gerechten Kammacher—In der alten Sonne*). Unfortunately, this promise is not fulfilled in the ensuing three sections.

Instead of proceeding systematically to establish his introductory remarks, Bühner begins very haphazardly to dwell upon a number of stylistic characteristics common to both authors: framework-*Novellen* in which Hesse is concerned with his droll *Leute von Gerbersau* and Keller with his bizarre *Leute von Seldwyla*,[18] the use of detailed background in the initial pages, the simplicity of thought and language, the peculiar use of adjectives (*e.g.*, "blutlose Gerechtigkeit"), and a tendency to personify the abstract (*e.g.*, "die Seele rümpft leise die Nase," pp. 27-28). Nor are differences entirely ignored: Hesse's freer use of the first person, his more intimate descriptions of nature, and the more musical than plastic quality of his prose.

Accepting the usual assumption that Keller is both a realist and a romanticist, Bühner then endeavors to show that Hesse, too, fits into this mixed category. He refers to the prevailing realism of Hesse's backgrounds, characters, and language, to his preoccupation with memories, and to his fascination by the remote and fantastic.

In the concluding pages of his study, instead of expounding

upon the likenesses between Hesse's and Keller's *personae*, Bühner manages quite successfully to show how decidedly Hesse's people differ. They are not the brusque, virile, flesh and blood creations of the optimistic Keller, but the timid, inept creations of a more pessimistic author.

Except for Bühner's brochure and the scanty allusions to Keller in the studies of Kuhn and Waldhausen, only Theodor Klaiber's survey of Keller's influence upon Hesse merits any consideration (*Gottfried Keller und die Schwaben* [1919], pp. 93-101). After calling attention to Hesse's early acclaim of Keller in *Hermann Lauscher* (1920, p. 195), and *Peter Camenzind* (end of first chapter), and his appreciation of *Grüner Heinrich* ("Gedanken bei der Lektüre des *Grünen Heinrich*," *März*, 1, i [1907], 455-459), Klaiber touches upon their common reverence for life and their faith in its reasonableness and purposiveness; and he perceives a marked kinship in both the substance and form of their works. In their ironic manner, both writers are kindly disposed to the fringe elements of society, to its beggars, vagabonds, and other stray people. Gerbersau, with its smug and foolish philistines, its odd characters, its "gelassene Lebenskünstler" and "unselige Lebensdilletanten," is a veritable Swabian Seldwyla. Klaiber finds Giebenrath's (*Unterm Rad*) experiences as a mechanic, the rather ludicrous escapades of Heller and Hürlin (*In der alten Sonne*), and Ladidel's motley collection of worthless articles particularly Kelleresque. He notes, too, that like Keller's, many of Hesse's stories end in a happy return to a simple, a more natural way of life (*e.g., Peter Camenzind, Ladidel, Karl Eugen Eiselein*). Notwithstanding, Klaiber admits that Hesse is more than just an echo of Keller. He is less austere. He is a more nervous person, whose characters seem to be more subdued. His is a softer temperament, and its expression is more lyrical. He is much more uncontained in his attachment to nature.

Together, Bühner, Kuhn, Waldhausen, and Klaiber represent the beginnings of a fruitful Keller-Hesse study. There is here no dearth of contentions and suggestions, but all still waits for the confirmation of a more inclusive and detailed study. Such a study would demand a close scrutiny of *Peter Camenzind* (despite Ball's conviction that there is little of Keller in this novel and probably more of Stifter, [1947, p. 117]), of *Unterm Rad,* of all three collections of the Gaienhofen *Novellen*, of *Knulp* (first part published in 1908), and perhaps even of "Meine Kindheit" of *Hermann Lauscher*, as H. R. Schmid would suggest (*Hermann Hesse*, p. 33). Nor should one overlook Hesse's appreciations and reviews ("Der Briefwechsel zwischen Storm und Keller," *Die Rheinlande*, 4 [1904], 518-519; "*Martin Salander*," *März*, 4, iii [1910], 148-150; "Der alte *Grüne Heinrich*," *März*, 7 [Dec. 1913], 884-888; "Beim Lesen des *Grünen Heinrich*," *Schweizerland*, 4 [1917-18], 51-53; "*Seldwyla* im Abendrot," *Vossische Zeitung*, July 13, 1919; "Gedanken über Gottfried Keller," *Der Lesezirkel*, 18 [1931], 141-144; his introductions (*Don Correa* [Bern, 1918] and a recent edition of *Grüner Heinrich*), and his many stray references to Keller (*Gertrud* [1927], pp. 16, 25-27; *Das Meisterbuch* [Berlin, 1913], pertinent references in the foreword; *Nürnberger Reise*, p. 13; "Besuch bei einem Dichter," *Gedenkblätter* [1947], p. 120; "Unterbrochene-Schulstunden," *Späte Prosa* [1951], pp. 99-100).

Heta Baaten

While Ball presents a reasonably detailed sketch of Hesse's ancestry, and H. R. Schmid refers very frequently to this family background, it was not until Heta Baaten concerned herself with this problem that it received more than nominal attention ("Der Romantiker Hermann Hesse," 1934). Only that half of her dissertation which deals with his family was ever published: *Die pietistische Tradition der-Familie Gundert und Hesse* (1934, 42 pp.).

In her effort to shed light upon this Pietism, Baaten presents the relevant biographical details of the Gundert family from Hesse's great-great-grandfather, Joh. Christian Gundert, to his illustrious grandfather, Hermann Gundert; and of the Hesse family, she pays particular attention to Hesse's grandfather and father. Going beyond mere biography, she strives to filter from this pietistic tradition an attitude toward the world, and a conception of God, man, and of sin. She concludes, from a confusion of data centered about involved religious issues, that the Gundert-Hesse families emphasized salvation through Christ, believed in the inherent sinfulness of man, and were uncompromising in their renunciation of all that was of this world ("das natürlich-menschliche und geistig kulturelle Leben," p. 38).

Since Baaten's publication breaks off at this pont, it remains of interest only to the biographer or to the student of Pietism, but has no direct bearing upon Hesse and his art. That the second half of the dissertation ("Eine geistesgeschichtliche Untersuchung seines Werkes auf dem Hintergrund der pietistischen Tradition seiner Familie") remained unpublished, is most unfortunate. The problem has still to be investigated.

Richard B. Matzig

Steppenwolf marks a belated and less turbid sequel to the expressionism of *Demian* and *Klingsor* and re-echoes the spirit of cultural decline permeating *Blick ins Chaos*. Thomas Mann terms it an experimental novel no less daring than James Joyce's *Ulysses* or André Gide's *Counterfeiters* (introduction to English translation of *Demian*, 1947). It should occasion little surprise that this novel has received more individual attention than any other of Hesse's works except *Glasperlenspiel*.[19] On the other hand, that *Steppenwolf* should be greeted by many critics and even by friends with a curious mixture of awe, bewilderment, antagonism, and even disgust ("Nachwort," *Krisis*), as though it served to betray some cause, is rather difficult to understand. *Steppenwolf* is a stepchild in neither substance nor form, but a logical climax to the post-war period of "Demianism" with its emphasis upon *Eigensinn*, its quest for the self, and its philosophy of *Gemüt ist Schicksal*.

Of the many studies centered about *Steppenwolf*, that of R. B. Matzig (*Der Dichter und die Zeitstimmung* [1947], 51 pp.), though perhaps not the most penetrating in its analysis, is certainly widest in its scope. By way of introduction, a few general remarks are made about Hesse and about his art, the confusion of literary movements preceding and culminating in Expressionism are briefly outlined, and Hesse's work previous to *Steppenwolf* and beginning with *Demian* is closely linked with the expressionistic spirit of the times with its concern for the essence of things, the absolute, the soul. Concluding this introduction, and as the immediate prelude to his discussion of *Steppenwolf*, Matzig touches specifically upon the notorious *Krisis* poems, most of which were not included in the *Gedichte* of 1942. The satanic self-exposure and self-castigation, the pathetic yearning and frantic eroticism, the cynicism and anti-intellectualism, and the jazz and whisky of these poems, give ample warning of the breaking storm.

Proceeding to *Steppenwolf* itself, Matzig first recalls Hesse's own introductory interpretation of Haller's plight. This is not only the unfortunate story of a hypersensitive artist or a psychopathic intellectual caught in the chaos between a dying and a yet unborn culture, but a document recording the disease and agonies of a whole age. Matzig then retraces Haller's life. Attention is drawn to his lonely existence in an insipid bourgeois world which he both hates and envies, to his thoughts of suicide, to the mad dance-hall world of Hermine, Maria, and Pablo, and to the magic theater, Goethe, Mozart, and recuperation. Concise character sketches follow, and the study concludes with a few remarks about style.

For the most part, Matzig's is a running commentary rather than an analysis, and as such, it leaves basic problems unresolved. The dichotomy of *Geist* and *Natur* is treated inadequately. The symbolic significance of Hermine, Maria, Pablo, Goethe, Mozart, and the magic theater receives too little consideration. Hesse's criticism of the intellectuals and their disgraceful rôle in German history, and his tirade against music are left untouched. No attempt is made to delve into the *Steppenwolf* personality. And while *Steppenwolf* may truly be one of the few lasting works of art left by Expressionism, this can hardly be convincingly established by mere allusions to its impressionistic tendencies, naturalistic detail, and wild, free associations.

Matzig's is an excellent survey. It provides an appropriate setting for *Steppenwolf,* broaches the more important problems of substance and form, but stops just short of the detailed analysis which the novel more than merits.

H. L. Wüstenberg

The importance of H. L. Wüstenberg's pamphlet (*Stimme eines Menschen. Die politischen Aufsätze und Gedichte Hermann Hesses* [1947], 23 pp.) lies mainly in the fact that it focusses attention upon a subject which had been neglected for two decades, Hesse's political essays and poems. Unfortunately, limiting his text proper to little more than twelve pages, Wüstenberg can do no more than survey the field, touching upon Hesse's emphasis upon the individual, upon moral responsibility and willingness to suffer, upon his appeal for humanity, for love and international brotherhood, and upon his lack of concern for immediate political problems and theories. Although it only breaks ground, this brief study, which was actually written in 1945, is a beginning; and now that all of Hesse's so-called political essays are readily available under one cover (*Krieg und Frieden*; reviewed by Otto Basler in the 1947 ed. of Ball's book, pp. 305-316), it is high time that they were given the close analysis they warrant.

Wilhelm Schwinn

Schwinn's brochure (*Hermann Hesses Altersweisheit und das Christentum* [1949], 39 pp.) is much weightier and far more thorough. It is with our age of religious, moral, and intellectual anarchy in mind, a time when a reëxamination of the intrinsic values of human existence and a renewed affirmation of the true Christian way of life is most pressing, that Schwinn turns to Hesse and his *Glasperlenspiel*. As the title of his study would indicate, Schwinn is interested only in the wisdom reflected in Hesse's last novel and in what bearing this wisdom may have on Christianity.

Examining the course of Knecht's gradual *Erwachen*, Schwinn notes Hesse's special emphasis upon self-knowledge, growth, meditation, and upon a harmonious interplay of life's two forces ("lebenskräftige geistige Existenz," p. 26). Hesse's view of our modern Christian world is clearly critical, and to a great extent, justly so; for the genuinely Christian spirit which once prevailed has become a skeptical, secularized attitude of spirituality to which true prayer and religious meditation have become foreign, and while the Christian Church scoffs at the autonomy of the mind and bewails the godlessness of our age, it itself affords human life little direction. Despite this criticism, however, Hesse has remained within the pale of Christianity. His world of thought has much in common with Christian belief and the two are far from incompatible. Castalia is akin to a monastery, Knecht's affirmation of life, love, and of service are basically Christian, and his *Erwachen* approaches a spiritual conversion.

Schwinn is convinced that mutual, beneficial influence is

possible between Hesse's wisdom and Christianity. While the
Church would benefit, were it to heed the criticism directed
against it, Hesse might do well to become more cognizant of God
and his grace, of revelation, and of the beyond. According to
Schwinn, Hesse is too much of this world and has erroneously
reduced the problem of divinity and man to the worldly conflict of *Geist* and *Natur*. His faith in meditation as a panacea for
life's problems reflects an unawareness of the power of sin. His
Oriental mysticism and relativity can have no appeal or value for
the Christian, and his *Heiterkeit* can be no substitute for the
love God stirs in man's soul.

Schwinn's treatment is anything but that of a rabid sectarian.
Though evidently written from a Lutheran pastor's point of view,
it is not the usual stereotyped chiding by orthodoxy, but reflects a
great deal of thought and a sincere personal concern. It is "ein
gewagter Versuch" (p. 39), as Schwinn himself admits, but it
is a very discreet one.

Karl Schmid

The title and subtitle of Schmid's pamphlet (*Hermann Hesse
und Thomas Mann. Zwei Möglichkeiten europäischer Humanität* [1950], 48 pp.) might better have been inverted, for it is
with Germany, a new humanism, and a Europe more united in
spirit, that he is primarily concerned. Only in the light of this
interest, and chiefly by way of illustration, is brief reference
made to Mann, and even briefer to Hesse.

Schmid deplores the present discord in Europe, is severely
critical of the aristocratic and irresponsible Faustian spirit
which has prevailed in Germany and has separated her from
the European community ever since the successful reaction of
Romanticism against the healthier, the more rational, and more
European bourgeois culture of the eighteenth century, and sees
promise of a better future only in the greater "europäisches Bewusstsein" (p. 12) of a new humanism. It is in Hesse and Mann,
the most widely known German writers of recent decades, decidedly different from one another yet both thoroughly German
in spirit, that Schmid finds the two kinds of humanism represented which could make just such a supranational attitude possible for the Germans.

In the brief comparative study of Hesse and Mann which is
intermittently woven into the main theme, a very limited effort

is made to characterize each by drawing attention to a few familiar biographical details, juxtaposing some basic differences, and noting a loosely analogous trend in their developments. Hesse, the child of nature, with his penchant for solitude and meditation, heir to the Swabian metaphysical tradition of Schelling and to the lyrical tradition of Mörike, and drawn to such kindred spirits as Grillparzer, Eichendorff, and Stifter, is contrasted with Mann, the city dweller, the more sociable world traveller, a descendent of the German *Aufklärung*, of Nicolai, Lessing, and closely akin to Fontane. Despite these differences, both are rooted in Romanticism—Hesse overly fascinated by music; Mann overly attached to Schopenhauer, Nietzsche, and Wagner; each scornful of the healthy bourgeois, his common sense and ability to cope with life—and both eventually repudiate Romanticism, deny the German culture fostered by it, and appeal for a European humanism.

Of the "zwei deutsche Wege zu europäischer Humanität" (p. 46) represented in *Glasperlenspiel* and *Dr. Faustus*, Schmid sees more hope in Mann's. Hesse's humanism, though no feeble ideology, can promise but little, for it is of too Oriental a nature, too concerned with *la condition humaine* (*e.g.*, it bypasses such important realities of life as sex and economy). Schmid therefore concludes: "Einer letzten ernstlichen Wirklichkeit—nicht einer metaphysischen, sondern einer existentiellen—ermangelt die Glasperlenspielvision, so rein und schön sie ist" (p. 34). In marked contrast, Mann's humanism remains thoroughly ensconced in Western tradition, looks forward to a more rational civilization and to a more plausible "rationalistische Humanisierung" (p. 37).

In a more comprehensive study of Hesse and Mann, humanism would undoubtedly be one of the most significant problems to be investigated.[20] Schmid's work is but the briefest beginning, in no way enhanced by his unreserved acclaim of reason and his indiscriminate rejection of all that smacks of Romanticism, but certainly incisive and very suggestive. Schmid himself broaches other vital issues which such a comparative study might include: Hesse and Mann with reference to Nietzsche[21] and to Schopenhauer;[22] their kinship with and attitude toward Romanticism; and their reception abroad. To these might be added the problem of *Geist* and *Natur*, expanded to embrace the problem of the artist and society,[23] and that of art and disease. Under the heading Hesse, Mann, and Germany, their attitudes to Wilhelmine Germany, to the Weimar Republic, and to the Third Reich might be compared, and the history of each writer in Germany traced. Both invite a study in terms of Goethe and in terms of the *Bildungsroman*. Nor should their friendship and mutual appreciation go unnoticed.[24] Other topics are suggested by the brief comparative studies that have appeared: Robert Faesi, "Kurgäste: Manns *Zauberberg* und Hesses *Kurgast*," *Basler Nachrichten*, Sonntagsblatt, Nov. 8, Nov. 15, 1925; Anni Carlsson, "Gingo Biloba," *"Neue Schweizer Rundschau*, 15 (1947), 79-87; G. Szczesny, "Hans Castorp, Harry Haller und die Folgen," *Umschau*, 2 (1947), 601-611; H. G. Thurm, "Thomas Mann, Hermann Hesse und wir Jungen," *Umschau*, 2 (1947), 612-615; Joseph Müller-Blattau, "Sinn und Sendung der Musik in Thomas Manns *Dr. Faustus* und Hermann Hesses *Glasperlenspiel*," *"Geistige Welt*, 4 (1949), 29-34; Alfredo Dornheim, "Musica Novelesca y Novela Musical. Concepción musical de las últimas novelas de Hermann Hesse y Thomas Mann," *Revista de Estudios Musicales* (Universidad Nacional de Cuyo, Mendoza, Argentina), 1 (August 1949), 131-172; G. W. Field, "Music and Morality in Thomas Mann and Hermann Hesse" (*University of Toronto Quarterly*, 24 [1955], 175-190).

Marcel Schneider ("Thomas Mann et Hermann Hesse," *La Table Ronde*, 3[1950], 139-144) broaches a novel comparison of Leverkühn and Peter Camenzind: artists of the same generation reacting against the same cultural climate, one by turning to the devil, the other to nature. Hans Mayer (*Thomas Mann. Werk und Entwicklung* [1950], p. 328) proposes that Mann's *Vertauschte Köpfe* is, among other things, a burlesque parody of *Siddhartha*. Oskar Seidlin's "geospiritual generalizations" constitute an interesting but sketchy comparison of Mann and Hesse ("Hermann Hesse: The Exorcism of the Demon," *Symposium*, 4 [1950], 347). Mann is considered an heir of Goethe, a Westerner whose concern is justice and the dignity of man, and whose supreme vision is a Third Humanism. Hesse is considered an heir of Dostoyevsky, an Easterner whose concern is grace and saintliness, and whose supreme vision is the eschatological Third Kingdom. Hesse possesses none of Mann's olympic equanimity, his works are not as wide in range, as deep in meaning, or as clear in outline; but his heart pulsates more visibly, and he is more beset by the timeless tragedy of man's existence.

J. F. Angelloz

In his bird's-eye view of Hesse's life and art, Angelloz (*Das Mütterliche und das Männliche im Werke Hermann Hesses* [1951], 31 pp.) perceives four major stages of development: decadence, reaction, *Ich*-quest and the mother-world, retreat and the father-world. For fifteen years preceding *Demian*, and in the manner of Thomas Mann, Hesse sought to shake himself free from the weary *fin de siècle* spirit. His heroes, quite like Tonio Kröger, are lonely outsiders torn between the mother-world and the father-world, between *Logos* and *Eros*, artists desperately seeking to justify their existence and to come to terms with life. Search for the self, for *Mutter Eva*, and an awareness of life's endless polarities, begin with *Demian*. The father-element is not introduced until *Steppenwolf*. The two worlds of *Logos* and *Eros* are finally balanced in *Narziss und Goldmund*, and with *Glasperlenspiel* Hesse retreats into the disciplined father-world of spirit, without ever really having achieved any synthesis of *das Mütterliche* and *das Männliche*.

With his own concluding remark, "mehr Probleme angeschnitten als Lösungen vorgeschlagen, mehr angeregt als gefördert," Angelloz himself best characterizes his pamphlet. While the subject he broaches is pregnant with possibilities, the argument is one of debatable generalities. The interesting parallel development between Mann and Hesse remains on a plane of vague allusions. The father-world and mother-world are never clearly distinguished. In reference to *Demian*, these two principles are erroneously equated with the home, the pious, ordered world of the father, and the wicked outside world of the servants; and love, which one moment is considered a trait of the mother-world, is the next attributed to the father-world (p. 11). How *Narziss und Goldmund* can represent both a balance of *Logos* and *Eros* (p. 8) and a last victory of *Eros* (p. 19), is inconceivable, and that *Siddhartha* and *Morgenlandfahrt* represent flight from the Western world to an Eastern wisdom which is no longer concerned with the father-mother polarity, cannot even be considered.

From *Demian* to *Glasperlenspiel*, *das Mütterliche* and *das Männliche*, *Logos* and *Eros*, *Geist* and *Natur*, or whatever terminology may be preferred to represent the polarity of human existence, is Hesse's constant concern. To resolve this problem adequately would entail a close analysis of all his prose and poetry from 1917 to the present. Even then, common agreement would be most unlikely, but conclusions would at least be reasonably well established.

Hermann Lorenzen

Lorenzen is fully aware that Hesse is no professional educator offering a finished pedagogical system (*Pädagogische Ideen bei Hermann Hesse*, [1955], 72 pp.). He is convinced, however, that much can be derived from his works that could be of great value to the modern pedagogue. With this in mind, Lorenzen dwells upon those basic aspects in Hesse's *Weltanschauung* that have a definite bearing upon pedagogy.

Attention is first drawn to Hesse's concept of polarity (*Geist* and *Natur*, the individual and society, freedom and restraint), to his acceptance of this fact of life, and to his emphasis upon the necessity of learning moderation and of achieving a healthy balance in this dualism. Lorenzen then turns to the three stages of man's development as outlined in Hesse's "Ein Stückchen Theologie" (*Neue Rundschau*, 43, i [1932], 736-747). The individual's progression from innocence to sin and despair, and ultimately to grace and redemption, is essentially a process of self-realization. For Hesse, however, a finding of oneself is also a finding of one's place in society. His individualism is, therefore, not anarchistic but based on belief in the inherent goodness of man. Life must be a continuous growth and every moment of this awakening is just as important as the goal itself.

Lorenzen notes that formal education, according to Hesse, can justify itself only if it furthers this process. The traditional schoolmaster must, therefore, give way to a guide. Youth must be allowed to make its own mistakes and to become independent and responsible as soon as possible. The student and his development must become more important than that which is taught. Demands made upon a student should always be commensurate with his potentialities. Education should be a human experience and not a meaningless experiencing of facts. And the formative powers of aesthetic experience, simple observation, and actual doing are not to be ignored. From this, Lorenzen concludes that Hesse belongs to the tradition of Rousseau, Pestalozzi, Fröbel, and Berthold Otto, and that his views are in accord with current pedagogical theories.

In his interest in the practicality of Hesse's views on education, Lorenzen pursues an important problem which both Geffert and Boersma fail to consider. Unfortunately, he stresses only those of Hesse's pedagogical ideas which are more or less compatible with present trends in the field of education. Hesse has not always extolled moderation, renunciation, sacrifice, and service. Nor has he always been as mindful of the individual's usefulness to society as Lorenzen suggests. The pedagogically unacceptable extremes of Hesse's works cannot be brushed aside casually as mere exaggerations (p. 29). Nor are *Demian* and *Steppenwolf* merely examples of that blind individualism which can only lead to despair, and which should, therefore, be avoided (p. 32) ; for Hesse they represented necessary paths which led from despair to hope.

Lorenzen's study almost suggests a deliberate attempt to make Hesse acceptable to educators. On the other hand, Friederich Lieser, the only other critic who has given serious consideration to this problem, doubts that Hesse's educational ideal would be feasible in general education. Obviously the problem needs more study, and both points of view should be reëxamined.

Anni Carlsson, Walter Kramer, Gerhard Kirchhoff, Rudolf Adolph

Carlsson's *Hermann Hesses Gedichte* (1943, 13 pp.), Kramer's *Hermann Hesses Glasperlenspiel und seine Stellung in der geistigen Situation unserer Zeit* (1949, 22 pp), and Kirchhoff's *Reine Gegenwart. Über Hermann Hesses Glasperlenspiel* (1952, 28 pp.) are dealt with under "Poetry" and *"Glasperlenspiel"* in Chapter III of Part Two. Adolph's, *Hermann Hesse, Schutzpatron der Bücherfreunde* (1952, 23 pp.) was unavailable for examination.

3

The third category of pamphlets consists of a heterogeneous collection of private or special publications, rather personal miscellanies, all of which have appeared since 1947. The first of these (*Die Sendung Hermann Hesses*, 24 pp.), published upon the occasion of Hesse's seventieth birthday, consists of three separate articles. Ivan Heilbut's introductory item, and the most meaty of the three ("Hermann Hesses Sendung in unserer Zeit," pp. 2-15), is one of those enigmas which one would prefer to leave alone. It is difficult to decide whether profound thoughts which resist simple expression are being pondered, or whether only ordinary notions lie concealed behind abstruse language. After hovering about in this ether for four pages, Heilbut finally descends and proceeds to outline those factors which determined Hesse and conditioned his art. Attention is drawn briefly to Hesse's background and his life, to his refusal to sacrifice his ideals in times of stress, to his emphasis upon the individual, and to his predilection for the lonely outsider who is versed neither in the art of life nor the art of love. Passing references are made to *Peter Camenzind, Steppenwolf,* and to *Glasperlenspiel.* Life of our life that Hesse's writings are, they can help restore faith in humanity, and are a source of that moral force which is necessary to bring about a world united in spirit.

Anna Jacobson's article ("Hermann Hesse. Anlässlich der Auszeichnung durch den Nobelpreis," pp. 16-21) is less tenuous and decidedly more concise. Her point of departure is Hesse's *Eine Bibliothek der Weltliteratur* (1944), and her principal theme is Hesse and books. She dwells upon Hesse's passion for reading while yet a child, his years of apprenticeship in a bookshop, his interest in books of the Middle Ages and the Orient, and the books he himself has edited. Digressing briefly, Jacobson draws attention to the autobiographical nature of Hesse's art, alludes to his kindred Romanticists of the nineteenth century, and concludes by pointing out an affinity of spirit between Hesse, Romain Rolland, and Thomas Mann.

Of Georg N. Shuster's short, concluding article ("Die Seele eines Künstlers," pp. 22-24) no more need be said than that the substance and style of *Steppenwolf* and *Glasperlenspiel* are very briefly remarked upon.

Hermann Hesse (1948, 29 pp.) consists of Thomas Mann's "Für Hermann Hesse" (pp. 3-14), André Gide's "Bemerkungen zum Werk Hermann Hesses" (pp. 15-27), and Hans Carossa's poem "Schutzgeist" (pp. 28-29). Both Mann and Gide give expression to that high esteem in which Hesse has generally been held by fellow authors of rank. In a very personal tone, Mann recalls his visits in Montagnola after his flight from Germany in 1933, lingers over their differences and similarities, draws attention to the general nature of Hesse's art, to his interest in world literature, to his activities as an editor, and to his very German nature.

It is about this very German nature that Gide's article centers. He is convinced that the German, with his detached, romantic disposition, his inclination towards a sentimental, aimless hovering about in the *clair-obscur* of the soul, is easily swept away by an almost primitive attachment to nature; furthermore, with his characteristics of self-denial and passivity, he is susceptible to extreme ideologies. Gide extols Hesse as one of the very few Germans who have refused to become victims of themselves and to sacrifice their moral integrity by falling prey to totalitarianism.

That such assertive individualists as Hesse and Gide should be drawn together in mutual appreciation, was almost inevitable. Yet, though each was well acquainted with and fascinated by the work of the other long before 1933, it was not until then that a sporadic correspondence began, and not until 1947, a few years before Gide's death, that they finally met in person. Their admiration was that of kindred spirits. Each perceived in the other a rebel individualist divorced from established dogma and institutions, a lonely seeker of new norms (see Hesse, *Erinnerung an André Gide*, [1951], 21 pp.).

The four artistically bound pamphlets prepared by Erich Weiss of the *Westdeutsches Hermann Hesse-Archiv* are undoubtedly of greater interest to the bibliophile than to the scholar. *Mein Mentor Hermann Hesse* (1948, 15 pp.) is Otto Korrodi's confession of faith in the artist and the man, and in *Schwäbische Vettern* (1948, 15 pp.), Ludwig Finckh, a good friend and fellow Swabian writer, presents a detailed genealogical study of Hesse's forbears. *Dank des Herzens* (1949, 23 pp.) comprises only poems dedicated to Hesse upon his seventy-second birthday, and each of the three very brief items (Wilhelm Schussen, "Hermann Hesse und die Schmetterlinge," 6 pp.; Max Hermann-Neisse, "Besuch bei Hermann Hesse," 2 pp. in verse; Karl Kloter, "Weg zum Dichter," 4 pp.) of *Besuch bei Hermann Hesse* (1949, 24 pp.) recalls a visit with Hesse, expresses great respect and praise for him, and emphasizes his intimate association with nature.

To these miscellaneous collections may be added: *Stimmen zum Briefbuch von Hermann Hesse* (1951, 20 pp.), comprising brief expressions of praise and gratitude by Hedda Eulenberg, Max Rychner, and "an old pedagogue," together with two letters written by Hesse in July, 1951; *Hermann Hesse als Badener*

Kurgast (1952, 26 pp.), consisting of Hesse's "Die Dohle" and extracts dealing with Baden, Robert Mächler's "Hermann Hesses Badener Psychologie," pp. 11-15, and Uli Münzel's "Hermann Hesse als Badener Kurgast," pp. 17-21; *Hermann Hesse* (1955, 37 pp.), comprising brief eulogies by Arthur Georgi and Robert Jokusch upon the awarding of the *Friedenspreis des Deutschen Buchhandels* to Hesse, Richard Benz' "Festansprache" (pp. 15-24), a very appreciative survey of Hesse's life and works, and Hesse's "Dankadresse"; and *Ein paar Leserbriefe* (1955, 39 pp.), twelve recent letters received by Hesse.

The February 1953 issue of *Du. Schweizerische Monatsschrift*, which is dedicated entirely to Hesse, is an excellent supplement to Ball's biography. In its sixty-two pages, extracts from Marie Hesse's diary (Adele Gundert, *Marie Hesse*) and a whole series of family photographs from Hesse's childhood to recent years are intermingled with such diverse items as Albrecht Goes, "Rede auf Hermann Hesse" (see "Pamphlets," 1), Othmar Schoeck's composition, "Ravenna," reports of encounters with Hesse, stylistic analyses of three poems (see "Poetry" in the following chapter), and a few water colors and poems by Hesse himself.

The American-German Review, October-November, 1956 (40 pp.), represents a similar composite, dedicated to Hesse. R. C. Wood's editorial on the author is followed by a brief Hesse chronology, and by Hesse's "Haus zum Frieden" (written in 1910) and "Klage und Trost," a poem dedicated to Ludwig Finckh. A water color and some photographs have also been added.

4

Like these miscellanies, all the bibliographical studies of the fourth category of pamphlets have been published since 1947. Of these, Horst Kliemann's, *Das Werk Hermann Hesses. Eine bibliographische Übersicht*, 8 pp. (*Sonderdruck* of his article in *Europa-Archiv*, 1 [1947], 604-609), his *Hermann Hesse und das Buch. Bemerkungen zu einer Hesse-Bibliographie*, 12 pp. (*Sonderdruck* of his article in *Deutsche Beiträge*, 1 [1947], 353-360), and *Verbesserungen und Ergänzungen zu Hermann Hesse. Eine Bibliographische Studie* (1948, 12 pp.) supplement the major Kliemann/Silomon bibliography of 1947. Siegfried Unseld's *Das Werk von Hermann Hesse. Ein Brevier* (1952, 72 pp.) presents a wealth of interesting biographical and bibliographical information, and Martin Pfeifer's *Bibliographie der im Gebiet der DDR seit 1945 erschienenen Schriften von und über Hermann Hesse* (1952, 15 pp.; supplemented in 1955, 63 pp.) affords the only picture of the general interest in Hesse in East Germany. These bibliographies are discussed in Chapter II of Part Three.

III

ARTICLES IN BOOKS, IN PAMPHLETS, AND IN PERIODICALS

Preceding 1927

The literary criticism centered about Hesse falls into three distinct periods. Of these, the first and least significant ended with the year 1926. The second began very auspiciously in 1927 but soon faltered under the Nazis and faded away with the war. The third, beginning in 1945, with unexpected international acclaim and a wave of enthusiastic criticism, has not yet exhausted itself.

During the first of these periods there appeared no books about Hesse, only one pamphlet (Alfred Kuhn), and one dissertation (Georg Zelder, "Mundartliche Einflüsse in der Sprache Hermann Hesses" [1922], 109 pp.). Of the one hundred and twenty-six periodical articles and the seventy-six newspaper items listed by Ernst Metelmann (*Schöne Literatur*, 28 [1927], 306-312), very few surpass the significance of the average review. During these earlier years, *Peter Camenzind* seems to have been the most popular book by far. *Unterm Rad* received considerably less attention, and the various collections of poetry and *Novellen*, and *Gertrud, Rosshalde*, and *Siddhartha*, even less. Despite the wild popular acclaim of *Demian*, relatively little was written about this work. Hesse's other publications remained almost unnoticed.

While most of the works published from 1918 to 1927 were eventually to receive their due consideration, the earlier publications have remained badly neglected. Only in four of the many books and dissertations which have appeared since 1927 (Ball, Geffert, H. R. Schmid, and *Schriftsteller der Gegenwart* [1956], pp. 12-42) have they been treated more than cursorily, and while repeated references are made to them in the many pamphlets of recent years, it is only occasionally that they are even briefly characterized (Bühner, Hafner, and Levander). These earlier works fare no better in the periodical literature which has accumulated since 1927 (H. Wiegand, "Hermann Hesse Jugendbildnis," *Neue Rundschau*, 45, i [1934], 119-122); Anni Carlsson, "Zu Hermann Hesse: *Eine Stunde hinter Mitternacht*," *Neue Schweizer Rundschau*, 13 [1948], 191-193; W. von Schöfer,

"Hermann Hesse, *Peter Camenzind* und das *Glasperlenspiel*," *Die Sammlung*, 3 [1948], 597-609; G. Hafner, "Hermann Hesses Anfänge," *Welt und Wort*, 7 [1952], 229-230) ; Suzanne Debruge, "L'Art de conter. Hermann Hesse: Trois histoires de la vie de Knulp," *Langues Modernes*, 48 (1954), 328-332.

Of the articles written before 1927, there are only a few to which specific attention need be drawn. The earliest of these is Theodor Klaiber's "Hermann Hesse," *Die Schwaben in der Literatur der Gegenwart* (1905), pp. 87-104. Hesse's first five publications are surveyed and ably characterized in both substance and form. While he considers *Romantische Lieder* and *Eine Stunde hinter Mitternacht* to be the works of an apprentice, the *Künstlerkunst* of a sentimental, linguistically talented youth enraptured by his own pose, he feels that *Hermann Lauscher, Gedichte,* and *Peter Camenzind* reflect a broadened horizon of experience and expression, and augur better works to come.

Almost from the very beginning, Hesse's readers and critics seem to have been far more interested in what he has had to say than how he has said it. For most, he has been nothing more than a seismograph faithfully recording the cultural disturbances of his age, an author with an uncanny ability to give expression to the emotional and intellectual problems of his time. This exaggerated emphasis upon substance, to the neglect of form, is very evident in Agnes Waldhausen's "Hermann Hesse," *Mitteilungen der Literarhistorischen Gesellschaft* 5 [1901]), 4-32. Centering her attention about *Peter Camenzind,* she presents a well annotated résumé of the novel, appends a brief appreciation of its art, and concludes with a few general remarks about *Unterm Rad, Hermann Lauscher, Diesseits,* and *Nachbarn.* While Waldhausen's synopsis of *Peter Camenzind* reflects a sound grasp of the substance, her appreciation of its art is hardly more than a token gesture. She notes that the apparently loosely constructed tale is actually given a close-knit continuity by constant recollection of the past and many allusions to the future.[25] She points out telling stylistic characteristics reminiscent of Keller. She praises the clarity of the language and remarks upon the vivid descriptions of nature and the contrasting hazy portrayal of human beings. Unfortunately, not one of these pertinent observations receives detailed consideration.

Waldhausen's brief allusions to Hesse's other works are quite insignificant. She dismisses *Unterm Rad* as not being a work of art at all, terms *Hermann Lauscher* a variegated, romantic composite, and finds that the little comedies and tragedies comprising *Diesseits* and *Nachbarn* again recall Keller, although they do lack the playful humor and careful composition of the *Seldwyla* tales.

Analyzing *Peter Camenzind, Unterm Rad, Diesseits* and *Gertrud* in terms of his theme ("Der Glücksgedanke bei Hermann Hesse," *Die Grenzboten*, 71, i [1912], 477-485), Wilhelm Hartung confirms what Hesse has often maintained: "die unglücklichsten Tage meines Lebens gäbe ich schwerer hin als alle heiteren" (*Gertrud*, 3rd sentence). Hesse's ideal of happiness is not fulfillment, but sad, romantic dreaming; and his attitude towards life is one of contented resignation, with wine and memories to console him. Hartung's article gives an indication of the nature of Hesse's pre-1914 popularity, and at the same time explains the later lack of appreciation for these earlier works. The strong romantic sentiment which distinguishes these writings was apparently very much in accord with the sentimentality current before the war, but could no longer be appreciated by, or answer the needs of the more cynical, disillusioned readers of the postwar world.

After dwelling upon Hesse's yearning and dreaming, Otto Hartwich ("Die grosse Sehnsucht," *Kulturwerte aus der modernen Literatur* [1912] Vol. 3, 50-79) appropriately characterizes *Peter Camenzind* as "nicht die Entwicklungsgeschichte eines Menschenlebens, sondern die der grossen Sehnsucht im Rahmen eines Menschenlebens" (p. 52). Camenzind's *grosse Sehnsucht*, first engenderd by nature, then fostered by learning, by art, by a feeling of moral inadequacy, by St. Francis of Assisi, and even by death, is eventually overcome in tolerance, kindness, understanding, and love. Hartwich considers Hesse's presentation of this theme not only highly artistic, but also psychologically sound. He attributes the great popularity of *Peter Camenzind* to Hesse's skill in depicting that enervating yearning which is such a common human affliction.

Sebastian Wieser's article affords further insight into the general pre-war attitude toward Hesse ("Hermann Hesse," *Die Bücherwelt*, 12 [1915], 201-209). For him, Hesse is a good bourgeois author who writes chiefly to entertain his fellow bourgeois, and who is concerned in a pleasant, melancholy way with the oddities and minor tragedies of the *Kleine Welt*, and with the storm and stress of youth. He is loved by those who have a romantic, vagabond temperament, by the suffering student, the young idealist, and the lover. His work blends the romantic with the naturalistic and fits into the established tradition of Goethe, Eichendorff, and Keller. However, Wieser would not recommend Hesse for general consumption. Although his writings are not only aesthetically satisfying but entertaining, and even, upon occasion, instructive, Hesse is a pantheistic author, "kein positiv gläubiger Christ," who fails to make demands upon the reader, to lift and to strengthen him spiritually. There has been no dearth of such criticism to the very present.

Of the other remaining earliest articles, only one of which was available for examination, the following merit mention: Theodor Klaiber, "Hermann Hesse," *Monatsblätter für deutsche Literatur*, 8 (1903), 11-15; H. A. Köstlin, "Zur Theologenerziehung (Hermann Hesse: *Unterm Rad*," *Monatsschrift für Pastoraltheologie*, 2 (1905), 305-308; F. D. Schmid, "Hermann Hesse," *Berner Rundschau*, 1 (1906), 66-68; Gerhart Böhme, "Hermann Hesse: *Peter Camenzind* und *Diesseits*," *Eckart*, 1 (1907), 675-679; R. Schmid-Gruber, "Hermann Hesse," *Über den Wassern*, 1 (1908), 299-304; W. A. Thomas-San-Galli, "Hermann Hesse und die Musik," *Der Merkur*, 5 (1914), 413-418 (see "Music"); H. Meyer-Benfey, "*Knulp*," *Die literarische Gesellschaft*, 3 (1917), 18-27.

Though Hesse was youth's ideological hero for some years following *Demian*, this enthusiasm did not result in the appearance of more numerous or profound articles. Inconsequential reviews continued to prevail until 1927; among these, Hanns Elster's introduction to *Im Pressel'schen Gartenhaus* (Dresden: Deutsche Dichterhandschriften, 1920, Vol. 6, 7-22) is quite exceptional (see "Surveys"). *Blick ins Chaos* managed to incur the ire of a few critics (Gustav Zeller, "Offener Brief an Hermann Hesse," *Psychische Studien*, 47 [1920], 622-630; Gertrud Bäumer, "Medusa," "Perseus," *Die Frau*, 28 [1921], 193-199, 225-235), and an occasional writer, as usual, took issue with Hesse's attitude toward religion (Albrecht Oepke, "Indische Mission im Kreuzfeuer moderner Kritik. Hermann Hesse: *Aus Indien*," *Evangel.-luther. Missionsblatt*, 76 [1921], 193-199). Using Hesse as a convenient reference point, Otto Zarek ("Notizen über einen deutschen Dichter," *Neue Rundschau*, 34, i [1923], 367-373) expounds upon the fate which seems peculiar to the German soul:

loneliness, persistent need for reorientation and reëvaluation, and constant search for new forms and modes of artistic expression. Wilhelm Kunze presents a good descriptive survey of Hesse's works from the beginning to *Siddhartha* ("Hermann Hesse," *Die Schöne Literatur*, 24 [1923], 201-205). Rudolf Kayser touches lightly upon the psychological implications of *Kurgast* (*Neue Rundschau*, 36, ii [1925], 758-761). And Jean Édouard Spenlé ("Les derniers Romans de Hermann Hesse," *Mercure de France*, 185 [1926], 74-87) makes cursory remarks about *Peter Camenzind, Demian, Kurgast*, and *Kurzgefasster Lebenslauf*, and then centers his attention upon *Siddhartha*. This parable in liturgical prose is not only considered Hesse's masterpiece in terms of sheer art, but also the decisive turning point in his thinking and in his attitude toward life. After his earlier years of revolt and self-assertion, he is now prepared for renunciation and adjustment to the universal rhythm of life (Spenlé hardly foresaw *Krisis* and *Steppenwolf*). In this adjustment, Spenlé detects a debatable blending of Buddhism and Nietzscheism. Siddhartha is for him a younger brother of Zarathustra, who strives, like Buddha, for unity. However, he achieves unity not through denial and withdrawal, but through affirmation of and participation in life.

A number of articles published in the early Twenties were not available for examination. Six of these, nevertheless, deserve mention: Gustav Keckeis, "Ein Dichter des Diesseits," *Literarischer Handweiser*, 56 (1920), 397-402; Wilhelm Kunze: Über Hermann Hesse," *Der Bund*, 3 (1921), 158-162; "Studie über Hermann Hesse," *Die Drei*, 4 (1925), 831-840; Lulu von Strauss und Torney, "Hermann Hesse," *Die Tat*, 14 (1922), 694-698; Theodor Kappstein, "Hermann Hesse," *Rheinische Blätter*, 4 (1923), 106-111.

From 1927 to 1955

To avoid the useless repetition and the confusion of a chronological examination of all the significant articles in the period
from 1927 to 1945, then of the corresponding items from 1945
to 1955, a thematic approach combining these two periods has
been chosen. In surveying and comparing these two periods, it
it interesting to note the sharp decline of interest in Hesse during
the Nazi régime, and his abrupt rediscovery in 1947. Within one
year, almost as many books and pamphlets were published as had
ever appeared; and articles suddenly became very numerous,
longer, and decidedly more profound than before. Hesse had
finally come into his own, and though the exaggerated plaudits
of 1947 were to subside by 1949, his popularity has remained un-
shaken, and a steady flow of critical literature continues to the
present both in Germany and abroad.

While reviews prevailed before 1927, surveys and discussions
have since become more characteristic. The more significant of
these, together with a number of pertinent earlier articles, will
be scrutinized under the following headings: Surveys, Congratulatory Articles, Hesse and his Age, Hesse and Youth, Hesse and
Nature, Hesse and Music, Hesse and Psychology, *Geist* and
Natur, Hesse and Religion, *Glasperlenspiel*, and Poetry.

Surveys

To endeavor, even most briefly, to examine the vast number
of articles which survey Hesse's life and works, would entail endless, purposeless repetition. It should more then suffice to touch
upon a few of the most significant. The earliest of these is Hanns
Martin Elster's introduction to *Gertrud* (Berlin: Deutsche
Bücher Gemeinschaft, 1927, pp. 5-48).[26] Before Ball's work appeared, this was the only fairly detailed and reliable biography
of Hesse. Biographical details are supplemented by well-chosen
quotations which highlight the dominant characteristics of
Hesse's personality. In his survey of Hesse's writings, Elster
draws attention to the highly autobiographical nature of his
art, the neo-romantic atmosphere of melancholy and longing, the
lyrical expression, and the early aestheticism evocative of George
and Maeterlinck. He points out the influences of Keller, the
greater plastic quality and clarity of *Gertrud* and *Rosshalde,*

the expressionism of *Demian,* and, finally, the sheer beauty of
Siddhartha.

Another of the earlier surveys of some import, which is
closely akin to that of Elster, is Philipp Witkop's "Hermann
Hesse," *Die Schöne Literatur,* 28 (1927), 289-312. Largely because of the appended bibliography prepared by Metelmann, this
article continues to be a major reference point for critics. Significant, too, is René Bétemps' detailed descriptive recall of Hesse's
major prose works from *Peter Camenzind* to *Steppenwolf* ("Hermann Hesse," *Revue d'Allemagne,* 3 [1929], 517-534), and Max
Kretschmer's primarily biographical sketch, which draws heavily
upon Ball ("Hermann Hesse," *Schicksale deutscher Dichter*
[1932], Vol. 2, 253-278).

Of the more recent surveys, attention might first be drawn to
Nino Erné's brief but pithy "Hermann Hesse," *Geistige Welt,*
1, No. 4 (1947), 37-45. Like all such surveys, Erné's can do little
more than generalize. However, unlike most of these articles
(*e.g.,* J. Frerking, "Dank an Hesse," *Dank und Gedenken*
[1947], pp. 5-33), his is more than a mere chronological outline
of Hesse's works with a scattering of biographical details. The
brief and striking characterization of each item, the interwoven
comments, and the ability to rise above the individual work and
to perceive the inner development of the author, reflects more
than average understanding of Hesse's personality and art.
Although Erné's division of Hesse's writings and inner development into three stages is hardly novel, his emphasis upon one
particular figure and upon the major idea on each of these levels,
is quite original and sound. Peter Camenzind is considered the
most representative of Hesse's heroes preceding *Demian.* The Li-
Tai-Po, Thu-Fu poles of *Klingsors letzter Sommer* come to the
fore after *Demian.* They yield to the *Morgenlandfahrer* following *Narziss und Goldmund.* And while the individual's adjustment to life at large is Hesse's chief concern from *Peter Camenzind* to *Rosshalde,* the inner world becomes his quest from *Demian*
to *Steppenwolf,* and after *Narziss und Goldmund* he begins his
search for "den Weg ins Morgenland."

O. F. Bollnow has Hesse's essentially romantic *Weg nach
Innen, Weg nach Hause,* or *Weg in die Stille,* as one prefers, fall
into these same three stages ("Hesses Weg in die Stille" [1947],
Unruhe und Geborgenheit im Weltbild neuerer Dichter, [1953],
pp. 31-69). The first, marked by sweet melancholy and loneliness

and concerned primarily with "das äussere Leben" (p. 38), is curtly and questionably dismissed as that of "eine verhältnismässig unproblematische Natur" (p. 34). From *Demian* to *Narziss und Goldmund*, and largely under the influence of Nietzsche and psychoanalysis, Hesse's quest becomes one of self-knowledge and of self-realization, and he acclaims life in all its vibrancy, in all its good and evil. However, the *Heimat* which Hesse could not share with his Peter Camenzind and could not find in his restless fear-ridden inner quest, is realized only on the highest ethical plane of renunciation and service, in the *Entwerden* of *Morgenlandfahrt* and *Glasperlenspiel*.

The pointed survey of E. R. Curtius ("Hermann Hesse," *Merkur*, 1 [1947], 170-185) is again more than a simple recall of familiar biographical facts and chronological listing of Hesse's works. Of particular interest is his brief consideration of such ever recurring themes as the intimate friend, fish and water, birds and air, and the wolf and the forest. Equally suggestive, though somewhat provocative in their brusqueness, are his occasional appraisals. That Hesse's prose lacks an epic quality, may rightly characterize many of his tales, but do *Siddhartha* or *Narziss und Goldmund* fit into this generalization? That most of Hesse's poetry is "fleissige Reimerei" (p. 178), is perhaps a greater reflection upon Curtius' powers of appreciation than upon Hesse's art. And that Siddhartha's resolution of life's problems is more novelistic than philosophical, can hardly mean more than that Hesse's philosophy is evidently not that of his critic.

Congratulatory Articles

Of the innumerable brief, congratulatory articles which appeared in scattered newspapers, periodicals, and books throughout Europe and abroad, upon Hesse's fiftieth, sixtieth, seventieth, and seventy-fifth birthdays, all but a few consist of innocent eulogy and sweet sentiment, have very little scholarly significance and are hardly worth recording except for the sake of bibliographical completeness. The exceptions are very few: Gerhard Szczesny, "Hans Castorp, Harry Haller und die Folgen," *Umschau*, 2 (1947), 601-611; Anni Carlsson, "Gingo Biloba," *Neue Schweizer Rundschau*, 15 (1947), 79-87; Claude Hill, "Hermann Hesse and Germany," *German Quarterly*, 21 (1948),

9-15; Fritz Strich, "Dank an Hermann Hesse," *Der Dichter und die Zeit* (1947), pp. 379-394; Paul Böckmann, "Der Dichter und die Gefährdung des Menschen im Werk Hermann Hesses," *Wirkendes Wort*, 3 (1952), 150-162; Hans Mayer, "Der Dichter und das feuilletonistische Zeitalter," *Aufbau*, 8 (1952), 613-628.

In his *j'accuse*, Szczesny develops a theme which Hesse himself suggests in *Steppenwolf*. The unfortunate course of recent German history is attributed to those who, like Castorp and Haller, represent a bourgeoisie and an intelligentsia no longer aware of any political or social responsibility. Like taciturn Castorp in his sheltered mountain retreat, lost in indolent dream and vague speculation, the pre-1914 *Grossbürger* had removed himself from the political and social unpleasantnesses of the day, oblivious of the gathering war clouds. Like the cynical Haller revelling in the drama of his *Ich*, pursuing more intense experience in the realms beyond this profane world, the pre-1933 intellectuals held themselves aloof. They refused to soil their hands with political and social matters until finally the Nazis were firmly entrenched. Although they were pacifists, humanitarians, and held an abhorrence for dictatorships, concentration camps, and gas chambers, Germany's *Grossbürger* and intellectuals, by choosing to divorce themselves from reality and responsibility, left the destiny of their country in the hands of the unscrupulous, and thereby sealed their own fate.

Perceiving an interesting analogy between Thomas Mann's Joseph story and Hesse's *Glasperlenspiel*, Carlsson briefly outlines the salient parallels. Both are myths written in the very thick of political and cultural stress, apparently outside of this encroaching chaos, yet intimately associated with it. While, stylistically, the former is myth made life and the latter life become myth, each is a blending of tradition with the present, of East with West, and both present "ein paradigmatisches Antlitz des zwanzigsten Jahrhunderts" (p. 81), a psychology of our modern world. The heroes themselves are blood brothers, akin in their *Seelenleben*, in their fates as in their names, who experience the tragedy of the chosen, are implicitly obedient to the God-element, the *Geist*-force, and are sustained by a philosophy characterized by *Heiterkeit*.

In contrast to Carlsson's comparative-interpretive article, Hill's is very factual and informative. He clarifies the question of Hesse's nationality. He discusses his pacifism. He outlines the official and private reaction to this attitude both immediately after 1918 and again under the Nazis. While neither of these two articles does more than scratch the suface of its theme, both are very suggestive and merit close attention.

The articles of Strich and Böckmann are very similar in their scholarly approach to that of Carlsson. Belonging to the best tradition of *Geistesgeschichte*, each is concerned with problems that transcend details, and each presupposes an intimate acquaintance with Hesse and his art. Strich sees Hesse in terms of his loneliness and isolation, fostered by a world out of joint; and he sees his art as a mirror reflecting the spiritual discord of this world. Strich's understanding of Hesse, the man and the artist, and his ability to give expression to this understanding, is quite uncanny.

For Böckmann, Hesse's works not only bear witness to the tensions of the inner life of an individual, but also reflect the basic perils that beset man when his faith in the traditional religious and social myths has been weakened, and when he has begun even to lose faith in *Geist* as a guiding principle. In this plight, Hesse felt compelled not to present panaceas, but to try to lead the individual back to himself by bringing him to experience himself through memory and introspection, thereby making possible his reëstablishment in life. Writing was Hesse's "road back," a type of contemplation in which play and creative imagination were not only compatible with abstract thinking, but could actually foster faith in *Geist*, so that fantasy and thought, together, would help man overcome the perils to which his inner life was subject, and help him find himself and his place in the unity of reality. While Böckmann propounds this incontrovertible thesis at considerable length and in an inordinately abstruse manner, he makes only passing references to specific works. Böckmann continues to dwell upon this theme in his "Hermann Hesse," *Deutsche Literatur im zwanzigsten Jahrhundert* (1954), pp. 288-304.

The first publication of Hesse's works in the *Deutsche Demokratische Republik* in 1952 (see Willi Bredel, "Unsere Verantwortung," *Aufbau*, 8 [1952], 608-612) met with loud acclaim which insisted that Hesse was more appreciated and better understood in East than in West Germany, and insinuated that he, in turn, was quite in sympathy with the cause of the new republic. It is as an example of this alleged better understanding, that Hans Mayer's congratulatory article merits close attention.

The "feuilletonistische westdeutsche offizielle Literaturbetrieb" (p. 628) is criticized sharply, and a more penetrating reëvaluation of Hesse's works is undertaken. Erroneously assuming that *Morgenlandfahrt* was published in 1923, Mayer criticizes the title of Anni Carlsson's article ("Vom *Steppenwolf* zur *Morgenlandfahrt*," Ball, 1947) for the false chronological picture it gives, marvels at the appearance of Pablo and Goldmund long before *Steppenwolf* and *Narziss und Goldmund* were written, and concludes that *Morgenlandfahrt* must therefore be the very focal point of Hesse's art.[27] Those who would term Hesse Buddhistic are casually informed that his attitude has never been one of flight from the world and scorn for his fellow man. Nor are his *Doppelgänger* mere psychological phenomena or an innocent echo of Romanticism, but represent the two possible attitudes of an artist to reality: withdrawal from, or communion with society. Those who have considered Hesse an advocate of "unpolitischer Innerlichkeit" (p. 618), have failed to note that he has always concerned himself with the prospect of a new humanistic society, and that he removed himself from the fray of 1914-1918 only because the interests on both sides were imperialistic. And to assume, as is commonly done, that *Demian* marks a sharp and unexpected turning point in the life and art of Hesse, is again to fail to note that Hesse has always been vitally interested in the problem of art and society, and that this concern gives his work its unbroken continuity.

Focussing his attention upon this problem, Mayer concludes that Hesse is convinced that true art ("Dichtung der Echtheit und Humanität," p. 622), is impossible under rank, inhumane capitalism and imperialism; that bourgeois capitalism and with it art, as we have known it, are doomed to perish; and that nothing the humanistic artist may desire to do, be it to try to preserve our cultural traditions in a Castalia-like retreat (a failure), or to become an activist like Knecht (also a failure), can be of any avail against this inevitable *Untergang*. That Hesse only hints at, and does not venture to show the way to the new order and its art, is rather regrettable; for Mayer is quite certain that the democracy of East Germany is moving in that direction, and would like to give the impression that Hesse is of the same opinion.

If this careless, tendentious scholarship is to be taken as evidence of better understanding of Hesse behind the Iron Curtain, then little of any value can be expected from those quarters. The low level to which literary criticism has sunk in East Germany is very evident in the following exchange of articles between Richard Drews and Franz Leschnitzer: "Hermann Hesse bricht das Schweigen," *Weltbühne*, 5 (1950), 1449-51; "Hermann Hesses Verse," 7 (1952), 882-883; "Es geht um die Dichtung," 7 (1952), 1010-16; "Brief eines Genesenden an seinen Chirurgen," 7 (1952), 1205-06; "Nochmals auf den Operationstisch," 8 (1953), 434-437; "Hoffentlich letzter Nachtrag," 8 (1953), 437-439. A minor critic is severely censured by his Moscow master.

Hesse and his Age

Hesse and his age have never seen eye to eye. Each has repeatedly rejected the other. For Hesse, ours is a godless world where nature and her beauties have no place, and where ideals are no longer fashionable. The individual is lost in the masses, his mind is plagued by doubt and insecurity, his soul is stifled by machines and money, and his dignity and inner contentment are sacrificed for material progress and physical comfort (*Feuerwerk* [1946], 19 pp.). It is this barren civilization which Hesse disparages, and it is its mediocre bourgeois nucleus that he never ceases to castigate.

Though this attitude has done little to ingratiate Hesse with his fellow Germans, it has actually, in itself, never stirred up any appreciable ill feeling. It was not until Germany in particular was called to task for its nationalism and militarism, that animosity towards Hesse developed. Hesse's subsequent diagnosis of our Western culture and his acceptance of *Untergang* added fuel to this growing enmity. Hardly was his *Blick ins Chaos* (1920) off the press, when a general sharp disapproval began to be voiced.

Although Gertrud Bäumer ("Medusa," "Perseus," *Die Frau*, 28 [1921], 193-199, 225-235) readily acknowledges the cultural decline envisioned by Hesse, she firmly contests his diagnosis of this cultural trend and disparages his general attitude toward it. That European civilization is succumbing to an Asiatic ideal of relativity spreading westward from Russia, is doubtful. That decline is a historical necessity, is rejected. That a new order will follow upon the chaos which is now to be accepted and exhausted is unbelievable. For Bäumer, this "Rückkehr ins Ungeordnete,

Rückweg ins Unbewusste, ins Gestaltlose, ins Tier, Rückkehr zu allen Anfängen," represents a weak and will-less surrender and not a determined desire for spiritual rebirth. The relativity, the amorality, which Hesse is willing to accept, is to be attributed to the sentimentality of naïve or stubborn intellectuals who have lost their sense of values. And Hesse's conception of the individual and society only reflects an "Entlaufen aus der Weisheit, dem Segen und der Kraft der Bindung" (p. 196). In the process of domestication, the individual is not forced from without to submit to moral and religous patterns, suppressing his animal drives. He is compelled to conform by an inner necessity; for such conformation is the indispensable condition of the life of every individual.

Paying little further attention to *Blick ins Chaos*, Bäumer proceeds at great length to expound her own theories about *Untergang*. Nonchalantly assuming this phenomenon to be a peculiarly German one, she counters with her own diagnosis and prescription. In the wake of the materialism and class conflict of the nineteenth century, German Idealism ("die Religion des germanischen Geistes," p. 228) with its principle of "Leben und Form," began to wane. The Goethean way of life and religion, of creative vitality, discipline, and form, gradually yielded to laxness and enervation, and finally degenerated into the *Sichfallenlassen* and *Allesgeltenlassen* embraced by Hesse. Germany's hope for cultural rebirth is not to be sought in this passive resignation, but in discipline, thought, and deed, in a revitalized, reaffirmed German Idealism.

Bäumer's reaction to *Blick ins Chaos* recalls that of Gustav Zeller, a fellow student of Hesse's at Maulbronn ("Offener Brief an Hermann Hesse," *Psychische Studien*, 47 [1920], 622-630). Again Hesse is taken to task for his *Untergangsstimmung*, for his acclamation of Dostoyevsky, the herald of Bolshevism, and for the parallel he draws between Myschkin and Christ. That a German writer of note was preparing the way for the Eastern barbaric hoards which threatened Christian, German culture, rather than providing the spiritual and intellectual leadership necessary in such a crisis, was unforgivable.

The common attitude of Bäumer and of Zeller toward the cultural chaos considered impending in the years immediately following the First World War, smacks very much of the national conceit which was later to be exploited by Hitler, and beside

Hesse's conception of this decline, theirs is dwarfed in significance. Bäumer arbitrarily localizes the crisis, choosing to see it only in terms of Germany, and to consider its causes only in terms of a lost German Idealism. Zeller, in turn, perceives only a struggle between German culture and Eastern barbarism. Hesse, in contrast, transcends national boundaries and the more immediate and incidental national expression of *Untergang*, to arrive at a Spenglerian view of an entire civilization irresistibly approaching old age and inevitable death. Whether Bäumer's theory of decline and its restriction to Germany is plausible or not, and whether Zeller's fears are warranted or not, in their refutation of Hesse's views they fail to perceive that he is striking for the deeper, more fundamental causes of a wider and more significant historical phenomenon.

This rebuke seems to have been the only immediate reaction to *Blick ins Chaos*. Its passive acceptance of an allegedly necessary cultural decline, and its espousal of complete relativity could have no appeal to the spreading activism and nationalism of the Twenties. Circulation was very limited and the pamphlet was soon forgotten. Not until after the Second World War was it again to receive some notice.[28] In the guise of a letter to a friend and fellow admirer of Hesse, Nino Erné ("Ein Beitrag zum Thema: Hermann Hesse und Dostojewski," *Deutsche Beiträge*, 1 [1947], 345-353) recalls and agrees with the views expressed in "Die Brüder Karamasoff oder der Untergang Europas," the first of the three essays in *Blick ins Chaos*. Elaborating upon this theme, Erné corrects those of Hesse's readers who had chosen to suffer patiently and even forgivingly under the Nazis, accepting the holocaust in terms of the inevitable return to the amoral, primeval chaos of Hesse's *russischer Mensch*, the decline and death necessary for the cultural rebirth of tomorrow. The Nazis and their régime are not to be equated with the Karamazovs and the *Urwelt*. They were neither children at heart, persecuted outsiders naïve and repentant in their sins, nor was their order a return to a more original, natural state which promised a cultural renaissance. Hesse's *russischer Mensch* is not a symbol of the Nazis, but of the Harry Hallers, and it is this *Steppenwolf* type which is the forerunner of the Josef Knechts who will eventually emerge from our *Untergang*.

The reaction of the general public and of officialdom to Hesse's anti-war essays (*Krieg und Frieden*) and to his *Zarathustras*

Wiederkehr, with its appeal to Germany that she mend her ways,
suffer and repent for her guilt, was decidedly unfavorable, and
has generally remained so. The acclaim brought by *Demian* was
just as brief as it was intense. In the wake of a new and more
exciting ideology, youth's erstwhile guide rapidly fell into disrepute. Nor was the older generation ever fully to forgive this
turncoat. Engrained militarism and national pride, stung by defeat, winced under Hesse's rebuke, and ignoring his humanitarian
principles, saw in him only a traitor to the just German cause.
Gustav Zeller's reaction is characteristic of the immediate general
resentment which Hesse occasioned. So convinced is this staunch
militarist and monarchist that Germany's war guilt is but a
fairy tale, that he is actually amazed to find that an intelligent
German could even for a moment believe that Germany was to
blame for the First World War. Because he did not take up arms
in his country's hour of need, and because he was now reproach-
ing rather than consoling her in defeat, Hesse is curtly dispensed
as an infamous traitor, "ein Besudler des deutschen Namens"
(p. 627).

Gustav Hecht's "Offener Brief an Hermann Hesse" (*Deutsches
Volkstum,* 1929, ii, pp. 603-611), written upon the republication
of Hesse's anti-war essays (*Betrachtungen*), bears witness to
an animosity undiminished by the passing years. Hesse is censured just as bitterly and as maliciously as ever. His appeals for
peace are ridiculed, his emphasis upon love is scoffed at, and
his philosophy of acceptance is disparaged. By means of distor-
tions and misconstructions, Hecht is determined to make Hesse
appear absurdly self-contradictory.

That only one feeble and quite ineffective attempt was made to
counter Hecht's calumny is very telling. Rather than endeavor to
refute unjust accusations, expose obvious and deliberate mis-
interpretations, and draw attention to a misuse of quotations,
Franz Schall ("Um Hermann Hesse," *Deutsches Volkstum,* 1930,
ii, pp. 232-235) replies only with an exaggerated and equally
unconvincing eulogy of Hesse. Proudly and effusively he lingers
over Hesse's wartime duties and elaborates upon his incorrigible
spirit, his courage, and his loyalty. Such an infantile apology
could be of little avail against the rising tide of public resentment.

The recent publication of Hesse's war essays (*Krieg und
Frieden,* 1946) brought no evidence of any drastic change in

Germany's attitude toward them. Loud censure was merely replaced by silent disapproval. Few critics acknowledged the humanitarian spirit and the wisdom of these essays and greeted them warmly. Otto Basler, a Swiss and an intimate friend of Hesse ("*Krieg und Frieden*," Ball [1947], pp. 305-316), and Elisabeth Langgässer ("Weisheit des Herzens. Zu Hermann Hesses *Krieg und Frieden*," *Deutsche Zeitung und Wirtschaftszeitung*, Stuttgart, Oct. 18, 1949, p. 15) are two of the most noteworthy of these few.

That Hesse during the Nazi régime should be subjected to such acrid derision as that of Will Vesper ("Unsere Meinung," *Neue Literatur*, 36 [1935], 685-687), was to be expected. However, that such sharp repudiation as that of von Schöfer ("Hermann Hesse, *Peter Camenzind* und das *Glasperlenspiel*," *Die Sammlung*, 3 [1948], 597-609) and of H. G. Thurm ("Thomas Mann, Hermann Hesse und wir Jungen," *Umschau*, 2 [1947], 612-615) should continue sporadically after 1945, is certainly rather startling. Old animosities were not quickly forgotten, and German activist youth, still in search of a strong leader with ready answers to life's problems, was only too anxious to reject a mere fellow sufferer, especially one who continued to refuse to become involved in immediate political and social problems.

In his study of Romain Rolland and Hesse (*Études Germaniques*, 8 [1953], 25-35) Pierre Grappin, a French activist, is almost inclined to follow suit. Drawing primarily upon unpublished letters and diaries, Grappin traces the relationship between Rolland and Hesse, touching upon their correspondence, their occasional meetings (see *Briefe*, pp. 94-95), the attitude of one to the other, and the reaction of each to the wars of 1914 and 1939. He draws attention to Rolland's approval of Hesse's Goethean supranationalism and his censure, at the outset of the First World War, of the German writers and intellectuals who had added their voices to the campaign of hate, and to Rolland's discountenance of Hesse's subsequent withdrawal from the fray. Rolland became a militant humanitarian, an activist convinced that it was a writer's duty to fight for the cause of the oppressed, of international brotherhood, and even to take direct part in political action. Hesse preferred to withdraw gradually into his poetry and his Oriental contemplation. And in his most important message to the Germans (*Zarathustras Wiederkehr*), his appeal was to the individual—not for a cause, but for self-knowledge, self-acceptance, and willingness to suffer. Nor did Hesse, with the rise of the Nazis, and again unlike Rolland, deign to emerge from the security of his hermitage as a leader or guide (cf. Briefe, p. 204). Still reluctant to enmesh himself in political matters, and underestimating the attraction National Socialism held for young people, Hesse quietly continued to appeal primarily to the individual and did little more than hope vaguely that the Hitler régime would eventually spend itself.

While Grappin obviously shares Rolland's conviction that a writer must descend from his ivory tower in times of stress, his appreciation of Hesse's attitude[29] is far less benign and respectful than was Rolland's (e.g., in a letter to Hesse, dated January 31, 1936, he writes: "Vous êtes un de mes très rares frères d'art et de pensée, pour qui j'ai amour et respect; et je suis heureux de votre amitié" [Hesse/Rolland. Briefe, p. 106]). Nor does Grappin's evidence warrant the conclusion that Rolland was the guide and Hesse a student unable to follow in the footsteps of his master. It is to be hoped that the diaries to which Grappin makes repeated reference soon will be available in print for further scrutiny. As it is, the letters to which he refers, and which have since been published (1954, 118 pp.), would tend to contradict, rather than substantiate his conclusion.[30]

Oddly enough, Hesse had himself once sharply criticized the pacifists for almost the very reason for which he is taken to task by Grappin. Never particularly enthusiastic about those organized attempts to regenerate humanity which are more concerned with the reformation of society than with the more vital transformation of the individual (Briefe, p. 96), and which generally do little more than spend themselves in theory, Hesse had felt obliged to take issue with the pacifist movement of the First World War. In a newspaper article entitled "Die Pazifisten," Die Zeit (Wien, Nov. 7, 1915; see also "Den Friedensleuten," Die Propyläen, 13 [1915], 180-181), he first lauds the pacifists for their ideals and then censures them roundly and at much greater length for their apparent inability to perceive the need for more action and less talk, for their inordinate concern about the world of tomorrow, and for their persistent promotion of convictions and their contrasting lack of interest in the immediate alleviation of the suffering around them.

Hesse's negative appraisal of pacifism ("Es war nicht in

Ordnung, es war faul, etwas starr, etwas tot in diesem Ideal," *Propyläen*, 13 [1915], 181) drew the immediate and acrid rebuke of Alfred H. Fried, Europe's leading pacifist at that time ("Hermann Hesse und die Pazifisten," *Vom Weltkrieg zum Weltfrieden* [1916], pp. 90-94). Fried regrets Hesse's glibness and insincerity. He deplores Hesse's misrepresentation of pacifists as foolish dreamers. He severely criticizes his seeming ignorance both of their goal, which was not merely to ameliorate but to end wars, and of their extended efforts to help war victims.

In their accusations and counteraccusations, Hesse and Fried (and Romain Rolland) represent the extremes of a house divided against itself. Their discord stems from their difference in attitude. Each is a pacifist. One is determined to change the world by aggressive leadership; the other is inclined to appeal more passively for individual acceptance of suffering (*Briefe*, p. 355). One believes in the powers of reason; the other believes in the efficacy of service (*Briefe*, p. 65). Mutual respect might better have helped their common cause.

Though Hesse has persistently repudiated modern bourgeois society, he has never ceased to concern himself with it. His own plight and that of this world are inseparably interwoven. His art records both the spiritual suffering of the individual, and the dissolution of our bourgeois civilization. Not without reason does Herbert Roch ("Hermann Hesse," *Deutsche Schriftsteller als Richter ihrer Zeit* [1947], pp. 117-123) term Hesse, the "Chronist der bürgerlichen Passionsgeschichte" (p. 117). Despite the importance of the theme, a thorough study of Hesse and the bourgeois world has yet to be made. Surveying the problem, Roch has Hesse come to grips with this world and its authority on three major fronts: the home, the school, and life at large. Unfortunately, he does little more than outline this promising thematic approach.

The alternative approach is preferred by Claude Hill ("Hermann Hesse als Kritiker der bürgerlichen Zivilisation," *Monatshefte*, 40 [1948], 241-253). Viewing Hesse's work chronologically, he has his preoccupation with our bourgeois civilization fall into three stages. The *Demian* stage marks Hesse's first real concern with the outside world. Troubled within and without, he begins his *Weg nach Innen;* before he can come to terms with the bourgeois world, a greater self-knowledge and better understanding of modern civilization is necessary. In *Steppenwolf*, the second stage, Hesse describes the plight of the individual, the outsider like himself, and presents his completely negative appraisal of the bourgeois; for want of anything better, a gallows humor must temporarily resolve the problem. With *Glasperlenspiel* the problem is finally and conclusively settled; the bourgeois world has now become quite inconsequential for Hesse, a historical phenomenon characteristic of our chaotic age but nonexistent in the tomorrow of Knecht.

Hill is, correctly, aware that the problem of Hesse's attitude toward our civilization is closely joined to the problem of inner strife. One may be emphasized more than the other, but neither can be omitted entirely. Contrary to the title of his article, Hill dwells in great detail upon Hesse's inner-world, but only touches upon his attitude toward the bourgeois and their age. Furthermore, though it was not until the First World War that Hesse became intensively concerned with our civilization, unless some heed is given to his earlier works (*e.g.*, *Peter Camenzind, Unterm Rad*, "Ein Mensch mit Namen Ziegler," *Fabulierbuch*), a real understanding of his attitude toward the bourgeois world and of its influences upon him, is hardly possible. Nor can Hesse's various collections of essays be disregarded (*e.g.*, *Wanderung, Bilderbuch, Betrachtungen, Gedenkblätter*).

In *Glasperlenspiel*, Hesse does finally overcome the problem of the bourgeois world, but hardly as Hill has it. The fact that the bourgeois world plays no rôle in the novel does not mean that it will cease in due time to be of any consequence, cease eventually even to exist. Though this world is no longer in the foreground, it has most certainly not become a phenomenon of the past, nor has it ceased to be a power to be reckoned with. Castalia is but a little island surrounded and supported by the prevailing bourgeois world of politics, passions, and strife, a world which is approaching another war, a world for which Knecht leaves the province and into which he hopes to bring some rays of light. The bourgeois problem is solved, but surely only insomuch as Hesse no longer allows it to dominate his thinking.

Allowing his inquiry to fall into four parts, Peter Heller ("The Writer in Conflict with his Age," *Monatshefte*, 46 [1954], 137-147) dwells briefly upon Hesse's indifference to external reality; his marked disdain for the bourgeois; his aversion to politics, disinterest in public affairs, and his anti-technological bias; and finally upon his contempt for his own profession and for his public. Hesse's need to vindicate his existence as a writer before the tribunal of his own conscience, is considered the impelling psychological factor in this conflict. Like Hill, Heller draws primarily upon Hesse's works beginning with *Demian*, implying that the earlier works are not particularly pertinent to the theme. A brief perusal of these earlier writings would have revealed that Hesse courted these notions and attitudes long before the problematic Twenties and Thirties. Furthermore, encompassing only a portion of Hesse's works and giving no heed to chronology, Heller's study tends to present a very static picture of a conflict which is, in fact, marked by a steady development.

If we review the above articles dealing with Hesse and his age, it is quite obvious that, to date, the problem has hardly been more than outlined. Of its main aspects, not one has been adequately investigated. In a study of Hesse the *Kulturphilosoph*, *Blick ins Chaos*, the introduction to *Steppenwolf*, *Feuerwerk*, the introductory chapter to *Glasperlenspiel*, and *Briefe* (1951) are the major reference points. For Hesse's criticism of German nationalism and militarism, a study of *Krieg und Frieden* (1949), and *Briefe* is essential. To trace Germany's changing attitude toward Hesse down through the years, would entail a general perusal of the literary criticism centered about him, plus an examination of "Kurzgefasster Lebenslauf" (*Traumfährte*), *Briefe*, "Schluss des Rigi-Tagebuchs," "Ansprache in der ersten Stunde des Jahres 1946," "Brief an Adele," and "Ein Brief nach Deutschland" (*Krieg und Frieden*). And finally, an examination of Hesse's attitude toward bourgeois society, in particular, would involve almost all of his writings, with special emphasis upon *Demian*, *Steppenwolf*, *Wanderung*, *Bilderbuch*, and *Betrachtungen*.

Hesse and Youth

Were one to consider which single theme most distinguishes Hesse from his contemporaries among the German writers, one might rightly suggest that of childhood and youth. In such a poignant manner has Hesse been able to recreate the inner world of the child and the adolescent, that younger people have always tended to look upon him as their spokesman.

Not in his art alone (*Hermann Lauscher, Peter Camenzind, Unterm Rad, Diesseits, Nachbarn, Umwege, Schön ist die Jugend,*

Demian, Kinderseele), has Hesse shown his concern for youth. In his desire to aid the German prisoners of war, he helped to edit the *Deutsche Internierten-Zeitung* (1916-17), and was co-editor of the *Bücherei für deutsche Kriegsgefangene* (1918-19). Unable to stand by idly during the postwar period of disillusionment and confusion, he became co-founder and co-editor of the periodical, *Vivos Voco* (1919-21), which appealed to youth for a moral, spiritual, and intellectual reform. Hesse made a similar and even more direct appeal in his manifesto, *Zarathustras Wiederkehr* (1919). His title was chosen with German youth in mind, and lest the younger generation ignore the message of an author who, in years, represented a past from which it was striving to emancipate itself, Hesse published his work anonymously ("Zu Zarathustras Wiederkehr," *Vivos Voco*, 1 [Oct. 1919], 72).

Although German youth, as a whole, proved to be very fickle in its allegiance, a small minority of sensitive spirits has remained loyal throughout the years. In the course of the Twenties and well on into the Thirties, hundreds of troubled letters continued annually to pour into Montagnola, and since 1945 this endless stream of appeals has grown steadily. These are the letters which have helped to sustain Hesse when all else seemed lost or futile (*Briefe*, pp. 111-112, 122-123, 223, 270, 279, 307, 328, 331, 332, 339, 376, 421).

Until 1919, Hesse was never quite able to extricate himself from his memories of childhood and youth; the painful trail of these memories is unbroken in both prose and poetry from *Hermann Lauscher* to *Kinderseele*. His many problems as a child, his dreams, joys and fears, the parent-child relationship, his school days with their student-teacher friction, and the awakening of sex are recurrent themes. Only after years of romantically morbid preoccupation with the more sordid and pathetic aspects of his childhood and youth, was Hesse able to recognize the futility and even the danger of such an all-absorbing attachment (*Demian* [1919], p. 78). In *Demian* and *Kinderseele*, he steeps himself once more in the past; but now, through the cold light of psychoanalysis, he is finally able to rid himself of this obsession. Although childhood and youth ceased thereafter to dominate Hesse's thought, the theme continued to linger in the background of his art. It is present in *Narziss und*

Goldmund, in *Glasperlenspiel,* "Der lahme Knabe" (*Zwei Idyllen*), and in five of the eleven items of *Späte Prosa* (1951).

Despite the rôle childhood and youth have played in the works of Hesse, and despite the great attraction he has been for successive younger generations, neither theme has received more than passing notice. The brief articles of Klabund ("Allerlei," *Neue Rundschau,* 31, ii, [1920], 1109) and of G. Sieveling ("Hermann Hesse und wir Jüngsten," *Neue Züricher Zeitung,* Feb. 22, 1921) reflect the tremendous impression *Demian* made upon German youth. Jörn Oven's remarks ("Hermann Hesse: *Siddhartha,*" *Schöne Literatur,* 24 [1923], 331-332) reveal the growing hostility of activist youth in the Twenties. Von Schöfer and H. G. Thurm bear witness to the recurrence of this animosity after 1945. W. E. Süskind ("Hermann Hesse und die Jugend," *Neue Rundschau,* 38, i, [1927], 492-497) does no more than note the prevalence of the theme of youth, list the various problems involved, and marvel at Hesse's ability to attract and to stir successive generations. Two other relevant articles were not available for examination: Karl Rauch, "Hermann Hesse und die neue Jugend," *Junge Menschen,* 2, No. 4 (1921); W. Meridies, "Hermann Hesse und die Jugend," *Die neue deutsche Schule,* 1 (1927), 501-507.

Richard Buchwald brings the discussion of the problem more up to date and delves into it in much greater detail ("Hermann Hesse," *Bekennende Dichtung. Ricarda Huch, Hermann Hesse* [1949], pp. 33-87). Hesse's influence upon three generations of young readers is traced in a very novelistic manner. At the turn of the century, youth, in its reaction to an excessively sordid Naturalism, was first attracted by Hesse's return to the romantic tradition, to nature, to fantasy, and to song. The postwar generation found in Hesse a disillusioned and searching spirit like its own. His way of life, attitude toward modern culture, and his resolution of inner conflict was for them an example and a challenge. The third wave, another postwar generation, has found hope in Hesse's continued faith in man, and in his humanitarian *via activa* of the spirit.

That Hesse's influence upon the first two generations was both widespread and intense, is not to be doubted. However, that Hesse has again, in more recent years, become a decisive factor in the life of German youth, is a very questionable assertion. And as he chooses to ignore the successive waves of animosity

which Hesse has had to suffer, Buchwald cannot possibly present
a truly representative picture of Hesse and German youth. Such
a picture is perhaps to be found in Rudolf Kurth's "Die Jugend
und Hermann Hesse," *Die Sammlung*, 11 (1956), 72-85.

Hesse and Nature

Like Peter Camenzind, Hesse has always been fascinated by
nature; and like his beloved St. Francis of Assisi, he has never
ceased to find new strength and spiritual rejuvenation in this
attachment (*Franz von Assisi*, p. 52). Until *Demian*, in both
prose and poetry, nature is a mirror for Hesse's every mood, a
setting for his thought, an escape from himself, and a refuge
from life. This love of nature also marked the first stage of
Hesse's lifelong criticism of modern civilization. He advocated
a return to the beauty and simplicity of nature as the only hope
for a cultural regeneration. Since *Demian*, nature has played
a less conspicuous rôle in Hesse's writings. His attitude toward
her became progressively less subjective and more contained;
feeling gradually yielded to observation and contemplation. In
the meantime he began to pay his homage through a new medium,
painting.

And yet, though nature has remained a prevailing theme in
Hesse's prose and poetry, and even in his many essays, it has
received only casual attention. Geffert (pp. 7-12), H. R. Schmid
(pp. 63-69), and Lützkendorf (pp. 44-47) are aware of the
back-to-nature appeal of *Camenzind*; they draw attention to
Hesse's fondness for mountains, trees, flowers, butterflies, and
clouds, and agree that these aspects of nature are of considerable
symbolic significance. Curtius ("Hermann Hesse," *Merkur*,
1 [1947], 170-185) broaches such important recurring themes
as fish and water, birds and air, the wolf and forest. Gnefkow
(pp. 38-56) perceives a kindship between Hesse's early worship
of nature and that of Wackenroder, and proposes that this attachment is but the old romantic quest for a *Natur-Ich-Gott-
Einheit*.

Mimi Jehle ("The Garden in the Works of Hermann Hesse,"
German Quarterly, 24 [1951], 42-50), in contrast to the usual
approach, centers her attention about one motif, convinced that
a study of this motif can lead to a better understanding of Hesse's
inner world and its development. In the garden she perceives a

symbol of childhood, of happiness and of harmony with nature. This is a symbol, too, of middle-class life. She is aware of the merging of the garden and mother motifs, and notes further that the garden is a constant refuge, a place for meditation and for religious experience. As usual, however, the development of these themes does not proceed beyond descriptive recall.

The problem of Hesse and nature, like the problem of Hesse and youth, has yet to receive the scrutiny it merits; the surface has hardly been scratched.[32]

Hesse and Music

While nature generally provides the framework for Hesse's art, it is music which pervades its atmosphere. Nature and music seem to have been the two forces which have done most to sustain Hesse and to mold his work. In the extreme subjectivity of his younger years, nature weeps in his sorrow, rejoices in his happiness, and, in her example, strengthens his acclaim of *Eigensinn*. Of music, on the other hand, Hesse can write, "Keiner andern Göttin dank' ich so viele/Tröstliche, schmerzliche, innige Freuden wie dir!" (*Gedichte* [1942], p. 332). It is music which sustains in adversity, which is life's very justification (*Gertrud* [1927], p. 52), and which has been Hesse's "letzter und innigster Trost" ("Erinnerung an Hans," *Gedenkblätter* [1947], p. 252) in his frequent despair. In the chaos of our modern culture, it is music again, of all the arts, which still remains comparatively uncontaminated, "ein lebendiger Baum . . . an dessen Ästen auch heute noch Paradiesäpfel wachsen können" ("Kurzgefasster Lebenslauf," *Traumfährte*, p. 120). Nature and music have been Hesse's refuge from a crass reality of materialism, mechanism, politics, and wars.

One need but briefly scan Hesse's many intimate essays and his more autobiographical tales, to note that the world of music has always been a very immediate one. Even as a child, the church organ held a strong attraction for him ("Meine Kindheit," *Hermann Lauscher*). He learned to play both violin and flute. Through his older stepbrothers Karl and Theodor Isenberg, he became familiar with eighteenth-century composers. He and his first wife, Maria Bernoulli, were drawn together by their common love of music; and while he was in Gaienhofen, Hesse became intimately acquainted with the composer Othmar Schoeck, whose friendship prompted him to write a libretto, and who later set many of Hesse's poems to music ("Erinnerungen an Othmar Schoeck," *Gedenkblätter*).

Like his antecedents, the Romanticists of the nineteenth century, Hesse is steeped in music. Like them he would quaff music "wie die Götter Necktar schlürfen" ("Musikalische Notizen," *Neue Schweizer Rundschau*, 15 [1948], 600). He, too, looked upon music as the medium in which art could attain its purest and most sublime expression. His love for the wonders of music borders upon Wackenroder's worship of "die Sprache der Engel" (*Werke und Briefe*, ed. F. von der Leyen [1910], Vol. 1, 168). For both, music is "das Land der heiligen Ruhe" (*ibid.*, p. 165), where surrender brings with it a nirvana of peace and forgetfulness.

This remained Hesse's prevailing attitude toward music until *Steppenwolf*. In the throes of a serious psychological crisis, a sharp reaction took place. He now inveighed against the German intelligentsia's traditional courtship of music. To this preoccupation with a language without words, expressive of the inexpressible and giving form to the formless, Hesse now attributed the ignominious rôle of the German intellectual in the political history of his country. This uncontained passion was the fatal disease of the German spirit (*Steppenwolf* [1931], p. 168). Purging himself of music in its "rein sinnliche Dynamik" (*Glasperlenspiel* [1943], Vol. 1, 41), Hesse next began to seek in it a means of self-edification, and no longer a nirvana. His new attitude found its fullest expression in *Glasperlenspiel*. Music is still acclaimed the art of all arts; it is the very essence of Castalia's culture, the most perfect expression of its ideals; but it is the music of the classical era (1500-1800), permeated by a spirit of order, discipline, faith, and of optimism, "eine der Urquellen aller Ordnung, Sitte, Schönheit und Gesundheit" (Vol. 1, 203). It is not the music of *Gertrud*, of "Zuflucht, Erlösung, Vergessen" (1927, pp. 50-51), but the music of affirmation and acceptance.

To trace Hesse's changing taste in music, would be to trace the course of his inner development. It is the spirit of Chopin which permeates *Eine Stunde hinter Mitternacht, Lauscher*, and most of Hesse's early poetry. It is a laughing Mozart who hovers above *Steppenwolf* in the cold, clear atmosphere of the eternals who have transcended life's painful dichotomy. It is the stately figure of Bach (*Briefe*, pp. 321-323) which looms large on the horizons of Castalia. Though Hesse has felt himself akin in spirit to such composers as Chopin, Schubert, Beethoven, and Hugo Wolf, he has not failed to perceive in their music a process of dissolution. Like himself, these composers are *Nachkömmlinge*, are to Bach and to Mozart what he has considered himself to be to E. T. A. Hoffmann and to Novalis. Even more advanced in this dissolution is the highly instrumentalized music of Brahms (*Steppenwolf* [1931], p. 271) and of Wagner (*Briefe*, pp. 137-138); and the twentieth century with its jazz, its *Untergangsmusik*, which is still to be preferred to its academic music (*Steppenwolf* p. 60), serves only more acutely to recall the incomparable music of the past. As he grows older, Hesse is drawn ever closer to this music of 1500-1800, the music which reflects a "Bejahung des Menschengeschlechts, Tapferkeit, Heiterkeit" (*Glasperlenspiel*, Vol. 1, 68), and which is epitomized in Bach's *Passion of St. Matthew* and in Mozart's *Magic Flute*.

Hesse's lyrical temperament, his love and understanding of music have left their impression upon his poetry (*Betrachtungen*, p. 172). The very significant title of an early collection of poems, *Musik des Einsamen*, would not be an inappropriate characterization of his poems as a whole. Hesse's most typical poetic form has been the technically simple, melodious quatrain of the folksong, "Melodien ohne Noten," as H. R. Schmid aptly terms them (p. 51); and like the poetry of the Romanticists, his lyrics lend themselves freely to composition.[33] More immediately reflective of Hesse's interest in the world of music are the many poems which are dedicated to, or recall Chopin, Mozart, and Bach. Others have musical themes; and there are many more in which the figure of the lonely violinist with his melancholy strains appears. Hesse's love of music shows also in his editions of German folksongs (*Der Lindenbaum* [1910]; *Der Zauberbrunnen. Die Lieder der deutschen Romantik* [1913].

Music has left an equally deep impression on Hesse's prose. It is obviously a lyrical prose ("Vorrede eines Dichters zu seinen ausgewählten Werken," *Betrachtungen*, p. 172). Upon occasion, it is even free verse (*e.g.*, *Wanderung*). It is a descriptive, rather than a narrative or dramatic prose, and is characterized by rhythmic patterns. Most common of these patterns is a three-beat melody, a chant-like succession of movements, each trailing two refrains. Single words, phrases, clauses, sentences, and, less frequently, even paragraphs fall into this pattern (*e.g., Siddhartha*). This stylistic tendency seems most common to those works written when Hesse was more or less at peace with himself (*e.g., Eine Stunde hinter Mitternacht, Peter Camenzind, Wanderung, Siddhartha, Narziss und Goldmund,* and *Glasperlenspiel*), and almost totally absent in those works which bear witness to severe inner distress (*e.g., Demian, Steppenwolf*). This suggests a theme which bears more investigation.

The substance of Hesse's prose shows his attachment to music even more obviously. Although most of his tales are centered about the plight of the writer, the painter, or the sensitive intellectual, the figure of the musician always stands in the immediate background. Most of Hesse's heroes are musically inclined. Many, like himself, are violinists (*e.g.,* Lauscher, Lucius of *Unterm Rad,* the *Lateinschüler,* Kuhn of *Gertrud,* H. H. of *Morgenlandfahrt,* the *Magister Musicae* and Knecht of *Glasperlenspiel*). Others are pianists (*e.g.,* Richard of *Peter Camenzind,* Frau Dillenius and her brother Ludwig of "Eine Sonate," *Simplicissimus,* 11 [1907], 792-793, the young lady in "Juninacht" of *Am Weg,* Calwer of *Freunde* (1949), Mrs. Veraguth and her son Albert of *Rosshalde*). Ladidel (*Umwege*) plays a guitar, Pistorius (*Demian*) is an organist, Pablo, a saxophonist, and Knecht learns to play the flute. And although it is only in *Gertrud* that music and the musician become the focal point of interest, the tales in which the theme is entirely lacking are exceedingly few in number. In *Kurgast,* Hesse is annoyed by his fellow guests' rapt attention to mediocre music. In *Steppenwolf,* Harry Haller welters in the dance-hall's blare of jazz, is ridiculed by an impish Mozart, and watches Brahms and Wagner labor slowly by, burdened by their superfluous notes. In *Morgenlandfahrt's* Bremgarten, Othmar Schoeck plays Mozart to his companions, among whom wanders Hugo Wolf. And mathematics and music are the basis of the *Glasperlenspiel;* the name itself, we are told, originated with Bastien Perrot of Calw, musicologist at the *Musik Hochschule* in Cologne. Hesse's interest in music is just as evident in his many essays.[34]

Despite the obviousness of the theme and despite its relevance to a fuller understanding of Hesse, this problem of music was almost ignored until recent years. None of the many aspects briefly touched upon above has received adequate attention. Nowhere in their books do Ball (1947, pp. 146-148), Matzig (pp. 7, 12), Max Schmid (pp. 71, 112, 180), and Engel (pp. 30, 40, 90) give music any deliberate study, and of the seven articles concerned with the problem, only four are of any consequence.[35] W. A. Thomas-San-Galli ("Hermann Hesse und die Musik," *Der Merker*, 5 [1914], 413-418) merely becomes rhapsodical and diffuse in his emphasis upon the inherently musical quality of Hesse's art ("Er bringt die Musik in ihrem kosmischen Akkord, leitet sie aus dem Leben ins Leben." p. 418),[36] and expounds, with liberal quotations, upon Hesse's general attitude toward music: *i.e.*, his emphasis upon its suggestive powers, its important function in life, and his indifference to the theories and technicalities of music (see *Briefe*, p. 137). Lisa Kunstmann's article is too brief to be of any significance ("Musik und Prosa. Zu Hermann Hesses Dichtung," *Deutsche Monatshefte*, 2 [1926], 157-158). Emil Böhmer's general references to the musical nature of Hesse's writings are of no import, although his allusions to Chopin, Mozart, and to Bach are noteworthy ("Musik in Hermann Hesses Dichtung," *Ostdeutsche Monatshefte*, 15 [1935], 623-625).

In contrast to the very general nature of these articles, Hans Engel's study broaches a specific theme and treats it in considerable detail ("*Das Glasperlenspiel*," *Das Musikleben*, 1 [1948], 257-261). Drawing attention to most of the more important references to music in the novel and to the very significant rôle music plays in Castalia's educational system, Engel shows how Hesse's attitude to music has changed with the years. Where he had once been drawn to Chopin, Beethoven, and kindred romanticists, he was now attached to Bach, Mozart, Händel, and Purcell; and music was no longer merely an enticing passion and source of oblivion, but a major factor in man's ethical development.

J. Müller-Blattau touches upon another specific and challenging problem ("Sinn und Sendung der Musik in Thomas Manns *Dr. Faustus* und Hermann Hesses *Glasperlenspiel*," *Geistige Welt*, 4, No. 1 [1949], 29-34). As reflected in these novels, music is a most important force in life. In its discipline, it is a factor which heightens the development of the individual and the cultural evolution of society. But when not restrained, it is a demonic force which draws the individual and society into an abyss of dissolution.[37] Müller-Blattau uses Mann's *Faustus* to exemplify the latter. Leverkühn's life, in its musical development, moves from the order of the classical tradition to the chaos of modern music, which has become demonic and anticultural; and he goes from health to insanity and to death. His lot augurs the course of modern culture, "Abfall ins Dämonische" (p. 31). On the other hand, in a more optimistic spirit, and with his faith in the regenerative powers of music, Hesse looks to the future and to a cultural rebirth. The spirit of classical music revived is the life force of Castalia and its game. Knecht's life, guided by this spirit of restraint and harmony, is characterized by an upward progression and by fulfillment. That Hesse himself has detected a kinship between Leverkühn and his problematic Tegularius (*Briefe*, p. 270) would perhaps tend to confirm Müller-Blattau's interesting thesis. In all events, Hesse's remarks might be introduced in a more detailed reconsideration of this theory.

Though distractingly discursive, cluttered by protracted quotations, and very repetitive in its excessive length, Alfredo Dornheim's musical analysis of *Glasperlenspiel* is both informative and suggestive ("Musica Novelesca y Novela Musical. Concepción de las últimas novelas de Hermann Hesse y Thomas Mann," *Revista de Estudios Musicales* [Mendoza], 1 [August 1949], 131-172). He lingers over Nietzsche's conception of music, drawing attention to the long passage from Lü Bu We's *Frühling und Herbst* which is quoted in the introduction to *Glasperlenspiel*, and touching upon the Greeks and their attitude to music. Dornheim notes that Hesse's conception of music marks a return to Nietzsche's, with its acclaim of that grand and severe musical style conducive to relaxation of both mind and body. Furthermore, Hesse's attitude reflects a strong Chinese influence in its concern with cultural implications, and is based upon the Greek notion of music as a cathartic force.

Turning more immediately to *Glasperlenspiel*, Dornheim maintains that the novel is essentially musical in both structure and substance, a veritable symphony in prose. Just as great music does, *Glasperlenspiel* presents the totality of life and synthesizes its dichotomy, touches upon the full range of human emotions, and plays the entire scale of spiritual values. The game itself is closely akin to absolute music, and like the severe and serene music of Bach, is able to harmonize life's polarities.

Dornheim's first three associations are very novel. Since Nietzsche has undeniably been a formative factor in Hesse's life, his possible influence upon Hesse's attitude toward music bears further investigation. Nor can it be denied that Lü Bu We's philosophy of music has influenced, or perhaps better, confirmed Hesse's own views (see *Briefe*, pp. 137-138, 143). However, that Hesse's ideas may be partially based upon the Greek conception of music as a purifying force, is a very tenuous and certainly quite pointless argument. In his efforts to cope with *Glasperlenspiel*, Dornheim is not the first to resort to analogy for assistance. Before him, his countryman Guillermo Thiele had termed the novel "a great symphony, not orchestrated concretely, but in a mature language capable of expressing the most delicate shades of meaning" (*Boletín Bibliográfico* [1948], p. 19). And still earlier O. Basler had ventured to equate the work with a Gothic cathedral (Ball [1947], pp. 319-320). To endeavor to characterize by such vague analogy merely presents a new predicament without resolving the first.

G. W. Field's sweeping title, "Music and Morality in Thomas Mann and Hermann Hesse" (*University of Toronto Quarterly*, 24 [1955], 175-190), promises, but does not afford, a broader treatment of the theme broached by Müller-Blattau. Attention is again focussed primarily upon *Dr. Faustus* and *Glasperlenspiel*, and, as before, Mann is disparaged and Hesse warmly lauded. Mann is a pessimist; he is fascinated by the spirit of anarchy which prevails in music from Beethoven to Schönberg, and yields to its demonic forces. Hesse, on the other hand, celebrates the edifying power which characterizes the music of Monteverdi, Purcell, Scarlatti, Bach, Händel, Haydn, and Mozart. Unlike Mann, Hesse refuses to concede that the highest aesthetic attainment in music must involve moral compromise of the most dubious sort. For him, as for Shaftesbury and Schiller, the highest art and the highest virtue form a sort of *unio mystica* at the core of human culture.

The paths of Mann and Hesse seem to diverge sharply, as Müller-Blattau and Field would argue; but is this actually the case? Mann's preoccupation with disease and death, like Hans Castorp's, is unquestionably nothing other than an inverted attachment to life. A more encompassing and more cautious study would perhaps reveal that Mann's preoccupation with the destructive forces of music is also a peculiarly inverted faith, a faith, like Hesse's in the ultimate regenerative power of music.

Hesse and Psychology

The psychological approach to Hesse and his art has always been a highly controversial one (see H. R. Schmid; Mauerhofer). The critics who have concerned themselves with this approach usually exhibit a strong bias for or against it. Oscar Seidlin's "Hermann Hesse: The Exorcism of the Demon" (*Symposium*, 4 [1950], 325-348) is probably the most learned and challenging of the articles which touch upon Hesse and psychology. Characterizing Hesse's tales as a whole, Seidlin terms them myths which record the process of awakening to the self. For Hesse, however, this problem is not merely a personal psychological one, but essentially the general metaphysical problem of life itself.

This, in brief, is Seidlin's argument, and it is from this point of view that he interprets all of Hesse's writings. Peter Camenzind and Hans Giebenrath timidly approach the threshold of awakening only to return to the twilight from which they briefly emerged. Not until *Demian* is Hesse able to survey the chaos within himself. Only now, after his awakening, do the *Doppelgänger*, symbolic of the father and mother elements, rise above their earlier physical and psychological level, to become archetypes on the mythical plane. Hesse's ensuing attempts to cope with these elemental spiritual and vital forces and with the problems of individuation and time eventually lead to a theoretical acceptance of a "Paradoxical oneness of opposites, of time and eternity, individuation and Universal Self, life and death, mother and father . . ." (p. 344). However, the alternating extremes of Hesse's course, as reflected in his books, show that, in fact, the tension between these poles is insoluble.

The originality of Seidlin's attitude is refreshing and stimulating, and the clear and forceful presentation of his ideas is extremely persuasive. However, there are too many casual assertions and generalizations, and too few specific references to individual works. Hesse's art seems to have been subordinated to a theory, which, though plausible, is too confining.

Seidlin maintains quite emphatically that Hesse's problem is essentially religious and metaphysical, not psycho-physical. He concedes only that the latter is partially the case before *Demian*, but insists that it is not the case thereafter. As Seidlin expresses it: "What Freud tries to repair is the disturbance of man's functional existence in the world; the malady which Hesse exposes time and time again is the disturbance of man's authenticity, his *Eigentlichkeit*, as Heidegger puts it. Freud is a reformer who points at curable diseases, Hesse is an existentialist who points at the malaise inherent in the *condition humaine*" (p. 340).[38]

Unfortunately, Seidlin tries to substantiate this theory more by criticizing Freud than by analyzing Hesse. Yet even his persistent attempts to discount Freudianism, particularly the Oedipus complex, are relatively ineffective. In opposition to those who perceive the workings of an Oedipus complex in *Demian*, Seidlin argues, and rightly so, that Mrs. Eva is not mother, but mother-image, not a psycho-physical reality, but a myth. The evidence for this is the fact that she is not Sinclair's mother, who does not appear in the book at all, but the mother of Sinclair's double. Seidlin forgets that Sinclair's mother does appear, in one of his many dreams, and as a lover (*Demian* [1919], p. 147). In dreams then, Sinclair desires to kill his father, is his mother's lover, and suffers deeply of remorse and guilt. Can an Oedipus tendency be more obvious? Seidlin acknowledges that Hesse's descents into the subconscious may at times read like samples from a psychoanalyst's handbook (p. 337); but, in defense of his anti-Freudianism, he retorts that "the direction of Hesse's genius was established long before he was ever exposed to Freud" (p. 337), that he "learned from the original masters, the German Romanticists, Dostoevsky, Nietzsche" (p. 335). Such contentions may be quite true, but even so, they can do no more than establish that Hesse was not directly influenced by Freud or his technique of analysis; they can hardly invalidate the application of Freud's theories in interpretation. Continuing in a somewhat compromising tone, Seidlin concedes that *Demian* and *Steppenwolf* may conditionally be considered applied Freudianism; but he insists that "they are at least as closely related to the great midwifery of Socratic dialogues; they are records of a merciless exorcism and conquest of the dark powers which we have to lift to the surface in order to know ourselves" (p. 337). In view of the above statement, Seidlin's conception of the Socratic *gnothi seauton* seems hardly to differ from Freud's *know thyself*. In each case the *Weg nach Innen* seems quite identical, except that Seidlin prefers to think of Demian, Narziss, and the many related figures in Hesse's works, as Socratic midwives rather than as Freudian psychoanalysts. In direct substantiation of his theory, Seidlin actually offers little more than his own intuitive conviction. Can one, as Seidlin apparently does, deliberately disregard Hesse's own repeated assertion that his art is confessional in form and in function, akin in many respects to psychoanalysis? ("Aus einem Tagebuch des Jahres 1920," *Corona*, 3 [1932], 208). Do O. F. Bollnow's conclusions not sound much more plausible than Seidlin's assertions?

> Den *Demian* kann man geradezu als psychoanalytisches Lehrgedicht betrachten, so eng schliesst sich Hesse hier an diese Lehren an, aber dieselben Gedanken durchziehen in ähnlicher Weise auch die andern Werke, der psychoanalytisch verstandene Traum bleibt bei ihm ein besonders beliebtes Mittel der dichterischen Darstellung, und in veränderter Form bleibt das psychoanalytische Wissen noch bis in das *Glasperlenspiel* hinein wirksam (*Unruhe und Geborgenheit im Weltbild neuerer Dichter* [1953], p. 47).

That Hesse, like all great artists, has always striven for the lofty plane on which Seidlin puts him, is not to be doubted (*Corona*, 3 [1932], 208). It is a moot point whether he reaches and remains on this height from *Demian* forward. Seidlin's unqualified assertion that he does, is evidence of a decided oversimplification of Hesse's struggles. When, if ever, does a work of art which is confessional in substance and admittedly therapeutic in its purpose cease to have personal, psychological significance? Only upon those rare occasions when Hesse ceases to be autoanalytic is he fully able to penetrate beyond his circumstantial *Ich* to the mythical plane of Jung's archetypes (as Mann does in his Joseph novels); and surely this can only be the case in *Siddhartha*, *Narziss und Goldmund*, and *Glasperlenspiel*.[39] In the remaining tales from *Demian* to the present, though his concern undoubtedly extends beyond the self, Hesse is unable to free himself from his own, immediate troubles. Hesse's concluding remarks in *Krisis* certainly point less to the malaise of the *condition humaine*, than to an immediate and very personal psychological problem:

> Es ist in ihnen [*Krisis* poems] nicht bloss von dem nochmaligen Aufflackern der Lebenstriebe im Alternden die Rede, sondern mehr noch von einer jener Etappen des Lebens, wo der Geist seiner selbst müde wird, sich selbst entthront und der Natur, dem Chaos, dem Animalischen das Feld räumt. In meinem Leben haben stets Perioden einer hochgespannten Sublimierung, einer auf Vergeistigung zielenden Askese abgewechselt mit Zeiten der Hingabe an das naiv Sinnliche, und Kindliche, Törichte, auch und Verrückte und Gefährliche. . . . (p. 81).

Seidlin's existentialist theory, in itself an excellent antidote to the enthusiasm of the Freudians (*e.g.*, H. R. Schmid), is probably valid only in respect to the three novels mentioned above. To extend this theory to the main body of Hesse's writings is an exercise in futility.

Seidlin's antipathy toward Freudianism broaches the very controversial issue of the critic, the artist and his art, and psychoanalysis (see, *e.g.*, Frederick J. Hoffmann, *Freudianism and the Literary Mind* [1945]). Some critics are opposed to the application of any form of psychoanalysis in literary criticism. On the other hand, the extremists of the Freudian school confuse the author and his work with the patient and his dreams, and proceed to dissect a work of art accordingly (*e.g.*, Albert Mordell, *The Erotic Movement in Literature* [1919]). Less partial critics are careful to distinguish literary criticism and psychological analysis as two different activities. They recognize, nevertheless, that psychoanalysis can be of help in understanding the personality of the artist in question and in interpreting his work; furthermore, much can be contributed to the psychology of art in this way (*e.g.*, Frederick Clarke Prescott, *The Poetic Mind* [1922]; Herbert Read, "Nature of Criticism," *Collected Essays on Literary Criticism* [1938]).

Hesse has not been averse to expressing himself on this matter. In his very candid article, "Künstler und Psychoanalyse" (*Almanach für das Jahr 1926* [Internationaler Psychoanalytischer Verlag, Wien], pp. 34-38)—written in 1918 when his active interest in Freudianism was at its height[40]—his general attitude is clearly outlined. Enthusiasm for the new science is very evident.[41] Psychoanalysis can help to restore the confidence and self-assurance of the artist who has lost faith in himself and his calling.[42] It can afford the artist what Hesse would term "das innigere Verhältnis zum eigenen Unbewussten" (pp. 37-38), the inexhaustible source of his creation. However, by way of admonition and warning, the younger writers of the day are reminded that creative activity will always remain a matter of intuition and not of analytic talent and that the technique of analysis has no place in artistic creation (see also "Recent German Poetry," *Criterion*, Oct., 1922, p. 90ff.). Adding to the theme in his "Tagebuch des Jahres 1920" (*Corona*, 3 [1932]), Hesse dwells at length upon the confessional element in his art and religious confession, and then draws a loose parallel between the purpose of his art and the purpose of psychoanalysis. His writing goes hand in hand with his *Weg nach Innen,* which will lead, he hopes, to "das Annehmen des Chaos" (p. 208) : "Dies ist auf andrem Gebiet dasselbe was die Psychoanalyse vom Patienten verlangt, und zum Teil ist ja mein Erlebnis auch durch Freud und Jung angeregt" (p. 208).

A few years later, though still full of admiration for Freud's genius, Hesse frankly expresses doubts as to Freud's ability to plumb the mysteries of life by his method of rational psychoanalysis ("Erinnerung an Lektüre," *Neue Rundschau,* 36 [1925], 966). And in a still later direct reference to Freud, Hesse outlines in a somewhat acrid tone the evils of the "Dilletantenanalyse" which has found its way into the field of literary criticism: *i.e.,* the prevalent tendency to explain away a masterpiece in terms of the same psychic disturbances which occasion Mrs. Smith's anxiety neurosis, to discuss an artist's accomplishments as though they were no more than the dreams of the common neurotic, or to see a cause and effect relationship between neurosis and art. Basically depreciatory in nature, that type of analysis can shed no light upon the aesthetic value of a work of art, nor can it even, in its indirectness, contribute much of value to an understanding of the artist ("Notizen zum Thema Dichtung und Kritik," *Neue Rundschau,* 41, ii [1930], 769-773; see also *Briefe,* p. 78).

It is to be noted that Hesse does not, as freely as does Kafka ("Meditations," *A Franz Kafka Miscellany* [1940], p. 74), discount psychoanalysis *per se;* nor, though he recognizes that psychoanalysis has a place in life and indirectly also in art, does he acclaim Freud with the enthusiasm of Thomas Mann ("Freud and the Future," *Freud, Goethe, Wagner,* tr. Lowe-Porter [1937]). But reiterating his respect for Freud, he directs his criticism first against the misapplication of Freudianism by incompetent dilettantes who are neither medical men nor real literary critics, and secondly, against the prevalent application of the Freudian technique in artistic creation.

Hesse himself has frequently been criticized for resorting to this analytic technique in some of his own works, particularly in *Demian, Klein und Wagner,* and *Steppenwolf.* H. David-Schwarz adds *Narziss und Goldmund* to this list (*"Narziss und Goldmund* in zwei verschiedenen Auffassungen," *Psychologische Rundschau,* 3 [1931], 7-13). As a work of art, the novel is dismissed as a tediously didactic "bruchstückhafte Anhäufung von Schondagewesenem" (p. 8). In terms of psychology, however, it is considered a masterpiece, a "psychoanalytischer Roman in analytischer Form" (p. 8), surpassing even *Demian*. For David-Schwarz, *Narziss und Goldmund* is obviously little more than a convincing and very readable case history.

W. Dehorn's article is of much greater consequence ("Psychoanalyse und Neuere Dichtung," *Germanic Review*, 7 [1932], 245-262, 330-358). Attention is focussed chiefly upon the problem of today's cultural crisis, and upon the efforts which the more outstanding German writers have made to resolve this problem. Examining Hesse's works from this point of view (pp. 339-344), and in sharp contrast with Seidlin, he finds little of that universal element, of that existentialism upon which the latter dwells. Instead, he notes, disparagingly, that Hesse remains immersed in the *Triebpsychologie* of Freud, and that this is generally true also of Thomas Mann, Stefan Zweig, Arthur Schnitzler, and Hugo von Hofmannsthal ("psychoanalytischer Impressionismus," p. 355). Preoccupied with "Nerven und Krankheitsgeschichten," these impressionists fail to come to grips with the basic ethical and religious factors involved in the crisis of modern man (the *Tiefenpsychologie* of Jung), and thus never really penetrate to the malaise of the *condition humaine*.

In the short chapter allotted to Hesse in her dissertation of 1938 (*Der Muttergedanke als Zeitausdruck*), Ingeborg Heiting broaches a theme which bears more investigation and which could contribute considerably to an understanding of Hesse's personality. Though Heiting is primarily interested in the *Muttergedanke* as a cultural, historical phenomenon of the nineteenth and twentieth centuries, she recognizes that this fascination is just as much a personal, psychological matter for every author preoccupied with it. In her brief references to Hauptmann, Hesse, Wiechert, and to Kolbenheyer, she endeavors to show how the myth of mother superiority, with its emphasis upon a mystical creative force, has changed to "das neue Frauenbild" of National Socialism, with its healthier emphasis upon *Muttertum* and not *Muttergedanke* (p. 8). Hauptmann's *Muttergedanke* is the playful escapism of a spirit that has grown weak and tired; Hesse's reflects the fatigue of decadence and the desire for oblivion. With Wiechert the halo about *Mutter* fades, and in Kolbenheyer "echtes Muttertum" finally emerges (p. 50).

Steeped in the doctrines of National Socialism, Heiting is less interested in a better understanding of Hesse's personality than in casting aspersions upon it. To resolve this theme of *Mutter-gedanke* adequately and to determine its personal implications, would demand much more than random references. To begin with, the actual relationship between Hesse and his mother should be analyzed. In doing this, attention should be given to the autobiographical episodes in which Hesse's mother appears, *e.g.*: "Meine Kindheit," *Hermann Lauscher*; "Aus Kinderzeiten," *Diesseits*; "Garibaldi," *Nachbarn*; *Schön ist die Jugend*; "Eine Gestalt aus der Kindheit," *Am Weg*; and *Kinderseele*. A comparative study of the women in Hesse's works before and after *Demian* would also be very revealing. The enigmatic *Mutter Eva* symbol of *Demian* and *Narziss und Goldmund* continues to beg for interpretation. And even Hesse's dichotomy of *Geist* and *Natur* would have to be drawn into the argument.

Unlike Dehorn and Heiting, Eric Peters is interested solely in the psychology of Hesse, in the personal and not the cultural implications of his art ("Hermann Hesse. The Psychological Implications of his Writings," *German Life and Letters*, 1 [1948], 209-214). Delving into a theme more appropriate for a book than for a short article, Peters is compelled to limit his discussion to that work which, in his opinion, does most to expose Hesse psychologically, to *Kurgast*, with its free and ironic self-analysis. However, rather than weigh the psychological implications, as expected, he merely recalls Hesse's frank acknowledgement of his schizophrenic and manic-depressive proclivities, his attempts to justify these, and his recognition of the duality of human nature. He also attempts to associate the Christian concept of original sin with Hesse's belief that to live means to be sullied and troubled by guilt. From this idea of original sin, Peters proceeds to the theme of redemption and suggests that Hesse, like Dostoyevsky, believes in "redemption through sin." That Hesse is imbued with ideas about the sinfulness of life is a very questionable contention; and if Hesse were to think about achieving redemption, it would surely be through love and service, and hardly through sin, close though saint and sinner have always been in his thinking (see *Briefe*, p. 271; *Blick ins Chaos*, pp. 2, 3, 5; H. R. Schmid, "Der Verbrecher und der Heilige," pp. 158-177).

Though psychologically far less technical than Peters' study, Dr. Göppert-Spanel's affords a vastly deeper insight into Hesse's inner self ("Hermann Hesses Werk als Spiegel seiner Seelenentwicklung," *Universitas*, 6 [1951], 637-644). Interweaving select biographical details with pertinent references to his art, Göppert-Spanel manages to present both an informative and critical picture of Hesse's inner self and its development. He considers extreme egocentricity and an obsession with loneliness to be the bane of Hesse's existence. With a natural penchant for introspection, and frustrated from childhood in his need for intimacy and warmth, Hesse readily succumbed to an all-excluding preoccupation with himself and to the resultant horror of isolation. Neither at home nor in school, neither in friendship nor in marriage was that community of spirit, the *Wir* transcending the *Ich* and the *Du*, to be found. Hesse's heroes are also sensitive outsiders. His children are lonely and fear-ridden, his youths maltreated and unappreciated, and his lovers are helplessly incapable of love.

Göppert-Spanel rightly terms Hesse "einen Dichter der Einsamkeit" whose motto might appropriately be his poem "Seltsam im Nebel zu wandern," and whose life was a long *Weg nach Innen.* That Hesse never actually realized his hoped-for oneness of reality, is attributed to his confining self-love, to his *Nicht-über-sich-hinaus können.* Only in Knecht's devotion and service to young Tito does Göppert-Spanel perceive a belated but apparently successful effort to establish an intimate rapport with a fellow human being. But even now the consequences are lost in the vague implications of Knecht's sudden demise. Hesse seems unable to do more than to veil fulfillment by means of an indefinite symbolism.

That Hesse has always been a lonely outsider engrossed with himself almost to the complete exclusion of everything else, is an obvious observation. The causes and nature of this self-preoccupation are much more deep-seated and elusive. In his emphasis upon Hesse's extreme self-love, and his suggestion that the only other love of which Hesse was capable, an all-embracing love, is again only another form of self-love, Göppert-Spanel broaches a vital issue and makes a plausible assertion; a more detailed reconsideration is warranted. That Hesse's loneliness is to be attributed not only to *Wesensschicksal,* but also to *Lebensschicksal,* in other words, to say that he has never actually loved nor has ever really been loved, is another debatable assertion.

For a sound study of this theme of self-love (and self-hatred), lightly touched upon by Göppert-Spanel, a perusal of almost all of Hesse's tales, with particularly close examination of *Klingsors letzter Sommer, Siddhartha,* and *Kurgast* is necessary. Of the many essays pertinent to the subject, most significant are: "Von der Seele," "Eigensinn," *Betrachtungen;* "Der Weg der Liebe," *Sinclairs Notizbuch;* "Aus dem Tagebuch eines Wüstlings," *Simplicissimus,* 27 (1922) 19, 30.

Suzanne Debruge ("L'Oeuvre de Hermann Hesse et la Psychanalyse," *Études Germaniques,* 7 [1952], 252-261) is less interested in the psychology of the artist than in his art. She argues that it is valid to use psychoanalytic insights in literary interpretation, particularly when symbols born of the collective unconscious have become the very heart of a work of art (as in the works of Hesse following his own experience with psychoanalysis). But rather than analyze the enigmatic symbolism of just one of Hesse's tales, the very most one would expect in a brief article, Debruge chooses to consider *Demian, Steppenwolf,* and *Narziss und Goldmund,* and consequently remains on the level of description. She makes little effort to delve into the significance of the many enigmatic characters, situations, and dreams in these works.

It can no longer be questioned that the theories of Freud and Jung can shed light upon Hesse's art and are perhaps the only means of resolving its symbolism. Unfortunately most literary critics are at best but amateur psychoanalysts, and most psychoanalysts have little understanding of art and even less time for literary criticism.[43]

Geist and *Natur*

Not all critics have been equally happy about Hesse's choice of the terms *Geist* and *Natur* to express the many conflicting forces of life. Much controversy has revolved about the nature of the implied dichotomy, about Hesse's changing attitude toward it, and about its ultimate resolution. Hesse himself is not unaware of the arbitrary oversimplification inherent in his use of such a formula (see the "Tractat" of *Steppenwolf*).[44]

In a brief extract from his dissertation ("The Writer's Image of the Writer," 1951), Peter Heller presents an excellent introduction to this problem ("The Creative Unconscious and the Spirit," *Modern Language Forum,* 38 [1953], 28-40). Though he would term the dichotomy one of Soul and Spirit, he readily concedes that in a less restricted sense Soul might better be defined as a battleground for the polarity of Nature and Spirit.

He delves into Hesse's never too clearly defined and never fixed conception of the two realms of the Soul and the Spirit. The realm of the Soul is the maternal sphere, with an ambiguous embrace of the idyllic, the innocent, the harmless, of chaos and nihilism, love and cruelty, passion and coldness, pity and incestuous desire, good and evil. The realm of the Spirit is the paternal, the conscious, formative disciplinary force, the guardian of cultural tradition and the revolutionary protagonist of the future, at times associated with prosaic Philistine consciousness and morality, or with academic intellect, and at other times equated with Divinity. Heller draws attention to Hesse's everchanging attitude toward these opposites. He shows how Hesse was eventually to accept the tension and conflicts occasioned by this dichotomy as the necessary mainspring of creative energy, how he was to recognize the Soul as the source of inspiration and the Spirit as the creative force, and to aspire either to spiritualize the Soul or render the Spirit incarnate.

While this portion of Heller's argument is convincingly documented, his more casual concluding contention is hardly persuasive. That the ultimate stage of perfection envisaged by Hesse suspends the *principium individuationis*, is beyond question (Hesse's *Entwerden*). However, that this stage of harmony and unity represents a paradoxical return to a primordial, maternal abyss, that Hesse's ultimate solutions merely reintroduce the initial predicament, is a very questionable argument. Does Hesse's final resolution of life's problems not indicate ascent to a level aware of values and distinctions and their necessity, despite their relativity, rather than regression to this primordial abyss? Is it not a religious stage in which Hesse can, through faith, discern unity in the apparent diversities of reality, an ethical plane on which man is united with his fellow men in love and service, the plane of Christ and of Lao Tse, not that of the "russischer Mensch" pictured in *Blick ins Chaos*?

Like many of the articles in which Hesse is taken to task for one reason or another, Gerhard Kuhlmann's reflects only a casual reading acquaintance ("Dichter und die Entscheidung," *Die Christliche Welt*, 45 [1931], 166-169). Kuhlmann erroneously assumes that Hesse depicts the lives of Narziss and Goldmund in terms of the individual and the serious choice confronting him, and that his alleged preference for Goldmund's way of life is meant to be of more than personal significance. Hesse's novel is more correctly a descriptive presentation of life's two roads, each seen with its mixed array of virtues and vices and acclaimed as it is. To be a *Geistesmensch* or a *Naturkind* is not a question of choice for Hesse, but one of self-acceptance. His concern in *Narziss und Goldmund* is therefore not Kuhlmann's philosophical problem of choice, but the psychological need to accept that way of life determined by the predominant half of one's nature.

In view of Kuhlmann's false assumptions, his argument stressing the complexity of the problem of decision is hardly to the point. His emphasis upon the impossibility of choosing between *Geist* and *Natur* without taking cognizance of the ethical implications (which Hesse allegedly neglects to do), is equally irrelevant, as is his contention that Hesse should accordingly have shown preference neither for Goldmund nor Narziss.

Paul Böckmann's ponderous essay is much more noteworthy ("Die Welt des Geistes in Hermann Hesses Dichten," *Die Sammlung*, 3 [1948], 215-233). In a general characterization of Hesse's writings, Böckmann emphasizes his incessant preoccupation with the inner world, "die Wunderwelt des seelisch-geistigen Lebens" (p. 219), his limited concern for the outer world, "die entzauberte und ernüchterte Welt," and his desire to realize that ultimate unity of *innen* and *aussen* which he can sense only briefly during his more intense moments of experience, "die Erlebnisaugenblicke" (p. 219).

Böckmann then proceeds to show how Hesse's works from *Demian* to *Glasperlenspiel* are all steps in the quest for ultimate unity, and how *Geist* prevails at every station. In *Demian* it is in "Geist und Polarität" that unity is sought, in *Siddhartha* it is in "Geist und Versenkung," in *Steppenwolf*, in "Geist und Humor," in *Narziss und Goldmund*, in "Geist und Kunst," and in Hesse's last novel, *Geist* is celebrated in the splendor of self-sufficiency.

It is quite obvious that Böckmann's overemphasis upon *Geist* has led him to an oversimplification of Hesse's problem. In this overemphasis, only one half of Hesse's dilemma is stressed, that of the relationship between the inner and the outer worlds. For Hesse this would be the less immediate half of the problem and would concern him only after the more acute, personal conflict between *Geist* and *Natur* was attended to. With the exception of *Siddhartha*, and *Glasperlenspiel*, where both parts of the dilemma are dealt with and resolved, most of Hesse's works are principally concerned with the inner tension caused by *Geist* and *Natur*. Though Böckmann makes casual mention of Hesse's *Weg nach Innen*, he actually pays no attention to this, the issue in question. Nor does he seem to be at all aware of the growing anti-*Geist* tendency following *Demian*, e.g.; Klein is too weak to embrace either *Geist* or *Natur;* Klingsor, exhausting both, gives preference to neither, while Louis der Grausame drinks deeply of life and ridicules *Geist;* the *Kurgast* wavers between the poles, first denouncing one and then the other; disdain for *Geist* is the very substance of *Der Mann mit den vielen Büchern;* the European and his intellect does not fare very well in "Der Europäer" (*Krieg und Frieden*) ; *Blick ins Chaos* gives evidence of anything but acclaim of *Geist,* and in *Nürnberger Reise* (pp. 102-103), Hesse muses bitterly over the futility and bravado of all pursuits which are motivated by *Geist.* Such evidence shows that Hesse's world of thought and experience has not always been as transfigured by *Geist* as Böckmann would have one believe.

Walter Naumann's approach to the problem of *Geist* and *Natur* is a very novel one ("The Individual and Society in the Work of Hermann Hesse," *Monatshefte,* 41 [1949], 33-42). Centering the problem of the individual and society about two typical tendencies of human nature, revolt against authority and quest for authority, he proceeds to equate these inclinations with the terms "nature" and "mind." That tendency which seeks to revolt is equated with the mother side of life, the dark, revolutionary forces of life, greed, sex, and death. That tendency which seeks authority is equated with the father side, where wisdom, obedience, reverence, and spiritual values are stressed. Naumann notes that Hesse's early heroes are outsiders, elect weaklings at odds with society. Assertive individualism and real revolt, however, do not begin until *Demian.* The mother-principle continues to prevail until *Glasperlenspiel.* The father-principle now comes to the fore, and individuality is subordinated to the authority of a new humanism.

Naumann's analogy between "mind" and "nature," and the search for and revolt against authority is interesting; but it is hardly a fortunate one. Is "nature" not more inclined to ignore restraints, to vegetate in its free self-expression, than to revolt? "Mind" seeks authority, but does it not also revolt in its quest for higher authority and greater truth? Can one accept "nature" as the driving force in Hesse's *Weg nach Innen,* as Naumann would? And how valid is his tangential contention that it is with "nature" that Protestantism and German Classicism are linked?

Tackling the problem from a somewhat more psychological standpoint, Maurice Benn manages to add to the accumulation of doubtful contentions ("An Interpretation of the Work of Hermann Hesse," *German Life and Letters*, 3 [1950], 202-211). Again it is maintained that Hesse submits to *Geist* until *Demian*, then gives free rein to *Natur*, only to turn again to *Geist* in *Glasperlenspiel*. Hesse's turn from the father-principle to the mother-principle is attributed to his realization that he had too long stifled his real being, which was by its very nature a child of the mother-world. That Hesse should then turn and submit to *Geist*, after his erstwhile emancipation from it, is difficult for Benn to understand. Futhermore, that Hesse should imply that a return to the mother-world of chaos must be of limited duration, and that from it a new moral order must emerge, seems very peculiar to Benn; he is convinced that Hesse is really not aiming at any establishment of new principles, for this would mean a return to *Geist* and a betrayal of *Natur*. Do these discrepancies really exist in Hesse's works, or are they not rather to be attributed to the false assumptions made by his critics?

In the views of Böckmann, Naumann, and of Benn, two extremes of interpretation are represented. Where, in actuality, there is a confusion of *Geist* and *Natur*, Böckmann perceives only *Geist;* Naumann and Benn see only *Natur*. To term the pre-*Demian* period one of *Geist* or one of *Natur*, is either to distort the interpretation of these terms or to misunderstand this part of Hesse's life. Neither principle is dominant during these earlier years. This was Hesse's bourgeois period of compromise and self-preservation; the intensities of life were carefully avoided (see "Tractat," *Steppenwolf*). Nor can *Geist* or *Natur* adequately characterize the period from Demian to *Narziss und Goldmund*. This is actually an experimental time during which Hesse acclaims one, then the other, all the while endeavoring to bring them into harmony. Furthermore, these critics fail to distinguish the two levels of the *Geist* and *Natur* problem: the psychological level of *Selbsterkenntnis, Werden*, and eventual inner harmony; and the subsequent ethical plane of *Lebenserkenntnis, Entwerden*, and eventual outer harmony.

Recalling the Kurgast's lament, "diese Doppelmelodie möchte

ich mit meinem Material, mit Worten, zum Ausdruck bringen und arbeite mich wund daran, und es geht nicht . . ." (*Kurgast* [1925], p. 158), Safinaz Durumann ("La Melodie à deux Voix de Hermann Hesse," *Dialogues*, 2, No. 2 [1951], 87-99) would have both *Narziss und Goldmund* and *Glasperlenspiel*, each in its own way, represent the eventual realization of this passionate desire. The melodious co-existence of *Geist* and *Natur* in *Narziss und Goldmund* suggests an equilibrium possible only on the plane of space ("l'immobile perfection de l'espace," p. 90). It is, however, only in *Glasperlenspiel*, with its introduction of the time factor which occasions "un dualisme double tant spatial que temporel qui se retrouve dans la construction, dans le tissage en contre-point des thèmes ainsi que dans la fluidité et dans le rythme de leur évolution spiraléiforme," and with its "rythme des alternances cycliques, la polyphonie d'une seule vie humaine" (p. 90), that life's polarity is actually transcended and a real synthesis achieved. Durumann's is an extremely novel thesis; but it needs more than his intricate diagrams and brief references to become intelligible and convincing.

While the dichotomy of human existence has never ceased to disturb Hesse, the very nature of reality, its inexorable flux, has certainly afforded him no consolation. His long quest for a *Heimat* was a desire for refuge from these painful realities. Death came to represent such a refuge for Hesse, and became a *leitmotif* in his art. It is upon this concern with death that Denise Riboni dwells ("Le thème de la mort chez Hermann Hesse," *Suisse Contemporaine*, 7 [1947], 99-105).

Riboni rightly perceives that in *Narziss und Goldmund* omnipresent death no longer represents just a return to the womb, but has become the most vibrant factor of life itself. In love it is the vital stimulus, because life is intensified in death's presence. In art it is the motivating force, because art is a brief arresting of flux. Had this study been extended to *Glasperlenspiel* and to Hesse's later poems, Riboni might have noted a decreasing interest in death with a growing affirmation of life. Life itself was eventually to afford Hesse the harmony he long expected to find only in death.

Hesse's poetry records the course of his inner conflicts and development, perhaps more fragmentarily, yet certainly no less distinctly than his prose. Nevertheless, except for Adolf Beck

("Dienst und reuelose Lebensbeichte im lyrischen Werk Hermann Hesses," *Festschrift. Paul Kluckhohn und Hermann Schneider* [1948], pp. 445-467; see also Joseph Mileck, "The Poetry of Hermann Hesse," *Monatshefte*, 46 [1954], 192-198), no critic has chosen to analyze Hesse's poetry from this point of view.

Beck takes up the basic problem of *Geist* and *Natur*. Unlike most critics, he does more than merely trace Hesse's efforts to reconcile these opposing principles and to establish rapport between himself and the world. Exposing himself to obvious criticism, Beck ventures to propound that Hesse's problem is essentially a religious-psychological one, with greater emphasis upon religion than upon psychology. According to Beck, Hesse's poetry reveals the tragic plight of the soul in an age where religion has become secularized. *Verlorenheit, Einsamkeit, Heimatlosigkeit* are consequences of this secularization, and Hesse's repeated attempts to break forth from the confines of his *Ich-Welt*, and his constant yearning for *Heimat* and *Sein*, constitute a struggle to return to God, "am Herzen Gottes Bergung zu finden" (p. 466).

The first of Hesse's four attempts to solve his problem is his *Weg nach Innen*, a mystic merging of the *Ich* and the soul (the Demian stage). The second is his acclaim of a Dionysian way of life (the Klingsor stage). The third is the road back to the *grosse Mutter*, to the eternal life-death tension (the stage of Narziss and Goldmund). And the fourth attempt is the way of *Geist* and the evolution of the self (the stage of Knecht). It is, however, not until Hesse is capable of Christian love that *Heimat* is finally found, that the *Ich* is able to transcend itself and, through confession and example, to aid its fellow beings.

Beck's views represent yet another conception of Hesse's problem of life. What H. R. Schmid, Max Schmid and Oskar Seidlin, respectively, perceive to be a Freudian-psychological, a Klages-metaphysical, and a Heidegger-existentialist problem, Beck terms a religious question, a personal consequence of the secularization of Christianity. A synthesis of all four extremes might come closest to the true nature of this problem.

Almost as an afterthought, remarking upon the wider cultural-historical implications of Hesse's problem, Beck disparages the encroachment of the Oriental spirit into the West. The attitudes of the East, ever present in Hesse's search for *Heimat*, present even in his acclaim of *Geist*, can only bode evil, pose a threat to the "abendländischer Geist der Selbstbegrenzung und Selbstverantwortung des Ich" (p. 467). In his negative attitude toward the East, Beck reflects the general reaction of orthodox Christianity (see Schwinn, Kohlschmid).

Hesse and Religion

That revolt would leave its mark upon Hesse's attitude toward religion, was inevitable. Early revolt against the severity of an impassioned Pietism that was convinced of the evil of human nature and the necessity of breaking the will for the sake of salvation, was to extend itself to a revolt against Christianity itself. For a time, Hesse considered himself a freethinker, an atheist. Then he professed pantheism, delving into old mythologies and theologies (*Gedenkblätter* [1947], p. 236), and into theosophy (*Gertrud* [1927], p. 151). Eventually, he turned to the study of Eastern religions and philosophies, first to those of India, and then to those of China (*Eine Bibliothek der Weltliteratur* [1946], pp. 57-62, 92-94). However, schools of philosophy and religious sects, whether Western or Eastern, with their stereotyped systems and dogmas, and the consequent restraint imposed upon the individual, could only repel Hesse (*Briefe*, pp. 159-160). Nowhere did his quest halt for very long. Appealing aspects of East and West were blended in a fluid way, and his religion and philosophy were soon marked by an eclecticism and a perpetual becoming.

Hesse's revolt against authority, against the encumbering trappings and human frailties so characteristically present in religious institutions, combined with his quest for the basic truths common to all enlightened, humane religions (*Briefe*, pp. 224-225, 310-311, 330, 378-381), was to take him beyond the pale of Christian orthodoxy. This was not without the disapproval and the repeated censure of good Catholics and Protestants alike. As early as 1915, he is roundly reprimanded for his lack of respect for the Christian dogmas, for a Feuerbach-like atheism thought to have been transmitted through Gottfried Keller, and for his allegedly derogatory allusions to Catholicism in "Pater Mathias" (*Umwege*), and to Protestant mission work in "Robert Aghion" (*Aus Indien*). His love for St. Francis of Assisi is discounted as "eine ethische Schwärmerei," and his loneliness and suffering are attributed solely to his departure from the straight and narrow path of the true Christian (Sebastian Wieser, "Hermann Hesse," *Die Bücherwelt*, 12 [1915], 201-209).

Albrecht Oepke's censure is of a somewhat different nature ("Hermann Hesse," *Moderne Indienfahrer und Weltreligionen* [1921], pp. 8-15). Together with Waldemar Bonsels (*Indienfahrt* [1916]) and Graf Hermann Keyserling (*Reisetagebuch eines Philosophen* [1919]), Hesse is taken to task for abetting the spread of false impressions, thus contributing to the general apathy and hostility towards Christian mission work in India. In a polemic tone, Oepke takes offense at Hesse's depiction of the ineffectiveness of mission work in *Aus Indien,* and at his unfavorable representation of a missionary in "Robert Aghion." He also reproaches him for his godless type of Oriental mysticism.

Max Jordan rebukes Hesse mildly for his agnosticism, his pessimism, for his lack of decision in dealing with life's problems, and for his rejection of human life as senseless and hopeless ("Die Sendung des Dichters, ein offener Brief an Hermann Hesse," *Benediktinische Monatsschrift*, 13 [1931], 398-405). Convinced that an author must be a guide for his fellow men, and that, beyond mere pleasure, art must afford spiritual sustenance, Jordan entreats Hesse to mend his ways, to affirm existence, to trust in God, and thereby to become a light for less fortunate fellow humans.

In his return letter ("Die Sendung des Dichters," *Benediktinische Monatsschrift*, 14 [1932], 28-34), Hesse acknowledges the sincerity of Jordan's intentions, but rightly reminds him that his admonition may not be fully justified, based, as it admittedly is, upon the occasional newspaper article, rather than upon the main body of his art. A closer acquaintance with Hesse's work would have made it quite apparent that he constantly affirms life despite its insufferability, convinced, as he is, that behind even its present chaos, there is harmony and meaning. The extreme pessimism of his frequent gloomy articles is to a great extent a deliberate exaggeration meant to combat popular foolish optimism. His apparent loss of faith in humanity is only directed against the thoughtless, frivolous world of today, with its blind faith in machinery and progress and its smug self-satisfaction. His way of life, his *Weg nach Innen,* has served as a guiding light for many, even though he has always refused to take upon himself the rôle of the wise leader with panaceas for life's ills. Finally, his whole life has always been steeped in religion, although he ceased while still a youth to profess any orthodox faith and became an errant seeker destined to do homage to an unknown "verhüllter Gott" (p. 32).

When Hesse's reply to Jordan was again published in the *Briefe* of 1951 (pp. 80-89), the latter felt constrained to take his adamant adversary to task a second time ("Offener Brief an Hermann Hesse," *Benediktinische Monatsschrift*, 28 [1952], 424-431). Hesse, persistent in his disdainful attitude toward the church, is destined to continue to stand perplexed in life's confusion, unwilling to see its unity and incapable of perceiving its meaning: "In der Spätreife Ihres Lebens verharren Sie trotzig zwischen Gott und dem Nichts" (p. 425). Hesse's continued aversion to, and tragic misunderstanding of "dogmatisch festgelegte Meinungen" (p. 426) is deplored, and Jordan expounds upon the relationship of truth and dogma. And that Hesse should venture in his birthday greeting to André Gide (*Briefe*, pp. 420-421) to equate Catholicism and Protestantism with Communism, to refer to all three as "Kollektiven, Maschinerien" in which human beings are reduced to a common factor, leaves Jordan appalled and irate. Man's hope for salvation is the church, and the church alone can offer an effective bulwark against encroaching Communism. Convinced that Hesse and such kindred spirits as Thomas Mann, André Gide, and Bertrand Russell are unwittingly furthering the very chaos which would not tolerate their existence, Jordan implores them to reconsider their ways.

Criticism of Hesse's concept of religion and particularly of his attitude toward Christianity has continued to be quite prevalent in more recent years. Adolf Beck considers the plight of those who maintain such views as Hesse's to be the inevitable consequence of the secularization of Christianity. Peter Hedinger-Henrici regrets Hesse's acclaim of Abraxas and his refusal to choose between God and the Devil ("Hermann Hesse als Erzieher," *Schweizerisches Evangelisches Schulblatt*, 83 [1948], 329-344). Wilhelm Schwinn maintains that Hesse is evidently not fully aware of the powers of sin and evil and not cognizant of the grace of God. Hermann Pongs, in his reference to *Narziss und Goldmund*, concludes: "kein Funken echter Frömmigkeit durchglüht dies schöne Schein-Mittelalter, es bleibt neuromantisch-ästhetische Fassade. Das Ja zu dieser Welt wird vom Nein durchkreuzt, mit dem Hesse der *Una Sancta Ecclesia* ihren

Muttermantel raubt und ihn allein der grossen Eva-Mutter:
Welt umlegt . . ." (*Im Umbruch der Zeit* [1952], pp. 152-153).
And while one faction extols *Glasperlenspiel* for its "Weltfrömmigkeit" (*e.g.*, Engel), another, more vociferous faction
disparages its secular spirit (*e.g.*, Kohlschmid).

Maurice Colleville has been able to view this subject with
some objectivity ("Le Problème religieux dans la vie et dans
l'oeuvre de Hermann Hesse," *Études Germaniques*, 7 [1952],
123-148). Supporting his entire discourse with a wide range of
apt quotations, Colleville first dwells upon Hesse's contradictory
recollections of the protestant-pietistic circle of his childhood.
This circle is sometimes remembered as a happy one, completely
dedicated to God yet permeated by a warm, tempered piety, a
world of comfort, music, excursions, and delicacies, a life in which
there is no "radikaler Bruch mit Welt und Sinnlichkeit" (p.
126). At other times, it is described as a severe world in which
an ominous "pietistisch-christliches Prinzip" (p. 128) prevails,
in which religious education is "grausam zuweilen für mich und
die Eltern" (p. 128), a world bent upon eradicating sin and crush-
ing the will, creating bad consciences and causing "Widerstreit
zwischen Welt und Gottesreich" (p. 127).

Colleville considers the somber picture to be "la vraie, la
plus profonde, la plus durable, la plus conforme à la réaltié"
(p. 126). However, in view of Hesse's own words, "Es gab
Konflikte und Bangigkeiten, man stand unter dem Gestez, aber
es gab auch Fröhlichkeiten und Feste . . ." (*Gedenkblätter*,
[1947], p. 206), and considering that these pictures almost always are presented simultaneously, they might better be re-
garded as complementary rather than contradictory, and equally
true or false.

In the second phase of his study, Colleville draws attention to
Hesse's gradual estrangement from his family, to his eventual
antipathy toward Pietism, his severe criticism of its incapacitat-
ing influence, and to his denunciation of its tormenting God.
In part three, he continues to show how this animosity became a
recurrent theme in Hesse's writings. That, in the Thirties,
Hesse should turn back to the great Pietists, and that these men
should become one of the sources of inspiration for *Glasperlenspiel*, is proof for Colleville of the indelible impression family
background had left upon him.

In answer to the question—"Se détache-t-il de sa confession

première pour se rallier ou se convertir à une autre Église?"—
Colleville submits as evidence a letter written by Hesse in 1950
and diverse appropriate quotations to show that Hesse seems
only to have acclaimed Christianity intermittently, in aesthetic
experience, and in sentimental recall of his parental home. His
quest has been primarily for a syncretic, supraconfessional religion which would incorporate the truths common to all religions. Colleville concludes that the religion ultimately embraced
by Hesse is one of direct communion with the divine, and of
supreme faith in man, the meaningfulness of life, and the unity of
the world's apparent diversity. It is a religion whose God seems
more pantheistic and philosophical than Christian, a religion for
which Christ is the great apostle of love and humaneness, and
whose saints are the great religous spirits, thinkers, and artists
of all times.

Colleville has but one serious regret; namely, that Hesse does
not appear to have learned tolerance, to have become a liberal
spirit (p. 132). Hesse's persistent acrid characterizations of
clerics, and the fact that he should consider Angelus Silesius' turn
from the Lutheran to the Catholic Church a pseudo-conversion,
treason against the spirit, he finds deplorable. In reply to this
criticism, Hesse reminds Colleville that it was not Silesius' conversion that he found regrettable,[45] but his subsequent activity
as a pamphleteer ("dieser Weg vom begnadeten Seher zum
militanten Kirchenmann [war] nicht eine Entwicklung sondern
ein Abstieg . . ." ["À propos du Problème religieux chez Hermann Hesse," *Études Germaniques*, 8 (1953), 182]).

In a letter of 1934 Hesse remarks: "Unter den Bekenntnissen,
die die Menschheit sich formuliert hat, verehre ich am höchsten
das der alten Chinesen und das der katholischen Kirche" (*Briefe*,
p. 155). Much has been said of Hesse and Pietism (Baaten and
Colleville), a good deal about Hesse and India (Lützkendorf and
Kunze), much less about Hesse and China (Gnefkow and
Koller),[46] and many general remarks have been made about
Hesse and Christianity as a whole.[47] But, except for a few
references by Colleville (p. 140), Hesse's enigmatic attitude toward the Catholic Church continues to remain uninvestigated
(see *Briefe*, pp. 134, 142, 150, 155, 162, 186, 198, 200; *Kurgast*
[1925], pp. 128-129; chapters four and five of *Glasperlenspiel;*
"Angelus Silesius," *Betrachtungen; Franz von Assisi;* "Mein

Glaube," *Neue Schweizer Rundschau*, 13 [1946], 664-667). A wider and more detailed reconsideration of the problem *Hesse and Religion* should include all five of these aspects, entailing a careful study of at least the following tales: "Walter Kömpff," *Nachbarn;* "Pater Mathias," *Umwege;* "Robert Aghion," *Aus Indien; Knulp, Demian, Siddhartha,* and *Glasperlenspiel.* Of the many relevant essays, particular attention should be given to: "Aus einem Tagebuch des Jahres 1920," *Corona*, 3 (1932), 192-209; "Chinesische Betrachtung," *Betrachtungen;* "Besuch aus Indien," *Bilderbuch;* "Kurzgefasster Lebenslauf," *Traumfährte;* "Ein Stückchen Theologie," *Neue Rundschau*, 43, i (1932), 736-747; "Erinnerung an Hans," "Nachruf auf Christoph Schrempf," *Gedenkblätter.* Very pertinent, too, are the following items: *Eine Bibliothek der Weltliteratur;* "An einen jungen Kollegen in Japan," *Krieg und Frieden* (1949) ; "Rückblick," *Neue Schweizer Rundschau*, 19 (1951), 78-81; "Der Einsame an Gott," "Besinnung," *Gedichte; Vivos Voco*, 1 (1919-20), 200-201, 204, 780, 816; *Vivos Voco*, 2 (1922), 482; and *Briefe* with their constant reference to religion.

Glasperlenspiel

Although *Glasperlenspiel* is the last of Hesse's major writings, and although it was hardly available in Germany before 1946, it has already occasioned more criticism than any other single work. Combined, this material amounts to almost a thousand pages, and the bulk of it appeared in the very short period from 1947 to 1952. To deal separately with only the most important of the articles would result in endless and confusing repetition. A thematic cross-section analysis is much more likely to clarify the results of all this activity.

The articles which deal with *Glasperlenspiel* fall roughly into three classes. Many are hardly more than brief reviews, and as such, merit no consideration. Of those that treat a specific theme, only seven are of any import: Anni Carlsson, "Gingo Biloba," which has been dealt with under "Congratulatory Articles"; J. Müller-Blattau, "Sinn und Sendung der Musik in Thomas Manns *Doktor Faustus* und Hermann Hesses *Glasperlenspiel*," Alfredo Dornheim, "Musica Novelesca y Novela Musical," and G. W. Field, "Music and Morality in Thomas Mann and Hermann Hesse," treated in "Hesse and Music"; Amalie Bonitz, "Der

Erziehungsgedanke in Hermann Hesses *Glasperlenspiel*," touched upon in "Books," under Geffert; Wilhelm Schwinn, *Hermann Hesses Altersweisheit und das Christentum*, which is discussed in the chapter on pamphlets; and finally Gottfried Koller, "Kastalien und China," which will be dealt with below. The greatest number are general survey articles.

Most of the survey articles follow a common pattern. Hesse's lengthy exposition of Western European civilization is reviewed in all its chief points. Castalia is described in its origin, historical significance, its inhabitants, institutions, and its ideals. Attention is drawn to the development, intricacies, and meaning of the glassbead game. Knecht's life is summarized; usually only casual reference is made to the *Lebensläufe* and to Knecht's poems. Brief comments are generally woven into this résumé. Vague allusions are made to philosophical influences, to other prominent writers, and to other novels of the same nature. While many of the tale's more significant problems are mentioned, any real analysis is seldom attempted.

In their attitude toward, and general evaluation of *Glasperlenspiel*, the survey articles present three main points of view. Reverent eulogy is the most common. A few critics maintain a neutral attitude, confining themselves to a description of the novel. And a very small number unreservedly disparage the novel in both substance and form. Of this anti-Hesse faction, two critics deserve individual attention.

In almost righteous indignation, Werner Kohlschmid endeavors to stem the flood of laudatory articles about *Glasperlenspiel* which followed in the wake of Hesse's Nobel Prize of 1946 ("Meditationen über Hermann Hesses *Glasperlenspiel*," *Zeitwende*, 19 [1947], 154-170, 217-226). The critics who take unscrupulous advantage of Hesse's position in the limelight are called to task for their unqualified and irresponsible acclaim of Hesse as one of the staunch, modern representatives of the "Ideal einer europäischen Humanität" (p. 154), and the panegyrists who indiscriminately maintain that Hesse's novel excels Goethe's *Meister* (*e.g.*, Engel), are asked to reëxamine their criteria.

Following this introduction, Kohlschmid subjects *Glasperlenspiel* to a thorough but somewhat tedious scrutiny. How to classify and how to evaluate this work affords him considerable anxiety. After methodically considering many of the established epic forms, he vaguely concludes: "Das Werk ist eine Allegorie, die den Mythos des ewigen Humanismus, einer edlen, beispielhaften, zuchtvollen, erudierten Menschlichkeit ausdrückt. Es bedient sich als Hilfsmittel geschichts- und bildungsutopischer Formfiktion, die aber nicht die Form des Ganzen ausmachen" (p. 162). In his evaluation, he finds that the chronicle-like language of the novel, though admittedly in keeping with the subject matter, is limited and tedious, and, with its interspersed psychoanalytical jargon, is unpleasantly mannered. And while the *Lebensläufe* are of some artistic value, the poems are exceedingly mediocre, and neither can convincingly be attributed to the schoolboy Knecht. The latter, moreover, is not depicted persuasively, revealing in neither action nor word any of the greatness Hesse attributes to him (E. von Vietsch expresses similar views; *Neues Europa*, 3, No. 6 [1948], 38-40).

Turning his attention to the substance of the novel, Kohlschmid proposes three possible interpretations for Knecht's death. The Tito episode could symbolize an ultimate and necessary synthesis of Castalia and the outside world, of *Geist* and *Natur*, an ideal achievement made possible by the spirit of self-sacrifice Castalia engenders in its sons. It could also reflect the ultimate impossibility of such a synthesis. Or it could represent the ultimate physical inability of the *Geistesmensch* to cope with the practical world. While each of these possibilities is plausible, not one is found to be beyond objection. The first is not convincingly borne out by the story; the final events in Knecht's life are purely personal and of no such symbolic significance, and to assume that a Castalia is needed to sober Tito, is absurd. To accept the second possibility, is to ignore the synthesis attained by Jakobus. To accept the third, is to have Hesse acknowledge the impossible, the bankruptcy of Castalia's "humanistisch-ästhetische Geistigkeit."

It is this ideal, Hesse's answer to the cultural crisis of the Western world, that disturbs Kohlschmid most of all. Little can be expected of a humanism which borders upon snobbish eclecticism, of an ideal based upon the dated "Humanitätsopt mismus" of the nineteenth century. He discounts "Reine Methoden, Formen, Versenkung und Atemübungen" as mere formalities. They are not the concrete thoughts and the decisions, conditioned by religion, which alone can be of help in our crisis. In short, Hesse fails to perceive the true nature of the world's ills, the religious nature: "*Das Glasperlenspiel* löst die Krise vom Menschen aus, ohne Gott. Es erreicht nicht die Grenze religiöser Problematik" (p. 225).

Kohlschmid's determination to counteract the prevalent uncritical praise of *Glasperlenspiel* leads him to assume a severely negative attitude; and what seems to him to be an absence of the religious factor persuades him to conclude that 'die Entscheidung des ludi magister ist nicht die unsrer Wirklichkeit entsprechende" (p. 226). His animosity blinds him to Hesse's humanitarian ideal of love, service, and sacrifice, and to his religous affirmation of life.

While Kohlschmid's article is severely critical, that of Wolfgang von Schöfer is a diatribe ("Hermann Hesse, *Peter Camenzind* und das *Glasperlenspiel*," *Die Sammlung*, 3 [1948], 597-609). It is based on the very extremes of misinterpretation. The sheer impossibility of Castalia is evidence enough for him to conclude that the novel was psychologically motivated: "das Phantasiegebilde, den Ausweichtraum eines Schwachen, der alle Problematik beiseitezuschieben versucht und sich eine Welt vorstellt, in der man die Qualitäten, die ihm fehlen, nicht braucht. . . . der Traum eines alten Mannes, der mit dem Leben endgültig nicht fertig geworden ist, der es aufgegeben hat, eines Schwachen und Empfindlichen, der sich nicht eine sublimierte Geistwelt, sondern eine sentimentale Scheinwelt aufbaut" (pp. 606-607).

He dispenses with the art of the novel in a manner no less depreciatory: "ein wahres Schwelgen in Worten" (p. 601), "Kitsch" (p. 602), "Formlosigkeit der Sprache" (p. 603), "im Ganzen eine schlaffe, pedantische, energielose Diktion" (p. 604). He expends just as little sympathy upon the substance: "ein philosophisches Schlaraffenland in dem jede Problematik von vornherein ihrer Auflösung in einer rosaroten Harmonie sicher ist" (p. 601); "diese Halbheiten, dieses Nichtverstehen, das Nichtergriffensein . . . das sich bis zum Grotesken steigert" (p. 603); "es ist vieles halb und ungenau und falsch in diesem Buch" (p. 602). Von Schöfer concludes that *Glasperlenspiel* is essentially an insincere book and dangerous for postwar Germany: "Darin liegt seine Gefahr, dass es mit Geschick versucht, unser Unterscheidungsvermögen zu betrügen und uns wie ein Falschmünzer Unechtes für Echtes zu geben" (p. 608).

In his hostility, von Schöfer fails to realize that Hesse does not claim that he has found a cure for humanity's ills. He merely desires to show that man's best efforts to solve the problems of existence will be futile, unless he is bent on self-knowledge, is prepared for the strain and sacrifice of self-realization, and is willing, in an adjustment to life characterized by *Frömmigkeit, Heiterkeit, Bejahung, Ehrfurcht, Dienst,* and *Liebe,* to be prompted and sustained by *Geist* and *Meditation.* However, for a detailed and competent repudiation of von Schöfer's acrid allegations, see: Paul Böckmann, "Ist das *Glasperlenspiel* ein gefährliches Buch? Eine Replik," *Die Sammlung,* 3 (1948), 609-618; and for a purposeless prolongation of the controversy, see: von Schöfer, "Aktualität und Überzeitlichkeit der Literatur," *Die Sammlung,* 4 (1949), 346-350.

Although the criticism centered about *Glasperlenspiel* consists mainly of description, there is no dearth of casual remarks pertaining either to the merits of the substance or to the artistic quality of the novel. A cross section of these remarks reveals a very wide range of opinion. With respect to substance, we find mainly broad generalizations. Extending a gracious courtesy to his fellow writer, Thomas Mann terms the novel "das sublime, aus allen Quellen der Menschheitskultur, abend- und morgenländischen, gespeiste Alterswerk . . ." (539, p. 247).[48] For R. B. Matzig the novel represents "die Summa von Hesses Lebensweisheit" (12, p. 102). It is Goethean in thought and wisdom for L. Freyberger (401, p. 368). O. Engel feels that Goethe's *Wilhelm Meister* hardly achieves a corresponding depth of concentration (4, p. 28). W. Nestle quite candidly terms *Glasperlenspiel* superior to *Wilhelm Meister* in "Umfang, Tiefe und Gedankenreichtum" (583, p. 10). E. Vietta dissents: "Aber er wagt sich ins Universale, das ihm nicht wie Goethe gegeben ist" (687, p. 691). A. Goes calls the work "eines der wichtigsten Bücher unsrer Zeit, einer der grossen Erziehungsromane der Weltliteratur" (32, p. 22). O. Basler terms it "ein gotischer Dom, mit allen feierlichen Bezügen eines solchen: trotzig, himmelanweisend, überlegen zeugend für das Dennoch, und auf die Menschenschinder wirkend wie das Kruzifix auf Satanas" (1, pp. 319-320).

In contrast, despite the novel's monumental stature and ponderous theme, O. Seidlin perceives a certain lack of profundity: "Hesse hat den Fehler begangen, das Unaussprechliche zu klar und direkt aussprechen zu wollen; das Unzulängliche wird hier zu deutlich Ereignis, und vergessen ist Fausts Wort: 'Am farbigen Abglanz haben wir das Leben,' selbst wenn es sich auch um das Leben im reinen Geiste, in Kastalien, handelt" (656, p. 307). And at the extreme end of negative appraisal, von Schöfer dismisses the book as sheer nonsense, "eine Stimme aus dem Limbus des Geistes" (636, p. 604), an example of modern art become a "gesellschaftliche Pose und zur exklusiven Esoterik eines aristokratischen Zirkels von Eingeweihten" (635, p. 347).

In addition to these general characterizations, considerable attention has been focussed upon a few, more specific issues. Of these, Knecht's unexpected and ambiguous death seems to have afforded the critics their greatest concern. As usual, opinions are widely divergent. O. Engel is willing to accept this abrupt ending as he would any of life's inexplicables: "Auch das Leben bricht den Faden, wo und wann es will. . ." (4, p. 73). O. F. Bollnow considers it a deliberate enigma, proof of Hesse's belief in the ineffableness of life's final mystery (87, p. 58). Fritz Kraus deems it a most appropriate "existentiellen Schluss" (495, p. 13). Maintaining that the novel's conclusion is neither makeshift nor detrimental to the proportions of the whole, Hilde Cohn goes on to insist vaguely that "both in structure and content, [it] reveals the nature of the work" (350, p. 347). W. Kohlschmid insists that the conclusion only reflects Hesse's inability to give "eine leuchtende Gestaltung" to the sacrifice motif apparently intended in Knecht's death (147, p. 159). For H. H. Groothoff it marks a regrettable indecisive halting in midstream: "nur . . . im letzten Augenblick der Entwicklung des Lebens des Josef Knecht . . . versagt der Roman" (422, p. 278). Von Faber du Faur candidly comments: "Hier aber handelt er [Knecht] sinnlos, lässt sich seine Handlungen von einem Unreifen diktieren" (385, p. 191). And while E. von Vietsch concludes that Knecht's death is absolutely banal, the simple consequence of insufficient foresight (686, p. 39), to E. Vietta it verges upon the comical (687, p. 691).

The opinions concerning the underlying significance of this final episode are no less diverse. As noted above, Kohlschmid suggests three possible interpretations. While he himself dismisses all three on one pretext or another, other critics generally favor the theory of synthesis, and consider Knecht's death not a tragedy, but a symbol of the service and of the sacrifice necessary for this synthesis (see *Briefe*, p. 231). Giving poetic expression to this theory, O. Basler describes the last scene as "das Mysterium von Stirb und Werde" (1, p. 323).

Not only does Wilhelm Grenzmann perceive in Tito this same promise of better things to come, but to him Knecht's departure from Castalia represents Hesse's rejection of man's flight from his dichotomous self and from the process of history (an insight for which Grenzmann is indebted to Theodor Litt, *Die Geschichte und das Übergeschichtliche* [1949], pp. 22-29). At the same time, Knecht's departure exemplifies Hesse's belief in the interdependence of *Geist* and *Sinnlichkeit* and in the necessity of historical flux (117, pp. 106-120). Hans Mayer perceives a decidedly different kind of rejection in Knecht's departure and death. To him they mean failure and the inevitable decline of our capitalistic culture (550, p. 625). For Gerhard Kirchhoff, Knecht's departure is a repudiation of Castalia, though not of its ideals, for Knecht's path leads but "in ein anderes, dem Absoluten ähnlicheres Kastalien" (6, p. 128). Hermann Pongs, on the other hand, considers this same departure as "Abstand und Abschied also von der einst so geliebten Goethewelt und ihre Symbolweite" (178, p. 20). Even before Pongs, Theodor Litt expressed a similar sentiment, terming Knecht's departure "eine Abweichung von Goethes pädagogischer Provinz." However, he considered this deviation from Goethe's "geschichtsverneinende Haltung," this rejection of Castalia and its "Geschichtslosigkeit," to be an auspicious one, a step beyond Goethe, and a warning for those German intellectuals of today who are inclined to withdraw into a world of thought, turning their backs upon the chaos, the historical fact about them (156, p. 29). For Marie-Louise Blumenthal, Knecht's departure again suggests a relapse, a return to the egocentricity which is contrary to the ideals of Castalia. She is almost inclined to agree with Magister Alexander: "Ist Josef Knecht nicht eigentlich doch ein Abtrünniger, ein Fahnenflüchtiger, der des Verzichtes auf Weltwirklichkeit überdrüssig und seines hohen Dienstes müde geworden, der Pädagogischen Provinz den Rücken kehrt, um draussen in der Welt versäumtes Schicksal, versäumtes Dasein nachzuholen . . ." (322, p. 484).

On the other hand, Max Schmid is convinced that the old

conflict between *Geist* and *Seele* has, in *Glasperlenspiel*, become one between a passive, aesthetic way of life and an active, ethical way. He therefore discounts the theory of synthesis, and says that Knecht sacrifices himself in affirmation of the ethical way of life (18, p. 210). And Hilde Cohn, rather than perceive Knecht's death in terms of the dichotomy of *Geist* and *Natur*, prefers to consider it as the last transformation in a long process of gradual awakening, as much "ein Akt der Berufung" as Knecht's first encounter with the *Magister Musicae* (350, p. 357). Harvey Gross is convinced that the novels written by Hesse after the First World War are essentially allegorical, and that their heroes personify the cleft soul of Western civilization. He suggests that the Knecht-Tito episode is a political allegory which represents the ultimate tempering of the forces of Russia and the East by the humanism of Western Europe (423, pp. 132-140).

In reply to a letter from a young enthusiast who was particularly perplexed by, and concerned about Knecht's death, Hesse writes:

Er hätte, klug und fein, es unterlassen können, trotz seiner Erkrankung den Sprung ins Bergwasser zu tun. Er tut ihn dennoch, weil etwas in ihm stärker ist als die Klugheit, weil er diesen schwer zu gewinnenden Knaben nicht enttäuschen kann, und er hinterlässt einen Tito, dem dieser Opfertod eines ihm weit überlegenen Mannes zeitlebens Mahnung und Führung bedeuten und ihn mehr erziehen wird als alle Predigten der Weisen. . . . Aber schliesslich ist es gar nicht so wichtig, ob Sie es verstehen werden, ich meine: mit dem Verstand diesen Tod Knechts begreifen und billigen. Denn dieser Tod hat ja seine Wirkung auf Sie schon getan. Er hat in Ihnen, so wie er es in Tito getan hat, einen Stachel hinterlassen, eine nicht mehr ganz zu vergessende Mahnung, er hat eine geistige Sehnsucht und ein geistiges Gewissen in Ihnen geweckt oder bestärkt, welche weiter wirken werden, auch wenn die Zeit kommt, wo Sie mein Buch und Ihren Brief vergessen haben werden. Hören Sie nur auf diese Stimme, die jetzt nicht mehr aus einem Buch, sondern in Ihrem eigenen Inneren spricht, sie wird Sie weiter führen (*Neue Rundschau*, 1948, pp. 244-245). [49]

Interesting though this commentary may be, it fails to settle this enigmatic issue conclusively. One is reminded of Hesse's remarks to a friend: "Das Du Dich meines Buches weniger mit denkerischer Analyse als mit Gefühl, Stimmung und Assoziationen bemächtigt hast, finde ich ganz in der Ordnung" (*Briefe*, p. 232).

The second major problem which has called forth a sharp variance of opinion, is the question of religion. While some deplore the prevailing secular spirit of *Glasperlenspiel*, others laud it for its deeply religious spirit. O. Engel, the most apt spokesman for the first group, maintains that the novel reflects the deep religiosity of a man for whom thought and religious experience have become one (4, p. 16), a religiosity which, according to H. H. Groothoff, has transcended Christian piety to become a "Weltfrömmigkeit" reminiscent of the spirit of Goethe's day (422, p. 274). The tempered critical attitude of W. Schwinn is quite representative of the attitude of Christian orthodoxy as a whole: while the merits of Hesse's *Lebensweisheit* are recognized, the absence of the Christian way of life, centered about the church and its tenets, is regretted (54). W. Kohlschmid, representative of a smaller faction, is decidedly sharper and more extreme in his criticism. He adamantly dismisses the novel as the work of a man who would endeavor to reckon with life without God (489, p. 225).

Despite these two extremes of opinion, which consider the spirit of *Glasperlenspiel* to be either something more or something less than Christian, one cannot but notice the many aspects of the novel which unmistakably recall Christianity. Though it is left on the shadowy horizon, the Catholic Church remains the only other major force combatting worldliness. The ideals of these two institutions are apparently not irreconcilable, for a number of higher church dignitaries are also *Glasperlenspieler*. It is to prepare the way for a better understanding that Knecht is sent to Mariafels. The consequent firm friendship which develops between Knecht and Jakobus may perhaps augur a future reconciliation between Castalia and the Catholic Church. Furthermore, in its island existence, its discipline, its subjugation of the individual, its exclusion of women, its emphasis upon values transcending the material world, and in its ideal of love, service, and affirmation of life, Castalia is obviously indebted to the Christian monastic tradition. The *Magister Ludi* is like an abbot, and his ritual, the glass-bead game, is akin to the celebration of the mass. The teachers and administrators of Castalia are like monks, and the chosen students are their novices. Is it really possible that Hesse retained only the shell of Christianity? The few remaining minor points broached by the critics need only passing attention. The vague time-element of the novel should not have puzzled the many people it has, for in a footnote accompanying the separate publication of the "Einleitung" (*Neue Rundschau*, 45, ii [1934], 638), Hesse himself suggests that it was written about 2400, A.D., at a time when Knecht's life and death had already become somewhat legendary. In the same footnote the novel is termed "eine utopische Dichtung," a characterization which many critics, apparently unaware of Hesse's own acknowledgment, have contested repeatedly and zealously (later Hesse uses the term more cautiously, see *Briefe*, pp. 227, 230, 232, 264). Hesse's neglect of women, the banning of marriage in Castalia, and his resolution of the problem of sex (available and willing maidens), have called forth an occasional disapproving remark (385, p. 185; 565, p. 269). To the often posed question as to why women play no rôle in his novel, Hesse replies in a letter of June, 1950 (*Briefe*, p. 385, also p. 234). The pros and cons of Knecht's departure are frequently touched upon, and it is generally conceded that he is not a traitor to his cause.

And finally, a number of more curious critics have managed to detect familiar places and particular figures behind Hesse's mythical world. In its geography and atmosphere, Castalia (evidently named after the celebrated spring of inspiration on Mt. Parnassus) recalls the Württemberg of the nineties (385, p. 182). "Der ältere Bruder" in his garden is none other than Hesse himself in Montagnola (12, p. 103). In *Magister Ludi*, Thomas von der Trave, Hesse is obviously paying his respects to Thomas Mann. Carlo Ferromonte is just as obviously a word translation of Karl Isenberg, a nephew who was once very close to Hesse (*Briefe*, pp. 314, 345), and the name Dubois reaches back to Hesse's maternal grandmother. Jakob Burckhardt is somewhat more difficult to detect in the person of Pater Jakobus (*Briefe*, p. 314), as is Nietzsche in the brilliant, egocentric and emotionally unstable Fritz Tegularius. Bastian Perrot of Calw, musicologist at the School of Music in Cologne, recalls both the Perrot machine shop in which Hesse worked as a youth, and the famous study by Albert Freiherr von Thimus (*Die harmonikale Symbolik des Altertums* [Cologne, Vol. 1,

1868, Vol. 2, 1876]) which Hesse may well have used in the writing of his novel. Clangor and Collofino, of the Latin motto, are no other than Hesse's old schoolmate, Franz Schall (*Briefe*, p. 97; "Gedenkblatt für Franz Schall," *Gedenkblätter*), and Feinhals, an erstwhile close friend who was a cigar manufacturer in Cologne. Hirsland recalls Hirsau next to Calw on the edge of the Black Forest. The monastery Mariafels recalls the Mariabronn of *Narziss und Goldmund*, which in turn suggests the Maulbronn from which Hesse had once fled. But to what do Escholz and Waldzell allude? When Josef arrives in Escholz he is assigned to House Hellas, the same House to which Hans Giebenrath of *Unterm Rad* is assigned, and the very House in which Hesse had lived while at Maulbronn. Does the *Magister Musicae* at Monteport allude to Hesse in Montagnola, and is Ludwig Wassermaler perhaps Max Wassmer, Hesse's old friend from Bremgarten, or the painter Louis Moilliet, alias Louis der Grausame? Did Hesse have another friend, Otto Basler, in mind when he created the *Joculator Basiliensis* who reduced music and mathematics to a common denominator? To whom could the literary historian Plinius Ziegenhalss, Bertram, and Alexander allude? And who is the *Pariser Gelehrte* who wrote *Chinesischer Mahnruf?* Rector Zbinden recalls "Der Schlossergeselle" (*Simplicissimus*, 10 [1905], 14-15), and Veraguth recalls *Rosshalde*, but what is the story behind these names? Was the name Tito to suggest the uncertain lot of Knecht's ward? Before Knecht enters Castalia he is a *Lateinschüler* at Berolfingen at the edge of Zaberwald. Could Hesse have had in mind the Latin School at Göppingen which he attended before his admission to Maulbronn, and which is not too far from the Black Forest? Ludovicus crudelis is of course none other than Louis der Grausame of *Klingsors letzter Sommer* (Louis Moilliet). While the name Knecht may partly have been suggested by Goethe's Meister, neither it nor Designori seems to allude to any particular person; they were probably chosen primarily for their antithetical implications. And what is the mystery behind Chattus Calvensis II? Chattus, the Latin for Hesse, was a name given to H⸌ ₁ann by Rector Bauer at Göppingen. But why Hesse the Second? Can Hesse have had in mind as the First, the sixteenth century humanist Hermannus Hesse, whose name appears a number of times in the *Index librorum prohibitorum?* Though Hesse himself had not yet officially been put on the *Schwarze Liste* of the Nazis, he certainly realized that it was only a matter of time before his name would be included.[50]

The scanty and nebulous attempts to characterize the art of *Glasperlenspiel*, can hardly be considered very consequential. The comparatively ineffective practice of defining by means of loose analogy has been widespread. The repeated casual references to the poetic novel of the eighteenth century (*e.g.*, 401, p. 368), or to the later, romantic novel, can only suggest vague notions, and general comparisons with such works as Goethe's *Wilhelm Meister*, Novalis' *Heinrich von Ofterdingen*, Stifter's *Nachsommer* or Mann's Joseph novels, affords no great insight into the form, language, and symbolism of Hesse's novel. In view of these associations, it has not been difficult to term *Glasperlenspiel* an *Erziehungsroman* or a *Bildungsroman*. These claims, however, have yet to be established through detailed study. Drawing attention to the novel's lack of body—"es fehlt ihm an Fülle, es fehlt ihm an Welt"—O. Seidlin suggests that it might even better be called a *Novelle* (656, pp. 306-307). Proceeding a step further, Hilde Cohn brushes aside the notion that *Glasperlenspiel* is an *Entwicklungsroman*, maintaining that it is neither a development nor a novel, but is in fact a *Novelle*, and Knecht's sudden and surprising death is its *pointe* (350, p. 350). A. Carlsson prefers to term the novel a myth (344), W. Kohlschmid calls it an allegory (489, p. 162), and for both it is a stylized reflection of our twentieth-century culture.

Going beyond these analogies and the quarrel over genre, critics have noted that *Glasperlenspiel* reflects the slower tempo, the clearer atmosphere, and the calmer observation of the author's later years; that it is a blending of two themes, the history of an institution and the story of a man (as yet, neither the mere mechanics nor the artistic merits of this interweaving of themes has received any marked attention); that it is largely descriptive in its presentation, essayistic in its endless discussions, and ironic in its playful spirit.

In the evaluation of this work, there is a sharp divergence of opinion. As usual there is no dearth of effusive eulogy. For O. Engel there seems to be little doubt that *Glasperlenspiel* is superior to *Wilhelm Meister* in its "innere Verdichtung" (4, p. 28). While noting that the Romanticists were unable to proceed beyond the fragment, A. Carlsson remarks that Hesse creates "ein straff gegliedertes, dreidimensional gebautes Ganzes, dessen Teile sich mit innererNotwendigkeit aneinanderschliessen und den Plan des Dichters bis ins letzte verwirklichen" (345, p. 198). Not to be outdone in abstruse language, L. Freyberger speaks of the novel's "dichterische Lauterkeit und Vollkommenheit . . . etwas Selbstverständliches in sich selbst Beruhendes und Bedingtes" (401, p. 368).

That *Glasperlenspiel* reveals a superior artistry, is refuted by the opposition, more boldly than convincingly. It is in the very perfection of the novel that O. Seidlin detects a flaw: "das Licht ist zu klar, die Luft zu kühl, der Grat zu scharf konturiert" (656, pp. 306-307). (Countering Seidlin, G. Kirchhoff sees in this very criticism but another indication of the plane of absolute, timeless reality that Hesse attains in his novel; 6, pp. 128-129). Perceiving an ineffective manner of fabrication in the loose form of the novel, H. H. Groothoff concludes that it is "nicht in allen Zügen und Partien überzeugend" (422, p. 279). And von Schöfer, in his extremely negative vein, arbitrarily discounts the work as "ein schwaches Buch, ein Buch ohne Energie" (636, p. 608).

The language, like the form of the novel, has occasioned another wide range of appraisals. O. Engel merely maintains that Hesse's language has become epic and its music softer (4, p. 77). L. Freyberger refers to its Goethean clarity and freshness, and to its very poetic quality (401, p. 368). A. Carlsson cannot restrain her enthusiasm: "Sie [die Sprache] hat die Einfachheit einer gesammelten Kraft und Gültigkeit, die nur auf das Wesentliche gerichtet ist, und zugleich das innere Licht, die durchgeistigte Anmut einer letzten poetischen Sublimierung. Ihre stille Selbstverständlichkeit ist die Gussform derselben geläuterten Menschlichkeit, die der Alt-Musikmeister Kastaliens dem jungen Josef Knecht mahnend vor Augen hält" (345, p. 201). W. Kohlschmid insists that the language is that of the pulpit and chancery, a language mannered but without style (489, p. 163). In response to von Schöfer's scoffing, P. Böckmann, acknowledging a stilted academic tone, nevertheless maintains that the language is fully in accord with the substance (324, p. 617).

Those critics who have been disturbed by, or have maligned *Glasperlenspiel* for its clutter of vague descriptions and abstruse allusions (565, pp. 266-268), ought to look up Gottfried Koller's

"Kastalien und China," *Annales Universitatis Saraviensis,* 1 (1952), 5-18. Drawing upon Richard Wilhelm's *I Ging. Das Buch der Wandlung* (1923), Koller shows clearly how those very passages which have proved to be so annoyingly enigmatic—Knecht's sojourn in the bamboo grove, his sober introduction to "Stäbchenzählen," his pious preoccupation with the "Grammatik und Symbolik der Orakelsprache" of *I Ging* with its "vierundsechzig Zeichen," and Knecht's game which, in its structure and dimensions, was to be akin to the old "konfuzianisch rituelle Schema des chinesischen Hausbaus"—are immediately meaningful to the student of sinology. The great extent to which Hesse depends directly upon *I Ging* and not upon playful imagination, is shown by the replies of the oracle (1943, Vol. 1, 200; 231); they are but translations from the Chinese. Koller notes, too, that the game itself, in its idea and technique, in its *Zeichensprache*, is indebted to Chinese writing, just as Hesse himself implies (Vol. 1, 54-55).

Of the many other stray remarks made about the art of *Glasperlenspiel*, W. Kohlschmid's contention that Knecht is a most unconvincing figure, giving no evidence in word or deed of the greatness, the wisdom Hesse would attribute to him, bears investigation (489, p. 217), as does von Faber du Faur's suggestion that Knecht's constant reference to the dangers threatening Castalia serves only to weaken the justification of his departure from the province (385, p. 190). Interesting, too, is von Faber du Faur's conviction that the novel is actually a fragment, that Hesse had originally intended to lead Knecht out into "ein fruchtbares Weltleben"; a balance in the form of the work is thinkable only in such a continuation (385, p. 194). Unfortunately, though he would detect evidence in support of this theory in the *Lebensläufe* and in the poems, von Faber du Faur does not venture to elaborate upon the issue.

Although *Glasperlenspiel* has attracted opinions ranging from effusive eulogy to rank disparagement, what has been done hardly represents more than the first stage of criticism, that of description and generalization. Detailed analysis has scarcely been begun.[51] Of the three divisions into which the novel falls, the *Lebensläufe*, though they merit attention both as independent units and as integral aspects of a whole, have fared worst, by-passed by most critics as though they were appendages of no import.[52] In a closer analysis of these three tales, which show the three stages of life awaiting Knecht, there may lie a better understanding of his philosophy of life and of his departure from Castalia. And though not as pressing, two comparative studies are very inviting, and might prove to be exceedingly revealing: the first and obvious one, of Goethe's *Wilhelm Meister* and *Glasperlenspiel;*[53] and the second, a comparison with Mann's *Dr. Faustus.*[54]

Poetry

Although Hesse's artistic temperament has probably found its freest and most complete expression in his poetry, and though a good portion of this poetry is likely to outlive much of his prose, it is still largely upon his prose that his reputation continues to be based. Until the collected *Gedichte* of 1942, Hesse's verse publications presented a very chaotic picture. Periodically after *Romantische Lieder* (1899), there appeared collections of new poems. There were also slightly revised editions, several small volumes of selected poems, and a confusion of *Einblatt-, Privat-, Sonder-,* and *Gelegenheitsdrucke,* ranging from one to twenty-five pages in length. Except for *Gedichte* (1902), *Musik des Einsamen* (1916), and *Vom Baum des Lebens* (1934), these publications were all rather limited in their circulation, passing out of print after only a few editions.

A relatively complete list of these various collections of verse can be found in the Kliemann/Silomon bibliography (pp. 31-33, 65-66) and its supplement of 1948. Here, too, are listed the first lines of one hundred and fifty-two poems (pp. 162-166) which Hesse did not include in the *Gedichte* of 1942 (see "Nachwort" for Hesse's own comments). Many of these poems appeared in earlier publications, some only in newspapers and periodicals, and eleven were written later than 1942.[55] Included, too, is a very incomplete list of the poems which have been set to music (pp. 67-70), and though mention is also made of those translated into other languages, no list of these is appended.[56]

No thorough critical study of Hesse's poetry has yet been made.[57] In their brief characterization of the earlier poems at the outset of the century, Carl Busse (introduction to the *Gedichte* of 1902) and Alfred Kuhn (*Hermann Hesse. Ein Essay* [1907], pp. 21-25) seem to have established the type of critical analysis which has prevailed, more or less, to the present. We learn that the poems are marked by a simplicity of form, sheer musicality, and an unconcealed subjectivity. The poetry is romantic, revealing moods of fatigue, loneliness, memory, and of grief; it is heavy with fragrance and intense in its yearning and melancholy. Except for giving factual information concerning subsequent collections of poems, most of the books, pamphlets, and articles published since 1907 do little more than re-echo the pronouncements of Busse and Kuhn.[58]

The first critic to venture beyond this sort of general characterization was H. R. Schmid (pp. 27-29, 38-52). He presents a thematic analysis based on such topics as youth, love, death, nature, and wanderlust. Revealing his antipathy for the decadent artist, he regrets that the poems lack vitality, joy, and humor and are filled with laments. Although he concedes that much of this poetry is likely to live on, he does so with reluctance and the remark: "er spielt dieselbe Geige; es ist ein altes Meisterinstrument, das einen verborgenen Sprung hat" (p. 39). Johannes Pfeiffer has expressed a similar sentiment more recently: "Aber so poetisch und so anziehend Hesses Lyrik auch sein mag . . . hat sie etwas unverkennbar Vorläufiges, ja manchmal geradezu Dillettantisches" ("Über die gegenwärtige Situation der deutschen Lyrik," Die Sammlung, 7 [July/August 1952], 293). E. R. Curtius, with much less ado, dismisses Hesse's poetry as "fleissige Reimerei" ("Hermann Hesse," Merkur, 1 [1947], 178). W. Kohlschmid lingers over the "mittelmässige Qualität" of the poems in Glasperlenspiel (Zeitwende, 19 [1947], 218-220).

The descriptive surveys of A. Carlsson ("Zur Gesamtausgabe von Hermann Hesses Gedichten," Neue Schweizer Rundschau, 11 [1943], 109-121) and of H. Bode (pp. 37-72) are eulogistic in tone. Both authors are aware of the gradual stylistic development of Hesse's verse. Carlsson rightly perceives an evolution in the form, cadence, imagery, and atmosphere of the poems. The simple pattern of the folksong yields to a more intricate form. The rhythm changes as it becomes a vehicle for thought rather than for nostalgic feeling. The images evoked become clearer and more plastic. A romantic half light yields to the crystal atmosphere of the Glasperlenspieler. O. Engel has appropriately termed this transformation Hesse's "Weg der Objektivierung, des Reifens, der Entsagung" (pp. 7-15).

Also aware of the change in Hesse's poetry, R. C. Andrews undertakes to characterize what he vaguely terms the earlier and the later poems ("The Poetry of Hermann Hesse," *German Life and Letters*, 7[1953], 117-127). Like most critics, he notes that in the earlier poems Hesse mourns a great deal over his lost childhood, and that nature is a sanctuary for him in his joys and sorrows. However, Andrews does not regard Hesse as an outcast in quest of a *Heimat*, but as an unrepentant hedonist; and his nostalgia, not as that of a romantic observer, but as that of a sensualist. In this early poetry Andrews perceives an unashamed Bacchanalianism and the sour after-taste of satiety. The poem "Nelke" (*Gedichte* [1942], p. 241) is for him the clearest expression of this "apotheosis of physical love and seduction" (p. 120). In a few isolated instances, Andrews' remarks may not be too far-fetched, but beyond that they can hardly be said to apply.

About the form of these earlier poems Andrews makes the usual general remarks. He then goes on to say that Hesse's early poems show an ability to paint word pictures of nature, and he calls attention to Hesse's plastic awareness of color and shape (p. 120). Subsequently, in what approaches self-contradiction, he remarks that Hesse's early poems leave memories of themes rather than of forms, "for form with Hesse is derivative rather than original" (p. 121).

In Hesse's later poems, Andrews sees a curtain of philosophy and mysticism drawn across the Bacchanalianism of his early manhood. In a mystical pantheism, man and nature become one; in a Heraclitean acceptance of life, death loses its fear. After considerable vacillation, *Geist* is finally given precedence over *Natur;* and the miracle of love heals this elemental rift in man. Andrews' argument is more than tenable, but his efforts to establish it are disquieting. As proof of Hesse's new, deeper communion with nature, "Adagio" (*Gedichte*, p. 242) is cited, a poem written before the First World War. "Spruch" (*Gedichte*, p. 168), which appeared about 1908, is proof of Hesse's new mystical pantheism, a confession of faith which seeks to crystallize itself in sensuous imagery, as in "Ländlicher Friedhof" (*Gedichte*, p, 217), also written before 1914. And when Andrews discusses Hesse's new philosophy of eternal recurrence, he refers to "Oktober" (*Gedichte*, p. 187) which again dates back to about 1910. These are not stray oversights. Half of the references supposed to pertain to Hesse's later poetry are pre-1914. Fully two-thirds of the poems cited in his discussion of the earlier works were written after 1914. This persistent disregard for the time factor and the added omission of page references do not enhance a study which deals specifically with an earlier and a later period.

While still other critics have noted the development in Hesse's poetry (Matzig [1947], pp. 111-113; N. Erné, *Deutsche Beiträge*, 1 [1947], 384-386), only one general comparative study of stanza forms, syntax, language, meters, rhyme patterns, and imagery has yet been made (Joseph Mileck, "The Poetry of Hermann Hesse, "*Monatshefte*, 46 [1954], 192-198) ; and no more than a handful of single poems has been subjected to a detailed stylistic analysis ("Blütenzweig," M. Schmid, pp. 17-23; "Leise wie die Gondeln . . ." *Neue Züricher Zeitung*, Feb. 7, 1953; "Ravenna," Werner Weber, *Du. Schweizerische Monatsschrift*, 13 [Feb. 1953], 47-48; "Flötenspiel," Suzanne Debruge, *ibid.*, 48; "Landstreicherherberge," J. F. Angelloz, *ibid.*, 48-49; "Landstreicherherberge," Robert Hippe, *Wirkendes Wort*, 4 (1954), 273-274).[59]

IV

GENERAL INTEREST IN HESSE

More has been written about Hesse since he received the Nobel Prize in 1946 than in all the years preceding. Of the twenty books and dissertations which have been published, twelve have appeared since 1947; and of the forty-two pamphlets, thirty-three postdate 1946. All but two of these items are in German. Twenty-five of the thirty unpublished German doctoral dissertations were accepted after 1946, and of the nine completed *Staatsexamensarbeiten*, not a single one predates 1947. Of the hundreds of articles about Hesse in books, periodicals, and newspapers, the major and certainly the more significant portion again postdates 1946, and again the German language prevails. Articles in other languages represent a small fraction of the total, and of these, about ninety percent follow the Nobel Prize award.

International interest in Hesse is of very recent origin. If translations may be considered a good criterion, then Hesse has found his greatest acclaim in Japan. Some twenty major works have appeared in Japanese since 1950, and of these, many are available in two or even three different translations. Of the twelve major items translated into Spanish, ten have appeared in Argentina, nine of these since 1947. In English-speaking countries, in France, Sweden, Italy, and in Demark, Hesse became a reasonably familiar figure much earlier in his career, though never widely acclaimed. Six of the eleven major English translations were published before 1947. Six of the ten more important French translations, six of the nine Swedish, five of the nine Italian, and all of the eight Danish translations also appeared before 1947. The Dutch, Norwegian, Finnish, Hungarian, Chinese, Greek, Portuguese, and Slavic translations are quite negligible in number.

The articles and the dissertations which have been written about Hesse in other than German speaking countries reflect the same recency of interest. Before 1947, Hesse seems to have attracted little or no attention in England. Since then, a mild interest has been shown by the appearance of five articles and one master's thesis. France's decidedly greater enthusiasm is a pleasant surprise; each of seven dissertations and all but five of twenty-two articles postdate 1946. That only three Japanese studies and no more than nine items in Spanish could be listed in the bibliography, is probably to be attributed more to the inaccessibility of the periodical literature of Japan and South America than to a dearth of scholarly interest. The critical literature in other languages is generally recent and quite inconsequential.

Apart from Germany and Switzerland, no country has shown as much scholarly interest in Hesse as the United States. Here, too, however, he was not really discovered until honored by the Swedish Academy. Of the thirty-seven periodical articles which have appeared in this country, a mere three predate 1946. Seven doctoral dissertations dealing exclusively with Hesse were submitted from 1948 to 1956. Two others, only partially devoted to Hesse, were accepted in 1951. Four of the seven master's theses and two of the four bachelor's theses were completed in 1949-50. Even in the field of textbooks, twelve of the seventeen publications which contain selections by Hesse were printed after 1947.

This present interest in Hesse has not been limited to dissertations, articles, and edited texts. Since 1946, quite a number of speeches have been made across the country. Hesse's life and works were discussed by Richard Jente at the University of North Carolina in 1947. Later the same year, Claude Hill read "Hermann Hesse als Kritiker der bürgerlichen Zivilisation" at the meeting of the Modern Language Association in Detroit. Hermann Barnstorff presented "Hermann Hesse's Conquest of Chaos" at the University of Cincinnati in 1949. In the autumn of 1952, Joseph Mileck read "Hermann Hesse and his Prose" at the annual meeting of the Philological Association of the Pacific Coast. Two papers were presented at the meeting of the Foreign Language Conference of the University of Kentucky in spring of 1953 (Jeanette H. Eilenberg, "Hermann Hesse and the Significance of his Works for Modern American Youth"; Joseph Mileck, "Hermann Hesse and his Poetry"); another two were read in Lexington in 1955 (M. B. Peppard, "Hermann Hesse's Ladder of Learning"; Joseph Mileck, "A Visit with Hermann Hesse"), and one more, in the spring of 1957 (Ruth J. Kilchenmann, "Hesses Stil als Ausdruck seiner Persönlichkeit"). Egon Schwarz presented "Zum 80. Geburtstag Hermann Hesses" at a meeting of the American Association of Teachers of German in Cambridge, 1956; and Ruth J. Kilchenmann is scheduled to present "Hesse als Herausgeber" at the meeting of the same organization in Madison, 1957.

Since 1946, more American universities have begun to include Hesse in their undergraduate literature work. He is inevitably touched upon in the courses in modern German literature, and a few English Departments have added Hesse to their courses in world literature. Hermann Barnstorff of the University of Missouri has managed to stir considerable interest in Hesse among his undergraduates over a number of years. In the summer of 1950, Ernst Rose of New York University devoted a complete undergraduate course to Hesse. Advanced undergraduates of the University of Buffalo have upon occasion centered their attention about Hesse in their tutorial work. An upper division course dealing with Thomas Mann and Hesse has been presented periodically during the summer sessions at the University of California at Berkeley, and a seminar centered about Mann and Hesse was given in the spring of 1956. Hans Jaeger has dealt with Hesse in his graduate courses at the University of Indiana, and in the spring of 1953, H. S. Boeninger included Hesse in his colloquium at Stanford University.

Hesse's favorable reception in America has not been entirely confined to scholarly periodicals and to the classroom. Although frequently quite noncommittal, and not without occasional misgivings and even vituperation (*e.g.*, "Whatever may have been the author's purpose [in *Demian*], he gives us a nightmare of abnormality, a crazed dream of a paranoic." *Boston Transcript*, April 14, 1923), the reviewers of Hesse translations have generally been quite impressed. In 1923, *Demian* was greeted as "an unusual piece of work . . . a book in a hundred" (*New York Times Book Review*, April 8, 1923). *Steppenwolf* made just as favorable an impression: "No review, whatever its length, could ever do justice to this amazing book" (*Bookman*, October, 1929). *Death and the Lover* was described as "An exceptionally rich and satisfying story, one that partakes of the quality of legendry and of the long-sustained melodic spirit of other times" (*Bookman*, January, 1933). *Magister Ludi* was termed "an amorphous, a nearly boundless fantasy. . . . It commands high respect as the confession of one of the most sincere of important authors . . ." (*Saturday Review of Literature*, October 15, 1949). And *Siddhartha* was characterized as "a beautiful little book, classic in proportion and style. It should be read slowly and with savor . . ." (*Nation*, November 17, 1951).

Notwithstanding, unlike Thomas Mann or even Franz Kafka, Hesse has never become a familiar figure in the intellectual circles of America. His reading public has remained a very small one. Even the determined efforts of his publishers to capitalize on the Nobel Prize award were quite fruitless. The new editions of *Steppenwolf* (1947) and of *Demian* (1948) have sold very poorly. *Magister Ludi* (1949), *Siddhartha* (1951), and *Gertrude* (1955) have fared little better. Immersed as he is in the romantic tradition of Novalis, a tradition which is neither understood nor appreciated by the American, Hesse is not likely to attract many readers here except for a few kindred spirits in our university circles, and for the German speaking intellectuals who have emigrated to America in the past two decades. Hesse is himself convinced that America will never prove receptive to his works (*Briefe,* pp. 358-359; *Beschwörungen,* pp. 98-99).

Part Three

BIBLIOGRAPHY

I

HESSE ARCHIVES IN EUROPE

Until the university libraries of Germany recover from the disastrous effects of the last World War, American Germanists undertaking longer and more thorough studies of Hesse might more profitably pursue their work at our own major institutions. Few, if any German universities have Hesse collections comparable to those at Harvard, Yale, New York, or at the University of California in Berkeley. Even when these German collections are fairly adequate, the materials are consistently so inaccessible and the library facilities so overtaxed, that reasonably unhampered research is impossible. However, incomparably more adequate than the best of these American and German university collections are the private archives which have sprung up in Germany and Switzerland. Only these continue to make travel abroad imperative.

Foremost of the private Hesse collections in Germany to which there is ready access is that of *Mittelschullehrer* Erich Weiss, the *Westdeutsches Hermann Hesse-Archiv* in Cologne (Unkeler Strasse 12, Köln-Klettenberg). Thanks to the prodigious effort of an enthusiastic and systematic collector, these archives have become the center of Hesse studies in Europe. Two or three dissertations and a number of lesser projects are completed here yearly, and to those unable to visit Cologne, material is mailed upon request.

Although established as recently as 1947, this collection leaves surprisingly little to be desired. Hesse's own works are well represented: his books, and many in their various editions, material published in books other than his own, books edited and prefaced by him, special and private publications, and items published in periodicals and in newspapers. The periodicals with which Hesse was once closely associated and in which he published most of his book reviews are less adequately represented. *März* is complete from 1907 to 1912, *Die Rheinlande* from 1904 to 1908, *Simplicissimus* from 1905 to 1922, and *Propyläen* (*Beilage zur Münchener Zeitung*) from 1903 to 1916. The *Neue Rundschau*, to which Hesse contributed regularly from 1910 to 1936, is very incomplete, and *Vivos Voco* (1919-1923) and *Deutsche Internierten-Zeitung* (1916-1917) both edited by Hesse among others, are not represented at all.

In addition to this printed material, the archives include many photographs of Hesse, his family, and his friends, a good sampling of his water colors, his letters to Weiss; a number of painted portraits, the latest bronze bust by Wilhelm Hager, and an extensive collection of scores (Hesse's poems set to music). Though far less complete than his collection of Hesse's own works, Weiss's accumulation of critical material is unusually extensive. No more than a dozen of the sixty-three books, pamphlets, and printed dissertations about Hesse are missing. As many as one quarter of the many articles published in books, periodicals, and in newspapers have been brought together. Almost one half of the unpublished German dissertations and *Staatsexamensarbeiten*, many seminar papers, a few unpublished speeches, and Ludwig Finckh's yet unpublished recollections of his early Gaienhofen days with Hesse, have found their way to Cologne.

Weiss's archives are systematically arranged and almost completely catalogued (about 2500 items). His bibliography of the poems which have been set to music already includes the names of more than three hundred composers. A bibliography of book reviews by Hesse is in progress, and ultimately Weiss intends to publish a bibliography embracing both Hesse's works and the literature about him.

The rather inaccessible Hesse collection of Horst Kliemann (Elisabethstrasse 8/III, München), business manager of *Oldenbourg Verlag* and bibliographer par excellence, is probably at least as extensive as that of Weiss. Not only are both Hesse's works and those of his critics well classified, but very useful compilations have been undertaken by Kliemann: a list of the first lines of Hesse's prose and poetry, a list of the books he has reviewed, of the periodicals to which he has contributed, of scores, of translations, of the illustrations in his books, and of dissertations; an index of places and of names, actual and fictitious, in Hesse's prose, and another of the people to whom he has dedicated works; a collection of Hesse's unpublished poetry and prose, of his water colors, of letters by him and others written to him, of photographs, portraits, and of unpublished critical material. Kliemann envisages, just as does Weiss, a sort of definitive Hesse bibliography.

Like Kliemann, Georg Alter has been a Hesse collector for more than three decades and has amassed a profusion of material (Kegelbahnstrasse 13, Oberhilbersheim, Rheinhessen). Unfortunately, never having considered his pastime of any but personal value, Alter has never seriously attempted to organize his accumulations. His collection of separate publications is very respectable. There are items among his private publications which have become quite scarce, and his letters from Hesse have accumulated with the passing of the years. However, much more important than this assortment are Alter's twenty haphazardly compiled *Sammelbände*. These represent a valuable, though poorly documented, confusion of material both by and about Hesse. Many of the older periodical and newspaper articles are found here and nowhere else.

Eleonore Vondenhoff, wife of the conductor of the symphony orchestra of Frankfurt am Main, did not begin her Hesseana until 1947 (Fontanestrasse 27, Frankfurt a.M.). Her collection, catalogued in its entirety and in great detail, already numbers more than 3500 items. All of Hesse's works published in book form are represented, many first editions, and most private and special publications. More significant are the hundreds of stray articles and book reviews published by Hesse in a multitude of different newspapers and periodicals, scarce items which have never appeared in books and have received little notice by scholars. Like Kliemann, in an effort to resolve the confusion occasioned by Hesse's habit of publishing many of his minor works under different titles, Eleonore Vondenhoff has compiled a very comprehensive catalogue of first lines together with their various titles. Her list of the authors and books discussed by Hesse in his book reviews can be just as helpful; and her assortment of photographs, of water colors and of numerous letters from Hesse, is an enviable one. It is only in its literature about Hesse that this collection in Frankfurt am Main does not rank with the best. Unfortunately, it is almost impossible for a stranger without a proper introduction to gain access to these archives.

There are only two collections of any consequence in Hesse's native Württemberg: that of the bibliophile Reinhold Pfau (Klopstockstrasse 53, Stuttgart W.), which is an accumulation similar to Alter's, and that of the *Schiller Nationalmuseum* in Marbach. Characteristically, those of Hesse's works that have been published in book form are well represented in Marbach, special publications less so, and periodical and newspaper articles least. Of the vast amount of critical material centered about

Hesse, Marbach has very little to show beyond the most readily available items. Its miscellany, however, is quite significant: five manuscripts by Hesse,[1] Carl Busse's manuscript of *Gedichte*, 1902, twelve poems typed and illustrated with water colors and pen sketches, another eleven only typed, thirteen poems hand-written, some one hundred and ninety typed or written letters and postcards by Hesse, a few letters and a collection of poems addressed or dedicated to Hesse, and a copy of the bust by Hager. Though stored away unsorted, all of this material, with the exception of the letters, is quite accessible.

Although this collection in Marbach is not at the present comparable to any of the first four collections discussed, it promises to become eventually the most significant Hesseana. The libraries of Alter and of Pfau will almost certainly be left to Marbach, and there is a very strong possibility that at least goodly portions of the others will also end there.[2] Lesser collectors in Württemberg and Baden traditionally leave their accumulations to the museum, and Marbach will undoubtedly inherit much of the intimate miscellany of Hesse's old Swabian acquaintances and of his remaining Swabian relatives (*e.g.*, the Gunderts in Kornthal and in Stuttgart). *Bundespräsident* Theodor Heuss, who began his long exchange of letters with Hesse as a literary critic in 1910, has intimated that this correspondence will also eventually go to Marbach. When asked how they intended to dispose of their many and significant letters from Hesse, Ludwig Finckh of Gaienhofen, Hesse's most intimate companion for more than a decade at the turn of the century, and Julia Hellmann of Möckmühl an der Jagst, Hesse's love of 1899, the beautiful Lulu of *Hermann Lauscher*, both remarked that everything would be left to Marbach. Though more noncommittal in his reply to the same question, Ernst Rheinwald, local historian in Calw and a very old friend of Hesse, can almost certainly be expected to dispose in like manner of his vast amount of unpublished material about Hesse's family background and his accumulation of letters from Hesse. Unfortunately, however, a large portion of Hesse's private correspondence, particularly that with his relatives, may never come to light. Much of it, like the hundreds of letters to his late sister Adele Gundert, will be returned to Montagnola, there, more likely than not, to be destroyed.

Unlike the private collections in Germany, those in Switzerland, Hesse's home since 1912, proved quite inaccessible for pur-

poses of research. But for the Hesseana of Armin Lemp (Clau-
siusstrasse 54, Zürich), bookdealer and Hesse bibliographer, all
of the significant collections seem to have been made by intimate
friends of the author. Most of Hesse's publications, many of
his manuscripts, large accumulations of water colors, photographs, letters, and miscellaneous personal items are undoubtedly to be found in the collections of his companion *Morgenlandfahrer*: Otto Basler of Burg in Aargau, Max Wassmer, owner of
the *Schloss* in Bremgarten, the rendezvous of the *Morgenlandfahrer*, and Hans C. Bodmer, Hesse's old friend and wealthy
patron of Zürich. Much significant material is very likely to be
found in the collections of the painters Cuno Amiet (Ochswand),
Gunter Böhmer (Montagnola), and of Ernst Morgentaler, of the
composer Othmar Schoeck (Zürich), of the publisher William
Matheson of *Olten, Verlag*, and particularly in those of Hesse's
three sons, Martin (Bern), Heiner (Zürich) and Bruno.

Just as most of the private collections in Germany will ultimately find their way to Marbach, many of these Swiss collections are likely to end in the *Landesbibliothek* in Bern, which
already has a respectable Hesseana. Hesse, himself, has already
deposited here many of the countless letters received from his
readers. However, most of the material of an intimate nature,
letters in particular, will undoubtedly gradually find its way back
to Hesse, to his wife, or to his sons, and either be burned or
made inaccessible for years to come. Dr. J. B. Lang's medical
record of Hesse's psychoanalysis is an example of this kind.

II

HESSE BIBLIOGRAPHIES

Earliest of the many and diverse bibliographical studies which deal with Hesse is Ernst Metelmann's "Hermann Hesse," *Die Schöne Literatur*, 28 (1927), 299-312. In the first section, Metelmann lists Hesse's books and pamphlets and a few of the books to which Hesse has contributed. Bibliographical details are adequate, and even translations into foreign tongues are noted. Part 2 consists of sixty-six periodical items not found in the preceding section; Part 3 adds fifty-five articles which appeared in periodicals and in newspapers; and Part 4 lists the books and the periodicals edited by Hesse himself. The last three sections deal with the literature about Hesse: a brief list of books and articles in books (thirteen items), one hundred and twenty-six periodical items (primarily reviews), and a selected list of seventy-six newspaper articles (again primarily reviews). Page references are carefully included in all but newspaper articles. Metelmann's work continues to be of considerable aid; it is still the major reference work for periodical and newspaper articles about Hesse up to 1927.

The bibliography which Hans R. Schmid included in his book, *Hermann Hesse* (1928), pp. 205-214, is loosely patterned after that of Metelmann. The first three sections, devoted to Hesse's own works, are not only less comprehensive than those of Metelmann, but also add little that is new. Of Schmid's selected list of Hesse's tales published in periodicals (twenty-nine), thirteen are not mentioned by Metelmann. Of his brief list of Hesse's articles published in periodicals and in newspapers (twelve), only two were overlooked by Metelmann. Schmid's collection of critical literature is again less extensive than Metelmann's. He mentions one book about Hesse and three others touching in part upon Hesse, which Metelmann does not list. He lists some thirty periodical and newspaper articles, twenty of which are again not found in Metelmann. A particular weakness of Schmid's bibliography is his failure to note the number of pages in the books both by and about Hesse, his omission of all page references when dealing with periodicals, and his careless treatment of newspapers and their dates.

Armin Lemp, in his bibliographical appendage to Max Schmid's work, *Hermann Hesse* (1947), pp. 243-288, is concerned almost exclusively with Hesse's book publications. A few books with introductions by Hesse, and a small number of his brief private publications seem to have been slipped in rather inadvertently. Lemp's list of yearly publications from 1899 to 1946 is presented with the detail of a bibliophile. Each item is thoroughly described, the table of contents of every volume of collected works is included, cross references are numerous and exceedingly helpful, and the many interpolated remarks about Hesse's career are very pertinent. Unfortunately Lemp's work was to remain a fragment; the more inclusive bibliography embracing works both by and about Hesse which he had envisaged was never compiled. Lemp chose, instead, to place his material at the disposal of Horst Kliemann, Hesse's major bibliographer.

As early as 1937, and then again in 1942, Kliemann was prepared to publish a Hesse bibliography. The times, however, were not auspicious, and it was not until 1947 that his various compilations finally began to appear in print.

The first two of these, though minor in their scope and thoroughness and hardly intended to be more than advance notice for a more comprehensive bibliography, continue nevertheless to be quite useful. The classified bibliography appended to Kliemann's "Hermann Hesse und das Buch" (*Deutsche Beiträge*, 1 [1947], 353-360), is particularly helpful. Part 1 lists forty items (in books, periodicals and newspapers) in which Hesse dwells upon writers and their profession, upon books, and upon readers. Twenty-eight of these references are not in Metelmann. Part 2 draws attention to fifteen poems in which Hesse deals with writers and their art. Part 3 comprises thirty articles (in books, periodicals and newspapers) by Hesse about specific writers. Of these only nine are found in Metelmann. Part 4 lists twenty-seven books edited by Hesse, eleven of which fail to appear in Metelmann. Kliemann's consistent omission of page references is an unfortunate oversight.

Kliemann's "Das Werk Hermann Hesses. Eine bibliographische Übersicht" (*Europa-Archiv*, 1 [1947], 604-609), represents the first real attempt to complement Metelmann's work in all its aspects. In Part 1, Hesse's book, pamphlet, and private publications are brought up to date, with attention given only to first editions. Part 2 again lists the books edited by Hesse (see previous bibliography), adding seventeen others with prefaces, or concluding remarks by him. Part 3 lists twenty-one other books with prose passages by Hesse, and Part 4 consists of ninety periodical and newspaper items, of which only one-third are mentioned by Metelmann. Part 5 represents a carelessly assembled potpourri of books, pamphlets, printed and unpublished dissertations. Some are entirely about Hesse or his *Umwelt*; others contain relevant passages, and a few have only casual references to Hesse. Only three of these twenty-two items are listed by Metelmann. Part 6 adds seventeen more books with articles about or references to Hesse, of which only five are found in Metelmann, and Part 7 comprises fifty-one periodical and newspaper articles, of which more than half are listed for the first time. Kliemann's concluding section presents a very incomplete list of translations into foreign tongues and into Braille. Again, but for Part 1, page references are only rarely included.

With the assistance of Karl H. Silomon, a fellow collector of Hesseana, Kliemann was able to publish his major opus soon after these preliminary compilations (*Hermann Hesse. Eine bibliographische Studie* [1947], 95 pp.). Section A, Part 1 (one hundred and nine items), devoted principally to Hesse's books, brochures, and private publications, an occasional foreign textbook, translations, and a few off-prints, is a bibliophile's delight. It surpasses even Lemp's excellent study in the detail and reliability of its information. Part 2 consists of a unique list of twenty-two *Einblatt- und Gelegenheitsdrucke*. Section B presents a very comprehensive and most thoroughly annotated list of books edited and prefaced, prefaced only, or with only a conclusion by Hesse (seventy-four items). Section C lists twenty-five other books with prose contributions by Hesse. All but four of these are listed in Part 3 of the bibliography in *Europa-Archiv*. Section D, dealing with literature about Hesse, is decidedly less adequate than the preceding sections. Part 1 (twenty-six items) is the same unsifted miscellany of books, pamphlets, printed and unpublished dissertations found in Part 5 of the bibliography in *Europa-Archiv*, except for four new items, three of which are periodical articles and should not have been listed in this category. Part 2 adds forty-three more books (primarily histories and lexicons of literature) with articles about Hesse or pertinent references to him. Page references neglected in Kliemann's previous studies are now almost always included.

The final three sections of the bibliography, Silomon's work, though somewhat divergent, are decidedly worthwhile additions. In Section E, Silomon lists by their first lines one hundred and fifty-two poems not published in *Gedichte* (1942). In F, he gives a very incomplete list of the Hesse poems set to music. G represents an equally limited list of books, pamphlets, and periodicals with water colors by Hesse.

That numerous errors should find their way into a bibliography of this magnitude and detail, was inevitable. In the *Verbesserungen und Ergänzungen* (1948), 12 pp., a goodly portion of these are corrected, and the work in sections A to D is supplemented by eighty additional items. However, the principal deficiency of Kliemann's otherwise indispensable bibliography continues; no attention is given either to works by or about Hesse in periodicals and in newspapers. But this too, among other weaknesses, Kliemann hoped to remedy in due time. In his "Bermerkungen zu einer Hesse-Bibliographie" (*Deutsche Beiträge*, 1 [1947], 381-384) he mentions a bibliography to be undertaken with the help of Dr. Hans-Joachim Bock "die zunächst alle Prosastücke in allen Abdrucksformen nach Überschriften und Textanfängen enthält und auch die noch fehlenden Abteilungen (Vertonungen, Verzeichnis der Buchbesprechungen Hesses, das malerische Werk Hesses, die Übersetzungen, das Echo im Ausland, die Illustration der Werke usw.) bringt. Erst dann wäre, damit zum ersten Male für einen modernen Dichter, die gesamte Breiten- und Tiefenwirkung seines Werkes erfasst," and in the preface of his *Verbesserungen* he remarks, "auch die Literatur über Hesse soll später zusammen mit weiteren Sonderthemen bibliographisch bearbeitet werden." Unfortunately, no further word has been heard of these intended supplements, and Kliemann's only somewhat related work since 1948, is his "Gliederung des Hesse-Archivs" (*Das Antiquariat*, 7 [1951], 43-44), a description of his own Hesseana.

Three more minor bibliographical studies were published in 1952. That of Klaus W. Jonas ("Hermann Hesse in Amerika. Bibliographie," *Monatshefte*, 44 [1952], 95-99), though far from exhaustive, presents a clear picture of Hesse's rather belated and mild reception in the United States. Section A lists nineteen translations into English published in the United States. Section B gives a yearly account of the works about Hesse in American publications, and in the *Neue Rundschau* by Germans living in America. Page references are not neglected. Almost half of the fifty-three items in Section B are reviews which have appeared in weeklies and newspapers. A few are private publications, two are unpublished doctoral dissertations, and the rest are articles in books and periodicals. To this, Jonas has added eight textbooks with selections by, and remarks about Hesse. His "Additions to the Bibliography of Hermann Hesse" (*Papers of the Bibliographical Society of America*, 49 [1955], 358-360), lists twelve new titles.

Martin Pfeifer's study (*Bibliographie der im Gebiet der DDR seit 1945 erschienenen Schriften von und über Hermann Hesse* [1952], 15 pp.) affords a similar picture of Hesse's reception in East Germany. Part 1 lists four books by Hesse; Parts 2 and 3, twenty-two items (books, periodicals, newspapers) with prose selections or poems by Hesse. Part 4 adds one book edited by him. Only one book about Hesse is listed in Part 5 and seven unpublished items (speeches, student papers, and dissertations) are found in Part 6. Twenty-six articles in books, periodicals, and newspapers are gathered in Part 7. Fifty-three other items with pertinent references to Hesse are given in Part 8. Parts 9-12 are rather tangential. They consist of reviews of five books about Hesse not published in East Germany, announcements and public programs dealing with Hesse (nine items), nine photographs of Hesse in various publications, and twenty poems set to music. Detailed and accurate information is given for each reference.

Continuing his compilation, Pfeifer published a greatly supplemented edition of his bibliography in 1955 (63 pp.). Two hundred and seventy-eight new items were added to the one hundred and fifty-one of the original edition. Many of these additions predate 1952; most of them, however, fall into the period from May 1952 to April 1955. Except for a slight change in the numbering, and the dropping of Part 10, this second edition continues the major divisions of the first. The separation of the articles about Hesse and articles in which Hesse is merely mentioned (Parts 5 and 6) into those appearing in books and those appearing in periodicals and newspapers, is a decided improvement upon the former confused mixture. It is in these two parts that most of Pfeifer's new items are listed.

Siegfried Unseld's bibliography, if such indeed it may be termed (*Das Werk von Hermann Hesse. Ein Brevier* [1952], 72 pp.), is in fact, a descriptive trade catalogue published by Suhrkamp upon the occasion of Hesse's seventy-fifth birthday. It is a compilation limited to Hesse's major book publications and is completely dependent upon the studies of Lemp and Kliemann. Much more important than Unseld's list of titles are the copious annotations in which he delves into the genesis of each item and presents a very informative running commentary on Hesse's life. Alternate pages bear apt quotations from Hesse's *Briefe* (1951).

A new edition of Unseld's study was published in 1955 (80 pp.). However, except for the addition of Hesse's recent major publications (*Piktors Verwandlungen*, 1954; *Beschwörungen*, 1955) and a few more excerpts from his *Briefe*, the two editions are identical.

BIBLIOGRAPHY

BIBLIOGRAPHY

The following represents the most comprehensive Hesse bibliography to date (June, 1957). Thirty percent of it is found scattered about in the nine studies discussed above; the rest has never been listed before. Since this was meant to be a scholar's, not a bibliophile's bibliography, only those details pertinent to scholarly research were incorporated. Except where otherwise indicated, every section was meant to be as complete as possible.

Abbreviations:
NR	Neue Rundschau
NSR	Neue Schweizer Rundschau
SRL	Saturday Review of Literature
NYT	New York Times
NYHT	New York Herald Tribune

WORKS BY HESSE

Until 1924, Hesse's books were published by various houses, of which the S. Fischer Verlag in Berlin was the most important. In 1925, S. Fischer began the *Gesammelte Werke in Einzelausgaben,* the familiar blue cover series which was interrupted under Nazi pressure, in 1938, after some twenty-two volumes had been published. The *Schweizerische Gesamt-Ausgabe,* intended to be a continuation of Fischer's work, and which now numbers more than a dozen volumes, was begun by Fretz & Wasmuth of Zürich in 1942. Since 1946, the Suhrkamp Verlag of Berlin and later also of Frankfurt am Main (formerly S. Fischer Verlag) has been supplementing the *Gesammelte Werke in Einzelausgaben.* In 1952, it published the *Gesammelte Dichtungen* in six volumes. In 1957, this edition was augmented by a seventh volume and appeared under the title *Gesammelte Schriften.* Not one of these sets is adequate by itself; all suffer major omissions. A reasonably complete, scholarly edition has yet to be prepared.

BOOKS AND PAMPHLETS, including important private publications. For an extensive list of *Einblatt-* and *Gelegenheitsdrucke,* see the Kliemann/Silomon bibliography pp. 31-33.

1 *Romantische Lieder* (Dresden, 1899), 44 pp.

2 *Eine Stunde hinter Mitternacht* (Leipzig, 1899), 84 pp. Published again in Zürich, 1941 (141 pp.), with a significant foreword by Hesse. Nine vignettes, written 1897-99.

3 *Hinterlassene Schriften und Gedichte von Hermann Lauscher* (Basel, 1901), 83 pp. Supplemented edition published in Düsseldorf, 1907, 189 pp. A miscellany of six items, written 1896-1901.

4 *Gedichte* (Berlin, 1902), 196 pp.

5 *Boccaccio* (Berlin, 1904), 75 pp. A monograph.

6 *Franz von Assisi* (Berlin, 1904), 84 pp. A monograph.

7 *Peter Camenzind* (Berlin, 1904), 260 pp.

8 *Unterm Rad* (Berlin, 1906), 294 pp.

9 *Diesseits* (Berlin, 1907), 308 pp. Five tales. The new edition, Zürich, 1930, 391 pp., was supplemented by "Schön ist die Jugend" and "Zyklon" from *Schön ist die Jugend,* and by "In der alten Sonne" from *Nachbarn.* All tales but "Aus Kinderzeiten" and "Eine Fussreise" were revised by Hesse 1928-30.

10 *Nachbarn* (Berlin, 1908), 317 pp. Five tales. "Karl Eugen Eiselein" was omitted after the 5th edition.

11 *Faust und Zarathustra* (Vortrag gehalten in der Bremer Ortsgruppe des Deutschen Monisten-Bundes, am 1. Mai 1909, Bremer Verlag von Otto Melchers), 32 pp.

12 *Gertrud* (Berlin, 1910), 301 pp.

13 *Unterwegs* (München, 1911), 58 pp. Poems. A supplemented edition was published in 1915, 111 pp.

14 *Umwege* (Berlin, 1912), 309 pp. Five tales.

15 *Aus Indien* (Berlin, 1913), 198 pp. Notes and Poems written during Hesse's trip to the East, and the *Novelle,* "Robert Aghion." See 44.

16 *Anton Schievelbeyns Ohnfreiwillige Reisse Nachher Ostindien* (München, 1914), 15 pp. See 62.

17 *Rosshalde* (Berlin, 1914), 304 pp.

18 *Am Weg* (Konstanz, 1915), 87 pp. A miscellany of eight items, written 1903-14.

19 *Knulp. Drei Geschichten aus dem Leben Knulps* (Berlin, 1915), 146 pp.

20 *Musik des Einsamen* (Heilbronn, 1915), 84 pp. Poems.

21 *Zum Sieg* (Stuttgart: Die farbigen Heftchen der Waldorf-Astoria, No. 3, about 1915), 16 pp.

22 *Hans Dierlamms Lehrzeit* (Berlin, 1916), 23 pp. A tale.

23 *Lektüre für Kriegsgefangene* (Bern, 1916), 7 pp.

24 *Schön ist die Jugend* (Berlin, 1916), 118 pp. Two tales.

25 *Alte Geschichten* (Bern, 1918), 55 pp. Two tales. See 62.

26 *Zwei Märchen* (Bern, 1918), 52 pp. See 29.

27 *Demian. Die Geschichte einer Jugend.* Von Emil Sinclair (Berlin, 1919), 256 pp.

28 *Kleiner Garten. Erlebnisse und Dichtungen* (Wien, 1919), 142 pp. A miscellany of eighteen items. See 44, 48, 54, 62, 76.

29 *Märchen* (Berlin, 1919), 182 pp. Seven tales. Supplemented in 1955 by "Flötentraum" ("Märchen," *Am Weg*), and "Piktors Verwandlungen" (1922).

30 *Zarathustras Wiederkehr. Ein Wort an die deutsche Jugend* (Bern, 1919), 43 pp. See 82.

31 *Blick ins Chaos.* Drei Aufsätze (Bern, 1920), 43 pp. See 48.

32 *Gedichte des Malers.* Zehn Gedichte mit farbigen Zeichnungen (Bern, 1920), 23 pp.

33 *Im Pressel'schen Gartenhaus* (Dresden, 1920), 22 pp. See 62.

34 *Klingsors letzter Sommer* (Berlin, 1920), 215 pp. Three tales.

35 *Wanderung.* Aufzeichnungen mit farbigen Bildern vom Verfasser (Berlin, 1920), 117 pp.

36 *Ausgewählte Gedichte* (Berlin, 1921), 82 pp.

37 *Elf Aquarelle aus dem Tessin* (München, 1921).

38 *Siddhartha. Eine Indische Dichtung* (Berlin, 1922), 147 pp.

39 *Italien* (Berlin, 1923), 23 pp. Poems.

40 *Die Offizina Bodoni in Montagnola* (Hellerau, 1923), 16 pp. First appeared in *Neue Züricher Ztg.*, Nov. 4, 1923.

41 *Sinclairs Notizbuch* (Berlin, 1923), 109 pp. A miscellany of twelve items, written 1917-20. See 27, 48, 82.

42 *Kurgast. Aufzeichnungen von einer Badener Kur* (Berlin, 1925), 160 pp. A private printing appeared in 1924 under the title: *Psychologia Balnearia oder Glossen eines Badener Kurgastes.* (Montagnola), 135 pp.

43 *Piktors Verwandlungen.* Ein Märchen (Chemnitz, 1925), 18 pp. (without illustrations). Of the many handwritten and illustrated copies of this tale, especially prepared by Hesse upon request, the copy given to "einer lieben Frau" in 1922 was published by Suhrkamp in 1954.

44 *Bilderbuch.* Schilderungen (Berlin, 1926), 320 pp. Fifty-three items, written 1901-24.

45 *Die Nürnberger Reise* (Berlin, 1927), 124 pp.

46 *Der Steppenwolf* (Berlin, 1927), 289 pp.

47 *Verse im Krankenbett* (Bern, 1927), 20 pp.

48 *Betrachtungen* (Berlin, 1928), 333 pp. A miscellany of forty-seven items, written 1904-27.

49 *Krisis.* Ein Stück Tagebuch (Berlin, 1928), 85 pp. Poems.

50 *Eine Bibliothek der Weltliteratur* (Leipzig, 1929), 85 pp. This edition was supplemented in 1946 (Zürich, 95 pp.) by the addition of "Magie des Buches" (first appeared in 1921), pp. 68-85, and "Lieblingslektüre" (1945), pp. 89-95.

51 *Trost der Nacht.* Neue Gedichte (Berlin, 1929), 192 pp.

52 *Der Zyklon und andere Erzählungen* (Berlin, 1929), 86 pp. Three tales. See 24, 29, 34.

53 *Narziss und Goldmund* (Berlin, 1930), 417 pp.

54 *Zum Gedächtnis unseres Vaters.* Von Hermann und Adele Hesse (Tübingen, 1930), 85 pp.

55 *Jahreszeiten.* Zehn Gedichte mit Bildern von Hesse (Zürich, 1931), 41 pp.

56 *Weg nach Innen.* Vier Erzählungen (Berlin, 1931), 433 pp. See 34, 38.

57 *Hermann Hesse* (Auszüge), ed. Alfred Simon (München, 1932), 32 pp. (Deutsches Schrifttum, Deutsche Akademie in München).

58 *Die Morgenlandfahrt* (Berlin, 1932), 113 pp.

59 *Kleine Welt..* Erzählungen (Berlin, 1933), 380 pp. Seven revised tales from *Nachbarn, Umwege,* and *Aus Indien.*

60 *Mahnung. Erzählungen und Gedichte* (Gotha, 1933), 58 pp.

61 *Vom Baum des Lebens,* Ausgewählte Gedichte (Leipzig, 1934), 79 pp.

62 *Fabulierbuch.* Erzählungen (Berlin, 1935), 341 pp. Twenty-three items, written 1907-27.

63 *Das Haus der Träume.* Eine unvollendete Dichtung; begun in 1914 (Olten, 1936), 85 pp. (*Der schwäbische Bund,* 2 [Nov. 1920]).

64 *Stunden im Garten.* Eine Idylle (Wien, 1936), 63 pp. See 113.

65 *Gedenkblätter* (Berlin, 1937), 272 pp. A supplemented edition was published in Zürich, 1947, 317 pp. Seventeen items, written 1902-45.

66 *Neue Gedichte* (Berlin, 1937), 98 pp.

67 *Der Novalis. Aus den Papieren eines Altmodischen* (Olten, 1940), 59 pp. Written about 1900, first published in *März* 1 [1907]. See 89.

68 *Kleine Betrachtungen.* Sechs Aufsätze (Bern, 1941), 37 pp. Written 1928-33.

69 *Die Gedichte* (Zürich, 1942), 448 pp. An edition supplemented by eleven later poems was published in Zürich, 1947.

70 *Das Glasperlenspiel. Versuch einer Lebensbeschreibung des Magisters Ludi Josef Knecht, samt Knechts hinterlassenen Schriften* (Zürich, 1943); Vol. 1, 452 pp.; Vol. 2, 442 pp.

71 *Zwischen Sommer und Herbst* (Montagnola, 1944), 9 pp. Written 1929. See 68.

72 *Berthold.* Ein Romanfragment (Zürich, 1945), 100 pp. Written in Gaienhofen, 1907-08.

73 *Der Blütenzweig.* Eine Auswahl aus den Gedichten (Zürich, 1945), 80 pp.

74 *Der Pfirsichbaum und andere Erzählungen* (Zürich, 1945), 48 pp. Five items, written 1926-45.

75 *Rigi-Tagebuch* (Bern, 1945), 24 pp. See 82, 106.

76 *Traumfährte.* Neue Erzählungen und Märchen (Zürich, 1945), 244 pp. Twelve items, written 1910-32.

77 *Zwei Aufsätze:* Über Gedichte," "Über einen Teppich" (Montagnola, 1945), 12 pp. See 48, 297.

78 *Dank an Goethe* (Zürich, 1946), 94 pp. Four essays about Goethe, written 1911-32.

79 *Danksagung und moralisierende Betrachtung* (Montagnola, 1946), 8 pp. See 82.

80 *Der Europäer* (Berlin, 1946), 73 pp. Five essays, written 1918-45. See 82, 106.

81 *Feuerwerk* (Olten, 1946), 19 pp. An essay written in 1930.

82 *Krieg und Frieden. Betrachtungen zu Krieg und Politik seit dem Jahre 1914* (Zürich, 1946), 265 pp. A supplemented edition was published in Berlin, 1949, 230 pp. Twenty-nine essays, written 1914-48.

83 *Statt eines Briefes* (Montagnola, 1946), 4 pp.

84 *Geheimnisse* (Zürich, 1947), 23 pp. See 120.

85 *Haus zum Frieden. Aufzeichnungen eines Herrn im Sanatorium* (Zürich, 1947), 35 pp. Written in 1910. Also in *American-German Review*, Oct.-Nov., 1956.

86 *Eine Konzertpause* (1947), 16 pp. (a reprint of article which had appeared in the *Neue Züricher Ztg.*). See 302.

87 *Stufen der Menschwerdung* (Olten, 1947), 29 pp. ("Ein Stückchen Theologie"). See 291.

88 *Berg und See.* Zwei Landschaftsstudien (Zürich, 1948), 51 pp.

89 *Frühe Prosa* (Zürich, 1948), 303 pp. See 2, 3, 67.

90 *Die Stimmen und der Heilige. Ein Stück Tagebuch,* 1918 (Montagnola, 1948), 15 pp. Appeared as "Ein Stück Tagebuch," in *Betrachtungen* (1928).

91 *Aus vielen Jahren.* Gedichte, Erzählungen und Bilder (Bern, 1949), 129 pp.

92 *Begegnungen mit Vergangenem* (Montagnola, 1949), 3 pp.

93 *Freunde.* Eine Erzählung, 1908-09 (Montagnola, 1949), 31 pp. See 226.

94 *Glück* (St. Gallen, 1949), 29 pp. See 106.

95 *Hermann Hesse. Alle Bücher dieser Welt,* ed. Karl H. Silomon (Murnau, 1949), 80 pp. A wide range of excerpts in which Hesse touches upon writers and books.

96 *Hermann Hesse. Gerbersau,* eds. Ernst Rheinwald, Otto Hartmann (Tübingen, Stuttgart, 1949); Vol. 1, 409 pp.; Vol. 2, 430 pp. Primarily a collection of early tales centered about Hesse's Swabia.

97 *Wege zu Hermann Hesse. Eine Auswahl,* ed. Walter Haussmann (Stuttgart, 1949), 88 pp.

98 *Aus dem Tagebuch eines Entgleisten* (1950), 4 pp.

99 *Jugendgedichte* (Hamm, 1950), 187 pp.

100 *Magie des Buches* (Frankfurt am Main, 1950), 20 pp. See 50.

101 *Aus einem Notizbuch* (St. Gallen, 1951), 5 pp.

102 *Bericht aus Normalien. Ein Fragment aus dem Jahre 1948* (Montagnola, 1951), 24 pp. See 120.

103 *Briefe* (Berlin, 1951), 431 pp. The edition of 1954 includes a *Nachwort* by Hesse, pp. 433-434.

104 *Erinnerung an André Gide* (St. Gallen, 1951), 23 pp.

105 *Eine Handvoll Briefe* (Zürich, 1951), 60 pp. See 103.

106 *Späte Prosa* (Berlin, 1951), 194 pp. Eleven items, written 1944-50.

107 *Die Verlobung und andere Erzählungen* (Berlin, Darmstadt, 1951), 299 pp. See 59.

108 *Glück* (Wien, 1952), 143 pp. All eleven items included appear in previous publications. See 29, 44, 48, 62, 63, 76, 106.

109 *Grossväterliches* (St. Gallen, 1952), 15 pp. See 120.

110 *Herbstliche Erlebnisse. Gedenkblatt für Otto Hartmann* (St. Gallen, 1952), 20 pp. See 120.

111 *Lektüre für Minuten. Ein paar Gedanken aus meinen Büchern und Briefen* (Bern, 1952), 27 pp.

112 *Gesammelte Dichtungen*, 6 vols., (Berlin and Frankfurt, 1952). Very incomplete.

113 *Zwei Idyllen: Stunden im Garten, Der lahme Knabe* (Berlin and Frankfurt am Main, 1952), 85 pp.

114 *Engadiner Erlebnisse. Ein Rundbrief* (Zürich, 1953), 39 pp. See 120.

115 *Hermann Hesse. Eine Auswahl*, ed. Reinhard Buchwald (Berlin, 1953), 138 pp.

116 *Beschwörungen. Rundbrief im Feb. 1954* (St. Gallen, 1954). See 120.

117 *Diesseits; Kleine Welt; Fabulierbuch* (Berlin, 1954), 987 pp. See 9, 59, 62.

118 *Hermann Hesse/Romain Rolland. Briefe* (Zürich, 1954), 118 pp.

119 *Über das Alter* (Olten, 1954), 15 pp. See 120.

120 *Beschwörungen. Späte Prosa* (Berlin, 1955), 295 pp. A miscellany of nineteen items, written 1947-55.

121 *Tagebuchblatt. Ein Maulbronner Seminarist* (Montagnola, 1955), 20 pp. See 120.

122 *Aquarelle aus dem Tessin* (Baden-Baden, 1955). Text with twelve paintings, written 1927.

123 *Der Wolf und andere Erzählungen* (Zürich, 1955), 24 pp. See 18.

124 *Abendwolken; Bei den Massageten* (St. Gallen, 1956), 20 pp. Two essays. See 322.

125 *Gedichte und Prosa* (Berlin, 1956), 32 pp. A miscellany.

126 *Der Zwerg* (Bamberg, 1956), 42 pp. (Biographische Bibliographie, pp. 35-42). See 62.

127 *Festliches Tessin* (Frankfurt am Main, 1957). Twenty-six water colors by Hesse and Gunter Böhmer.

128 *Gesammelte Schriften*, 7 vols. (Frankfurt, 1957). This is an expansion of the *Gesammelte Dichtungen* (1952); *Betrachtungen, Krieg und Frieden* (1949), *Briefe*, all but the first part of *Beschwörungen*, and fifteen other essays, written from 1928 to 1956, comprise the seventh volume.

129 *Der Trauermarsch. Gedenkblatt für einen Jugendfreund* (St. Gallen, 1957), 24 pp.

SHORT STORIES, ARTICLES, AND POEMS IN BOOKS AND PAM-
PHLETS (items not found in the collections of the preceding sec-
tion). But for two very recent items, books with introductions by
Hesse are not included. For a comprehensive list of books edited
and prefaced, or just prefaced by Hesse, see the Kliemann/
Silomon bibliography, pp. 35-41.

130 "Vom Wandern und Reisen," *Dürerbund Flugschrift* (München,
1905).
131 "Liebesopfer. Zwölf Monatssprüche," *Simplicissimus-Kalender*, 1907.
132 "Selma Lagerlöf," *Prospect des Verlages A. Langen* (München, 1907).
133 "Der Umgang mit Büchern: Vom Lesen; Das Buch," *Moderne Kultur.*
Ein Handbuch der Lebensbildung und des guten Geschmacks (Stuttgart, 1907), Vol. 2, 391-399, 399-402.
134 *Vom Lesen und von guten Büchern.* Eine Rundfrage veranstaltet
von der Redaktion der *Neuen Blätter für Literatur und Kunst*
(Wien, 1907), 16 pp. Contains a contribution by Hesse.
135 "Ein altes Buch," *Sieben Schwaben* (Heilbronn, 1909). See 67.
136 "Autobiographischer Beitrag," Franz Brümmer's: *Lexikon der deut.*
Dichter und Prosaisten, 6th ed. (Leipzig, 1913), Vol. 3, 191.
137 "Dichter und Buchhändler," *Festbuch zur Pfingsttagung dtsch. Buch-
handlungsgehilfen* (Leipzig, 1914).
138 "Der Weg zur Kunst ("Der Dichter," *Märchen*, 1919), *O mein
Heimatland* (Zürich, 1914), pp. 76-81.
139 "Wieder in Italien: Spaziergang am Comersee; Bergamo, San
Vigilio," *Das Bodenseebuch* (Konstanz, 1914), pp. 39-46.
140 ". . . noch ein Dritter gefallen," *Deutsche Sturmflut*, Vol. 1 of
Kriegsnovellen 1914/15, ed. Heinrich Goebel (Berlin, 1915), pp. 42-47.
141 "Auf dem Eise," *Kriegsweihnachten 1915* (Stuttgart: Die farbigen
Heftchen der Waldorf-Astoria, No. 17-18, 1915).
142 *Das Jugendbuch* (St. Gallen, 1915), 160 pp. Contains an item by
Hesse.
143 *Nach der Schlacht.* Ein Kriegsbuch in Prosa und Lyrik (Hagen,
1915), 148 pp. Contains items by Hesse.
144 *Der Weltkrieg 1914-15* (St. Gallen, 1915). A number of literary contributions by Hesse are scattered through the five volumes.
145 "Bekenntnis zu Storm," *Gedenkbuch zu Storms hundertstem Geburts-
tage* (Braunschweig, 1916).
146 "Alte Geschichte," *Amalthea Almanach*, 1917-21, pp. 16-24.
147 "Die Halsbandgeschichte," *Wilhelm Schäfer. Zu seinem 50. Geburtstag* (München, 1918); a review which first appeared in *März*, 4,
No. 3 (1910).
148 "Über das Rauchen," *O mein Heimatland* (Zürich, 1918), p. 181.
149 "Das seltene Buch," *Der Spiegel. Anekdoten Zeitgenössischer Deutscher Erzähler* (Berlin, 1919), pp. 132-136.
150 "Seenacht," *Die Ernte* (Basel, 1920 pp. 33-38. *Simplicissimus*,
16 (1911), 467-469.

151 "Überwindung der Einsamkeit," *Jahresbuch deutscher Dichter* (Stuttgart, 1920).

152 "Die Brinvilliers," *Die Ernte* (Basel, 1921), pp. 123-128.

153 "Warisbühel," *Die Ernte* (Basel, 1922), pp. 81-90. *Berner Woche in Wort u. Bild*, 1917.

154 "Künstler und Psychoanaylse," *Almanach f. d. Jahr 1926* (Wien: Internat. Psychoanalyt. Verlag, pp. 34-38). *Frankfurter Ztg.* July 16, 1918.

155 *Ostwart-Jahrbuch* ed. Viktor Kubczak, (Breslau, 1926), pp. 156-157 (Hesse's view of our age of *Untergang*).

156 *Verkannte Dichter unter uns*. Eine Rundfrage von Eduard Korrodi, *Neue Züricher Ztg.*, Ostern 1926, 56 pp. Contains a contribution by Hesse.

157 "Ausflug in die Stadt," *Das Bodenseebuch* (Konstanz, 1928).

158 "Herbst," *Die Ernte* (Basel, 1928), pp. 151-153.

159 "Inneres Erlebnis," *Ewige Gegenwart* (Berlin, 1928), pp. 22-41.

160 "Reisebilder. Ein Spaziergang in Würzburg. Bilderschauen in München," *Das Bodenseebuch* (Konstanz, 1930), pp. 17-21.

161 *Dichterglaube* (Eckart-Verlag, 1931), pp. 123-127.

162 "Martins Traum," *O mein Heimatland* (Zürich, 1931), pp. 124-127.

163 "Schriftsteller," Eugen Gömöri's: *Das Problem der Todestrafe* (Wien, 1931).

164 "Verbummelter Tag," *Menschen auf der Strasse* (Stuttgart, 1931), pp. 30-35.

165 *Mozarts Opern*. Programmheft des Züricher Stadttheaters vom 29. Oktober, 1932.

166 "Geselle Zbinden," *Das Bodenseebuch* (Lindau, 1933). See 179, 197.

167 "Magnolia und Zwergbaum," *O mein Heimatland* (Zürich, 1933), pp. 144-147.

168 "Über Wieland," *Wieland-Festschrift* (Biberach, 1933).

169 "Der Traum," *Das Bodenseebuch* (Lindau, 1934).

170 "Tessiner Kapellen," *O mein Heimatland* (Zürich, 1936), pp. 77-84.

171 "Eine Reise-Erinnerung," *O mein Heimatland* (Zürich, 1938), pp. 69-76.

172 "Kleines Bekenntnis (zu Schopenhauer)," *Jahrb. d. Schopenhauer-Gesellschaft* (Heidelberg, 1938).

173 "Sommerschreck," *Die Ernte* (Basel, 1939), pp. 71-74. *Simplicissimus*, 1906, p. 348.

174 "Über Wilhelm Busch," *Mittlg. d. Wilh. Busch-Gesellschaft*, (Sonderheft, 1939).

175 "Das Kind. Eine thebaische Legende," *Die Ernte* (Basel, 1945).

176 "San Vigilio (1913)," *Freundesgabe für Eduard Korrodi zum 60. Geburtstag* (Zürich, 1945), pp. 238-242.

177 *Jugend. Die Frage der Jugend* (München, 1946), 104 pp. (includes an item by Hesse).

178 *Das junge Mädchen—der junge Mann* (Dortmund, 1946), 4 pp. (includes a contribution by Hesse).

179 "Der fremde Schlosser," *Die Ernte* (Basel, 1947), pp. 31-35. See 166, 197.

180 "Führung und Geleit," *Hans Carossa. Eine Bibliographie zu seinem 70. Geburtstag* (Murnau, 1948), pp. 15-16.

181 *Les Prix Nobel en 1946* (Stockholm, 1948), pp. 112-113. Mentions influences of Schopenhauer, Nietzsche, Burckhardt, Spinoza, Plato.

182 "Ein Satz über die Kadenz," *Gruss der Insel an Hans Carossa*, (Insel-Verlag, 1948), pp. 148-149.

183 *Tiere in Not. Drei Tiergeschichten* (Bern, 1949), 16 pp. (one by Hesse).

184 *Gartenfreuden.* Eine Bilderfolge mit einem Geleitwort von Hesse (Zürich, 1950), 16 pp.

185 "Gruss an die französischen Studenten zum Thema der diesjährigen Agrégation," *Katalog der Buchhandlung Martin Flinker* (Paris, 1951), pp. 9-12 (pertinent remarks about *Peter Camenzind*).

186 "Vollendung" (a poem), Hanna und Ilse Jursch, *Hände als Symbol und Gestalt* (Berlin, 1951), p. 41.

187 "Geleitwort," of Alfredo Baeschlin's: *Ein Künstler erlebt Mallorca* (Schaffhausen, 1953), 100 pp.

188 *Trunken von Gedichten. Eine Anthologie geliebter deutscher Verse*, selected and commented upon by T. Mann, H. Hesse, G. Benn (Zürich, 1953), 221 pp.

189 *Dichter über Dichtung* (Darmstadt, 1954), 400 pp. (includes an item by Hesse).

190 "Dankadresse," *Hermann Hesse. Vier Ansprachen anlässlich der Verleihung des Friedenspreises des deutschen Buchhandels* (Frankfurt a.M., 1955), pp. 27-31. See also *Börsenblatt für den deutschen Buchhandel*, No. 86, 1955, pp. 701-702.

191 "Krieg und Frieden. Bekenntnisse aus 40 Jahren," *Dichten und Trachten* (Berlin; Frankfurt: Jahresschau des Suhrkamp Verlags, 1955), pp. 5-19 (all excerpts are taken either from *Krieg und Frieden*, or *Hermann Hesse/Romain Rolland. Briefe*).

192 "Meine Dichtungen sind alle ohne Absichten entstanden. . ." A foreword to Hermann Lorenzen, *Pädagogische Ideen bei Hermann Hesse* (Mülheim-Ruhr, 1955), p. 5.

193 *Wenn das Herz erwacht. Erzählungen für Mädchen* (Wien, Heidelberg, 1956), 264 pp. (includes an item by Hesse).

SHORT STORIES; ARTICLES, AND POEMS IN PERIODICALS (items not found in the preceding two sections, or listed there under other titles).

194 "Hans Amstein," *NR*, 15 (1904), 1109-20.
195 "Abends (Erzählung)," *Die Rheinlande*, 5 (1905), 6-7.
196 "Eine Nacht auf Wenkenhof," *Jugend*, No. 3, 1905, pp. 47, 49.
197 "Der Schlossergeselle," *Simplicissimus*, 10 (1905), 14-15. See 166, 179.
198 "Abschiednehmen," *Simplicissimus*, 11 (1906), 404-405.
199 "Casanova's Bekehrung," *Süddeutsche Monatshefte*, 3, No. 4 (1906).
200 "Dichterische Arbeit und Alkohol," *Das literarische Echo*, 9 (Oct. 1906), 107.
201 "Das erste Abenteuer," *Simplicissimus*, 10 (1906), 596.
202 "Karneval," *Simplicissimus*, 10 (1906), 558.
203 "Kastanienbäume," *Simplicissimus*, 11 (1906), 4.
204 "Legende," *Simplicissimus*, 11 (1906), 284-285.
205 "Maler Brahm," *Simplicissimus*, 11 (1906), 628-629. Hesse's first attempt to write his *Klingsor*.
206 "Schattenspiel," *Simplicissimus*, 11 (1906), 88-9, 103.
207 "Unterwegs. Ein Reisefragment," *Berner Rundschau*, 1906 ("Eine Fussreise im Herbst," *Diesseits*, (1907).
208 "Gubbio," *März*, 1, ii (1907), 233-236.
209 "Legende vom indischen König," *NR*, 18 (1907), 1128-30.
210 "Die Legende vom verliebten Jüngling," *Simplicissimus*, 12 (1907), 640-641, 647 ("Der Verliebte Jüngling," *Fabulierbuch*, 1935).
211 "Montefalco," *März*, 1, ii (1907), 380-382.
212 "Eine Sonate," *Simplicissimus*, 11 (1907), 792-793.
213 "Sor acqua," *März*, 1, i (1907), 61-71.
214 "Tippelschickel," *März*, 1, i (1907), 119 (a poem not found in Hesse's collected poems).
215 "Aventiure," *Nord und Süd*, 32, No. 1 (1908).
216 "Cäsarius von Heisterbach," *März*, 2, iii (1908), 33-39.
217 "Grindelwald," *März*, 2, iv (1908), 450-458.
218 "In den Felsen," *März*, 2, ii (1908), 51-59.
219 "Die Kulturellen Werte des Theaters," *Nord und Süd*, 32, No. 4, (1908).
220 "Eine Liebesgeschichte," *März*, 2 (1908): iii, 354-360, 454-459; iv, 45-51 ("Die Verlobung," *Nachbarn*, 1908).
221 "Die Schreibmachine," *März*, 2, i (1908), 377-378.
222 "Taedium vitae," *NR*, 19 (1908), 1053-68.
223 "Übersetzungen," *März*, 2, iii (1908), 239-240.
224 "Winterglanz," *Die Rheinlande*, 8 (1908), 24-25.
225 "Aus der Werkstatt," *Die Rheinlande*, 9 (1909), 94-96.
226 "Freunde," *Velhagen und Klasings Monatshefte*, 23, iii (1909), 49-83. See 93.
227 "Ein Gespräch am Abend," *März*, 3, i (1909), 119-125.
228 "Das hohe Lied," *März*, 3, i (1909), 287-291.

228   BIBLIOGRAPHY

229 "Mwambo," *Propyläen* (Beil. z. *Münchener Ztg.*), 7 (1909), 218-219.

230 "Silbernagel," *Simplicissimus*, 14 (1909), 124-125.

231 "Vom Naturgenuss," *März*, 3, iii (1909), 384-387.

232 "Wintertage in Graubünden," *Propyläen* (Beil. z. *Münchener Ztg.*), 7 (1909), 202-203.

233 "Der Beruf des Schriftstellers," *Wissen und Leben*, 3, No. 13 (1910).

234 "Doktor Knölges Ende," *Jugend*, No. 41, 1910, pp. 967-968.

235 "Der Monte Giallo," *Simplicissimus*, 15 (1910), 125, 131, 135.

236 "Eine Rarität," *März*, 4, i (1910), 164 (appeared in *Österr. Rundschau*, 1905 as "Das Büchlein" and later at various times as "Das seltene Buch."

237 "Der Schnitter Tod," *Die Rheinlande*, 10 (1910), 32-33.

238 "Schweizer Bürgerhäuser," *März*, 4, i (1910), 108-111.

239 "Ein Wandertag. Idylle," *März*, 4, iii (1910), 201-211, 289-298 ("Ein Wandertag vor hundert Jahren," *Fabulierbuch*, 1935).

240 "Im Garten," *Die Rheinlande*, 11 (1911), 101-103.

241 "Herr Piero," *Westermanns Monatsschriften*, 110, ii (1911), 891-900 ("Der Erzähler," *Fabulierbuch*, 1935).

242 "Der lustige Florentiner, *Propyläen* (Beil. z. *Münchener Ztg.*), 8 (1911), 554-555.

243 "Nachtpfauenauge," *Jugend*, No. 24, 1911, pp. 617-620.

244 "Vom Schriftsteller," *März*, 5, iv (1911), 184-187.

245 "Der Städtebauer," *Die Rheinlande*, 11 (1911), 26-28.

246 "Über das Lesen," *Die Rheinlande*, 11, No. 12 (1911).

247 "Eine Wolke," *Jugend*, No. 49, 1911, p. 1334.

248 "Eine Goethebibliothek," *Der Bücherwurm*, 2 (1912), 211.

249 "Kurgast," *Jugend*, No. 39, 1912, p. 1042.

250 "Untersee," *Propyläen* (Beil. z. *Münchener Ztg.*), 9 (1912), 626-627.

251 "Von der alten Zeit," *Propyläen* (Beil. z. *Münchener Ztg.*), 9 (1912), 449-450.

252 "Winterferien," *Die Rheinlande*, 12 (1912), 24-26.

253 "Abschied," *Die Schweiz*, 17 (1913), 265-267.

254 "Aus einem alten Skizzenbuch," *Die Rheinlande*, 13 (1913), 391-392.

255 "Fragment aus der Jugendzeit," *Velhagen u. Klasings Monatshefte*, 27 (May 1913), 77-87.

256 "Hermann Hesse als Buchhändler," *Börsenblatt für den deutschen Buchhandel*, No. 268, 1913.

257 "Nachtgesicht," *Jugend*, No. 37, 1913, p. 18.

258 "Die Ostindienreise. Ein Manuskript aus d. 17. Jahrh.," *März*, 7 (July 1913), 116-131 ("Anton Schievelbeyn's Reisse," *Fabulierbuch*).

259 "Erinnerung an Asien," *März*, 8 (Aug. 1914), 190-193.

260 "Das Landgut," *Die Rheinlande*, 14 (1914), 169-170.

261 "Ein Tag ausserhalb der Zeit," *Propyläen* (Beil. z. *Münchener Ztg.*), 12 (1914), 503-504.

262 "*Wilhelm Meisters Lehrjahre*. Eine Einführung," *Eckart*, 8 (1914), 297-312. See 78.

263 "Die drei Brüder," *Die Rheinlande*, 15 (1915), 305-307.

264 "Den Friedensleuten," *Propyläen* (Beil. z. *Münchener Ztg.*), 13 (1915), 180-181.

265 "Grindelwalder Tage," *Die Rheinlande*, 15 (1915), 76-78.

266 "Musik," *Die Schweiz*, 19 (1915), 147-150.

267 "Bücher-Zentrale für deutsche Kriegsgefangene, Bern," *Die Eiche*, 4 (1916), 241-243.

268 "Für unsere Landsleute in Kriegsgefangenschaft," *Propyläen* (Beil. z. *Münchener Ztg.*), 13 (1916), 292-294.

269 "Denket unserer Gefangenen," *März*, 11, ii (1917), 545-546.

270 "Kubu," *Simplicissimus*, 22 (1917), 42-43, 48.

271 "In einer kleinen Stadt (Eine unvollendete Romanhälfte)," *Velhagen u. Klasings Monatshefte*, 32, No. 5 (1918), 1-11.

272 "Die Braut," *Velhagen u. Klasings Monatshefte*, 33, No. 4 (1918), 365-368.

273 "Seltsame Geschichte," *Wieland*, 5 (Oct. 1919), 6-8.

274 "Zu Zarathustras Wiederkehr," *Vivos Voco*, 1 (October 1919), 72-73.

275 "*Demian*," *Vivos Voco*, 1 (July 1920), 658.

276 "Die Frau auf dem Balkon," *Wieland*, 5 (Feb. 1920), 6-10.

277 "Heimkehr. Erster Akt eines Zeitdramas," *Vivos Voco*, 1 (April-May 1920), 461-474.

278 "Wanderschaft," *Wieland*, 6 (May 1920), 2-4.

279 "Die Dichter," *Die Schweiz*, 25 (1921), 241-251 (a verse drama written in 1900).

280 "Aus dem Tagebuch eines Wüstlings," *Simplicissimus*, 27 (1922), 19, 30.

281 "Verrat am Deutschtum," *Vivos Voco*, 3 (1922), 62-63.

282 "Hochsommerabend im Tessin," *Velhagen u. Klasings Monatshefte*, 38, ii (1924), 495-496.

283 "Die Sehnsucht unserer Zeit nach Weltanschauung," *Uhu*, 3, No. 2 (1926).

284 Wilhelm Meridies, "Zum deutschen Bildungsroman der Gegenwart," *Literarischer Handweiser*, 64 (1928), 491 ff. (Besprechungen von Hesse et al.).

285 "Gedanken über Casanova," *NSR* 23, No. 3 (1930).

286 "Notizen zum Thema Dichtung und Kritik," *NR*, 41, ii (1930), 761-773.

287 "Zu Christian Schrempfs 70. Geburtstag," *NR*, 41, i (1930), 552-558.

288 "Gedanken über Gottfried Keller," *Der Lesezirkel*, 18 (1931), 141-144.

289 "Aus einem Tagebuch des Jahres 1920," *Corona*, 3 (1932), 192-209.

290 "Mozarts Opern," *Programmheft des Züricher Stadttheaters*, Oct. 29, 1932.

291 "Ein Stückchen Theologie," *NR*, 43, i (1932), 736-747. See 87.

292 "Eduards des Zeitgenossen unzeitiger Traum," *Simplicissimus*, 38, No. 13 (1933).

293 "Erinnerung an S. Fischer," *NR*, 45, ii (1934), 571-573.

294 "Zu Christoph Schrempfs 75. Geburtstag," *NR*, 46, i (1935), 539-543.

295   "Der Berg," *Neue Schweizer Bibliothek* (Zürich), Vol. 47, 5-16. See 88.

296   "Erinnerungen an Klingsors Sommer," *NSR*, 12 (1944), 208-209.

297   "Über den von Frau M. Geroe-Tobler gewebten Teppich in meinem Atelier," *Werk*, 32 (1945), 190-192. See 77.

298   "Mein Glaube" (written in 1931), *NSR*, 13 (1946), 664-667.

299   "Beschreibung einer Landschaft. Ein Stück Tagebuch," *NR* (Spring 1947), 196-205. See 88.

300   "Romantisch" (written about 1900), *Deutsche Beiträge*, 1 (1947), 386-388.

301   "Drei Gedichte," *NSR*, 16 (1948), 29-31.

302   "Musikalische Notizen," *NSR*, 15 (1948), 598-616. See 86.

303   "Nicht abgesandter Brief an eine Sängerin," *Musica*, 2 (1948), 116-121; see preceding item (singer is Ria Ginster).

304   "Gedenkblatt für Adele (15. August 1875 - 24. September 1949), *NSR*, 17 (1949), 360-366.

305   "Eine Arbeitsnacht," *Das Antiquariat*, 6 (1950), 81-82 (written 1928).

306   "Rückblick (Ein Fragment aus der Zeit um 1937)," *NSR*, 19 (1951), 78-81.

307   "Werkstatt-Gedanken," *Welt und Wort*, 7 (1952), 227-228.

308   "Nachruf für Marulla," *NSR*, April 1953. See 120.

309   "Vom Altsein," *Du. Schweizerische Monatsschrift*, Feb. 13, 1953, p. 39. See 120.

310   "Die Gedichte eines Jahres," *NSR*, 22 (1954), 293-296.

311   "Am Schreibtisch," *Universitas*, 10 (1955), 1277-82. See 352.

312   "Lesungen aus dem Werk des Dichters," *Börsenblatt für den deutschen Buchhandel*, No. 86, 1955, 703-704.

313   "Wiederbegegnung mit zwei Jugendgedichten," *Westermanns Monatshefte*, No. 9 (1956), 27-28 ("Bergnacht"; "Bootnacht").

314   "Klage und Trost" (Ludwig Finckh zu seinem 80. Geburtstag gewidmet), *American-German Review*, Oct.-Nov., p. 21 (a poem).

ARTICLES AND POEMS IN NEWSPAPERS (items not found in the preceding three sections).

315 "Stimmungsbilder aus Oberitalien," *Schweizer Hausfreund* (Beilage des *Basler Anzeigers*), No. 37-43, 1901, p. 43.

316 "Die Kunst des Müssiggangs," *Die Zeit* (Wien), May 28, 1904, pp. 105-107.

317 "Über das Reisen," *Die Zeit* (Wien), April 30, 1904, pp. 55-57.

318 "Sommerreise," *Münchener Neueste Nachr.*, Sept. 2, 1905.

319 "Der Schnitter Tod," *Basler Nachrichten*, No. 31, 1911.

320 "An den Kaiser" (Prolog zur Kaiserfeier der deutschen Kolonie, Bern), *Suddeutsche Ztg.*, Feb. 4, 1915 (a poem not included in Hesse's collected poems).

321 "In eigener Sache," *Neue Züricher Ztg.*, Nov. 2, 1915.

322 "Die Pazifisten," *Die Zeit* (Wien), Nov. 7, 1915. See 264.

323 "Wieder in Deutschland," *Neue Züricher Ztg.*, Oct. 10, 1915.

324 "Krieg und Christentum," *Protestantenblatt*, July 5, 1916, pp. 422-423.

325 "Kirchenkonzert," *Deutsche Internierten-Zeitung*, Dec. 25, 1918, pp. 11-12.

326 "Erinnerungen an Konrad Haussmann," *Neue Züricher Ztg.*, Feb. 16, 1922.

327 "Aus Indien und über Indien," *Berl. Tageblatt*, Sept. 24, 1925.

328 "Sehnsucht nach Indien," *Berl. Tageblatt*, Dec. 21, 1925.

329 An article concerned with the attitude of *Simplicissimus* during the war, in *Neue Züricher Ztg.*, Sept. 4, 1926.

330 "Abendstunde in einer kleinen Kneipe," *Berl. Tageblatt*, Jan. 26, 1927.

331 "Hesse trifft Stevenson," *Frankfurter Ztg.*, Sept. 11, 1927.

332 "Bei den Massageten (Ironische Reise)," *Berl. Tageblatt*, Sept. 25, 1927. See 124.

333 "Über den Koffer gebückt," *Münchener Neueste Nachr.*, Sept. 15, 1928.

334 "Unentbehrliche Nacht," *Berl. Tageblatt*, Dec. 25, 1928.

335 "Notizen im Speisesaal," *Berl. Tageblatt*, Oct. 20, 1929.

336 "Beim Kofferpacken," *Vossische Ztg.*, June 8, 1930.

337 "An einem Regensonntag," *Thüringer Allgemeine Ztg.*, Aug. 1931.

338 "Schmetterling zu Weihnacht," *Vossische Ztg.*, Dec. 15, 1931.

339 "Was die Morgenpost beschert," *Münchener Neueste Nachr.*, Jan. 24, 1932.

340 "Reise auf dem Ozean," *Münchener Neueste Nachr.*, July 26, 1932.

341 "Kleine Reise," *Vossische Ztg.*, Aug. 14, 1932.

342 "Sommernachtsfest," *Vossische Ztg.*, June 25, 1933.

343 "Umbrischer Vorfrühlingstag," *Neue Züricher Ztg.*, March 18, 1934.

344 "Ein Protest," *Neue Züricher Ztg.*, Jan. 18, 1936.

345 "Briefe die uns doch erreichten," *Deutsche Postzeitung* (Berlin), 1940, p. 144.

346 "Schneeberger Schnupftabak," *Hamburger Fremdenblatt*, April 4, 1942.

347 "Christoph Schrempf," *Stuttgarter Ztg.*, April 27, 1946.
348 "Nachtgedanken," *Der Morgen* (Berlin), Jan. 5, 1947.
349 "Traumtheater," *National-Ztg.* (Basel), April 24-25, 1948. See "Nächtliche Spiele," in *Beschwörungen* (1955).
350 "Preziosität," *Neue Züricher Ztg.*, July 3, 1948.
351 "Notizen aus diesen Sommertagen," *National-Ztg.*, Sonntagsbeilage (Basel), August 7-8, 1948.
352 "Stunden am Schreibtisch," *National-Ztg.* (Basel), June 12, 1949. See 311.
353 "Herbstwanderung," *National-Ztg.*, Sonntagsbeilage (Basel), Sept. 10, 1950.
354 "Andere Wege zum Frieden," *Neue Zeitung* (München), Oct. 28, 1950.
355 "Mahnruf Hermann Hesses," *Das Volk, Thüringische Landesztg.*, Nov. 13, 1950, p. 1.
356 "Ein paar Basler Erinnerungen," *Die Weltwoche* (Zürich), March 22, 1951, p. 17.
357 "Hermann Hesse warnt vor Antibolschewismus," *Leipziger Volkszeitung.* Aug. 9, 1951, p. 1.
358 "Hermann Hesse mahnt das deutsche Volk," *Das Volk, Thüringische Landesztg.*, Aug. 10, 1951, p. 2.
359 "Vom Überschätzen und Unterschätzen," *Neue Zeit* (Berlin), June 29, 1952, p. 5.
360 "Überfahrt im Herbst," *Die Union* (Chemnitz), Oct. 30, 1952, p. 2.
361 "Ein Wintergang," *Die Union* (Dresden), Jan. 10, 1954, p. 3.
362 "Ferienberichte und Erinnerungen," *Neue Züricher Ztg.*, August 27, 1954, pp. 3-4.
363 "Altern" (a poem), *Neue Zeit* (Berlin), Oct. 21, 1954, p. 3.
364 "Letzter Gruss," *Aufbau* (New York), August 26, 1955, p. 4 (upon occasion of T. Mann's death).
365 "Ohne Krapplack," *Die Brücke zur Welt* (Sonntagsbeilage zur *Stuttgarter Ztg.*), October 8, 1955. See 122.

REVIEWS.

März (Hesse was co-editor from 1907 to 1912) :

366 "Unbekannte Schätze," 1, i (1907), 246-250.
367 "Gedanken bei der Lektüre des *Grünen Heinrich,*" 1. i (1907), 455-459.
368 "Mörike für Wohlhabende," 1, i (1907), 577-578.
369 "Der endgültige Novalis," 1, ii (1907), 424.
370 "Gedichtbücher," 1. iv (1907), 86-90.
371 *"Heinrich Stillings Jugend,"* 1, iv (1907), 263.
372 *"Abu Telfan,"* 1, iv (1907), 346-347.
373 "Die grosse Mörike Ausgabe," 2, i (1908), 284-285.
374 "Neue Erzähler," 2, i (1908), 559-561.
375 *"Neue Gedichte* von Ricarda Huch," 2, i (1908), 575.
376 "Romane," 2, ii (1908), 334-336.
377 "Sommerbücher," 2, ii (1908), 465-470.
378 *"Die Bernsteinhexe,"* 2, iii (1908), 247-248.
379 "Über Heidenstams *Karl XII,"* 2, iv (1908), 155-156.
380 "Handzeichnungen Schweizer Meister," 2, iv (1908), 238.
381 "Billige Bücher," 2, iv (1908), 254-260.
382 *"Henrik Steffens,"* 2, iv (1908), 398-399.
383 "Auf Erden," 2, iv (1908), 490-491.
384 "Exzentrische Erzählungen," 3, ii (1909), 57-63.
385 "Der Verlag Eugen Diederichs," 3, ii (1909), 318-320.
386 "Gute neue Romane," 3, ii (1909), 373-379.
387 "Neue Bücher," 3, iii (1909), 400-402.
388 "Die grossen Russen," 3, iii (1909), 495.
389 "Klassiker Ausgaben," 3, iv (1909), 76.
390 "Spukgeschichten aus Transvaal," 3, iv (1909), 158-159.
391 "Romane und Novellen," 3, iv (1909), 197-201.
392 "Wohnhausneubau," 3, iv (1909), 309-310.
393 *"Der Lindenbaum,"* 3, iv (1909), 490-491.
394 *"Des Knaben Wunderhorn,"* 4, i (1910), 85-86.
395 "Gedichte einer Toten," 4, i (1910), 86.
396 "Gute neue Bücher," 4, i (1910), 108-111.
397 "Westöstliche Dichtungen," 4, i (1910), 161-163.
398 "Thomas Manns *Königliche Hoheit,"* 4, i (1910), 281-283, (rather negative remarks).
399 "Charles de Coster," 4, i (1910), 325.
400 "Sprüche und Widersprüche," 4, i (1910), 406.
401 "Gute Lektüre," 4, ii (1910), 204-207.
402 "Ein Leben Leonardos," 4, ii (1910), 511-512.
403 "Geijerstam," 4, ii (1910), 512.
404 "Die Halsbandgeschichte," 4, iii (1910), 80.
405 "Ferienlektüre," 4, iii (1910), 120-128.
406 *"Martin Salander,"* 4, iii (1910), 148-150.
407 "Leutholds *Gedichte,"* 4, iii (1910), 168.
408 *"Sprüche des Confusius,"* 4, iii (1910), 168.

409   "Nochmals Leutholds *Gedichte*," 4, iii (1910), 256.
410   "Briefe eines Unbekannten," 4, iii (1910), 336.
411   "Basler Kultur," 4, iii (1910), 365-368.
412   "Graf Federigo Confaloniere," 4, iii (1910), 415-416.
413   "Erich Schmidts kleiner Goethe," 4, iii (1910), 493.
414   "Eichendorff," 4, iv (1910), 264.
415   "Mauthners Wörterbuch," 4, iv (1910), 352.
416   "Neue Erzählungen," 4, iv (1910), 408-414.
417   "Neuausgaben," 4, iv (1910), 504-512.
418   "Gedichte von Emanuel von Bodman," 5, i (1911), 165-167.
419   "Klassische Illustratoren," 5, i (1911), 144.
420   "Ein österreichischer Studentenalmanach," 5, i (1911), 184.
421   "Drugulindrucke," 5, i (1911), 288.
422   "Der alte Pitaval," 5, i (1911), 382-383.
423   "Künstler und Gelehrte," 5, i (1911), 472.
424   "Poetischer Büchersturz," 5, ii (1911), 65-70.
425   "Briefe des Enea Silvio," 5, ii (1911), 184.
426   "Der deutsche Balzac," 5, ii (1911), 429-430.
427   "Goethebücher," 5, iii (1911), 47-48.
428   "Bücherschau," 5, iii (1911), 120-122, 159-160.
429   "Gedichte von Wilhelm von Scholz," 5, iii (1911), 190-191.
430   "*Der Junge Goethe*," 5, iii (1911), 208.
431   "Eine neue Romanbibliothek," 5, iii (1911), 248.
432   "*Cäsarius von Heisterbach*," 5, iii (1911), 328.
433   "Reisen und Abenteuer," 5, iii (1911), 410-412.
434   "Vom Philister," 5, iii (1911), 412.
435   "Wissenschaftliche Volksbücher," 5, iii (1911), 456.
436   "*Tausend und eine Nacht* in Auswahl," 5, iii (1911), 496.
437   "Aus dem preussischen Kasernenleben um 1780," 5, iv (1911), 118-119.
438   "Vom Schriftsteller," 5, iv (1911), 184-187.
439   "Schöne Bücher," 5, iv (1911), 296-300, 345-347.
440   "Ein Dichter," 6, i (1912), 36-37.
441   "Biedermeier," 6, i (1912), 80.
442   "Holbein," 6, i (1912), 199.
443   "Eine chinesische Geschichte," 6, i (1912), 200.
444   "Thule," 6, i (1912), 200.
445   "Chinas Verteidigung gegen europäische Ideen," 6, i (1912), 240.
446   "Bibliothek der Romane," 6, i (1912), 240.
447   "Menschen und Schicksale," 6, i (1912), 279-280.
448   "Biedermeier-Moritaten," 6, i (1912), 317-319.
449   "*Tristan und Isolde*," 6, i (1912), 319-320.
450   "Mondespfeil," 6, i (1912), 320.
451   "*Don Quixote*," 6, i (1912), 440.
452   "*Der Junge Goethe*," 6, i (1912), 440.
453   "Wertvolle Neuausgaben," 6, ii (1912), 110-112.
454   "Aus Hippels Buch *Über die Ehe*," 6, ii (1912), 159-160.
455   "Etwas für Gottfried Kellerfreunde," 6, ii (1912), 160

456 "Jeremias Gotthelf," 6, ii (1912), 199-200.
457 *"Jacques le fataliste,"* 6, ii (1912), 280.
458 "Der Hodscha Masuddin," 6, ii (1912), 320.
459 "Ludwig Finckh, *Gedichte,"* 6, ii (1912), 348-350.
460 "Deutsche Lyrik aus Österreich," 6, ii (1912), 360.
461 "Albert Welti," 6, ii (1912), 375-376.
462 "Anselm Feuerbachs *Briefe,"* 6, ii (1912), 398-399.
463 "Almquist," 6, ii (1912), 440.
464 "Gedichte von Christian Morgenstern," 6, ii (1912), 501-502.
465 *"Gockel, Hinkel und Gackeleia,"* 6, iii (1912), 39-40.
466 "Liliencrons Werke," 6, iii (1912), 40.
467 "Sommerlektüre," 6, iii (1912), 112-114.
468 "D. W. B.," 6, iii (1912), 199-200.
469 "Inselverlagbücher für fünfzig Pfennig," 6, iii (1912), 240.
470 "Beethovens Briefe," 6, iii (1912), 319-320.
471 "Christian Wagner," 6, iii (1912), 320.
472 "Thackeray," 6, iii (1912), 320.
473 "Eulenbergs *Neue Bilder,"* 6, iii (1912), 360.
474 "Ein Rodinbuch," 6, iii (1912), 360.
475 "Geschichte von Bruno Frank," 6, iii (1912), 381-382.
476 "Für Italienfreunde," 6, iii (1912), 400.
477 "Klassische Dichtungen," 6, iii (1912), 505-507.
478 "Töpffers humoristische Bilderfolgen," 6, iv (1912), 40.
479 "Ein amerikanischer Roman," 6, iv (1912), 120.
480 "Hamburger Attentat," 6, iv (1912), 120.
481 "Briefe von Jakob Burckhardt," 6, iv (1912), 200.
482 "Bücherglosse," 6, iv (1912), 239-240.
483 "Etwas für Weihnachten," 6, iv (1912), 439-440.
484 "Kinder- und Bilderbücher," 6, iv (1912), 472-474.
485 "Welti-Publikationen," 6, iv (1912), 527-528.
486 "Der alte *Grüne Heinrich,"* 7 (Dec. 1913), 884-888.
487 "Apologie des Krieges. Max Schelers *Genius des Krieges und der deutsche Krieg,"* 9 (May 1915), 167-168.

Vivos Voco (Hesse was co-editor from 1919 to Dec. 1921) :

488   "Über die neuere französische Literatur," 1 (October 1919), 76-80.
489   1 (Nov.-Dec. 1919), 201-205.
490   1 (Jan. 1920), 268-270.
491   1 (Feb. 1920), 334-336.
492   1 (March 1920), 397-400.
493   1 (April-May 1920), 518-528.
494   1 (June 1920), 588-592.
495   1 (July 1920), 658-661.
496   1 (Sept. 1920), 730-733.
497   1 (Nov. 1920), 780-782.
498   1 (Nov. 1920), 815-819.
499   2 (March 1921), 109-111.
500   2 (May 1921), 157-160.
501   2 (July 1921), 275-277.
502   2 (Oct. 1921), 348-349.
503   2 (Dec. 1921), 419-421.
504   2 (Jan. 1922), 481-484.
505   2 (Feb. 1922), 543-548.
506   2 (April-May 1922), 637-639.
507   2 (June 1922), 705-707.
508   3 (Sept.-Oct. 1922), 155-158.
509   3 (Nov.-Dec. 1922), 224.
510   3 (Jan.-Feb. 1923), 290-291.
511   3 (March-April 1923), 359-360.
512   3 (May-July 1923), 417-418.

Neue Rundschau:

513   "Die schöne Bibel," 20 (1909), 461.
514   "Noch eine Mörike Ausgabe," 21 (1910), 432.
515   *"Palmström,"* 21 (1910), 1316.
516   "Wie geht es mit Jean Paul?" 25 (1914), 423-426.
517   "Deutsche Erzähler," 26 (1915), 188-208.
518   "Zu *Expressionismus in der Dichtung*," 29 (1918), 838-843.
519   "Hinduismus," 34 (1923), 668-670.
520   "E. T. A. Hoffmanns Werke," 35 (1924), 1199.
521   "Der Pyramidenrock," 36 (1925), 220-221.
522   "Üble Aufnahme," 36 (1925), 266-271.
523   "Erinnerung an Lektüre," 36 (1925), 964-972.
524   "Von der Gegenwart vergangener Literaturen," 36 (1925), 1280-94.
525   "R. M. Rilkes *Gesammelte Werke*," 39, i (1928), 222-223.
526   *"Hugo Balls Leben in Briefen und Gedichten,"* 41, i (1930), 720.
527   "Bücher Ausklopfen," 42, ii (1931), 829-833 (about Spengler).
528   "Beim Lesen eines Romans," 44, i (1933), 698-702.
529   "Erinnerung an ein paar Bücher," 45, i (1934), 454-458.
530   "Über einige Bücher," 45, ii (1934), 321-328 (about Freud and Jung).

531 "Notizen zu neuen Büchern," 45, ii (1934), 744-750.
532 "Notizen zu neuen Büchern," 46, i (1935), 325-334.
533 "Bemerkungen zu neuen Büchern," 46, i (1935), 664-672 (about Kafka).
534 "Anmerkungen zu Büchern," ii (1935), 551-558 (about Rilke, George).
535 "Notizen zu neuen Büchern," 46, ii (1935), 664-672.
536 "Anmerkungen zu neuen Büchern," 47, i (1936), 208-215.
537 "Anmerkungen zu Büchern," 47, ii (1936), 1004-08.

Stray Periodicals and Newspapers:

538 "Zum achten September (Mörike)," *Die Rheinlande*, 4 (1904), 493-494.
539 "Der Briefwechsel zwischen Storm und Keller," *Die Rheinlande*, 4 (1904), 518-519.
540 "Goethes Briefe," *Die Rheinlande*, 4 (1904), 589-590.
541 A review in *Vom Lesen und von guten Büchern*, Wien, 1907 (Eine Rundfrage veranstaltet von der Redaktion der *Neuen Blätter für Lit. u. Kunst*).
542 "Chinesische Flöte," *Die Propyläen*, (Beil. z. *Münchener Ztg.*), 5 (1907), 132.
543 "R. Wilhelms *Confucius*," *Die Propyläen* (Beil. z. *Münchener Ztg.*), 7 (1910), 637.
544 "Julius Grill, R. Wilhelm: *Lao-Tse*," *Die Propyläen* (Beil. z. *Münchner Ztg.*), 8 (1911), 533.
545 "*Als Vagabund um die Erde*," *Der Bücherwurm*, 2 (1912), 250.
546 "Chinesische Anekdoten," *Die Propyläen* (Beil. z. *Münchener Ztg.*), 9 (1912), 227.
547 "*Nervöse Leute* von Kurt Wolff," *Die Propyläen* (Beil. z. *Münchener Ztg.*), 12 (1914), 186.
548 "Chinesische Novellen," *Die Propyläen*, (Beil. z. *Münchener Ztg.*), 12 (1914), 646.
549 "105 Chinesische Erzählungen," *Die Propyläen* (Beil. z. *Münchener Ztg.*), 12 (1914), 756.
550 "Kriegslektüre," *Die Zeit* (Wien), No. 4478.
551 "Romain Rolland. *Johann Christof*," *Berl. Tageblatt*, May 4, 1915.
552 "Jüngste deutsche Dichtung," *Schweizerland. Monatsheft für Schweizer Art und Arbeit*, 2 (1916), 399-401.
553 "Ein süddeutscher Dichter (Emil Strauss)," *Die Schweiz*, 20 (1916), 233-236.
554 "Beim Lesen des *Grünen Heinrich*," *Schweizerland*, 4 (1917-18), 51-53.
555 "Seldwyla im Abendrot," *Vossische Ztg.*, July 13, 1919.
556 "Unsere jüngste Dichtung," *Vossische Ztg.*, July 30, 1920.
557 "Jean Paul," *Neue Züricher Ztg.*, June 21-22, 1922.
558 "Recent German Poetry," *Criterion* (London), Oct. 1922, pp. 89-93.
559 "Die heutige deutsche Literatur," *Neue Züricher Ztg.*, Jan. 7, 1924.
560 "Über einen vergessenen Dichter (Heinrich Leuthold)," *Frankfurter Ztg.*, May 4, 1924.
561 "Verkannte Dichter unter uns," *Neue Züricher Ztg.*, April 4, 1926.

562 "Franz Kafkas Nachlass," *Der Lesezirkel*, 16 (1929), 61-63.

563 "Nya Tyska Böcker," *Bonniers Litterära Magasin*, 4 (1935): No. 3, 26-34; No. 7, 50-57; No. 9, 22-29. 5 (1936): No. 1, 32-39.

564 "Ritter Halewijns Lied," *Münchener Neueste Nachr.*, Aug. 8, 1939.

565 "Strindberg," *Neue Züricher Ztg.*, July 2, 1947.

566 "Notiz von Hesse über Schestows Essay über Buber," *Deutsche Beiträge*, 3 (1949), 192.

567 "Mein stärkster Bucheindruck, 1954" *Neue Deutsche Literatur*, 3 (1955), 114.

LETTERS BY HESSE (starred items are included in the *Briefe*, 1951).

568 "Ein Brief," *Simplicissimus*, 11 (1906), 220.

569 "Ein Briefwechsel," *Velhagen u. Klasings Monatshefte*, 22, i (1907), 81-86.

570 A reply to an inquiry by the Redaktion der *Neuen Blätter für Literatur u. Kunst*, in *Vom Lesen und von guten Büchern* (Wien, 1907).

571 "Aus dem Briefwechsel eines Dichters," *Die Gegenwart*, No. 39-40, 1908.

572 "Ein Brief," *Der Schwabenspiegel* (Wochenschrift der *Württemberger Ztg.*), March 10, 1908, p. 172.

573 A reply to an inquiry by Hermann Bahr in the latter's: *Die Bücher zum wirklichen Leben* (Wien, 1908).

574 "Der junge Dichter. Ein Brief an viele," *März*, 4, i (1910), 441-443.

575 "Zwischen Winter und Frühling. Ein Brief," *Die Rheinlande*, 12 (1912), 111-112.

576 "Jünglingsbrief," *Die Schweiz*, 18 (1914), 547-549.

577 *Brief ins Feld* (München Pasing, 1915), 14 pp.

578 "Brief ins Feld," *Propyläen* (Beil. z. *Münchener Ztg.*), 13 (1915), 227-228.

579 "Ein Mönchsbrief," *Die Schweiz*, 20 (July 1916), 375-379.

580 "Hassbriefe," *Vivos Voco*, 2 (July 1921), 235-239.

581 "Brief an einen jungen Deutschen (1919)," *Betrachtungen* (1928), pp. 153-159.

582 "Brief an einen Philister (1915)," *Betrachtungen* (1928), pp. 36-45.

*583 "Die Sendung des Dichters," *Benediktinische Monatsschrift*, 14 (1932), 28-34. A reply to Max Jordan's letter, *ibid.*, 13 (1931), 398-405.

584 *Neue Literatur*, 37 (1936), 57-58. A reply to Will Vesper's article, *Neue Literatur*, 36 (1935), 685-687.

585 A letter addressed to the Swiss people in the periodical *Civitas Nova* 1 (1938).

586 "Ein Brief," *Die Ernte*, (Basel, 1941), pp. 73-76.

587 "Ein Brief," *Kleine Betrachtungen* (1941).

588 A letter to Fritz Brun, 1941, in *Kleine Festgabe für Fritz Brun* (Bern, 1941).

589 A letter to Paul Ilg, dated Jan. 29, 1903, in Franz Larese's: *Paul Ilg, ein Thurgauer Dichter* (Bischofszell, 1943), 16 pp.
590 A letter to Albert Steffen, 1944, in *Das Albert Steffen Buch* (Basel, 1944).
591 *Zwei Briefe* (St. Gallen, 1945), 7 pp. (a letter from Thomas Mann and Hesse's answer).
592 "Antwort auf Schmähbriefe aus Deutschland," *Neue Züricher Ztg.,* August 23, 1946.
593 An exchange of letters with J. Berna: *Schweizer Annalen,* 3 (1946-47), 241-243.
594 *Antwort auf Bittbriefe* (Montagnola, 1947) 3 pp.
*595 *Der Autor an einen Korrektor,* 1946 (Bern, 1947), 14 pp.
596 "Ein Briefwechsel aus dem Jahre 1937" (Hesse an Horst Lange), *Der Ruf, Blätter der jungen Generation,* 1, No. 17 (1947).
597 "Verehrter Herr Bierbaum (1907)," in Gotthilf Hafner's: *Hermann Hesse* (1947), pp. 31-32.
598 "Der wohlgenutzte Ruhm. Aus einem Brief von H. Hesse," *NR,* 1947, p. 258 (to T. Mann).
599 "Zwei Briefe über das *Glasperlenspiel,*" *National-Ztg.* (Basel, Oct. 5, 1947.
600 A letter to the Ephorus des Uracher Seminars, May 1934, in Gotthilf Hafner's: *Hermann Hesse* (1947), p. 58.
*601 *Blätter vom Tage. Briefe* (Montagnola, 1948), 16 pp.
602 "Ein Briefwechsel," *NR,* 1948, pp. 244-245.
603 "Nicht abgesandter Brief an eine Sängerin," *Musica,* 2 (1948), 116-121 ("Musikalische Notizen," *NSR,* 15 [1948], 598-616).
604 "An einen jungen Kollegen in Japan (1947)," *Krieg und Frieden* (1949), pp. 213-219.
*605 *An einen jungen Künstler* (Montagnola, 1949), 11 pp.
606 "Auszüge aus zwei Briefen," *NSR,* 17 (1949), 54-55.
607 "Brief an Adele (1946)," *Krieg und Frieden* (1949), pp. 181-194.
608 "Ein Brief nach Deutschland (1946)," *Krieg und Frieden* (1949), pp. 195-205.
609 "Lieber Herr St.," *Aufbau* (New York), Sept. 23, 1949, p. 14.
610 "Versuch einer Rechtfertigung, Zwei Briefe wegen Palästina (1948)," *Krieg und Frieden* (1949), pp. 220-225.
611 Excerpt from a letter written in 1940 in *Krieg und Frieden* (1949), pp. 165-168.
612 A letter to Paul Wiegler in *Sinn und Form* 1, No. 5 (1949), 15-16 (written about 1930).
613 Letters to A. von Bernus, 1904, in *Worte der Freundschaft für Alexander von Bernus* (Nürnberg, 1949), pp. 89-90.
*614 "Brief-Mosaik I," *NSR,* 17 (1950), 673-696; "Brief-Mosaik II," *NSR,* 18 (1950), 195-221 (all but six letters in these two collections are in *Briefe*).
*615 "Briefmosaik zur geistigen Lage," *Universitas,* 5 (1950), 769-778. 909-918 (all but one of these in *Briefe*).

*616   *Das junge Genie. Brief an einen Achtzehnjährigen*, (St. Gallen, 1950), 14 pp.

*617   "Lieber Herr Thomas Mann," *NR*, 61 (1950), 151-152.

*618   *Zwei Briefe: An einen jungen Künstler; Das junge Genie* (St. Gallen, 1950), 15 pp.

619   Three letters sent to Lulu Hellmann and one to Ludwig Finckh 1899, in Finckh's: *Die Verzauberung* (Ulm, 1950).

*620   *Brief an einen Schwäbischen Dichter*, 1950 (Olten, 1951), 17 pp.

621   *Briefe* (Berlin, 1951), 431 pp. The edition of 1954 includes a *Nachwort* by Hesse, pp. 433-434.

*622   "Briefe nach Deutschland. Neues Brief-Mosaik," *Universitas* 6 (1951), 1-12 (all but two of these in *Briefe*).

*623   *Eine Handvoll Briefe* (Zürich, 1951), 60 pp.

624   Letter to Dr. W. Weber, 1951, in *Neue Züricher Ztg.*, July 1951.

625   Two letters written in 1951, in *Stimmen zum Briefbuch von Hermann Hesse* (Montagnola, 1951).

626   *Dank für die Briefe und Glückwünsche zum 2. Juli 1952* (Privatdruck).

627   *Geburtstag. Ein Rundbrief* (Montagnola, 1952), 4 pp.

628   "Ein peinlicher Brief an den französischen Dichter Krug," *Deutsches Pfarrerblatt*, 52 (1952), 526.

629   An excerpt from a letter sent to Theodor Heuss in 1910, in *Dank an Hermann Hesse* (1952), p. 30.

630   Portion of a letter by Hesse in *Hermann Hesse als Badener Kurgast* (St. Gallen, 1952), p. 18.

631   Three letters to Redaktion des März, 1910, in Hannsludwig Geiger's: *E's war um die Jahrhundertwende* (München, 1953), pp. 175-176.

632   Portion of a letter in which Hesse replies to Colleville's remonstrance (*Études Germaniques*, 7 [1952], p. 132) against his criticism of Angelus Silesius (*Betrachtungen*): "À propos du Problème religieux chez Hermann Hesse," *Études Germaniques*, 8 (1953), 182.

633   "Brief eines Studenten an Hesse und dessen Antwort," *Neue Züricher Ztg.*, July 2, 1954, p. 8.

634   "Briefwechsel zu einem Gedicht von Hermann Hesse," *Neue Züricher Ztg.*, Jan. 17, 1954, p. 4.

635   *Hermann Hesse/Romain Rolland. Briefe* (Zürich, 1954), 118 pp.

636   "Ein Leserbrief und die Antwort des Autors," *NSR*, March, 1954.

637   "Rundbrief im Februar," *Neue Züricher Ztg.*, Feb. 5, 1954, pp. 4-5.

*638   "Verehrter, lieber Herr Dr. Benz," *Festschrift zum 70. Geburtstag von Richard Benz* (Hamburg, 1954), pp. 17-19.

639   Letters sent by Hesse to Th. Heuss in *Begegnungen mit Th. Heuss*, eds. Hans Bott, Hermann Leins (Tübingen, 1954), pp. 255-259.

*640   "Brief an einen Kriegsgefangenen in Frankreich," "Brief an eine Gruppe junger Menschen in Berlin," Axel Lindqvist, *Lebende Vergangenheit* (Stockholm, 1955), pp. 277-278; 258.

641   "Rundbriefe," *Beschwörungen* (1955), pp. 61-261. Twelve letters from 1947 to 1954.

642   Portion of a letter to a pastor in East Germany, *Beschwörungen* (1955), pp. 237-238.

643 A portion of a letter to Thomas Mann in Klaus W. Jonas' *Fifty Years of Thomas Mann Studies* (University of Minnesota, 1955), xiv.
644 "Weltanschauliche Briefe politischer Richtung," *Schweizer Monatshefte*, 36 (1956), 189-194.

HESSE IN TEXTBOOKS FOR ENGLISH SPEAKING STUDENTS.

645 *Deutsches Geistesleben der Gegenwart*, ed. Otto Koischwitz, Alfred A. Knopf, 1928 (a short selection from *Demian*).

646 *Modern German Short Stories*, ed. H. F. Eggeling, Clarendon Press, England, 1929 (*Das Nachtpfauenauge*).

647 *Knulp. Drei Geschichten aus dem Leben Knulps*, eds. Wm. Diamond and Christel B. Schomaker, Oxford University Press, 1932.

648 *Schön ist die Jugend; Der Zyklon*, ed. Theodore Geissendoerfer, Prentice-Hall, 1932.

649 *In Dichters Lande: Erlebtes und Gestaltetes*, ed. Jane F. Goodloe, F. S. Crofts & Co., 1939 (*Tragisch*).

650 *Intermediate German Readings*, ed. James A. Chiles, Ginn and Co., 1940 (*Ein Abend bei Doktor Faust*).

651 *Graded German Reader for Beginners*, ed. Edwin H. Zeydel, 2nd ed., Appleton-Century-Crofts, 1947 (poem, *Allein*).

652 *Drei Nobelpreisträger: Hauptmann, Mann und Hesse*, ed. Claude Hill, Harper and Brothers, 1948 (*Im Presselschen Gartenhaus*).

653 *Kinderseele. Drei Erzählungen*, ed. K. W. Maurer, London, 1948 (*Meine Kindheit, Kinderseele, Erinnerung an Hans*).

654 *Zwei Erzählungen: Der Novalis; Der Zwerg*, eds. Anna Jacobson and Anita Ascher, Appleton-Century-Crofts, 1948.

655 *Deutsche erleben die Zeit 1914-45*, eds. Hanna Hafkesbrink and Rosemary Park, Houghton Mifflin, 1949 (an excerpt from *Betrachtungen*).

656 *Aus Nah und Fern*, ed. Lore Foltin, Houghton Mifflin, 1950 (*Ein Mann mit Namen Ziegler*).

657 *Drei Erzählungen: Der Lateinschüler; Die Verlobung; Die Heimkehr*, ed. W. C. Peebles, American Book Co., 1950.

658 *36 German Poems*, ed. K. S. Weimar, Houghton Mifflin Co., 1950 (poem, *Manchmal*).

659 *Worte und Wörter. An Intermediate German Reader*, eds. W. F. Michael and G. Schulz-Behrend, Urania Press, 1950 (*Wenn der Krieg noch zwei Jahre dauert*).

660 *German Short Stories of To-day*, eds. Hildegard Schumann and G. M. Wolff, D. C. Heath & Co., 1951 (*Kurzgefasster Lebenslauf*).

661 *Wie sie es Sehen*, eds. E. Davis, A. Gardner, Wm. McClain, J. Mileck and H. Zohn, Henry Holt & Co., 1952 (*Marmorsäge*).

662 *Kinderseele und Ladidel. Zwei Erzählungen*, ed. W. M. Dutton, D. C. Heath & Co. (no date, probably 1952).

663 *Aus unserer Zeit*, eds. I. C. Loram, L. R. Phelps, W. W. Norton and Co., 1956 (*Der Wolf; Ein Abend bei Doktor Faust*).

TRANSLATIONS.

The translator, the place of publication, and the date of the first edition are added whenever possible. The German title is included whenever the work involved is not readily recognized in the foreign title.

JAPANESE

664 *Hoshigusa no Tsuki,* trans. Kenji Takahashi, Kyôto, 1950, 251 pp. (*Heumond*).

665 *Haru no arashi,* trans. Kenji Takahashi, Tokyo, 1950 (*Gertrud*).

666 *Hyôhaku no Hito,* trans. Mayumi Haga, Kyôto, 1950 (*Knulp*). Again with title *Hyôhaku no Tamashii,* trans. Morio Sagara, 1952. Again as *Knulp,* trans. Toshio Uemura, Tokyo, 1953.

667 *Kohan no ie,* trans. Mayumi Haga, Kyôto, 1950 (*Rosshalde*).

668 *Seishun wa Uruwashi,* trans. Kenji Takahashi, Kyôto, 1950 (*Schön ist die Jugend*). Again as *Seishun wa Utsukushi,* trans. Kôji Kunimatsu, Tokyo, 1952.

669 *Sekai Bungaku o dô Yomuka,* trans. Kenji Takahashi, Tokyo, 1950 (*Eine Bibliothek der Weltliteratur*).

670 *Shishû,* trans. Kenji Takahashi, Tokyo, 1950, 306 pp. (poems).

671 *Shishû,* trans. Kenji Takahashi, Tokyo, 1950, 208 pp. (poems).

672 *Chi to ai,* trans. Kenji Takahashi, Kyôto, 1951 (*Narziss u. Goldmund*). Again as *Yûjô no Rekishi,* trans. Kôichi Fujioka, Tokyo, 1953.

673 *Demian,* trans. Kenji Takahashi, Tokyo, 1951. Again in 1952 by Morio Sagara.

674 *Kôya no Okami,* trans. Mayumi Haga, Kyôto, 1951 (*Steppenwolf*).

675 *Sharin no Shita,* Kenji Takahashi, Tokyo, 1951 (*Unterm Rad*). Again trans. Rokurobê Akiyama, Tokyo, 1953.

676 *Jittaruta,* trans. Mayumi Haga, Kyôto, 1952 (*Siddhartha*). Again as *Siddhartha,* trans. Tomio Tezuka, Tokyo, 1952.

677 *Kon'yaku,* trans. Kenji Takahashi, Kyôto, 1952 (*Kleine Welt*).

678 *Kyôshû,* trans. Kenchû Hara, Tokyo, 1952 (*Peter Camenzind*). Again by Shôji Ishinaka, Tokyo, 1952. Again as *Seishun Hôkô,* trans. Taisuke Seki, Tokyo, 1953.

679 *Naimen eno Michi,* trans. Mayumi Haga, Kyôto, 1952 (*Weg nach Innen*).

680 *Shi-Shû,* trans. Kenji Takahashi, Tokyo, 1952, 306 pp. (*Die Gedichte*).

681 *Chi to ai no monogatari,* trans. Kôichi Satô, Tokyo, 1953 (*Fabulierbuch*).

682 *Hôrô,* trans. Kenji Takahashi, Kyôto, 1953 (*Die Wanderung*).

683 *Kodokusha no Ongaku,* trans. Kenji Takahashi, Kyôto, 1953 (*Musik des Einsamen*).

684 *Kôya no Okami* etc, trans. Morio Sagara *et al.,* Tokyo, 1953, 456 pp. (*Steppenwolf, Demian, Heumond, Hermann Lauscher*).

685 *Kyôshû; Haru no arashi; Sasurai no Hito; Seishun wa Uruwashi,* trans. Mayumi Haga, Kenji Takahashi, Tokyo, 1953, 434 pp. (*Peter Camenzind, Gertrud, Knulp, Schön ist die Jugend*).

686 *Seishun Jidai*, trans. Mayumi Haga, Kyôto, 1953 (*Hermann Lauscher*).
687 *Seishun Jidai*, trans. Kunitarô Yamato, Tokyo, 1953 (*Hermann Lauscher, Der Zyklon*).
688 *Seishun wa Uruwashi*, trans. Kôji Kunimatsu, Tokyo, 1953, 243 pp. (*Schön ist die Jugend, Lateinschüler, Ladidel, Heumond*).
689 *Seishun wa Utsukushi*, trans. Taisuke Seki, Tokyo, 1953, 120 pp. (*Schön ist die Jugend, Eine Fussreise im Herbst*).
690 *Sensô to Heiwa*, trans. Mayumi Haga, Kyôto, 1953 (*Krieg und Frieden*).

ENGLISH

691 "In the old Sun," trans. P. Coleman, *German Classics*, ed. K. Francke, Vol. 19, New York, 1914, 325-372. (*Nachbarn*)
692 *Gertrude and I*, based upon *Gertrud*, by Adele Lewisohn, New York, 1915.
693 "Brothers Karamasov—The downfall of Europe," trans. Stephen Hudson, *Dial*, 72 (1922), 607-618. Same translation under title "A prophet of Catastrophe," *Living Age*, 314 (1922), 606-613.
694 "Recent German Poetry," *Criterion*, Oct. 1922, pp. 89-93.
695 *Demian*, trans. N. H. Priday, New York, 1923; New York, 1948, with a foreword by T. Mann.
696 *In Sight of Chaos. The Brothers Karamasoff. Thoughts on Dostoevsky's Idiot*, trans. Stephen Hudson, Zürich, 1923.
697 "Journey with Stevenson," *Living Age*, 333 (1927), 812-814 ("Hesse trifft Stevenson," *Frankfurter Ztg.*, Sept. 11, 1927).
698 *Steppenwolf*, trans. B. Creighton, New York, 1929.
699 "Notes on the theme: Imagination, Writing and Criticism," trans. E. W. T., *This Quarter*, Sept. 1931, pp. 20-34 ("Erinnerung an Lektüre," *NR*, 36, 1925, 964-972).
700 *Death and the Lover*, trans. G. Dunlap, New York, 1932 (*Narziss u. Goldmund*).
701 "Jacob Boehme's Calling," trans. E. B. Ashton, *Heart of Europe*, eds. Klaus Mann, Hermann Kesten, New York, 1934, pp. 928-930 (*Betrachtungen*).
702 "A Life in Brief," trans. Mervyn Savill, *Horizon. A review of Lit. and Art*, Sept. 1946, pp. 175-190 ("Kurzgefasster Lebenslauf," *Traumfährte*).
703 "Bad Poetry," trans. R. T. House, *Poetry*, 70 (1947), 202-205 "Schlechte Gedichte," *Betrachtungen*).
704 *Magister Ludi*, trans. Mervyn Savill, London, New York, 1949 (*Glasperlenspiel*).
705 "Hermann Hesse. Within and Without," trans. T. K. Brown III, *The World's Best*, ed. Whit Burnett, New York, 1950, pp. 830-840. ("Innen und Aussen," *Fabulierbuch*).
706 *Siddhartha*, trans. Hilda Rosner, New York, 1951.
707 "The Brothers Karamazov or The Downfall of Europe. Thoughts on reading Dostoevsky," trans. Harvey Gross, *Western Review*, 17 (1953), 185-195.

708 "Dream Journeys: A Record," trans. Denver Lindley, *Partisan Review*, 5 (1954), 473-482 ("Traumfährte." *Traumfährte*).
709 "Tragic," trans. Denver Lindley, *Partisan Review*, 5 (1954), 482-491 ("Tragisch," *Traumfährte*).
710 *Gertrude*, trans. Hilda Rosner, London, 1955.
711 "Youth, Beautiful Youth," trans. Richard and Clara Winston, *German Stories and Tales*, ed. Robert Pick, New York, 1955, pp. 1-38 (*Schön ist die Jugend*).
712 *The Journey to the East*, trans. Hilda Rosner, London, 1956; New York, 1957.
713 *The Prodigy*, trans. W. J. Strachan, London, 1957 (*Unterm Rad*).

SCATTERED POEMS

714 "In the Fog; Talk in a Gondola," trans. Margarete Münsterberg, *A Harvest of German Verse*, New York, 1917.
715 "Night," trans. L. Lewisohn, *Nation*, 116 (1923), 303.
716 "Spring Song; Night," trans. Ludwig Lewisohn, *Anthology of World Poetry*, ed. Mark Van Doren, New York, 1928, pp. 939-940.
717 "Fog," trans. G. Mueller, *Books Abroad*, 1947, p. 152.
718 "He walked in darkness," trans. A. Robison, *Poet Lore*, 53 (1947), 147.
719 "Midsummer," trans. H. Salinger, *Books Abroad*, 1947, p. 66.
720 "Brother death," trans. O. Seidlin, *Monatshefte*, 40 (1948), 204.
721 "Ende August; Ich bin ein Stern," trans. K. W. Maurer, *German Life and Letters*, 1 (1948), 200-203.
722 "Im Nebel, Böse Zeiten," trans. O. Seidlin, *Contemporary Poetry*, summer 1948, pp. 4-5.
723 A Translation of the poems in *Glasperlenspiel* by Eric Peters, in *Magister Ludi*, trans. Mervyn Savill, London, New York, 1949.
724 Salinger, Hermann, *Twentieth-Century German Verse*, Princeton University Press, 1952 (eight poems by Hesse translated into English).
725 "Good Friday; Brother Death," trans. Marianne Leibholz, *German Life and Letters*, 6 (1953), 129.
726 "In sight of Africa," trans. Margaret Richey, *German Life and Letters*, 6 (1953), 129-130.

SPANISH

727 *Demian*, Buenos Aires, 1930. Again by Luis Lópes Ballesteros y de Torres, Mexico, 1940.
728 *El lobo estepario*, trans. Manuel Manzanares, Buenos Aires, 1943. (*Steppenwolf*).
729 *La ruta interior*, trans. Annie dell Erba, Buenos Aires, 1946. (*Der Weg nach Innen*).
730 *Peter Camenzind*, trans. Jesús Ruiz, Barcelona, 1947, Buenos Aires, 1948.
731 *Siddhartha*, Buenos Aires, 1947.
732 *Bajo la rueda*, trans. Jesús Ruiz, Barcelona, 1948 (*Unterm Rad*).
733 *Narxiso y Goldmundo*, Buenos Aires, 1948.

734   *El juego de abalorios*, trans. Aristides Gregori, Buenos Aires, 1949 (*Glasperlenspiel*).

735   "Sobre las poesías de Goethe," *Boletin del Instituto de Estudios Germánicos de la Universidad de Buenos Aires*, Numéro especial dedícado a Goethe, No. 9, 1949, pp. 5-8 ("Über Goethes Gedichte," *Dank an Goethe*).

736   *Ensueños*, trans. Alfonso Pintó, Barcelona, 1950 (*Traumfährte*).

737   *Gertrudis*, trans. Jorge Pinette, Buenos Aires, 1950.

738   *Pequeño Mundo*, trans. Aristides Gregori, Buenos Aires, 1951 (*Kleine Welt*).

739   *A una hora de medianoche*, trans. Alfredo Cahn, Buenos Aires, 1955 (*Eine Stunde hinter Mitternacht*).

FRENCH

740   *Peter Camenzind*, trans. J. Brocher, 1910. Again by Fernand Delmas, Paris, 1950.

741   *Knulp*, trans. Geneviève Maury, Montrouge-Seine, 1925.

742   *Siddhartha*, trans. Jos. Delage, Paris, 1925.

743   *Le dernier été de Klingsor*, trans. René Bétemps, *Revue d' Allemagne*, 3 (1929).

744   *Demian*, trans. Denise Riboni with preface by F. Bertaux, Paris, 1930.

745   "Âme d'enfant," trans. Mag. Fizaine, *Oeuvres libres*, Vol. 118, Paris, 1931, pp. 341-377 (*Kinderseele, Klingsors letzter Sommer*).

746 ' *Le Loup des Steppes*, trans. Juliette Pary, Paris, 1931.

747   *Anthologie de la poésie allemande*, trans. René Lasne, Georg Rabuse, Paris, 1943 (three poems by Hesse).

748   "Les jours de la peste," trans. D. Riboni, *Suisse Contemporaine*, 7 (1947), 106-113 (extract from *Narziss u. Goldmund*).

749   *Le voyage en Orient*, trans. Jean Lambert with preface by André Gide, Paris, 1948 (*Morgenlandfahrt*).

750   *Narcisse et Goldmund*, trans. Fernand Delmas, Paris, 1948.

751   *Knulp; Un Conte; La Fontaine du cloître de Maulbronn*, trans. Geneviève Maury, Montrouge, 1949.

752   Piot, André, *Hermann Hesse. Poèmes*, Paris, 1952, 73 pp. (twenty-eight poems).

753   *Le jeu des perles de verre*, trans. Jacques Martin, Paris, 1955.

SWEDISH

754   *Peter Camenzind*, trans. Kerstin Måås, Stockholm, 1905.

755   *Gertrud*, trans. Sigrid Abenius, Stockholm, 1913.

756   *Demian*, Stockholm, 1925.

757   *Stäppvargen*, trans. Sven Stolpe, Stockholm, 1932 (*Steppenwolf*).

758   "Nya Tyska Böcker," *Bonniers Litterära Magasin*, 4 (1935): No. 3, 26-34; No. 7, 50-57; No. 9, 22-29. 5 (1936): No. 1, 32-39.

759   *Själens Spegel*, trans. A. Österling, Stockholm, 1939 (*Klein u. Wagner, Kinderseele*).

760 "Fjörde Krigsåret; I Natten; Sommernatt," trans. Joh. Edfelt, *Tolkningar av Tysk, Engelsk och Amerikansk Lyrik,* Stockholm, 1940. pp. 21-24.

761 "Auf Wanderung; Blume, Baum, Vogel; Im Leide; Pfeifen, Belehrung," trans. into Swedish by B. Malmberg, E. Blomberg, A. Österling, G. M. Silfverstolpes, in Joh. Edfelt's *Strövtåg,* Stockholm, 1941, pp. 44-54.

762 *Siddhartha,* trans. Nils Holmberg, Stockholm, 1946.

763 *Drömfärder,* trans. A. Österling & Nils Holmberg, Stockholm, 1948 (*Traumfährte*).

764 *Klingsors sista Sommar; Osterlandsfärden,* trans. Arvid Brenner, Stockholm, 1950.

765 *Glaspärlespelet,* trans. Nils Holmberg, Stockholm, 1952.

766 "Tragiskt," trans. A. Österling, *All världens berättare,* 11, No. 7, (1955), 33-39.

767 "Dammiga böcker," *Bokvännen,* 11 (1956), 49-51.

DANISH

768 *Peter Camenzind,* trans. Ira Wennerberg, Copenhagen, 1907.

769 *Rosshalde,* trans. Svend Drewsen, Copenhagen, 1922.

770 *Under Hjulet,* trans, Soffy Topsøe, Copenhagen, 1922 (*Unterm Rad*).

771 *Demian, trans.* Axel Thomsen, Copenhagen, 1923.

772 *Knulp,* Holstebro, 1930.

773 *Sol og Maane,* trans. C. V. Östergaard, Copenhagen, 1936 (*Narziss u. Goldmund*).

774 *En Barnesjael og to kulturelle Essays,* trans. Clara Hammerich, Copenhagen, 1944 (*Kinderseele*).

775 *Steppeulven,* trans. Karen Hildebrandt, Copenhagen, 1946 (*Steppenwolf*).

776 "Uafsendt brev til en sangerinde," trans. Karen and Frede Schandorf Petersen, *Danske Musiktidskrift,* 26 (1951), 115-121.

777 "Bogens magi," trans. Tage Skou-Hansen, *Heretica,* 5 (1952), 339-350.

778 "Lykki," trans. Henrik Hertig, *Heretica,* 6 (1953), 429-441 (*Glück*).

779 "Kronikkens tidsalder," trans. Conrad Raun, *Vindrosen,* 1 (1954), 230-239 (selection from *Glasperlenspiel*).

780 "Brev til Adele," trans. Axel Davidsen, *Perspektiv,* 3, No. 4 (1955), 43-48.

ITALIAN

781 *L'ultima estate di Klingsor, Klein e. Wagner,* trans. Barbara Allason, Milano, 1931.

782 *Narciss e Boccadoro,* trans. Cristina Baseggio, Milano, 1933.

783 *Voci della poesia di Hermann Hesse,* trans. Roberto Biscardo, Rome, 1933, 166 pp.

784 *Siddhartha. Poema indiano,* trans. Massimo Mila, Turin, 1945.

785 *Il lupo della Steppa,* trans. Ervino Pocar, Milano, 1946.

786 "Dall' infanzia di S. Francesco d'Assisi," trans. Rodolfo Paoli, *Ecclesia Rivista Mensile*, 7 (1948), 264-266 ("Aus der Kindheit des heiligen Franziskus von Assisi," *Fabulierbuch*).
787 *Storia di un vagabondo*, trans. Ervino Pocar, Milano, 1950 (*Knulp*).
788 *Peter Camenzind*, trans. Ervino Pocar, Milano, 1951.
789 *Demian*, trans. Ervino Pocar, Milano, 1952.
790 *Liriche*, trans. Emo Leonardi, Firenze, 1952, 59 pp.
791 *Il giusco delle perle di vetro*, trans. Ervino Pocar, Milano, 1955, (*Glasperlenspiel*).

DUTCH

792 *Siddhartha. Een droombeeld uit het land der Brahmanen*, trans. Boer-Breijer, 'S-Graveland, 1928.
793 *Narcis en Guldemond*, trans. John Kooy, Utrecht, 1939.
794 *Siddhartha; Klingsor's laatste Zomer; Klein en Wagner*, trans. B. H. den Boer-Breijer and G. Huib A. Verstegen, 'S-Graveland, 1949.
795 *Poverello*, trans. K. H. R. de Josselin de Jong, Delft, 1955, 31 pp.

NORWEGIAN

796 *Knulp*, 1930.
797 *Demian, Historien om Emil Sinclairs ungdom*, trans. Bjarne Gran, Trondheim, 1947.
798 *Peter Camenzind*.

FINNISH

799 *Alppien poika*, trans. Eino Railo, Helsinki, 1908 (*Peter Camenzind*).
800 *Arosusi*, trans. Eeva-Liisa Manner, Helsinki, 1952 (*Steppenwolf*).

HUNGARIAN

801 *Peter Camenzind*, 1920.
802 *Sziddhártha*.

CHINESE

803 *Schön ist die Jugend*, 1937.

PORTUGUESE

804 *Ele e o Outro*, trans. Manuela de Sousa Marques, Lisboa, 1952 (*Klein u. Wagner*).

GREEK

805 "Chioggia, und Die Zypressen von San Clemente," in German with Greek translations, Holzminden, Privatdruck, 1949, 9 pp.
806 *Poietike Techne*. A number of Hesse's poems in Greek translation are printed in this periodical's volume of 1947.
807 *Ho Aionas Mas*. A few more poems in this periodical's volume of 1949.

SLAVIC

808 Peter Camenzind, Russian, 1905.
809 Unterm Rad, Russian, 1906.
810 Rosshalde, trans. A. S. Polockoj, Russkaja Mysl'., 1914.
811 Tropa Mudrosti, Leningrad, 1924 (Siddhartha).
812 Siddhartha, Polish, 1932; Czechoslovakian, 1935.
813 Steppenwolf, Czechoslovakian, 1931; Polish, 1932.
814 Narziss und Goldmund, Polish, 1932.
815 "V Hmlách," trans. E. B. Lukáč, Books Abroad, 1947, p. 392 ("Im Nebel," in Solvak).
816 "U Magli," trans. Preveo Gustav Krklec, Republika 11 (Feb./March, 1955), 137 ("Im Nebel," in Croatian).

MISCELLANY

817 Twenty-six poems translated by students of the Technische Hochschule in Dresden into Gothic. Poems sent in manuscript form to Hesse in 1948 (see Briefe [1951], p. 278).
818 Professor Grant Loomis of the University of California expects shortly to publish a small volume of his translations of poems by Hesse.
819 Kliemann notes (Europa-Archiv, 1 [1947], 609) that the following works are available in Braille:

Franz von Assisi
Vom Baum des Lebens
Peter Camenzind
Demian
Diesseits
Es war ein König in Indien
Gedichte
Gertrud
Kurgast
Der Lateinschüler
Hermann Lauscher

Musik des Einsamen
Nachbarn
Narziss u. Goldmund
Unterm Rad
Nürnberger Reise
Rosshalde
Schön ist die Jugend
Siddhartha
In der alten Sonne
Umwege
Weg nach Innen

WORKS ABOUT HESSE

BOOKS AND PRINTED DISSERTATIONS:

1 Ball, Hugo, *Hermann Hesse. Sein Leben und sein Werk* (Berlin, 1927), 243 pp. Supplemented in 1933 by Anni Rebenwurzel's (Carlsson) "Vom *Steppenwolf* zur *Morgenlandfahrt*," pp. 237-258, and again in 1947 by her "Hermann Hesses *Glasperlenspiel* in seinen Wesensgesetzen," 306 pp. In 1947 the edition of 1933 was also supplemented by Otto Basler's "Der Weg zum *Glasperlenspiel*," pp. 272-340, and by Hesse's "Nachruf an Hugo Ball," pp. 341-342 (Zürich), 351 pp.

2 Bode, Helmut, *Hermann Hesse. Variationen über einen Lieblingsdichter* (Frankfurt a. M., 1948), 172 pp.

3 Dürr, Werner, *Hermann Hesse. Vom Wesen der Musik in der Dichtung* (Stuttgart, 1957), 120 pp.

4 Engel, Otto, *Hermann Hesse. Dichtung und Gedanke* (Stuttgart, 1947), 95 pp.

5 Geffert, Heinrich, *Das Bildungsideal im Werk Hermann Hesses. Eine erziehungswissenschaftliche Studie*, Fr. Manns Pädagog. Magazin, Heft 1127 (Langensalza, 1927), 106 pp.; doctoral dissertation, Hamburg, 1927.

6 Gnefkow, Edmund, *Hermann Hesse. Biographie* (Freiburg i. Br., 1952), 143 pp.; doctoral dissertation, Freiburg i. Br., 1951. Hesse's "Rückblick. Ein Fragment aus der Zeit um 1937," pp. 7-11; Gerhard Kirchhoff's "Das *Glasperlenspiel* als *Reine Gegenwart*," pp. 117-140.

7 Hafner, Gotthilf, *Hermann Hesse. Werk und Leben* (Nürnberg, 1954), 175 pp.

8 Kliemann, Horst; Karl H. Silomon, *Hermann Hesse. Eine bibliographische Studie. Zum 2. Juli 1947* (Frankfurt a. M., 1947), 95 pp.

9 Konheiser-Barwanietz, Christa M., *Hermann Hesse und Goethe* (Berlin, 1954), 98 pp.; doctoral dissertation, Bern, 1953.

10 Kunze, Johanna M. L., *Lebensgestaltung und Weltanschauung in Hermann Hesses Siddhartha* (Hertogenbosch, 1946), 84 pp.; Academisch Proefschrift, Amsterdam, 1946.

11 Lützkendorf, Ernst A. Felix, *Hermann Hesse als religiöser Mensch in seinen Beziehungen zur Romantik und zum Osten* (Burgdorf, 1932), 95 pp.; doctoral dissertation, Leipzig, 1931.

12 Matzig, Richard B., *Hermann Hesse in Montagnola. Studien zu Werk und Innenwelt des Dichters* (Basel, 1947), 119 pp. Published again in Stuttgart, 1949, 146 pp.

13 Mauerhofer, Hugo, *Die Introversion, mit spezieller Berücksichtigung des Dichters Hermann Hesse* (Bern u. Leipzig, 1929), 61 pp.; doctoral dissertation, Bern, 1929.

14 Mayer, Gerhard, *Die Begegnung des Christentums mit den asiatischen Religionen im Werk Hermann Hesses* (Bonn, 1956), 181 pp.; doctoral dissertation, Braunschweig, 1955.

15 Nadler, Käte, *Hermann Hesse. Naturliebe, Menschenliebe, Gottesliebe* (Leipzig, 1956), 143 pp.

16 Plümacher, Walter, *Versuch einer metaphysischen Grundlegung literaturwissenschaftlicher Grundbegriffe aus Kants Antinomienlehre mit einer Anwendung auf das Kunstwerk Hermann Hesses*, Bonner deutsche Studien, Bd. 1 (Würzburg, 1936), 81 pp.; doctoral dissertation, Bonn, 1936.

17 Schmid, Hans Rudolf, *Hermann Hesse*. Die Schweiz im deutschen Geistesleben, Bd. 56/57 (Frauenfeld, 1928), 218 pp.; in part, doctoral dissertation, Zürich, 1928.

18 Schmid, Max, *Hermann Hesse. Weg und Wandlung. Mit einem bibliographischen Anhang von Armin Lemp* (Zürich, 1947), 288 pp. This doctoral dissertation (Zürich, 1947) was first published without Armin's bibliography as *Konfliktwandel in Hermann Hesses Neueren Werken* (Zürich, 1947), 240 pp. Schmid's work was translated into English by A. A. Dawson, "Hermann Hesse. Growth of a poet" (M.A.), Southern Methodist University, 1949.

19 Weibel, Kurt, *Hermann Hesse und die deutsche Romantik* (Winterthur, 1954), 146 pp.; dissertation, Bern, 1953.

20 *Dank an Hermann Hesse. Reden und Aufsätze* (Frankfurt a. M., 1952), 122 pp.

21 *Schriftsteller der Gegenwart. Hermann Hesse* (Berlin, 1956), 147 pp. This teacher's guide was published by the "Kollektiv für Literaturgeschichte" in East Berlin. The first portion of the book, a general study of Hesse, is based largely on Dr. Margot Böttcher's unpublished "Hermann Hesse's Leben und Werk." The second portion consists of extracts from Hesse's works.

PAMPHLETS:

22 Adolph, Rudolf, *Hermann Hesse, Schutzpatron der Bücherfreunde* (Olten, 1952), 23 pp.

23 Angelloz, J. F., *Das Mütterliche und das Männliche im Werk Hermann Hesses*, Schriftenreihe der Saarländischen Kulturgesellschaft, 2 (Saarbrücken, 1951), 31 pp.

24 Baaten, Heta, *Die pietistische Tradition der Familien Gundert und Hesse* (Bochum-Langendreer, 1934), 42 pp. Part of a doctoral dissertation, Münster, 1932; see dissertations (on microfilm, University of California, Berkeley).

25 Basler, Otto, *Hermann Hesse, 60 Jahre. Gesprochen auf der Feier am 2. Juli 1937 im Studio Zürich* (Menzikon, 1937), 8 pp.

26 Baumer, Franz, *Hermann Hesse. Der Dichter und sein Lebenswerk* (Murnau, Olten: Lux-Lesebogen, 193, 1955), 32 pp.

27 Bühner, Karl Hans, *Hermann Hesse und Gottfried Keller. Eine Studie* (Stuttgart, 1927), 59 pp.

28 Carlsson, Anni, *Hermann Hesses Gedichte* (Zürich, 1943), 13 pp.

29 Engel, Otto, *Hermann Hesse. Ein Vortrag* (Zürich, 1947), 31 pp. Same as first part of 4.

30 Finckh, Ludwig, *Schwäbische Vettern. Hermann Hesse zum 71. Geburtstag am 2. Juli 1948*, Westdeutsches Hermann Hesse-Archiv (Köln, 1948), 15 pp.

31 Fuchs, Hella, *Hermann Hesse. Zu seinem sechzigsten Geburtstag* (Prag, 1937), 14 pp.

32 Goes, Albrecht, *Rede auf Hermann Hesse* (Berlin, 1946), 38 pp.

33 Hafner, Gotthilf, *Hermann Hesse. Werk und Leben. Umrisse eines Dichterbildes* (Reinbeck bei Hamburg, 1947), 87 pp. See 7.

34 Hecker, Joachim F. von, *Hermann Hesse. Zwei Vorträge* (Murnau, 1949), 64 pp.

35 Heilbut, Ivan; Anna Jacobson; George N. Shuster, *Die Sendung Hermann Hesses. Drei Beiträge zur Würdigung des Dichters* (New York, 1947), 24 pp. "Hermann Hesses Sendung in unserer Zeit," pp. 2-15; "Hermann Hesse. Anlässlich der Auszeichnung durch den Nobelpreis," pp. 16-21; "Die Seele eines Künstlers," pp. 22-24.

36 Huber, Hans, *Hermann Hesse* (Heidelberg, 1948), 72 pp.

37 Kirchhoff, Gerhard, *Reine Gegenwart. Über Hermann Hesses Glasperlenspiel* (Freiburg i. Br., 1952), 28 pp. See 6.

38 Kliemann, Horst, *Hermann Hesse und das Buch. Bemerkungen zu einer Hesse-Bibliographie*, 12 pp. Sonderdruck aus *Deutsche Beiträge*, 1 (1947), 353-360, 381-385.

39 ———, *Das Werk Hermann Hesses. Eine bibliographische Übersicht*, 8 pp. Sonderdruck aus *Europa-Archiv*, 1 (1947), 604-609.

40 ———; Karl H. Silomon, *Verbesserungen und Ergänzungen zu Hermann Hesse. Eine bibliographische Studie* (1948), 12 pp.

41 Kolb, Walter, *Ansprache und Rede für Hermann Hesse* (Frankfurt a. M., 1946), 16 pp.; speech made by *Oberbürgermeister* Kolb when Hesse received the *Goethepreis* in 1946.

42 Korrodi, Otto, *Mein Mentor Hermann Hesse,* Westdeutsches Hermann Hesse-Archiv (Köln, 1948), 15 pp.

43 Kramer, Walter, *Hermann Hesses Glasperlenspiel und seine Stellung in der geistigen Situation unsrer Zeit,* Wilhelmshaver Vorträge. Schriftenreihe der nordwestdeutschen Universitätsgesellschaft, No. 2 (1949), 22 pp.

44 Kuhn, Alfred, *Hermann Hesse. Ein Essay,* Beiträge zur Literaturgeschichte, ed. Hermann Graef, No. 45 (Leipzig, 1907), 54 pp.

45 Levander, Hans, *Hermann Hesse,* Studentföreningen Verdandis Småskrifter, No. 498 (Stockholm, 1949), 63 pp.

46 Lorenzen, Hermann, *Pädagogische Ideen bei Hermann Hesse* (Mülheim-Ruhr, 1955), 72 pp.

47 Mann, Thomas; André Gide; Hans Carossa, *Hermann Hesse* (St. Gallen, 1948), 29 pp. Mann, "Für Hermann Hesse" (1947), pp. 3-14; Gide, "Bemerkungen zum Werk Hermann Hesses" (1947), pp. 15-27; Carossa, "Schutzgeist" (a poem, 1946), pp. 28-29.

48 Matzig, Richard B., *Der Dichter und die Zeitstimmung. Betrachtungen über Hermann Hesses Steppenwolf* (St. Gallen, 1944), 51 pp.

49 Pfeifer, Martin, *Bibliographie der im Gebiet der DDR seit 1945 erschienenen Schriften von und über Hermann Hesse* (Zwickau-Planitz, abgeschlossen Ende Mai 1952), 15 pp.

50 ———, *Bibliographie der im Gebiet der DDR seit 1945 erschienenen Schriften von und über Hermann Hesse* (Leipzig, 1955), 63 pp.

51 Richter, Georg, *Hermann Hesse, der Dichter und Mensch* (Berlin, 1947), 48 pp.

52 Schmid, Karl, *Hermann Hesse und Thomas Mann. Zwei Möglichkeiten europäischer Humanität* (Olten, 1950), 48 pp.

53 Schussen, Wilhelm; Max Hermann-Neisse; Karl Kloter, *Besuch bei Hermann Hesse,* Westdeutsches Hermann Hesse-Archiv (Köln, 1949), 24 pp. Schussen, "Hermann Hesse und die Schmetterlinge," 6 pp.; Hermann-Neisse, "Besuch bei Hermann Hesse," 2 pp. in verse; Kloter, "Weg zum Dichter," 4 pp.

54 Schwinn, Wilhelm, *Hermann Hesses Altersweisheit und das Christentum* (München, 1949), 39 pp.

55 Unseld, Siegfried, *Das Werk von Hermann Hesse. Ein Brevier* (Frankfurt a. M., 1952), 72 pp. New edition, summer 1955, 78 pp.

56 Wüstenberg, H. L., *Stimme eines Menschen. Die politischen Aufsätze und Gedichte Hermann Hesses* (Konstanz, 1947), 23 pp.

57 *The American-German Review,* Oct.-Nov., 1956, 40 pp. This issue dedicated to Hesse but not devoted entirely to him, comprises: an editorial by R. C. Wood; Hesse's "Haus zum Frieden," and "Klage und Trost," a poem dedicated to Ludwig Finckh upon the occasion of his eightieth birthday; a brief Hesse chronology; a water color by Hesse; and photographs of Hesse and of various places associated with him.

58 *Dank des Herzens. Gedichte an Hermann Hesse,* Westdeutsches Hermann Hesse-Archiv (Köln, 1949), 24 pp.

59 *Du. Schweizerische Monatsschrift,* 13 (Feb. 1953), 62 pp. This issue, dedicated to Hesse, is a composite of extracts from his works,

a few poems, water colors, photographs, extracts from *Marie Hesse. Ein Lebensbild in Briefen und Tagebüchern,* a number of letters addressed to Hesse, and eight items about him (see periodicals: Birrer, Baeschlin, Korrodi, Käge, Weber, Angelloz, Debruge).

60 *Hermann Hesse als Badener Kurgast* (St. Gallen, 1952), 26 pp. Hesse: "Die Dohle" and extracts dealing with Baden; Robert Mächler, "Hermann Hesses Badener Psychologie," pp. 11-15; Uli Münzel, "Hermann Hesse als Badener Kurgast," pp. 17-21.

61 *Hermann Hesse. Vier Ansprachen anlässlich der Verleihung des Friedenspreises des deutschen Buchhandels* (Frankfurt a. M.: Börsenverein des deutschen Buchhandels E. V., 1955), 37 pp. Arthur Georgi, "Hermann Hesse und der Sinn des Friedenspreises," pp. 7-12; Richard Benz, "Festansprache," pp. 15-24; Hermann Hesse, "Dankadresse," pp. 27-31; Robert Jockusch, "Ansprache anlässlich des Empfangs zu Ehren des Preisträgers," pp. 35-37.

62 *Ein paar Leserbriefe an Hermann Hesse* (Frankfurt a. M.), 1955, 39 pp.

63 *Stimmen zum Briefbuch von Hermann Hesse* (Montagnola, 1951), 20 pp. Expressions of praise and gratitude by Hedda Eulenberg, Max Rychner, and "an old pedagogue," along with two letters written by Hesse in July 1951. See 104, 190.

ARTICLES AND PERTINENT PASSAGES IN BOOKS AND PAMPHLETS:

64 Aretz, Karl, "Ein Gruss an Hermann Hesse," *Das Bodenseebuch* (Konstanz, 1930), pp. 108-109.

65 Bahr, Hermann, *Kritik der Gegenwart* (Augsburg, 1922), pp. 92-98 (a severe criticism of Hesse's alleged misinterpretation of Dostoyevsky).

66 Ball, Hugo, *Die Flucht aus der Zeit* (Luzern, 1946); see index for numerous references to Hesse.

67 ———, "Vom Wesen Hermann Hesses," *S. Fischer Almanach* (Berlin, 1928), pp. 19-25. See 1.

68 Ball-Hennings, Emmy, *Briefe an Hermann Hesse* (Frankfurt a. M., 1956), 442 pp.

69 ———, *Hugo Ball. Sein Leben in Briefen und Gedichten* (Berlin, 1930); twenty letters addressed to Hesse.

70 ———, *Hugo Balls Weg zu Gott* (München, 1931), pp. 93-99, 118, 151-152, 154, 160-165.

71 Bartels, Adolf, *Jüdische Herkunft und Literaturwissenschaft* (Leipzig, 1925), p. 136.

72 Basler, Otto; F. K. Mathys; F. H. Weber, *Für Thomas Mann* (Basel, 1954), pp. 31, 57.

73 Becher, Johannes R., *Poetische Konfession* (Berlin, 1954), pp. 52-53.

74 ———, *Verteidigung der Poesie* (Berlin, 1952), pp. 384-385.

75 Beck, Adolf, "Dienst und reuelose Lebensbeichte im lyrischen Werk Hermann Hesses," *Festschrift. Paul Kluckhohn und Hermann Schneider* (Tübingen, 1948), pp. 445-467.

76 Behrens, Ada, *Der entwurzelte Mensch im Familienroman von 1880 bis zur Gegenwart* (Lübeck, 1932), 45 pp. (doctoral dissertation, Bonn, 1932).

77 Bennet, E. K., *A History of the German Novelle* (Cambridge, 1934), pp. 240-241.

78 Berger, Berta, "Hermann Hesse. Die Darstellung des seelischen Chaos," *Der Moderne Deutsche Bildungsroman* (Sprache und Dichtung. Forschungen zur Sprach- und Literaturwissenschaft, Heft 69, Bern-Leipzig, 1942), pp. 47-53.

79 Bernoulli, C. A., *Johann Jakob Bachofen und das Natursymbol* (Basel, 1924), p. 493 (*Demian*).

80 Bick, Ignatz, *Das Erziehungsproblem im modernen Roman seit dem Naturalismus* (Gelnhausen, 1931), 128 pp. (doctoral dissertation, Frankfurt a. M., 1931).

81 Binz, Arthur F., *Die abendliche Allee* (Würzburg, 1924), pp. 51-59.

82 Blei, Franz, "Hermann Hesse," *Das grosse Bestiarium der Modernen Literatur* (Berlin, 1922), pp. 39-40.

83 Bock, Werner, "Hermann Hesse. Premio Nobel de literatura de 1946"; "Hermann Hesse. El Caminante"; "Comunion de dos grandes Individualistas: André Gide y Hermann Hesse," *Idea y Amor De Goethe à Hesse* (Buenos Aires, 1952), pp. 165-173, 175-177, 179-183.

84   Böckmann, Paul, "Hermann Hesse," *Deutsche Literatur im Zwanzig-sten Jahrhundert*, eds. Hermann Friedmann, Otto Mann (Heidelberg, 1954), pp. 288-304.

85   Boeckh, Joachim G., *Literaturfibel* (Berlin, 1952), pp. 134, 156.

86   Böhmer, Gunter, "Malausflug mit Hermann Hesse," *Das Bodensee-buch* (Lindau, 1936), 4 pp.

87   Bollnow, Otto Fr., "Hermann Hesses Weg in die Stille,"*Unruhe und Geborgenheit im Weltbild neuerer Dichter* (Stuttgart, 1953), pp. 31-69.

88   Boucher, Maurice, "Les soubresauts de l'humanisme," *Le roman allemand contemporain et la crise de l'esprit* (Editions Stock, Paris, 1940). Only the proofs of this book, which was suppressed by the Nazis, are available at the Sorbonne, the Bibliothèque Nationale and at the École Normale Supérieure.

89   Braem, Helmut M., "1945-1953," *Deutsche Literatur im Zwanzigsten Jahrhundert*, eds. Hermann Friedmann, Otto Mann (Heidelberg, 1954), pp. 426-428 (*Glasperlenspiel*).

90   Brand, Guido K., *Werden und Wandlung* (Berlin, 1933), pp. 335-337.

91   Buchwald, Reinhard, "Hermann Hesse," *Bekennende Dichtung. Ricarda Huch, Hermann Hesse* (Zürich, 1949), pp. 33-87.

92   Busse, Carl, Introduction to the *Gedichte* of 1902 (Berlin: Grote).

93   Carossa, Hans, *Ungleiche Welten* (Wiesbaden, 1951), pp. 160-170.

94   Chen, Chuan, *Die chinesische schöne Literatur im deutschen Schrifttum* (Glückstadt-Hamburg, 1933), 108 pp. (doctoral dissertation, Kiel, 1933).

95   Curtius, Ernst Robert, "Hermann Hesse," *Kritische Essays zur europäischen Literatur* (Bern, 1950), pp. 202-223.

96   Edfelt, Johannes, "Hermann Hesse," *Europas Litteraturhistoria 1918-1939*, ed. Artur Lundkvist (Stockholm, 1947), pp. 576-583.

97   ———, "Nattens tröst," *Strövtag* (Stockholm, 1941), pp. 44-45.

98   Egger, Eugen, *Ein Weg aus dem Chaos* (Olten, 1951), pp. 160-161 (Ball-Hesse friendship).

99   Eichbaum, Gerda, *Die Krisis der modernen Jugend im Spiegel der Dichtung* (Erfurt, 1930), 165 pp. (doctoral dissertation, Giessen, 1929).

100 Eickhorst, William, *Decadence in German Fiction* (Denver, 1935), 179 pp. (for Hesse, see index).

101 Elster, Hanns Martin, "Hermann Hesses Leben und Werk," *Im Pressel'schen Gartenhaus*, (Dresden: Deutsche Dichterhandschriften, 1920), Vol. 6, 7-22 (Geleitwort).

102 ———, "Hermann Hesses Leben und Werk," *Gertrud* (Berlin: Deutsche Buchgemeinschaft, 1927), pp. 5-48 (Geleitwort); same as preceding item except for additional remarks about *Siddhartha* and *Bilderbuch*.

103 Engelmann, Susanne, An Introduction to *Der Zyklon* (Berlin, 1929).

104 Eulenberg, Hedda, *Im Doppelglück von Kunst und Leben* (Düsseldorf, 1952), pp. 391-392. See 63.

105 Faesi, Robert, *Thomas Mann* (Zürich, 1955), pp. 61, 62, 62, 64, 65, 72-75 (Hesse's *Kurgast* and Mann's *Zauberberg*).

106 Fankhauser, Alfred, *Von den Werten des Lebens* (Bern, 1922), pp. 83-94.

107 Finckh, Ludwig, *Ahnenbüchlein* (Görlitz), pp. 6-7; written in 1920.

108 Fink, Gertrud, *Ludwig Finckh. Leben und Werk* (Tübingen, 1936), pp. 13, 18-19, 22, 31-35.

109 Forst, John, *Indien und die deutsche Literatur von 1900 bis 1923* (Borna-Leipzig, 1934), pp. 25-29 (doctoral dissertation, New York University, 1935).

110 Franulic, Lenka, "Hermann Hesse," *Cien Autores Contemporáneos*, 3rd ed. (Santiago de Chile, 1952), pp. 397-405.

111 Frerking, Johann, "Dank an Hesse," *Dank und Gedenken. Hesse, Hauptmann und Werfel* (Hannover,1947), pp. 5-33.

112 Fried, Alfred H., "Hermann Hesse und die Pazifisten," *Vom Weltkrieg zum Weltfrieden* (Zürich, 1916), pp. 90-94.

113 Frohnmeyer, Ida, "In Erinnerung (Joh. Hesse)," *Die Ernte*, 21 (Basel, 1941), 65-72.

114 Gide, André, "Morgenlandfahrt," *Préfaces* (Neuchâtel-Paris), 1948, pp. 181-189. Foreword to *Le Voyage en Orient* (Paris, 1948). See 47.

115 Grenzmann, Wilhelm, *Gott und Mensch im jüngsten deutschen Roman* (Bonn, 1948), pp. 32-41 (*Glasperlenspiel*).

116 ———, "Hermann Hesse," *Deutsche Dichtung der Gegenwart* (Frankfurt a. M., 1953), pp. 100-108.

117 ———, "Hermann Hesse. Geist und Sinnlichkeit," *Dichtung und Glaube* (Bonn, 1950), pp. 106-120; (Bonn, 1952), pp. 114-129.

118 Grolman, Adolf von, *Kind und Junger Mensch in der Dichtung der Gegenwart* (Berlin, 1930), pp. 88-92, 123-127.

119 Groth, Helge, "Hermann Hesse," *Dichter des Humanismus im heutigen Deutschland* (Berlin, 1939), pp. 91-133.

120 Gundert, Adele, *Marie Hesse. Ein Lebensbild in Briefen und Tagebüchern* (Stuttgart, 1934), 283 pp.

121 Hartmann, Ursula, *Typen dichterischer Selbstbiographien in den letzten Jahrzehnten* (Bonn, 1940), 115 pp. (doctoral dissertation, Breslau, 1940).

122 Hartwich, Otto, "Die Grosse Sehnsucht. Hermann Hesse: *Peter Camenzind*," *Kulturwerte aus der modernen Literatur* (Bremen, 1912, Vol. 3, 50-80.

123 Hauser, Arnold, *Sozialgeschichte der Kunst und Literatur* (München, 1953), Vol. 2, 535.

124 Heiney, Donald W., "Hermann Hesse," *Contemporary Literature* (New York: Barrow's Educational Series Inc., 1954), pp. 189-193.

125 Heiting, Ingeborg, *Der Muttergedanke als Zeitausdruck in neuerer Literatur*, Köln, 1938), pp. 31-41 (doctoral dissertation, Bonn, 1938).

126 Hendriksen, Jørgen, ▪oduction to Clara Hammerich's tranlation: *En Barnesjael og t⌐ ▪▪lturelle Essays*. Hasselbalchs Kultur-Bibliotek, Vol. 38 (Copenhagen, 1944).

127 Hesse, Johannes, *Aus Dr. Hermann Gunderts Leben* (Calw, 1894), 368 pp.

128 Heuss, Theodor, "Einleitung," *Sieben Schwaben* (Heilbronn, 1909).

129 ———,"Hermann Hesse," *Reden, Aufsätze und Briefe aus den Jahren 1949-1955* (Stuttgart, 1955), pp. 77-84, 85, 427. See 20.

130 Holm, Korfiz, *Farbiger Abglanz* (München, 1947), p. 163.

131 Hoerschelmann, Rolf von, *Leben ohne Alltag* (Berlin, 1947), p. 19.

132 Holmberg, Olle, "Hermann Hesse," *Inte bara om Hamlet* (Stockholm, 1949), pp. 118-122.

133 Horst, K. A., "Das Literarische Kuckucksei," *Deutscher Geist zwischen Gestern und Morgen*, eds. Joachim Moras, Hans Paeschke (Stuttgart, 1945), pp. 371-372 (*Glasperlenspiel*).

134 Hunnius, Monika, *Mein Onkel Hermann. Erinnerungen an Alt-Estland* (Heilbronn, 1921), 126 pp.

135 ———, *Mein Weg zur Kunst* (Heilbronn, 1924), pp. 319-323.

136 Ihlenfeld, Kurt, "Hermann Hesses Friedensbotschaft," *Poeten und Propheten* (Witten, 1951), pp. 283-288.

137 Ilberg, Werner, *Traum und Tat. Romain Rolland in seinem Verhältnis zu Deutschland und zur Sowjet-Union* (Halle, 1950), p. 57.

138 Jerven, Walter, "Eine literarische Bodenseewanderung," *Das Bodenseebuch* (Konstanz, 1914), pp. 155-157 (*Unterwegs*).

139 ———, "Von unsern Bodenseedichtern," *Das Bodenseebuch* (Konstanz, 1930), pp. 181-182 (*Rosshalde*).

140 Kehr, Charlotte, *Der deutsche Entwicklungsroman seit der Jahrhuntertwende* (Dresden, 1939), 127 pp. (*Peter Camenzind*).

141 Kiener, H., *Thieme-Becker, Allgem. Lexikon der bildenden Künstler* (Leipzig, 1923), Vol. 16, 591.

142 Klaiber, Theodor, *Gottfried Keller und die Schwaben* (Stuttgart, 1919), pp. 93-102.

143 ———, "Hermann Hesse," *Die Schwaben in der Literatur der Gegenwart* (Stuttgart, 1905), pp. 87-104.

144 ———, "Hermann Hesse," *Württemberg unter der Regierung König Wilhelms II* (Stuttgart, 1916), pp. 512-515.

145 Klein, Johannes, "Hermann Hesse," *Geschichte der deutschen Novelle von Goethe bis zur Gegenwart* (Wiesbaden, 1954), pp. 468-470.

146 Kliemann, Horst, "Hermann Hesse und München," *Weihnachten mit Büchern* (Straubing: Attenkofersche Sort.-Buchhandlung, 1947), pp. 7-10.

147 Kohlschmid, Werner, "Miditationen über Hermann Hesses *Glasperlenspiel*"; "Das Motiv der entzweiten Welt" (Hesse, Werfel, Jünger), *Die Entzweite Welt. Studien zum Menschenbild in der neuen Dichtung* (Gladbeck, 1953), pp. 127-154, 155-166.

148 Kraeger, Heinrich, *Vorträge und Kritiken* (Oldenburg, 1911), pp. 210-215.

149 Kretschmer, Max, "Hermann Hesse," *Schicksale deutscher Dichter* (Langensalza, 1932), Vol. 2, 253-278.

150 K. H. M., "Italienbücher von Hesse, Alfons Paquet, Hanns Heinz Ewers," *Das Bodenseebuch* (Konstanz, 1914), pp. 165-168.

151 Lang, Renée, *André Gide und der deutsche Geist* (Stuttgart, 1953), p. 240.

152 Laux, Karl, *Joseph Haas* (Berlin, 1954), pp. 118-119, 187-188, 215, 281.

153 Leese, Kurt, *Die Mutter als religiöses Symbol* (Tübingen, 1934), pp. 26-28.

154 Lemp, Armin, "Hermann Hesse. Bibliographie," Max Schmid, *Hermann Hesse. Weg und Wandlung* (Zürich, 1947), pp. 241-288.

155 Lestiboudois, Herbert, "Geschenk und Gnade," *Literarische Miniaturen* (Hamburg, 1948), pp. 100-118.

156 Litt, Theodor, *Die Geschichte und das Übergeschichtliche* (Hamburg, 1949), pp. 22-29 (*Glasperlenspiel*).

157 Loerke, Oskar, *Tagebücher 1903-1939*, ed. Hermann Kasack (Heidelberg/Darmstadt, 1955), pp. 33, 115, 138, 140, 155, 159, 162, 261, 336, 350.

158 Lublinski, Samuel, *Der Ausgang der Modernen* (Dresden, 1909), pp. 186-187.

159 Magnat, G. E., "Hermann Hesse," *Die Sprache der Handschrift* (Luzern, 1948), pp. 125-128.

160 Maier, Hans, "Hermann Hesse siebzigjährig," *Ex Libris*, ed. Ernst Hauser (Zürich, 1947), pp. 99-101.

161 Mann, Erika, *Das Letzte Jahr* (Frankfurt a. M., 1956), pp. 6, 8-9, 24, 52.

162 Mann, Thomas, *Die Entstehung des Doktor Faustus* (Amsterdam, 1949), pp. 68-69 (*Glasperlenspiel*).

163 ———, "Hermann Hesse, Liberator of a stifling provincialism." Foreword to *Demian* (New York, 1947), v-xiv. See 47.

164 ———, "Hermann Hesse zum siebzigsten Geburtstag, 1947," *Altes und Neues* (Frankfurt a. M., 1953), pp. 225-231. See 163.

165 Marck, Siegried von, *Grosse Menschen aus unserer Zeit* (Meisenheim am Glan, 1954), 226 pp. (includes an essay about Hesse).

166 Marti, Fritz, *Lichter und Funken* (Zürich, 1914), pp. 400-409.

167 Mayer, Hans, "Hermann Hesse und das feuilletonistische Zeitalter," *Studien zur deutschen Literaturgeschichte* (Berlin, 1954), pp. 225-240.

168 ———, *Literatur der Übergangszeit* (Berlin, 1949), pp. 25-26, 28 (*Glasperlenspiel*).

169 ———, *Thomas Mann: Werk und Entwicklung* (Berlin, 1950), pp. 31-32.

170 Mjöberg, Jöran, *Livsproblemet Hos Lagerkvist* (Stockholm, 1951), pp. 6, 67, 77, 113.

171 Moser, Joachim H., *Goethe und die Musik* (Leipzig, 1949), p. 41.

172 Mueller, Gustav E., "Hermann Hesse," *Philosophy of Literature* (New York, 1948), pp. 205-216 (a slight elaboration of 574).

173 Müller, Lotte, *Der deutsche Unterricht* (Bad Heilbronn, 1952), p. 73.

174 Natorp, Paul, *Fjedor Dostojewskis Bedeutung für die gegenwärtige Kulturkrisis* (Jena, 1923), p. 36.

175 Oepke, Albrecht, "Hermann Hesse," *Moderne Indienfahrer und Weltreligionen. Eine Antwort an Waldemar Bonsels, Hermann Hesse, Graf Hermann Keyserling* (Leipzig, 1921), pp. 8-15.

176 Paulsen, Wolfgang, *Expressionism und Aktivism* (Leipzig-Bern, 1935), pp. 100-102.

177 Pfeiffer, Johannes, "Hermann Hesse: *Die Morgenlandfahrt,*" *Wege zur Erzählkunst* (Hamburg, 1953), pp. 117-123.

178 Pongs, Hermann, *Im Umbruch der Zeit. Das Romanschaffen der Gegenwart* (Göttingen, 1952), pp. 20-21, 151-154.

179 Rang, Bernhard, "Die Wandlungen des Epischen," *Deutsche Literatur im Zwanzigsten Jahrhundert,* eds. Hermann Friedmann, Otto Mann (Heidelberg, 1954), pp. 193-195 (*Glasperlenspiel*).

180 Rathenau, Walter, *Briefe* (Dresden, 1926), pp. 353-55, 357-360 (letters to Hesse in 1918).

181 Reich, Willi, "Musik in der Literatur," *Musica Aeterna* (Zürich, 1948), p. 165 (*Steppenwolf* and Mozart).

182 Rein, Heinz, *Die Neue Literatur* (Berlin, 1950), pp. 421-431.

183 Richter, Rudolf, "Hermann Hesses Horoskop," *Astrologisches Jahrbuch* (Dresden, 1929).

184 Rilke, R. M., *Theater, Bücher, Kunst* (Wien, 1934), pp. 108-110. See 611.

185 Roch, Herbert, "Hermann Hesse," *Deutsche Schriftsteller als Richter ihrer Zeit* (Berlin, 1947), pp. 117-123.

186 Röder, Gerhard, *Der Zwerg* (Torino, 1937), 34 pp. In his introduction to this textbook, Röder deals briefly with Hesse.

187 Rolland, Romain, *Au-Dessus de la Mêlée* (Paris, 1916), p. 128.

188 Rousseaux, André, "Hermann Hesse, Le Loup et L'Homme," *Littérature du Vingtième Siècle* (Paris, 1953), pp. 134-142.

189 Ruprecht, Erich, "Wendung zum Geist? Gedanken zu Hermann Hesses *Glasperlenspiel,*" *Die Botschaft der Dichter. Zwölf Vorträge* (Stuttgart, 1947), pp. 443-474.

190 Rychner, Max, "Hermann Hesse: *Briefe,*" *Sphären der Bücherwelt* Zürich, 1952), pp. 117-123. See 63.

191 ———, "Hermann Hesse: *Das Glasperlenspiel,*" *Zeitgenössische Literatur* (Zürich, 1947), pp. 243-254.

192 Sabais, H. W., "Hermann Hesse," *Das Greifenbüchlein. Ein Almanach* (Rudolstadt, 1947), pp. 54-56.

193 Samuel, Richard and R. H. Thomas, *Expressionism in German Life, Literature and the Theatre* (Cambridge, England, 1939), pp. 121-122.

194 Satô, Kôichi, "Mann and Hesse" (in Japanese), *Bücherei* (Tokyo, 1941), pp. 58-60.

195 Schoolfield, George, *The Figure of the Musician in German Literature* (Chapel Hill, 1956), pp. 136-137, 147-150, 156-168, 190-194 (*Peter Camenzind, Gertrud, Steppenwolf, Glasperlenspiel*).

196 Schröder, Rud. Alex., "Zu Hesses 60. Geburtstag 1937," *Die Aufsätze und Reden* (Berlin, 1939), Vol. 2, 592-397.

197 Schussen, Wilhelm, "Hermann Hesse und die Schmetterlinge," *Anekdote meines Lebens,* (Ravensburg, 1953), pp. 68-70. See 53.

198 Schwarz, Georg, "Hermann Hesse," *Die Ewige Spur. Schwäbische Dichterprofile aus einem Jahrtausend* (München, 1949), pp. 140-142.

199 Seidlin, Oskar, "The Exorcism of the Demon," *New Directions,* 14 (New Jersey, 1953), 109-131. See 657.

200 Spiero, Heinrich, *Geschichte des deutschen Romans* (Berlin, 1950), pp. 555-556.

201 Straub, E., Introduction and notes to *Peter Camenzind* (Paris, 1948).

202 Steen, Albert, "Hermann Hesse," *Almanach der Unvergessenen* (Rudolstadt, 1946), pp. 67-68.

203 Steinbüchel, Theodor, *Mensch und Wirklichkeit*, 2nd ed. (Frankfurt a. M., 1950), pp. 31-32.

204 Strich, Fritz, "Dank an Hermann Hesse," *Der Dichter und die Zeit* (Bern, 1947), pp. 379-394.

205 Suhrkamp, Peter, "Hermann Hesse zum 60. Geburtstag," *S. Fischer Almanach* (Berlin, 1937), pp. 18-24.

206 Takahashi, Yoshitaka, *Mann, Hesse, Carossa* (Tokyo, 1947), 200 pp.

207 Weber, Ernst, *Dichter und Jugendbildung* (Schriften für Lehrerfortbildung Nr. 21, Deut. Dichterpädagogik Teil 1, Wien-Leipzig, 1921), pp. 91-96 (*Unterm Rad, Knulp*).

208 Weber, Marta, "Hermann Hesse," *Im Vergangenen das Unvergängliche* (Zürich, 1942), pp. 191-198.

209 Weiss, Hansgerhard, *Romain Rolland* (Berlin-Leipzig, 1948), pp. 85-87.

210 Welter, Friedrich, *Justus H. Wetzel* (Berlin, 1931), pp. 34-36 (Hesse Vertonungen).

211 Wiechert, Ernst, *Eine Mauer um uns baue* (Mainz, 1937), p. 1.

212 ———, *Der Totenwald* (Zürich, 1946), p. 50.

213 Wiegler, Paul, "Hermann Hesse," *Peter Camenzind. Unterm Rad* (Berlin: Bibliothek fortschrittlicher deutscher Schriftsteller, 3rd. Ser., 1952), pp. 317-320.

214 Wilson, Colin, *The Outsider* (Boston, 1956), pp. 51-68 (the outsider in *Demian, Siddhartha, Steppenwolf, Narziss und Goldmund, Glasperlenspiel*).

215 Witkop, Philipp, "Hermann Hesse," *Volk und Erde. Alemannische Dichterbildnisse* (Karlsruhe, 1929), pp. 163-177. See 705.

216 Worbs, Erich, *Ewige Musik* (Berlin, 1954), pp. 21, 46, 65.

217 Wurster, Gotthold, *Der deutsche Finckh. Leben und Werk* (München, 1941), pp. 9-11, 15, 114.

218 Zeidler, Kurt, *Die Wiederentdeckung der Grenze* (Jena, 1925), p. 31 (*Demian*).

219 *Aus Dr. Hermann Gunderts Briefnachlass* (Stuttgart, 1900), 422 pp.

220 *Begegnungen mit Th. Heuss*, eds. Hans Bott, Hermann Leins (Tübingen), pp. 238-239, 245, 269, 276, 307.

221 *Deutsche Lyrik seit Rilke*, eds. B. Q. Morgan and Fernando Wagner (New York, 1939), pp. 181-183.

222 *Friedrich Gundert. Zum Gedächtnis* (Stuttgart, 1946), 111 pp.; six very informative letters to Hesse from 1944 to 1946.

223 "Hermann Hesse," *Deutscher Geist. Ein Lesebuch aus zwei Jahrhunderten*. Neue erweiterte Ausgabe (Berlin-Frankfurt a. M.: Suhrkamp, 1953), Vol. 2, 752-753.

HISTORIES OF LITERATURE (Books in which Hesse is more than merely mentioned) :

224 Abusch, Alexander, *Literatur und Wirklichkeit. Beiträge zu einer neuen deutschen Literaturgeschichte* (Berlin, 1952), pp. 77, 79, 83, 85, 338, 343.

225 Alker, Ernst, *Geschichte der deutschen Literatur* (Stuttgart, 1950), Vol. 2, 385-389, 480-483.

226 Bartels, Adolf, *Geschichte der deutschen Literatur* (Berlin-Hamburg, 1943), p. 601.

227 Beer, Johannes, *Deutsche Dichtung seit hundert Jahren* (Stuttgart, 1937), pp. 197-198.

228 Bernt, Alois, *Handbuch der deutschen Literaturgeschichte* (Reichenberg, 1928), pp. 733-734.

229 Biese, Alfred, *Deutsche Literaturgeschichte* (München, 1930), Vol. 3, 734-741.

230 Bithell, Jethro, *Modern German Literature* (London, 1939), pp. 314-320.

231 Bredel, Willi, *Über die Aufgaben der Literatur und Literaturkritik* (Berlin: Deutscher Schriftstellerverband, 1952), pp. 29-32.

232 Burger, Otto Heinz, *Annalen der deutschen Literatur* (Stuttgart, 1952), pp. 779-781, 808-809, 821-822.

233 Duwe, Willi, *Deutsche Dichtung des 20. Jahrhunderts* (Zürich-Leipzig, 1936), pp. 275-280.

234 Eggebrecht, Axel, *Weltliteratur* (Hamburg, 1948), pp. 282-284.

235 Eloesser, Arthur, *Die deutsche Literatur von der Romantik bis zur Gegenwart* (Berlin, 1931), pp. 528-529.

236 Engel, Edward, *Geschichte der deutschen Literatur* (Leipzig, 1908), Vol. 2, 382, 386-387, 391.

237 Eppelsheimer, Hanns W., *Handbuch der Weltliteratur* (Frankfurt a. M., 1950), Vol. 2, 239-240.

238 Fechter, Paul, *Geschichte der deutschen Literatur* (Gütersloh, 1952), pp. 526-531.

239 Floeck, Dr. Oswald, *Die deutsche Dichtung der Gegenwart* (Karlsruhe, Leipzig, 1926), pp. 110-111.

240 Geissler, Max, *Führer durch die deutsche Literatur des 20. Jahrhunderts* (Weimar, 1913), p. 208.

241 Grabert, Dr. W., *Geschichte der deutschen Literatur* (München, 1953), pp. 480-484.

242 Heinemann, Karl, *Deutsche Dichtung* (Leipzig, 1930), pp. 323-325.

243 Jenssen, Christian, *Deutsche Dichtung der Gegenwart* (Leipzig-Berlin, 1936), pp. 62-63.

244 Koch, Franz, *Geschichte deutscher Dichtung* (Hamburg, 1937), p. 281.

245 Koenig, Robert, *Deutsche Literaturgeschichte* (Bielfeld, 1925), Vol. 2, 451.

246 Kosch, Wilhelm, *Deutsches Literatur-Lexikon* (Bern, 1953), Vol. 2, 960-962.

247 Krüger, Herm. Anders, *Deutsches Literatur-Lexikon* (München, 1914), p. 188.

248 Kutzbach, Karl August, *Autorenlexikon der Gegenwart* (Bonn, 1950), pp. 152-155.

249 Laaths, Erwin, *Geschichte der Weltliteratur* (München, 1950), pp. 752-753.

250 Lang, Martin, "Von deutscher Dichtung," Hermann Stegemann, *Des Deutschen Vaterland* (neither place nor date given), pp. 737-738.

251 Lange, Victor, *Modern German Literature, 1870-1940* (Ithaca, 1945), pp. 100-101, 164-165.

252 Lavalette, Robert, *Literaturgeschichte der Welt* (Zürich, 1948), pp. 398-399.

253 Lechner, Hermann, *Grundzüge der Literaturgeschichte* (Innsbruck-Wien, 1950), pp. 336-339.

254 Lennartz, Franz, *Der Dichter unserer Zeit* (Stuttgart, 1941), pp. 173-176; 5th ed., 1952, pp. 196-201.

255 Leyen, Friedrich von der, *Deutsche Dichtung in neuer Zeit* (Jena, 1927), pp. 319-320.

256 Linden, Dr. Walter, *Geschichte der deutschen Literatur* (Leipzig, 1942), pp. 421-422.

257 Lüth, Paul E. H., *Literatur als Geschichte* (Wsiebaden, 1947), Vol. 1, 131-136.

258 Mahrholz, Werner, *Deutsche Literatur der Gegenwart* (Berlin, 1930), pp. 265-266.

259 Majut, Rudolf, *Geschichte des deutschen Romans vom Biedermeier bis zur Gegenwart* (Berlin, 1954), *Deutsche Philologie im Aufriss*, Vol. 2, 2392-93, 2468-69.

260 Martens, Kurt, *Die deutsche Literatur unserer Zeit* (München, 1922), pp. 208-212.

261 ———, *Literatur in Deutschland* (Berlin, 1910), pp. 41-42.

262 Martini, Fritz, *Deutsche Literaturgeschichte* (Stuttgart, 1949), pp. 492-496.

263 Meyer, Richard M., *Die deutsche Literatur des 19. und 20. Jahrhunderts* (Berlin, 1923), pp. 625-626.

264 Mumbauer, Johannes, *Die deutsche Dichtung der neuesten Zeit* (Freiburg i. Br., 1936), pp. 573-587.

265 Nadler, Josef, *Literaturgeschichte der deutschen Stämme und Landschaften* (Regensburg, 1928), Vol. 4, 790-791.

266 ———, *Literaturgeschichte des deutschen Volkes* (Berlin, 1938), Vol. 3, 696-697.

267 Naumann, Hans, *Die deutsche Dichtung der Gegenwart, 1885-1924* (Stuttgart, 1924), pp. 213-214.

268 Petry, Karl, *Handbuch zur deutschen Literaturgeschichte* (Köln, 1949), Vol. 2, 897-899.

269 Rein, Heinz, *Die neue Literatur* (Berlin, 1950), pp. 421-431.

270 Riemann, Robert, *Von Goethe zum Expressionismus* (Leipzig, 1922), pp. 381-382.

271 Röhl, Hans, *Geschichte der deutschen Dichtung* (Leipzig, 1931), p. 329.

272 Salzer, Anselm, *Illustrierte Geschichte der deutschen Literatur von*

den ältesten Zeiten bis zur Gegenwart (Regensburg, 1931), VoL 4, 448-454.

273 Scherer, Wilhelm, and Th. Schultz, *Geschichte der deutschen Literatur* (Wien, 1948), pp. 695-696.

274 Schmitt, F.; G. Fricke, *Literaturgeschichte in Tabellen* (Bonn, 1952), pp. 291-294.

275 Schneider, Manfred, *Einführung in die neueste deutsche Dichtung* (Stuttgart, 1921), pp. 119-124.

276 Schumann, Otto, and Franz Krezdorn, *Literaturführer* (Wilhelms-haven, 1953), pp. 288-290.

277 Schuster, W.; M., Wieser, *Weltliteratur der Gegenwart 1890-1931*, Vol. 2 (Berlin, 1931), 216, 217.

278 Soergel, Albert, *Dichtung und Dichter der Zeit* (Leipzig, 1928), Vol. 1, 944-957.

279 Vogelpohl, Wilhelm, *Deutsche Dichtung* (Stuttgart, 1952), pp. 150-151.

280 Walzel, Oskar, *Deutsche Dichtung von Gottsched bis zur Gegenwart* (Handbuch der Literaturwissenschaft, Potsdam, 1930), p. 344.

281 Wiegler, Paul, *Geschichte der deutschen Literatur* (Berlin, 1930), p. 814-816.

282 Witkop, Philipp. *Deutsche Dichtung der Gegenwart* (Leipzig, 1924), pp. 73-76.

283 *Cassell's Encyclopaedia of Literature* (London, 1953), Vol. 2, 1827.

284 *Columbia Dictionary of Modern European Literature* (New York, 1947), pp. 381-382.

285 *Der Romanführer*, ed. Wilhelm Olbrich (Stuttgart, 1950), pp. 259-271.

286 *Twentieth Century Authors. A Biographical Dictionary of Modern Literature* (New York, 1942), pp. 645-646.

287 *Die Welt-Literatur*, eds. E. Frauwallner, H. Giebisch, E. Heinzel (Wien, 1953), Vol. 2, 727-728.

ARTICLES IN PERIODICALS.

This represents a complete list of items from 1927 to 1957. Only fifty-seven articles preceding 1927 were considered significant enough to be included (for a more extensive list of items preceding 1927, see Metelmann, *Die Schöne Literatur*, 28 [1927], 306-310) :

288 Ackerknecht, Erwin, "Hermann Hesse," *Bücherei und Bildungspflege*, 1 (May-June 1921), 155-156, 159-160.

289 Ackermann, Werner, "Der Hermann Hesseliche Mensch. Betrachtungen eines Ketzers," *Das Stachelschwein*, Jan. 1928, pp. 8-15.

290 Amegú, Gubitsch y, "Hermann Hesse. Ensayo sobre la lírica sustancial," *Boletín del Instituto de Estudios Germánicos*, Universidad de Buenos Aires, 1939-40, pp. 151-168.

291 Anderle, H., "Der süddeutsche Mensch. Hermann Hesse zum 50. Geburtstag," Heimat, *Vorarlberger Monatshefte*, 8 (1927), 201-203.

292 Andrews, R. C., "The poetry of Hermann Hesse," *German Life and Letters*, 6 (1953), 117-127.

293 Angelloz, J. F., "Hermann Hesse," *Mercure de France*, 304 (1948), 485-493.

294 ———, "Landstreicherherberge," *Du. Schweizerische Monatsschrift*, 13 (February 1953), 48-49.

295 ———, "Das Mütterliche und das Männliche im Werk Hermann Hesses. Zum 75. Geburtstag des Dichters," *Freude an Büchern*, 3 (1952), 155-156.

296 ———, "L'Oeuvre de Hermann Hesse," *Critique*, May 1949, pp. 387-400.

297 ———, "Présentation de *Das Glasperlenspiel* par Hermann Hesse," *Études Germaniques*, 1 (1946), 428-431.

298 Anselm, F., "Hermann Hesse," *Poet Lore*, 53 (1947), 353-360.

299 Auernheimer, Raoul, "Der Roman eines Dichters. Hermann Hesse: *Peter Camenzind*," *Die Wage*, (Wien, 7 1904), 779-782.

300 Augustin, Elizabeth, "Hermann Hesses *Glasperlenspiel*, een protest tegen cadaver-gehoorzaamheid," *Litterair paspoort*, 4 (1949), 121-125.

301 Bach, Rudolf, "Brief an Hermann Hesse," *Deutsche Beiträge*, 1 (1947), 297-307.

302 ———, "Wandlung und Beharrung. Zum 60. Geburtstag Hermann Hesses," *NR*, 48, ii (1937), 46-52.

303 Baeschlin, Theodor, "Begegnung mit Hermann Hesse," *Du. Schweizerische Monatsschrift*, 13, (February 1953), 30-31.

304 ———, "Zu Hermann Hesses 75. Geburtstag," *Der Schweizer Buchhandlungsgehilfe*, 33 (1952), 81.

305 Baldus, A., "Hermann Hesse," *Das Deutsche Wort*, 13 (1937), 232-233.

306 Ball, Hugo, "Hermann Hesse und der Osten," *NR*, 38, i (1927), 483-491.

307 Ball-Hennings, Emmy, "Zwei Briefe an Hermann Hesse," *Schweizer Rundschau*, 1953, pp. 445-451.

308 Baser, Friedrich, "Vom Sinn des *Glasperlenspiel*," *Musica* (Kassel), 8, No. 12 (1954), 530.

309 Basler, Otto, "Hermann Hesses *Briefe* und *Späte Prosa*," *NSR*, 19 (1951), 146-153.

310 ———, "Hermann Hesses Weg zum *Glasperlenspiel*," *Schweizer Annalen*, 1 (1944), 637-648.

311 ———, "Lieber Herr Hesse," *NSR*, 20 (1952), 162-164.

312 Bauer, Paul, "*Das Glasperlenspiel*," *Die Lücke. Eine christlich-kulturelle Monatsschrift*, No. 11-12, 1947, pp. 20-21.

313 Bäumer, Gertrud, "Medusa," "Perseus," *Die Frau*, 28 (1921), 193-199, 225-235.

314 Becher, Hubert, "*Das Glasperlenspiel*," *Stimmen der Zeit*, 73, (1948), 146-148.

315 Benn, Maurice, "An Interpretation of the Work of Hermann Hesse," *Life and Letters*, 3 (1950), 202-211.

316 Benz, Richard, "Festanrede," *Börsenblatt für den deutschen Buchhandel* (Frankfurt a. M.), No. 86, 1955, pp. 699-701. See 61.

317 Berna, J., "Wache Nacht. Ein Briefwechsel mit Hermann Hesse," *Schweizer Annalen*, 3 (1946-47), 241-243.

318 Bernecker, Gabriele, "*Piktors Verwandlungen*," *Die Bücher-Kommentare* (Stuttgart), 4, No. 1 (1955), 1.

319 Bétemps, René, "Hermann Hesse," *Revue d'Allemagne*, 3 (1929), 517-534.

320 Birrer, Emil, "Hermann Hesse," *Du. Schweizerische Monatsschrift*, 13 (Feb. 1953), 2.

321 Blanchot, Maurice, "H. H."; "Le Jeu des Jeux," *Nouvelle Nouvelle Revue Française*, 4 (1956), 872-883, 1051-62.

322 Blumenthal, Marie-Luise, "Die Pädagogische Provinz und das Schicksal des Magisters Ludi Josef Knecht," *Die Sammlung*, 8 (1953), 478-484.

323 Böckmann, Paul, "Der Dichter und die Gefährdung des Menschen im Werk Hermann Hesses," *Wirkendes Wort*, 3 (1952), 150-162.

324 ———,"Ist das *Glasperlenspiel* ein gefährliches Buch? Eine Replik," *Die Sammlung*, 3 (1948), 609-618. A reply to von Schöfer, see 636.

325 ———, "Die Welt des Geistes in Hermann Hesses Dichten," *Die Sammlung*, 3 (1948), 215-233.

326 Böhm, H., "Neue Lyrik (Besprechungen von 20 Lyrikern)," *Kunstwart*, 42, ii (1929), 248-262; Hesse, pp. 249-250.

327 Böhme, G., "Hermann Hesse: *Peter Camenzind, Unterm Rad* und *Diesseits*." *Eckart*, 1 (1907), 675-679.

328 Böhme, S., "*Das Glasperlenspiel* (Studenten diskutieren einen Erziehungsroman)," *Die Neue Schule*, 3 (1948), 248-251.

329 Böhmer, Emil, "Musik in Hermann Hesses Dichtung," *Ostdeutsche Monatshefte*, 15 (1935), 623-625.

330 Bollnow, O. F., "Probleme der Anthropologie (zum *Glasperlenspiel*)," *Die Sammlung*, 2 (1946), 56-60.

331 Bonitz, Amalie, "Der Erziehungsgedanke in Hermann Hesses *Glasperlenspiel*," *Schola, Monatsschrift für Erziehung und Unterricht*, 3 (1948), 803-815. See also *Vierteljahrsschrift für wissenschaftliche Pädagogik* (Bochum), 29 (1953), 215-226.

332 Bonwit, Marianne, "Der Leidende Dritte," *University of California Publications in Modern Philology*, 36 (1952), 91-111; Peter Camenzind, p. 111.

333 Botta, P., *"Das Glasperlenspiel," Die Kirche in der Welt*, 1 (1948), 465.

334 Böttger, Fritz, "Freund der Wahrheit,—Kämpfer für den Frieden," *Deutschunterricht* (Berlin), 5 (1952), 350-353.

335 Boucher, Maurice, "Lettres allemandes (Hesse, Werfel, Jünger, Kasack, Carossa)," *Hommes et Mondes*, 15 (1951), 301-303.

336 Braemer, E., "Kastalien als pädagogische Provinz," *Die Neue Schule*, 3 (1948), 251-253.

337 Bredel, Willi, "Unsere Verantwortung," *Aufbau*, 8 (1952), 608-612.

338 Brod, Max, "Briefwechsel mit Hermann Hesse (zum jüdischarabischen Krieg)," *Literarische Revue*, 4 (1949), 188-191.

339 Bruder, Erhard, "Ludwig Finckh," *Neue Literatur*, 37 (1936), 196-205; Hesse, p. 199.

340 Brüll, Oswald, "Hermann Hesse und sein neues Buch: *Rosshalde*," *Nord und Süd*, 38 (August 1914), 196-203.

341 Buchwald, Reinhard, "Der Friedenspreisträger Hermann Hesse," *Anzeiger österreichischen Buch-, Kunst-, und Musikalienhandels*, 90 (1955), 85.

342 Busse, Carl, "Hermann Hesse: *Unterm Rad*," *Velhagen und Klasings Monatshefte*, 20 (Dec. 1905), 484-486.

343 Carlsson, Anni, "Dichtung als Hieroglyphe des Zeitalters: Hermann Hesses *Morgenlandfahrt*," *NSR*, 20 (1952), 165-168. See 20.

344 ———, "Gingo Biloba: Hermann Hesse zum 70. Geburtstag," *NSR*, 15 (1947), 79-87.

345 ———, "Hermann Hesses *Glasperlenspiel* in seinen Wesensgesetzen," *Trivium*, 4 (1946), 175-201. See 1.

346 ———, "Zu Hermann Hesse: *Eine Stunde hinter Mitternacht*," *NSR*, 10 (1942), 54-57.

347 ———, "Zur Gesamtausgabe von Hermann Hesses Gedichten," *NSR*, 11 (1943), 109-121. See 28.

348 Cast, G. C., "Hermann Hesse als Erzieher," *Monatshefte*, 43 (1951), 207-220.

349 Chastain, A., "Bericht über Hermann Hesse," *Neue Auslese aus dem Schrifttum der Gegenwart*, 2, No. 3 (1947), 15-18.

350 Cohn, Hilde, "The symbolic end of Hermann Hesse's *Glasperlenspiel*," *Modern Language Quarterly*, 11 (1950), 347-357.

351 Colleville, Maurice, "À propos du problème religieux chez Hesse," *Études Germaniques*, 8 (1953), 182.

352 ———, "Le problème religieux dans la vie et dans l'oeuvre de Hermann Hesse," *Études Germaniques*, 7 (1952), 123-148.

353 Como, Cesco, "Hermann Hesse. Eine psychische Studie," *Deutsche Heimat*, 6 (1903), 1669-74.

354 Cube, H., "Hermann Hesses *Glasperlenspiel,*" *Welt und Wort,* 2 (1947), 105.

355 Curtius, Ernst Robert, "Hermann Hesse," *Merkur,* 1 (1947), 170-185. See 95.

356 Cysarz, Herbert, "Jahrhundertwende und Jahrhundertwehen. Zur Forschung der Literatur seit dem Naturalismus," *Deutsche Vierteljahrsschrift f. Literaturwissenschaft u. Geistesgeschichte,* 7 (1929), 745-796; Hesse, 789-792.

357 David-Schwarz, H., "*Narziss und Goldmund* in zwei verschiedenen Auffassungen," *Psychologische Rundschau,* 3 (1931), 7-13.

358 Debruge, Suzanne, "L'Art de conter. Hermann Hesse: Trois histoires de la vie de Knulp," *Langues Modernes,* 48 (1954), 328-332.

359 ———, "Flötenspiel," *Du. Schweizerische Monatsschrift,* 13 (February 1953), 48.

360 ———, "Hermann Hesse en France," *Revue des Langues Vivantes,* 16 (1950), 270-271.

361 ———, "Hermann Hesse—Lebensabend," *Revue des Langues Vivantes,* 22 (1956), 373-374 (review of *Beschwörungen*).

362 ———, "Introduction à *Narziss et Goldmund* de Hermann Hesse," *Revue des Langues Vivantes,* 17 (1951), 76-79.

363 ———, "L'oeuvre de Hermann Hesse et la Psychanalyse," *Études Germaniques,* 7 (1952), 252-261.

364 ———, "Les vagabonds de Hermann Hesse," *Études Germaniques* 6 (1951), 48-53; for a résumé see *NSR,* 20 (1952), 191-192

365 Dehorn, W., "Psychoanalyse und Neuere Dichtung," *Germanic Review,* 7 (1932), 245-262, 330-358; Hesse, 339-344.

366 Delage, J., "Hermann Hesse," *Vie des Peuples,* 12 (1924), 689-690.

367 Diamond, William, "Hermann Hesses *Weltanschauung,*" *Monatshefte,* 22 (1930), 39-44, 65-71.

368 Dirks, Walter, "Die Musik und die Vollkommenheit," *Frankfurter Hefte,* 4 (1949), 245-246.

369 Doderer, Otto, "Lebensbetrachtungen zu Hermann Hesses *Betrachtungen* und Jakob Wassermann's *Lebensdienst,*" *Die Literatur,* 31 (1929), 274-275.

370 Dornheim, Alfredo, "Musica Novelesca y Novela Musical. Concepción musical de las últimas novelas de Hermann Hesse y Thomas Mann," *Revista de Estudios Musicales* (Universidad Nacional de Cuyo, Mendoza, Argentina), 1 (August 1949), 131-172.

371 Drews, Richard, "Brief eines Genesenden an seinen Chirurgen," *Die Weltbühne* (Berlin), 7 (1952), 1205-06.

372 ———, "Hermann Hesse bricht das Schweigen," *Die Weltbühne* (Berlin), 5 (1950), 1449-51.

373 ———, "Hermann Hesses Verse. Zum 75. Geburtstag des Dichters," *Die Weltbühne* (Berlin) 7 (1952), 882-883.

374 ———, "Hoffentlich letzter Nachtrag," *Die Weltbühne* (Berlin), 8 (1953), 437-439; Hesse p. 438.

375 Dürr, Erich, "Hermann Hesses Ich-Problem," *Die Literatur,* 30 (1927), 135-136.

376 Duruman, Safinaz, "La *Melodie* à deux *Voix de* Hermann Hesse," *Dialogues* (Istanbul), 2, No. 2 (1951), 87-99.

377 Ehrenberg, H., "Der Fünfzigjährige," *Gral*, 21 (1927), 769-771; *Getreue Eckart*, (July-Aug., 1927), 307-312.

378 Elster, Hanns Martin, "Hermann Hesse. Ein Bild des Dichters," *Deutscher Bote*, 32 (1925), 571-573.

379 Engel, H., "*Das Glasperlenspiel*," *Das Musikleben*, 1 (1948), 257- 261.

380 Engel, Otto, "Hermann Hesse," *Aussaat*, 1, No. 2 (1946), 8-10; 1, No. 3 (1946), 8-10. These two articles comprise the "Vortrag" of Engel's *Hermann Hesse. Dichtung und Gedanke* (Stuttgart, 1947). See 4.

381 Erné, Nino, "*Die Gedichte* von Hermann Hesse," *Deutsche Beiträge*, 1 (1947), 384-386.

382 ———, "Ein Beitrag zum Thema: Hermann Hesse und Dostojewski," *Deutsche Beiträge*, 1 (1947), 345-353.

383 ———, "Hermann Hesse," *Geistige Welt*, 1, No. 4 (1947), 37-45.

384 ———, "Hermann Hesse: *Traumfährte*," *Welt und Wort*, 4 (1949), 201-202.

385 Faber du Faur, Curt von, "Zu Hermann Hesses *Glasperlenspiel*," *Monatshefte*, 40 (1948), 177-194.

386 Fabian, E., "Deutscher, Europäer, Weltbürger," *Heute und Morgen* (Schwerin), 1947, pp. 370-373; pp. 450-454.

387 ———, "Hermann Hesse wurde 70 Jahre alt," *Heute und Morgen* (Schwerin), 1947, p. 138.

388 Faesi, Robert, "Hermann Hesses *Glasperlenspiel*," *NSR*, 11 (1943), 411-427.

389 Federmann, Hertha, "Hermann Hesses Neue Gedichte," *Hochland*, 29 (1931-32), 558-560.

390 Fiechtner, H., "Hermann Hesse in seinen Selbstzeugnissen," *Die literarische Welt*, No. 2 (1946).

391 Field, George W., "Music and Morality in Thomas Mann and Hermann Hesse," *University of Toronto Quarterly*, 24 (1955), 175- 190.

392 Finckh, Ludwig, "Die Ahnen des Dichters Hermann Hesse," *Genealogie und Heraldik*, 3, No. 1-2 (1951), 1-2.

393 Fischer, J. M., "Hermann Hesse. 75 Jahre alt," *Wirkendes Wort*, 3 (1952-53), 62-63.

394 Flaxman, S. L., "*Der Steppenwolf*. Hesses Portrait of the Intellectual," *Modern Language Quarterly*, 15 (1954), 349-358.

395 Flügel, Hans, "*Das Glasperlenspiel*," *Deutsche Rundschau*, 69 (Nov. 1946), 165-168.

396 Fontana, O. M., "Bitte an Hermann Hesse," *Das Tagebuch*, 8 (1927), 1072-74.

397 ———, "Hermann Hesse zum 70. Geburtstag," *Europäische Rundschau*, 2 (1947), 615-616.

398 Foran, Marion N., "Hermann Hesse," *Queens Quarterly*, 55 (1948), 180-189.

399 Frenzel, C. O., "Hermann Hesse—Dichter unserer Zeit," *Die Volksbühne*, 2, No. 12 (1952), 180-182.

400 Frey, Emmy, "Über Rilkes Gedichte," *Der Deutschunterricht*, 1 (August 1948); Hesse's "Schmetterlinge im Spätherbst," pp. 75-76.

401 Freyberger, Laurentius, "Hermann Hesse: *Glasperlenspiel*, ein Bekenntnis zum Geist," *Hochland*, 39 (1946-47), 363-368.

402 Friederici, Hans, "Die Indien-Rezeption in den Erzählungen Hermann Hesses," *Wissenschaftliche Zeitschrift der Friedr.-Schiller-Universität*, 5 (1955-56), 459-463.

403 Fuchs, K., "Hermann Hesse," *Universität* (Die Erlanger Halbmonatsblätter der Dozenten und Studenten der Friedrich-Alexander-Universität zu Erlangen), 1, No. 13 (1947), 173-175.

404 F. S., "Hermann Hesse—Bekenner und Idylliker. Zum 70. Geburtstag," *Aufbau*, 3, No. 7 (1947) 59-60.

405 Geheeb, Charlotte, "Neujahrsgruss nach Montagnola," *Börsenblatt für den Deutschen Buchhandel* (Leipzig), Jan. 2, 1954, pp. 24-26.

406 Georg, B., "Positive Zeitkritik. Gedanken zu Hesses neuem Werk *Das Glasperlenspiel*," *Die Schau*, 2 (1947), 27.

407 Georgi, Arthur, "Hermann Hesse und der Sinn des Friedenspreises," *Börsenblatt für den deutschen Buchhandel* (Frankfurt a. M.), No. 86, 1955, pp. 697-698. See 61.

408 Gerhard, I., "*Peter Camenzind* von Hermann Hesse," *Der alte Glaube*, 6, No. 3 (1904), 61-65.

409 Gey, P., "Der Dichter malt," *Daheim*, 64, No. 7 (1927).

410 Geyh, K. W. "Hermann Hesse als Künder einer neuen Zeit. Besprechung des *Glasperlenspiels*," *Geistige Welt*, 1, No. 1 (1946), 44-45.

411 Gide, André, "Geleitwort zur *Morgenlandfahrt*," *NSR*, 20 (1952), 190-191. See 47.

412 ———, "Zum Werk Hermann Hesses," *Universitas*, 2 (Sonderheft 1947), 135-137. See 47.

413 Gnamm, Dr., "Offener Brief an Hermann Hesse," *Universitas*, 1 (1946), 1048-50.

414 Goern, Hermann, "Der Maler Hermann Hesse," *NSR*, 20 (1952), 154-160. See 20.

415 Goes, Albrecht, "Ein Gruss zu Hermann Hesses 75. Geburtstag," *NR*, 63 (1952), 327-330.

416 ———, "Rede auf Hermann Hesse," *Du. Schweizerische Monatsschrift*, 13 (1953), 13-16; 52-58. See 32.

417 ———, "Rede zu einer Hermann-Hesse-Feier," *NSR*, 14 (1946), 387-407. See 32.

418 Göppert-Spanel, Dr., "Hermann Hesses Werk als Spiegel seiner Seelenentwicklung," *Universitas*, 6 (1951), 637-644; 761-768.

419 Gowan, B. L., "*Demian* by Hermann Hesse," *Monatshefte*, 20 (1928), 225-228.

420 Grappin, Pierre, "Romain Rolland et Hermann Hesse," *Études Germaniques*, 8 (1953), 25-35.

421 Griese, W. H., "François hat einen Bruder bekommen," *Der Kreis*, 5 (Sept. 1928), 541-542 (*Krisis* and François Villon).

422   Groothoff, H. H., "Versuch einer Interpretation des *Glasperlenspiels*," *Hamburgische Akademische Rundschau*, 2 (1947), 269-279.

423   Gross, Harvey, "Hermann Hesse," *Western Review*, 17 (1953), 132-140.

424   Grünberg, Karl, "Wie kommen die Schriftsteller an?" *Der Autor* (Berlin), 5, No. 1 (1951), 3-4.

425   Guder, Erich, "Gedichte Hermann Hesses bei Kindern der Volksschule," *Berliner Lehrerzeitung*, 6 (1952), 316-318.

426   Guilland, Antoine, "Hermann Hesse," *Semaine Littéraire*, 14 (1906), 337-339.

427   Gündel, Bernhard, "Gedanken über die geistige Struktur der Mathematik im Blickfeld von Hermann Hesses *Glasperlenspiel*," *Pädagogische Provinz*, 5 (1951), 463-468.

428   Günnel, Peter, "Hermann Hesse," *Der Bibliothekar*, 6 (1952), 459-463.

429   Günther, Gerhard, "Hermann Hesse," *Deutsches Volkstum*, 1930, i, pp. 448-454.

430   Hafner, Gotthilf, "Frankreich und Hesse," *Welt und Wort*, 10 (1955), 172.

431   ———, "Hermann Hesses Anfänge," *Welt und Wort*, 7 (1952), 229-230.

432   ———, "Hermann Hesse: *Gesammelte Dichtungen*," *Welt und Wort*, 7 (1952), 362.

433   ———, "Hermann Hesse: *Zwei Idyllen*," *Welt und Wort*, 7 (1952), 250.

434   ———, "Hesse: *Meiner Mutter*," *Der Deutschunterricht*, 1 (August 1948), 101-108.

435   Hänsel, L., "Hermann Hesse und die Flucht in den Geist. Gedanken zu *Glasperlenspiel*," *Wort und Wahrheit*, 3 (1948), 273-288.

436   Hartung, Ludwig, "Hermann Hesse: *Der Europäer*," *Welt und Wort*, 3 (1948), 129.

437   Hartung, Rudolf, "Hermann Hesses Spätwerk, *Das Glasperlenspiel*," *Die Fähre*, 2 (1947), 441-446.

438   Hartung, Wilhelm, "Der Glücksgedanke bei Hermann Hesse," *Die Grenzboten*, 71, i (1912), 477-485.

439   Haussmann, Walter, "Drei Gedichte von Hermann Hesse," *Der Deutschunterricht*, 6, No, 4 (1953), 34-42.

440   ———, "Hermann Hesse," *Studentische Blätter* (Tübingen), No. 4, (1947), 1-2.

441   Hecht, Gustav, "Offener Brief an Hermann Hesse," *Deutsches Volkstum*, 1929, ii, 603-611. See 625.

442   Hedinger-Henrici, P., "Hermann Hesse als Erzieher," *Schweizerisches Evangelisches Schulblatt*, 83 (1948), 329-334.

443   Heise, Wolfgang, "Fragwürdigkeit des reinen Geistes," *Die neue Schule*, 3 (1948), 253-254.

444   Heiseler, Bernt von, "Drei deutsche Meister. Hesse, Schröder, Carossa," *Zeitwende*, 23 (1951), 181-183 (*Späte Prosa*).

445   ———, "Neue Gedichtbücher," *Zeitwende*, 22 (1950), 370 (*Musik des Einsamen*).

446 Helbling, Carl, "Der Grundzug von Hermann Hesse," *Wissen und Leben*, 13 (1920), 800-803.

447 Heller, Peter, "The Creative Unconscious and the Spirit. A study of polarities in Hesse's image of the writer," *Modern Language Forum*, 38 (1953), 28-40.

448 ———, "The Masochistic Rebel in Recent German Literature," *Journal of Aesthetics and Art Criticism*, 11 (1953), 198-213; Hesse, pp. 205-206.

449 ———, "The Writer in Conflict with his Age. A Study in the Ideology of Hermann Hesse," *Monatshefte*, 46 (1954), 137-147.

450 Hering, G. F., "Über das *Glasperlenspiel*," *Die Gegenwart*, 2, No. 11-12 (1947), 31-33.

451 Heuschele, Otto, "Hermann Hesse. Zum 75. Geburtstag des Dichters am 2. Juli 1952," *Schwäbische Heimat*, 3 (1952), 185-188; *Deutsche Rundschau*, 78 (1952), 720-725.

452 ———, "Hermann Hesses Erzählungen," *Weltstimmen*, 24 (1955), 35.

453 Heuss, Theodor, "Hermann Hesse: *Diesseits*. Erzählungen," *NSR*, 20 (1952), 188-190; appeared in *Das literarische Echo*, September 1907, 1846-48.

454 ———, "Hermann Hesse. Zu seinem 60. Geburtstag," *Die Hilfe*, 43 (1937), 276-278.

455 Hill, Claude, "Hermann Hesse als Kritiker der bürgerlichen Zivilisation," *Monatshefte*, 40 (1948), 241-253.

456 ———, "Hesse and Germany," *German Quarterly*, 21 (1948), 9-15.

457 Hilscher, Eberhard, "Der Lyriker Hermann Hesse," *Neue Deutsche Literatur*, 4, No. 9 (1956), 109-118.

458 Hippe, Robert, "Vier Brunnengedichte. C. F. Meyer, R. M. Rilke, Hans Carossa, H. Hesse," *Wirkendes Wort*, 4 (1954), 268-274.

459 Hornung, Erik, "Hermann Hesses *Glasperlenspiel*—Idee und Vergegenwärtung," *Universitas*, 11 (1956), 1043-52.

460 Humm, R. J.,"Erste Begegnung mit Hermann Hesse," *NSR*, 20 (1952), 169-172.

461 Hunnius, Aegidus, "Hermann Hesse," *Neue Literatur*, 37 (1936), 239-240.

462 Jacobson, Anna, "Hermann Hesse. Anlässlich der Auszeichnung durch den Nobelpreis," *Monatshefte*, 39 (1947), 1-8. See 35.

463 Jaeger, Hans, "Heidegger's Existential Philosophy and Modern German Literature," *Publications of the Modern Language Association*, 67 (1952), 655, 670, 673, 676-677.

464 Jancke, Oskar, "Hermann Hesses Dichtersprache," *Die Literatur*, 43 (1941), 327-331.

465 ———, "Hermann Hesse und das *Glasperlenspiel*," *Welt und Wort*, 2 (1947), 216.

466 Jehle, Mimi, "The Garden in the works of Hermann Hesse," *German Quarterly*, 24 (1951), 42-50.

467 ———, "Das moderne deutsche Kunstmärchen," *Journal of English and Germanic Philology*, 33 (1934), 452-461; Hesse, pp. 457-458.

468 Johnson, Sidney M., "The Autobiographies in Hermann Hesse's

Glasperlenspiel," *German Quarterly*, 24 (1956), 160-171.

469 Jonas, Klaus W., "Additions to the Bibliography of Hermann Hesse," *Papers of the Bibliographical Society of America*, 49 (1955), 358-360.

470 ——, "Hermann Hesse in Amerika. Bibliographie," *Monatshefte*, 44 (1952), 95-99.

471 ——, "Thomas Mann and Hermann Hesse," *Deutsche Literatur* (Tokyo), May 1953, pp. 15-18.

472 Jordan, Placidus (Max), "Die Sendung des Dichters, ein offener Brief an Hermann Hesse," *Benediktinische Monatsschrift*, 13 (1931), 398-405.

473 ——, "Offener Brief an Hermann Hesse," *Benediktinische Monatsschrift*, 28 (1952), 424-431.

474 J. F., "Ein Freund des Friedens und der Wahrheit (Zu einem offenen Brief von Hermann Hesse), *Heute und Morgen* (Schwerin), 1951, p. 2.

475 Käge, Hans, "Begegnung mit Hermann Hesse," *Du Schweizerische Monatsschrift*, 13 (February 1953), 36.

476 Kappstein, Theodor, "Hermann Hesse. Ein deutsches Dichterporträt," *Rheinische Blätter*, 4, No. 2 (1923), 106-111.

477 Kayser, Rudolf, "*Der Kurgast*," *NR*, 36, ii (1925), 758-761.

478 Keckeis, G., "Ein Dichter des Diesseits," *Literarischer Handweiser*, 56 (1920), 397-402.

479 Klabund, "Allerlei," *NR*, 31, ii (1920), 1109.

480 Klaiber, Th., "Hermann Hesse," *Monatsblätter für deutsche Literatur*, 8 (1903), 11-15.

481 Klie, B., "*Glasperlenspiel*," *Umschau. Die Internationale Revue*, 2 (1947), 615-619.

482 Kliemann, Horst, "Bemerkungen zu einer Hesse-Bibliographie," *Deutsche Beiträge*, 1 (1947), 381-385.

483 ——, "Gliederung des Hesse-Archivs," *Das Antiquariat*, 7 (1951), 43-44.

484 ——, "Hermann Hesse und das Buch," *Deutsche Beiträge*, 1 (1947), 353-360.

485 ——, "Das Werk Hermann Hesses. Eine bibliographische Übersicht," *Europa-Archiv*, 1 (1947), 604-609.

486 Knab-Grzimek, Fränze, "Eine Nachfahrin der Bettina," *Welt und Wort*, 11 (1956), 312-313. (Emmy Ball-Hennings).

487 Knodt, K. E., "Hermann Hesse," *Monatsblätter für deutsche Literatur*, 6, No. 5 (1902), 225-228.

488 Köge, H. H., "Begegnung mit Hermann Hesse," *Freude an Büchern* (Wien), 4 (1953), 175-176.

489 Kohlschmid, Werner, "Meditationen über Hermann Hesses *Glasperlenspiel*," *Zeitwende*, 19 (1947), 154-170; 217-226. See 147.

490 Koller, Gottfried, "Kastalien und China," *Annales Universitatis Saraviensis*, 1 (1952), 5-18.

491 Korn, Karl, "Verspielte Perlen," *Berliner Hefte*, 2 (1947), 253-259.

492 Korrodi, Edward, "Begegnung mit Hermann Hesse," *Du. Schweizerische Monatsschrift*, 13 (February 1953), 35-36.

493 ———, "Hermann Hesse," *Universum,* 44 (1927), 1054.

494 Köstlin, H. A., "Zur Theologenerziehung (Hermann Hesse: *Unterm Rad),*" *Monatsschrift für Pastoraltheologie,* 2 (1905), 305-308.

495 Kraus, Fritz, "Vom lebendigen Geist. Anmerkungen zu Hesses *Glasperlenspiel,*" *Prisma,* 2, No. 17 (1948), 9-13.

496 Krieg, Walter, "Hermann Hesse, 75 Jahre alt," *Das Antiquariat,* 8 (1952), 388.

497 Kriteon, "Natur und Geist (Hermann Hesses *Narziss und Goldmund),*" *Schule der Freiheit,* 1 (1933), 345-348.

498 Kuhlmann, G., "Der Dichter und die Entscheidung. Zu Hermann Hesses *Narziss und Goldmund,*" *Christliche Welt,* 45 (1931), 166-169.

499 Kunstmann, Lisa, "Musik und Prosa. Zu Hermann Hesses Dichtung," *Deutsche Monatshefte,* 2 (1926), 157-158.

500 Kunze, Wilhelm "Hermann Hesse," *Die Schöne Literatur,* 24 (1923), 201-206.

501 ———, "Hermann Hesses Lyrik," *Weimarer Blätter,* 4 (1922), 323-328.

502 ———, "Studie über Hermann Hesse," *Die Drei,* 4 (1925), 831-840.

503 ———, "Über Hermann Hesse," *Der Bund,* 3 (1921), 158-162.

504 Kurth, Rudolf, "Die Jugend und Hermann Hesse," *Die Sammlung,* 11 (1956), 72-85.

505 Kusch, Eugen, "Hermann Hesses *Nürnberger Reise,*" *Die Neue Schau,* 11 (1950), 102-103.

506 Kusche, Lothar, "Bemerkung über Hermann Hesse," *Die Weltbühne* (Berlin), 7 (1952), 832.

507 Lambrecht, Paulus, "Hermann Hesse: *Siddhartha,*" *Vivos Voco,* 3 (March-April 1923), 260.

508 Lange, I. M., "Literatur im Zeitalter des Imperialismus. Der Formalismus der neuen Ära," *Der Deutschunterricht* (Berlin), 5, No. 3 (1952), 117-125; Hesse, p. 121.

509 Lanuza, Ed. Gonzalez, "Hermann Hesse: *Narciso y Goldmundo,*" *Sur* (Buenos Aires), December, 1948, pp. 87-90.

510 Largiader, Maria, "Brief an Hermann Hesse," *Wissen und Leben,* 15 (1922), 346-347.

511 Laserstein, Käte, "Ein Dichter der Kinderseele. Hermann Hesse zum 50. Geburtstag," *Schule und Elternhaus,* 4 (1927), 589.

512 ———, "Hermann Hesse," *Freie deutsche Bühne,* 9 (1927), 399.

513 ———, "Hermann Hesse," *Das blaue Heft,* 9, No. 13 (1927), 399-401.

514 Lehner, H. H., "Das Romantische bei Hermann Hesse," *Mainleite* (Schweinfurt), 1, No. 6, No. 7 (1950), 41, 50-51 respectively.

515 ———, "Das Sendungsbewusstsein des Künstlers Hermann Hesse zum 2. Juli, dem 78. Geburtstag," *Mainleite* (Schweinfurt), 6, No. 6 (1955), 113-116.

516 Lemm, R. A. von, "Die väterliche Seite der Ahnen Hermann Hesses," *Genealogie und Heraldik,* 3 (1951), 94-95.

517 Lenz, Hermann, "Hermann Hesse. *Das Glasperlenspiel,*" *Weltstimmen,* 17 (1946), 5-9.

518 Leschnitzer, Franz, "Es geht um die Dichtung," *Die Weltbühne* (Berlin), 7 (1952), 1010-16.

519 ———, "Nochmal auf den Operationstisch," *Die Weltbühne* (Berlin), 8 (1953), 434-437; Hesse, 435-436.

520 Lesser, J., "Nobel prizewinner," *Contemporary Review*, 171 (1947), 31-34.

521 Lestiboudois, Herbert, "Geschenk und Gnade," *Das junge Wort*, 2, No. 11 (1947). See 155.

522 ———, "Ein Ruf von Hermann Hesse," *Aufbau*, 2 (1946), 958-959.

523 ———, "Wanderung mit Hermann Hesse," *Heute und Morgen* (Düsseldorf), 7 (1952), 589-591.

524 Leuteritz, Gustav, "Der Zauberer von Montagnola. Weg und Wirken des Nobelpreisträgers Hermann Hesse," *Börsenblatt für den deutschen Buchhandel* (Leipzig), No. 9-10, 1946, p. 181.

525 Levander, Hans, "Hermann Hesse," *Studiekamraten*, 37 (1955), 108-116.

526 Libal, Erika, "Hermann Hesse. Ein Weg nach Innen," *Sonnenblumen. Zeitschrift für junge Mädchen*, 1, No. 2 (1947), 6-7.

527 Lieser, Friedrich, "Die Frage der Menschenbildung bei Hermann Hesse," *Bildung und Erziehung*, 8 (1955), 625-641.

528 Lingelbach, Helene, "Über das Geheimnis dichterischer Sendung im lyrischen Bekenntnis," *Die Horen*, 5 (1928-29), 1056-79; Hesse, p. 1068-69.

529 Lissauer, Ernst, "Zu Hermann Hesses Lyrik," *Das Literarische Echo*, 24 (1922), 730-733.

530 Litt, Theodor, "Die Geschichte und das Übergeschichtliche," *Die Sammlung*, 5 (1950), 6-19; *Glasperlenspiel*, 11-19. See 156.

531 Lorenzen, Hermann, "Kastalien—eine moderne pädagogische Provinz im *Glasperlenspiel* Hermann Hesses," *Pädagogische Rundschau*, 9 (1954-55), 264-268. See 46.

532 Lunding, Erik, "Den Tyske Utopi Som Tidstypisk Genre," *Salmonsen Leksikon Tidskrift*, 12 (1952), 832-839; Hesse, pp. 835-836.

533 Maass, Joachim, "Anmerkung zum Buch eines Magister Ludi," *NR*, April 1946, pp. 375-377; *Das Silberboot*, 3 (1947), 229-230.

534 ———, "Hermann Hesse—Antlitz, Ruhm und Wesen. Zum 70. Geburtstag des Dichters am 2. Juli 1947," *NR*, 1947, pp. 251-257.

535 Maier, Hans, "Hermann Hesse siebzigjährig," *Ex Libris*, 2 (1947), 99-101.

536 Malthaner, Johannes, "A Visit with Hermann Hesse," *Books Abroad*, 25 (1951), 236-237.

537 ———, "Hermann Hesses *Siddhartha*," *German Quarterly*, 25 (1952), 103-109.

538 Mann, Thomas, "Hermann Hesse," *Centaur* (Amsterdam), 1947-48, pp. 33-36.

539 ———, "Hermann Hesse. Einleitung zu einer amerikanischen *Demian*-Ausgabe," *NR*, 1947, pp. 245-250. See 47, 163.

540 ———, "Mein lieber Hermann Hesse," *NSR*, 20 (1952), 143. See 20.

541 ——, "Dem sechzigjährigen Hermann Hesse," *Neue Literatur*, 38 (1937), 424-426.

542 Marti, E. O., "Dank an Hermann Hesse," *Hortulus*, 2 (1952), 58-64.

543 Martini, Fritz, "Hermann Hesse. Träger des Friedenspreises des deutschen Buchhandels," *Der Werbende. Buch- und Zeitschriftenhandel* (Stuttgart), 63 (1955), 330.

544 Mathies, M. E., "Hermann Hesses *Glasperlenspiel*," *Hamburgische Akademische Rundschau*, 1 (1946), 32-35.

545 Matzig, R. B., "*Berthold* und *Knulp*," *NSR*, 13 (1945), 191-193.

546 ——, "Lebendige Romantik. Betrachtungen über Hermann Hesse," *Der Geistesarbeiter*, 22 (1943), 69.

547 ——, "*Narziss und Goldmund* und *Traumfährte*," *NSR*, 13 (1946), 770-771.

548 Maurer, K. W., "*Dank an Goethe* von Hermann Hesse," *The Gate*, 2, No. 2 (1948), 50-51.

549 Maurer, L., "Hermann Hesse und der Zeitkreis der Mutterwelt," *Rhythmus, Mitteilungen des Bodebundes*, 13 (1935), 17-27.

550 Mayer, Hans, "Der Dichter und das feuilletonistische Zeitalter. Über einige Motive im Werk Hermann Hesses," *Aufbau*, 8 (1952), 613-628. See 167.

551 ——, "Goethes Erbschaft in der deutschen Literatur," *Der Deutschunterricht* (Berlin), 2, No. 3 (1949), 36, 38.

552 ——, "Hermann Hesses *Morgenlandfahrt*," *Aufbau*, 8 (1952), 863-864.

553 Melchinger, Siegfried, "Hermann Hesse und die Altersweisheit," *Wort und Wahrheit*, 11 (1956), 162-164.

554 Meridies, W., "Hermann Hesse und die Jugend," *Die neue deutsche Schule*, 1 (1927), 501-507.

555 Mersmann, Heinrich, "Hermann Hesse," *Westermanns Monatshefte*, 93, No. 6 (1952-53), 71.

556 ——, "Dichter malen," *Westermanns Monatshefte*, 94, No. 2 (1953-54), 18-22.

557 Metelmann, Ernst, "Hermann Hesse Bibliographie," *Die Schöne Literatur*, 28 (1927), 299-312.

558 ——, "Unsere Meinung," *Neue Literatur*, 38 (1937), 371-372.

559 Meuer, A., "Demiurg oder der Untergang. Der andere Hermann Hesse," *Zwiebelfisch*, 25, No. 4 (1946-48), 3-7.

560 ——, "Friedenspreis des Buchhandels für Hermann Hesse," *Der Bürger im Staat* (Stuttgart), 5 (1955), 132.

561 Meyer, Th. A., "Hermann Hesse," *Württemberg. Monatsschr. im Dienst von Volk und Heimat*, 2 (1930), 88-95, 194-201.

562 Meyer-Benfey, H., "Hermann Hesse. Zu seinem 50. Geburtstag," *Magdeburg. Harz*, 1927-28, p. 333.

563 ——, "*Knulp*," *Die literarische Gesellschaft*, 3 (1917), 18-27.

564 Mileck, Joseph, "*Hermann Hesse/Romain Rolland. Briefe*," *Modern Language Notes*, 70 (1955), 627.

565 ——, "Hermann Hesse's *Glasperlenspiel*," *University of California Publications in Modern Philology*, 36 (1952), 243-270.

566 ———, "Hesse Bibliographies," *Monatshefte*, 49 (1957), 201-205.

567 ———, "Hesse Collections in Europe," *Monatshefte*, 47 (1955), 290-294.

568 ———, "The Poetry of Hermann Hesse," *Monatshefte*, 46 (1954), 192-198.

569 ———, "The Prose of Hermann Hesse: Life, Substance and Form," *German Quarterly*, 27 (1954), 163-174.

570 ———, "A Visit with Hermann Hesse and a Journey from Montagnola to Calw," *Modern Language Forum*, 41 (1956), 3-8.

571 Missenharter, H., "Hermann Hesse: *Märchen*," *Der deutsche Bund*, 1 (1919), 135-138.

572 ———, "Schwäbische Betrachtung," *Der Schwäbische Bund*, 2 (1920-21), 81-83.

573 Morgenthaler, Ernst, "Lieber Freund (Venedig, June 20, 1952)," *NSR*, 20 (1952), 161.

574 Mueller, Gustav E., "Hermann Hesse," *Books Abroad*, 21 (1947), 146-151. See 172.

575 ———, "Hermann Hesse. Reminiscence," *Books Abroad*, 21 (1947), 287.

576 Mühlberger, Josef, "Hermann Hesse: *Briefe*," *Welt und Wort*, 6 (1951), 327.

577 Müller-Blattau, J., "Die Musik in Thomas Manns *Doktor Faustus* und Hermann Hesses *Glasperlenspiel*," *Annales Universitatis Saraviensis*, 2 (1953), 145-154.

578 ———, "Sinn und Sendung der Musik in Thomas Manns *Dr. Faustus* und Hermann Hesses *Glasperlenspiel*," *Geistige Welt*, 4, No. 1 (1949), 29-34. See preceding item.

579 Müller-Seidel, W., "Autobiographie als Dichtung in der neuen Prosa," *Der Deutschunterricht* (Stuttgart), No. 3, 1951, pp. 29-50.

580 Näf, Hans, "Zu einem Begriff des Poetischen. Bei Anlass der Neuausgabe von Hermann Hesses *Morgenlandfahrt*," *NSR*, 13 (1945), 443-444.

581 Naumann, Walter, "The Individual and Society in the Work of Hermann Hesse," *Monatshefte*, 41 (1949), 33-42.

582 Nestele, Karl, "Hermann Hesse. *Das Glasperlenspiel*," *Der lachende Löwe*, January 1951, pp. 29-30.

583 Nestle, Wilhelm, "Hermann Hesses *Glasperlenspiel*," *Aussaat*, 1, No. 6-7 (1946), 10-11.

584 Oepke, Albrecht, "Indische Mission im Kreuzfeuer moderner Kritik. Hermann Hesse: *Aus Indien*," *Evangel.-luther. Missionblatt*, 76 (1921), 193-199. See 175.

585 Opitz, Fritz, "Der Dichter lebt in den Gestalten seiner Werke. Hermann Hesse im *Steppenwolf*," *Berliner Lehrerzeitung*, 6 (1952), 413-414, 437-438, 462-463.

586 Oven, Jörn, "Hermann Hesse: *Siddhartha*," *Schöne Literatur*, 24 (1923), 331-332 (a severe criticism of Hesse).

587 Park, C. W., "Note on Hermann Hesse's Verse," *Poetry*, 70 (1947), 206-208.

588 Pasinetti, P. M., "Novels from three Languages." *Sewanee Review*, 56 (1948); *Steppenwolf* is severely criticized pp. 171-174.

589 Penzoldt, Ernst, "Zum 75. Geburtstag von Hermann Hesse," *NSR*, 20 (1952), 146-148.

590 Peppard, Murray, "Hermann Hesse's Ladder of Learning," *Kentucky Foreign Language Quarterly*, 3 (1956), 13-20.

591 Peters, Eric, "Hermann Hesse. The Psychological Implications of his Writings," *German Life and Letters*, 1 (1948), 209-214.

592 Pfeiffer, Johannes, "Über die gegenwärtige Situation der deutschen Lyrik," *Die Sammlung*, 7 (July-August 1952), 281-300; Hesse, pp. 293-294.

593 Pfeifer, Martin, "Ein Dichter des Friedens und der Menschlichkeit," *Heute und Morgen* (Düsseldorf), 7 (1952), 585-588.

594 ———, "50 Jahre *Peter Camenzind*," *Arnstädter Kulturbote*, April 1954, pp. 17-18.

595 ———, "Hermann Hesse. Ein Kämpfer für den Frieden," *Heute und Morgen* (Schwerin), 1952, pp. 353-357. See 593.

596 ———, "Hermann Hesse und der Buchhandel," *Börsenblatt für den deutschen Buchhandel* (Leipzig), 122 (1955), 750-751.

597 Pistor, M., "Besuch beim Dichter Hermann Hesse," *Schweizer Garbe. Familienblatt*, 25 (1941-42), 603-605.

598 Pöggeler, Fr., "Aus Hermann Hesses *Glasperlenspiel*," *Pädagogische Provinz*, 3 (1949), 498.

599 Probizer, E. M., "L'India antica nelle opere di due moderni poeti tedeschi (Karl Gjellerup, Hermann Hesse)," *Nuova Antologia*, Settima Serie, Vol. 258 (1928), 87-105; *Siddhartha*, pp. 96-103.

600 Rainalter, E. H., "Hermann Hesse," *Die Gegenwart*, 43 (August 1914), 536-539.

601 Rang, Bernhard, "Oskar Maria Graf: *Wir sind Gefangene;* Hermann Hesse: *Steppenwolf*," *Der Kunstwart*, 41 (April 1928), 52-55.

602 Rasch, Wolfdietrich, "Hermann Hesse fünfundsiebzigjährig," *Die Literatur* (Stuttgart), 1, No. 8 (1952), 2.

603 Rauch, Karl, "Hermann Hesse und die neue Jugend," *Junge Menschen*, 2, No. 4 (1921).

604 Rauscher, Ulrich, "Hermann Hesses *Rosshalde*," *Das literarische Echo*, 17 (1914), 21-23.

605 Reinhold, Helmut, "Hermann Hesses Morgenlandfahrt mit Mozart," *Geist und Zeit*, 1, No. 5 (1956), 86-99.

606 Reinke-Ortmann, S., "Besuch in Montagnola," *Der Standpunkt. Die Zeitschrift für die Gegenwart*, 2, No. 3-4 (1947), 39-40.

607 Reisse, M., "Hesse als Lyriker," *Das Deutsche Wort*, 5 (1929), 24.

608 Reuter, Emil, "Hermann Hesse und die Menschlichkeit," *Die Brücke*, 3 (October 1948), 25-27.

609 Riboni, Denise, "Hermann Hesse et l'idée de l'unité," *Revue de Genève*, 14 (1928), 166-172.

610 ———, "Le thème de la mort chez Hermann Hesse," *Suisse Contemporaine*, 7 (1947), 99-105.

611 Rilke, R. M., "Hermann Hesse: *Eine Stunde hinter Mitternacht*,"

NSR, 20 (1952), 188; first appeared in *Boten für die deutsche Literatur*, September, 1899.

612 Ringer, P., "So war mein Leben—nicht arm, und nicht schlecht! Hermann Hesse z. 75. Geburtstag," *Zeitschrift der Buchgemeinschaft Ex Libris* (Zürich), 7, No. 5 (1952).

613 Roch, Herbert, "Studie über Hermann Hesse," *Die Hilfe*, 42 (1936), 403-406.

614 Rockenbach, Martin, "Rede und Antwort," *Orplid*, 5, No. 11-12 (1928), 185-186.

615 ———, "*Der Steppenwolf*," *Orplid*, 4, No. 5-6 (1927), 54-56.

616 Rose, Ernst, "The Beauty from Pao. Heine, Bierbaum, Hesse," *Germanic Review*, 32 (1957), 17-18 ("König Yu," *Traumfährte*).

617 Röttger, Fritz, "Freund der Wahrheit—Kämpfer für den Frieden," *Der Deutschunterricht*, 5 (1952), 350-353.

618 Russo, W., "Hermann Hesse. Zu seinem 50. Geburtstag," *Schatzgräber*, 6, No. 9 (1927), 1-3.

619 Rz. W., "*Elf Aquarelle aus dem Tessin*," *Die Schweiz*, 24 (1920), 711.

620 Saager, Adolf, "Hermann Hesses Biographie," *Lesezirkel*, 15 (Feb. 1928), 41-46.

621 ———, "Zu Hermann Hesses *Siddhartha*," *Wissen und Leben*, 17 (1924), 560-562.

622 Sander, E., "Zu Hermann Hesses 50. Geburtstag," *Der Bücherfreund*, 14, No. 6-7 (1927).

623 Schacht, Roland, "Rückblicke, Einblicke, Ausblicke," *Aufbau*, 2 (1946); *Der Europäer*, p. 1180.

624 Schäfer, W., "*Nachbarn* von Hermann Hesse," *NR*, 20 (1909), 782-783.

625 Schall, Franz, "Um Hermann Hesse," *Deutsches Volkstum*, 1930, ii, pp. 232-235; a reply to Hecht's criticism of Hesse, see 441.

626 Scheffler, Herbert, "Hesses *Narziss und Goldmund*," *Die Literatur*, 32 (1930), 575-576.

627 Scheffler, Karl, "Zwei Besprechungen über Hermann Hesse als Maler," *Kunst und Künstler*, 19 (1920-21).

628 Scheurmann, Erich, "Begegnung mit Hermann Hesse," *Deutsche Presse-Korrespondenz* (T. Oppermann Verlag, Hannover-Kirchrode), June 1951, pp. 11-12.

629 Schmid, F. D., "Hermann Hesse," *Berner Rundschau*, 1 (1906), 66-80.

630 Schmid, Karl, "Rede zur Feier von Hermann Hesses 75. Geburtstag, gehalten am 29. Juni 1925 im Züricher Schauspielhaus," *NSR*, 20 (1952), 131-139. See 20.

631 Schmid-Gruber, R., "Hermann Hesse," *Über den Wassern*, 1 (1908), 299-304.

632 Schneider, Gerhard, "Hermann Hesse und das *Glasperlenspiel*," *Wissenschaftliche Zeitschrift der Humboldt-Universität* (Berlin), 3 (1953-54), 219-234.

633 Schneider, Marcel, "Thomas Mann et Hermann Hesse," *La Table Ronde*, 3 (July 1950), 139-144.

634 Schoeck, Othmar, "Lieber Hesse!" *NSR*, 20 (1952), 145.

635 Schöfer, Wolfgang von, "Aktualität und Überzeitlichkeit der Literatur," *Die Sammlung*, 4 (1949), 346-350; a reply to Böckmann, see 324.

636 ――――, "Hermann Hesse, *Peter Camenzind* und das *Glasperlenspiel*," *Die Sammlung*, 3 (1948), 597-609.

637 Scholz, Wilhelm von, "Hermann Hesse: *Eine Stunde hinter Mitternacht*," *Das literarische Echo*, 2 (1899), 322-323.

638 Scholz-Wülfing, P., "Hermann Hesse: *Das Glasperlenspiel*," *Der Deutschunterricht* (Berlin), 1, No. 1 (1948), 34-35.

639 Schott, Rold, "Geburtstagsbrief an Hermann Hesse den grossen Europäer," *Das Silberboot*, 3 (1947), 225-228.

640 Schouten, H., "Hermann Hesse. *Glasperlenspiel*," *Duitse Kroniek* ('s Gravenhage), 3, No. 3 (1951), 75-78.

641 Schröder, Eduard, "Hermann Hesse," *Frankfurter Hefte*, 3 (1948), 841-845.

642 Schröder, Rudolf Alex., "Briefgruss an Hermann Hesse," *NSR*, 20 (1952), 140-142.

643 ――――, "An Hermann Hesse," *NR*, 48, ii (1937), 41-45.

644 Schuh, Willi, "Richard Strauss. Four last Songs," *Tempo*, Spring 1950, pp. 25-30.

645 Schühle, Erwin, "Linien in der Dichtung Hermann Hesses," *Die Christengemeinschaft*, September 1946, pp. 122-126.

646 Schultz de Mantovani, Fryda, "Hermann Hesse: *El juego de abalorios*," *Sur* (Buenos Aires), Oct., Nov., Dec., 1950, pp. 306-308.

647 Schultze, Friedrich, "Bekenner und Idylliker. Zum 70. Geburtstag des Dichters," *Aufbau*, 3, No. 7 (1947), 59-60.

648 ――――, "Das Glasperlenspiel," *Aufbau*, 3, No. 5 (1947), 455-457.

649 Schuwerack, Wilhelm, "Gedanken zum *Glasperlenspiel* von Hermann Hesse," *Begegnung*, 7 (1952), 329-331.

650 Schwarz, Georg, "*Beschreibung einer Landschaft*," *Welt und Wort*, 3 (1948), 170-171.

651 ――――, "Hermann Hesse beschreibt eine Landschaft," *Deutsche Presse-Korrespondenz* (Hannover-Kirchrode), July 1953, pp. 21-22.

652 ――――, "Hermann Hesse in seinem Gedicht," *Welt und Wort*, 4 (1949), 171-174.

653 ――――, "Hermann Hesse. *Späte Prosa*," *Welt und Wort*, 6 (1951), 200.

654 Schweter, W., "Eine Wanderung mit Hermann Hesse," *Vaterland*, 9 (1932), 24-30.

655 Seidl, F., "Hermann Hesse. Auseinandersetzung," *Scholle*, 5 (1928), 330-333.

656 Seidlin, Oskar, "Hermann Hesses *Glasperlenspiel*," *Die Wandlung*, 3 (1948), 298-308; see also *Germanic Review*, 23 (1948), 263-273.

657 ――――, "Hermann Hesse: The Exorcism of the Demon," *Symposium*, 4 (1950), 325-348. See 199.

658 Seyffarth, Ursula, "Hermann Hesse: *Die Gedichte*," *Welt und Wort*, 3 (1948), 83-84.

659 Siedler, W. J., "Ein stiller Jubilar," *Der Monat* (München), 4 (1952), 541.

660 Spenlé, J. E., "Les derniers romans de Hermann Hesse," *Mercure de France*, 185 (1926), 74-87.

661 Steen, Albert, "Hermann Hesse," *Der Quäker* (Bad Pyrmont), 26 (1952), 59-61.

662 Stein, Gottfried, "Hermann Hesse," *Begegnung*, 2 (1947), 161-164.

663 Stolz, Heinz, "Hermann Hesse." *Die Literatur*, 26 (1924), 324-327.

664 Strauss und Torney, Lulu von, "Hermann Hesse," *Die Tat*, 14 (1922), 694-698.

665 Süskind, W. E., "Hermann Hesse und die Jugend," *NR*, 38, i (1927), 492-497.

666 Szczesny, G., "Hans Castorp, Harry Haller und die Folgen," *Umschau. Die Internationale Revue*, 2 (1947), 601-611.

667 Tenschert, Roland, "Richard Strauss' Schwanengesang. *Vier letzte Lieder für Sopran und Orchester*," *Osterreichische Musik*, 5 (1950), 225-229.

668 Thiele, Guillermo, "Jugando con perlas de vidrio. Informe sobre la última novela de Hermann Hesse," *Boletín Bibliográfico*. Sección Lengua y Literatura Alemanas, Mendoza, 1948, pp. 17-46.

669 Thiess, F., "Hermann Hesse zum 70. Geburtstag," *Junior*, 1, No. 4, (1947), 18-19.

670 Thomas-San-Galli, W. A., "Hermann Hesse und die Musik," *Der Merker*, 5 (1914), 413-418.

671 Thurm, H. G., "Thomas Mann, Hermann Hesse und wir Jungen," *Umschau. Die Internationale Revue*, 2 (1947), 612-615.

672 Townsend, S. R., "The German Humanist Hermann Hesse (Nobel Prize Winner in 1946)," *Modern Language Forum*, 32 (1947), 1-12.

673 ———, "Die moderne deutsche Literatur in Amerika," *Die Sammlung*, 9 (1954), 237-243; Hesse, p. 241.

674 Trog, Hans, "Hermann Hesse: *Gertrud*," *Wissen und Leben*, 4 (1911), 509-511.

675 Türke, Kurt, "Das Überflüssige und seine Folgen," *Neue Deutsche Literatur* (Berlin), 2, No. 4 (1954), 166-167.

676 Über Wasser, Walter, "Der Maler Hermann Hesse," *Die Schweiz*, 24 (1920), 511-515.

677 Ude, Karl, "Hermann Hesse und Frankreich," *Welt und Wort*, 10 (1955), 104.

678 Uenuira, Toshio, "Thomas Mann and Hermann Hesse" (in Japanese), *Romanticism and Classicism*, 1 (Dec. 1934), 15-20.

679 Uhlig, Helmut, "Hermann Hesse," *Die Weltbühne*, 1 (1946), 383-384.

680 ———, "*Die Morgenlandfahrt*—Buch eines Übergangs," *Aufbau*, 4 (1948), 1009-11.

681 Uhlmann, A. M., "Wir Freunde des Friedens und der Wahrheit müssen zu unserem Glauben stehen. Zum 75. Geburstag des humanistischen und treuen Friedensfreundes Hermann Hesse am 2. Juli," *Börsenblatt für den deutschen Buchhandel* (Frankfurt a. M., 8 (1952), 459-461.

682 Uhse, Bodo, "Literatur und Nation," *Aufbau*, 9 (1953), 507.

683 Unger, Wilhelm, "Die Hermann Hesse Gemeinde," *The Gate*, 1, No. 1 (1947), 14-19.

684 ———, "Hermann Hesse. Zur Verleihung des Goethe-Preises und des Nobel Preises für Literatur an den grossen deutsch-schweizerischen Dichter," *The Gate*, 1, No. 1 (1947), 11-13.

685 Vesper, Will, "Unsere Meinung," *Neue Literatur*, 36 (1935), 685-687; 37 (1936), 239-242.

686 Vietsch, Eberhard von, "Wahrheit und Wirklichkeit im *Glasperlenspiel*," *Neues Europa*, 3, No. 6 (1948), 32-46.

687 Vietta, Egon, "Hermann Hesse. Das *Glasperlenspiel*," *Das Goldene Tor*, 2 (1947), 690-691.

688 Volkart, D., "Hermann Hesse: *Blick ins Chaos*," *Wissen und Leben*, 13 (July 1920), 854.

689 Vordtriede, Werner, "Hermann Hesse: *Das Glasperlenspiel*," *German Quarterly*, 19 (1946), 291-294.

690 Wagner, Gisela, "Kastalien und die Schulen auf dem Lande," *Pädagogische Provinz* (Frankfurt a. M.), 10, No. 2 (1956), 57-64.

691 Waldhausen, Agnes, "Hermann Hesse. Referat," *Mitteilungen der Literarhistorischen Gesellschaft* (Bonn), 5 (1910), 4-32.

692 Wantoch, H., "Hermann Hesse," *Masken*, 5 (1910), 305-310.

693 Weber, Werner, "Hermann Hesse. Das *Glasperlenspiel*," *Athena*, 1, No. 1 (1947), 84-86.

694 ———, "Im Presselschen Gartenhaus," *NSR*, 20 (1950), 150-153.

695 ———, "Ravenna," *Du. Schweizerische Monatsschrift*, 13 (February 1953), 47-48.

696 Werner, A., "Hermann Hesse," *South Atlantic Quarterly*, 52 (1953), 384-390.

697 Werner, B. E., "Hermann Hesse," *Deutsche Rundschau*, 212 (1927), 57-62.

698 Widner, Thomas, "Vom herbstlichen Geiste Kastaliens," *NSR*, 9 (1941-2), 373-377.

699 Wiedner, Laurenz, "Hermann Hesses Gedichte," *Das Silberboot*, 4 (1948), 52-53.

700 Wiegand, Heinrich, "Hermann Hesses Jugendbildnis," *NR*, 45, i (1934), 119-122.

701 ———, "Hermann Hesses *Morgenlandfahrt*," *NR*, 43, i (1932), 697-701.

702 Wiegler, Paul, "Vom *Demian* zu *Narziss und Goldmund*," *NR*, 41, ii (1930), 827-832.

703 Wieser, S., "Hermann Hesse, " *Die Bücherwelt*, 12 (1915), 201-209.

704 Wistinghausen, Kurt von, "Früchte des Alters. Über Ina Seidel und Hermann Hesse," *Die Christengemeinschaft*, 23 (1951), 220-221.

705 Witkop, Philipp, "Hermann Hesse," *Die Schöne Literatur*, 28 (1927), 289-299. See 215.

706 Wolfenstein, A., "Wölfisches Traktat," *Weltbühne* (Berlin), 23, ii (1937), 107-109.

707 Wood, R. C., "Hermann Hesse," *American-German Review* (Oct.-Nov. 1956), pp. 3-5, 38.

708 Wrobel, I., "Der deutsche Mensch," *Weltbühne* (Berlin), 23, 1i (1927), 332-337.

709 Wüstenberg, H. L., "Hermann Hesses politische Aufsätze und Gedichte," *NSR*, 13 (1945), 476-484. See 56.

710 ——, "Hermann Hesse und die Politik der Zeit," *Berliner Hefte*, 1 (1946), 204-211. Same as preceding item.

711 Wyss, H. A., "Hermann Hesses Frühzeit," *Schweizerische Monatshefte f. Politik u. Kultur*, 13 (1933), 135-137.

712 Zarek, Otto, "Notizen über einen deutschen Dichter," *NR*, 34, i (1923), 367-373.

713 Zeller, Gustav, "Offener Brief an Hermann Hesse," *Psychische Studien*, 47 (1920), 622-630.

714 Zoff, Otto, "Über Hermann Hesse," *Wieland*, 6 (May 1920), 11-12.

715 "An Hermann Hesse zum Nobelpreis," *Deutsche Blätter* (Santiago de Chile), 4, No. 34 (1946), 57.

716 "Auf Besuch bei Hermann Hesse," *Mitteilungsblätter der Aussiger Stadtbücherei*, 2, No. 7 (1937), 14.

717 "Baltische Köpfe: Hermann Hesse," *Baltische Rundschau* (Bovenden über Göttingen), 3, No. 7 (1952), 1.

718 "Brief an Hermann Hesse," *Du. Schweizerische Monatsschrift*, 13 (February 1953), 49-50.

719 "Die Bücher Hermann Hesses in unserer Bücherei," *Mitteilungsblätter der Aussiger Stadtbücherei*, 2, No. 7 (1937), 10.

720 "Der Dichter, Maler, Philosoph," *Aufstieg*, 3 (1951), 757-758.

721 "Echo der Zeitungen zu Hermann Hesses 50. Geburtstag," *Die Literatur*, 29 (1927), 707.

722 "Echo der Zeitungen zu Hermann Hesses 60. Geburtstag," *Die Literatur*, 39 (1937), 737.

723 "Fünf Jahre westdeutsches Hermann-Hesse-Archiv," *Heute und Morgen* (Düsseldorf), 7 (1952), 621-623.

724 "Hermann Hesse hat in diesem Sommer . . ." *Mitteilungsblätter der Aussiger Stadtbücherei*, 2, No. 7 (1937), 3.

725 "Hermann Hesse. Im englischen Blickwinkel," *Englische Rundschau*, 3, No. 7 (1953), 78.

726 "Hermann Hesse in Frankreich," *Neuphilologische Zeitschrift*, 1, No. 3 (1949), 67-68.

727 "Hermann Hesse. *Siddhartha*," *Velhagen u. Klasings Monatshefte*, 38 (1924), 574.

728 "Hermann Hesse. 70 Jahre," *Börsenblatt für den deutschen Buchhandel* (Frankfurt a. M), 3 (1947), 224.

729 "Hermann Hesse. Zu seinem 75. Geburtstag," *Der Leihbuchhändler* (Wiesbaden), 6 (1952), 89.

730 "Hermann Hesse zum 75. Geburtstag," *Der Bosch-Zünder*, 32, No. 7-8 (1952), 135.

731 "Hermann Hesse, zum 2. Juli 1952," *Blätter der Freiheit*, 4, No. 9-12 (1952), 16.

732 "Nobelpreise," *Börsenblatt für den deutschen Buchhandel* (Leipzig), No. 9-10 (1946), pp. 183-184.

733   "Der Traum vom reinen Menschen. Hermann Hesse zum 75. Geburts-
      tag," *Bodensee Hefte*, 3 (1952), 217-218.
734   "Unsere Meinung," *Neue Literatur*, 37 (1936), 58.
735   "Über Hermann Hesse," *Junge Menschen*, 5 (Dec. 1924), 208-209.
736   "Verleihung des Wilhelm-Raabe-Preises an   Hermann   Hesse,"
      Börsenblatt für den Deutschen Buchhandel (Leipzig), Dec. 9, 1950,
      p. 552.
737   "Der Weg zu Hermann Hesse," *Mitteilungsblätter der Aussiger
      Stadtbücherei*, 2, No. 7 (1937), 13.

ARTICLES IN NEWSPAPERS AND WEEKLIES.

Needless to say, this cannot claim to be an exhaustive list. It does, however, represent a good coverage of the period from 1927 to 1957. Only twenty-four earlier articles were considered significant enough to be included (for a longer list of items preceding 1927, see Metelmann, *Die Schöne Literatur*, 28 [1927], 310-311; and for a very extensive list of items which have appeared in newspapers and weeklies of East Germany since 1945, see Pfeifer, *Hermann Hesse. Bibliographie* [1955], pp. 29-37) :

738 Aburi, Hans, "Hermann Hesse," *Basilisk* (Sonntagsbeilage zur *National-Ztg.*, Basel), July, 1927.

739 Amrhein, Martin, "Der "immerwährende Freund," *Basler Nachrichten*, No. 272, 1947.

740 Ball, Hugo, "Vom Wesen Hermann Hesses," *Schwabenspiegel* (Beil. z. *Württ. Ztg.*), 22 (1928), 73.

741 Ball-Hennings, Emmy, "Begegnung mit Hermann Hesses," *National-Ztg.* (Basel), No. 296, 1946.

742 Basler, Otto, "Hermann Hesse," *Das Bücherblatt* (Zürich), No. 6, 1947.

743 ———, "Hermann Hesse, menschliches und dichterisches Bekenntnis," *National-Ztg.* (Basel), No. 291, 1947.

744 Bergholter, Jürgen, "Die Postkarte. Ein Dank an Hermann Hesse," *National-Ztg.* (Basel), Dec. 14, 1949, p. 2.

745 Bezold, K., "In Hesses alter Stube," *Schwabenspiegel* (Beil. z. *Württ. Ztg*). 26 (1932), 379.

746 Blum, Bernhard, "Erscheinung eines alten Mannes," *Die Brücke zur Welt* (Sonntagsbeilage zur *Stuttgarter Ztg.*), October 8, 1955.

747 Bock, H. J., "Hermann Hesse und sein *Glasperlenspiel*," *Die Wochenpost* (Stuttgart), 1, No. 26 (1946), 4.

748 Brandweiler, H., "Der Traumweg Hermann Hesses," *Tägliche Rundschau* (Berlin), July 2, 1947, p. 3.

749 Bronson, John, "*Death and the Lover*," *Bookman*, 76 (Jan. 1933), 91-92.

750 Buchwald, Reinhard, "Hermann Hesse," *Die Barke*, No. 3, 1955, pp. 1-2.

751 Burger, O. H., "Glasperlen. Étude über ein schwäbisches Thema," *Das Literarische Deutschland*, November 10, 1951, pp. 5-6.

752 B., Th., "Dem Dichter der menschlichen Seele," *Sächsisches Tageblatt* (Dresden), July 1, 1952, p. 4.

753 Carlsson, Anni, "Hesses späte Prosa," *Deutsche Universitätszeitung* (Göttingen), 6, No. 20 (1951), 12-14.

754 Carossa, Hans, "Besuch bei Hermann Hesse," *Das Literarische Deutschland*, March 5, 1951, p. 3.

755 Caspar, Günter, "Hermann Hesse — Humanist und Freund des

Friedens," *Neues Deutschland* (Berlin), July 2, 1952, Ausg. A. p. 4.

756   Chemnitz, E. W., "Offener Brief an den Verfasser von *Zarathustras Wiederkehr*," *Deutsche Internierten-Ztg.*, Feb. 28, 1919, pp. 12-14.

757   Craven, Thomas, "German Symbolism. *Demian*," *Dial*, 74 (1923), 619-620.

758   Deike, Günther, "Begegnung mit Hermann Hesse," *Abendpost* (Berlin), July 2, 1947.

759   Delbono, Francesco, "Beitrag zur Lyrik Hermann Hesses," *Italienische Kulturnachrichten*, 1954, No. 41-42, pp. 37-42.

760   Deubel, Werner, "*Steppenwolf*," *Didaskalia* (Beil. z. *Frankf. Nachr.*) Dec. 4, 1927, pp. 221-222.

761   Eggebrecht, Axel, "Eine gütige und verstehende Liebe," *Der Demokrat* (Schwerin), July 2, 1952. p. 3.

762   Engel, Monroe, "*Magister Ludi*," *Nation*, 169 (December 24, 1949), 626-627

763   Epping, F., "Hermann Hesse und der Krieg," *Zeitschrift f. Literatur, Kunst und Wissenschaft* (Beil. z. *Hamburgischer Correspondent*), 38 (Nov. 21, 1915).

764   Erler, I., "Hermann Hesse," *Deutsche Lehrer-Ztg.*, 29, No. 26 (1916), 337-339.

765   Eyberg, J., "Hermann Hesse und Klingsor," *Schwabenspiegel* (Beil. z. *Württ. Ztg.*), 27 (1933), 58.

766   Eyck, H. A. van, "Betrachtungen zu Hermann Hesses *Glasperlenspiel*," *Deutsche Woche* (München), 1, No. 25 (1955), 11.

767   Faesi, Robert, "Kurgäste: Th. Manns *Zauberberg* und Hermann Hesses *Kurgast*," *Basler Nachrichten*, Sonntagsblatt, Nov. 8, Nov. 15, 1925. See 105.

768   Farrelly, John, "*Demian*," *New Republic*, 118 (February 23, 1948), 24.

769   Finckh, Ludwig, "*Diesseits*," *Propyläen* (Beil. z. *Münchener Ztg.*), 4 (1907), 502-504.

770   Förster, Franz, "Hermann Hesse," *Thüringer Neueste Nachrichten* (Weimar), July 2, 1952, p. 3.

771   Freemantle, Anne, "Good and Evil. *Demian*," *NYHT Weekly Book Review*, Feb. 29, 1948, p. 27.

772   Frisch, Max, "Aus einem Tagebuch," *Basler Nachrichten*, Sonntagsblatt, No. 27, 1947.

773   Fritsch, Oskar, "Hermann Hesse und wir," *Der Tag* (Berlin), Oct. 26, 1921.

774   Fuss, Karl, "Hermann Hesse," *Propyläen* (Beil. z. *Münchener Ztg.*), 24 (1927), 313-314.

775   ———, "Hermann Hesse," *Schwabenspiegel* (Beil. z. *Württ. Ztg.*), 21 (1927), 202, 212.

776   ———, "Hermann Hesse als Alemannendichter," *Beilage besond. des Staatsanzeigers für Württemberg*, 1927, p. 194.

777   F. R. B., "Was Hesse am liebsten liest," *Nacht-Express* (Berlin), Oct. 30, 1947.

778   Gide, André, "Hermann Hesse," *Allgemeine Zeitung* (Mainz), Dec. 7, 1947. See 114.

779 ———, "Hermann Hesse zum 70. Geburtstag," *Neue Züricher Ztg.*, July 2, 1947. See 114.

780 Goern, Hermann, "Hesses innere Wahrhaftigkeit," *Der Neue Weg* (Halle), June 28, 1952, p. 3.

781 ———, "Schlichtes Christentum: tägliche Bewährung," *Der Neue Weg* (Halle), July 4, 1953, p. 5.

782 Grebert, Ludwig, "Hermann Hesse," *Didaskalia* (Beil. z. *Frankf Nachr.*), April 5, 1925, pp. 54-55.

783 Gutkind, C. S., "Freund und Führer. Hermann Hesse: *Demian*," *Frankfurter Ztg.*, Aug. 19, 1920.

784 G. C., "Der Pazifist im Elfenbeinturm," *Tägliche Rundschau* (Berlin), Oct. 8, 1949, Ausg. 2, p. 4.

785 Haering, Alfred, "Novalis redivivus," *Sonntag* (Berlin), May 4, 1947, p. 3.

786 Halsband, R., "*Siddhartha*," *SRL*, Dec. 22, 1951, p. 38.

787 Hammer, Franz, "Hermann Hesse," *Start* (Berlin), June 20, 1947, p. 4.

788 Hartley, L. P., "*Steppenwolf*," *Sat. Review*, June 1, 1929, 746.

789 Hartmann, Rolf, "Der friedliebende Hermann Hesse," *Neue Zeit* (Berlin), June 29, 1952, p. 5.

790 Hees, Martin, "Es ist lehrreich, zu beobachten . . ." *Tägliche Rundschau* (Berlin), June 6, 1946, p. 3.

791 Herrigel, Hermann, "Positiver Surrealismus," *Das Literarische Deutschland*, September 20, 1951, p. 1.

792 Hertel, Werner, "Hermann Hesse," *Verantwortung* (Dresden), June 28, 1952, p. 8.

793 Herzog, F. M., "Gruss an Hermann Hesse," *Basler Nachrichten*, Sonntagsblatt No. 26, 1947.

794 Heuss, Theodor, "*Das Glasperlenspiel*," *Rhein-Neckar-Ztg.*, Oct. 19, 1946.

795 ———, "Hermann Hesse, der vaterlandslose Geselle," *Neckar Ztg.*, Nov. 1, 1915.

796 Hill, Claude, "Herr Hesse and the Modern Neurosis. *Steppenwolf*," *NYT Book Review*, March 16, 1947, p. 5.

797 ———, "The Journey to the East," *Saturday Review*, June 1, 1957, pp. 12-13.

798 Hirsch, F. E., "*Demian*," *Library Journal*, 72 (1947), 1685.

799 ———, "Nobel Prize Novel. *Steppenwolf*," *Library Journal*, 72 (1947), 468.

800 Huch, Ricarda, "Loslösung vom Nationalgefühl. Eine Erwiderung an Hermann Hesse," *Tägliche Rundschau* (Berlin), April 12, 1946, p. 3.

801 Irvine, L. L., "*Steppenwolf*," *The Nation and Athenaeum*, May 11, 1929, p. 208.

802 Joho, Wolfgang, "Hermann Hesse zum 70. Geburtstag," *Sonntag* (Berlin), 2, No. 26 (1947), 5.

803 ———, "*Peter Camenzind* und wir," *Sonntag* (Berlin), 7, No. 20 (1952), 6.

804 J. M., "Verantwortungsbewusste Innerlichkeit," *Norddeutsche Ztg.* (Schwerin), July 1, 1952, p. 4.

805 J. R., "Hermann Hesse, Dichter und Humanist," *Freie Presse* (Zwickau), July 2, 1952, p. 4.

806 J. W., "Lyriker in Prosa und Poesie," *National-Ztg.* (Berlin), June 28, 1952, p. 7.

807 Kalenter, O., "Der junge Hermann Hesse," *Weltwoche*, 16, No. 785 (1948), 5.

808 Kantorowicz, Alfred, "Hermann Hesse," *Neues Deutschland* (Berlin), May 10, 1952, Ausg. A. p. 4.

809 ———, "Der Humanist Hermann Hesse," *Tägliche Rundschau* (Berlin), July 1, 1952, Ausg. 1, p. 4.

810 Kellermann, Bernhard, "Begegnung mit Hermann Hesse," *Sonntag* (Berlin), July 6, 1952, p. 6.

811 Kiessig, Martin, "Über Hermann Hesse," *Leipziger Volkszeitung*, March 12, 1947, pp. 2-3.

812 Klein, T., "Hermann Hesse, Wieland, Schiller," *Münchner Neueste Nachr.*, Oct. 4, 1921.

813 Kömig, Otto, "Hermann Hesse," *Arbeiter-Ztg.* (Wien), No. 151, 1947.

814 Korrodi, Ed., "An Hermann Hesse, den Dichter des *Demian*," *Neue Züricher Ztg.*, July 4, 1920.

815 ———, "Hermann Hesse, Preisträger des Gottfried-Keller-Preises," *Neue Züricher Ztg.*, No. 619, 1936.

816 ———, "Wer ist der Dichter des *Demian?*" *Neue Züricher Ztg.*, June 24, 1920.

817 Krafft, Johannes, "Das weise Buch eines weisen Dichters," *Der Neue Weg* (Halle), June 28, 1952, p. 3.

818 Kraus, Fritz, "Hermann Hesse, der Politiker," *Die Neue Ztg.* (München), No. 228, 1949.

819 Krauss, R., "Hermann Hesse," *Schwabenspiegel* (Beil. z. Württ. Ztg.), 23 (1929), 347.

820 Kronenberger, Louis, "*Death and the Lover*," *NYHT Books*, December 11, 1932, p. 18.

821 Krüger, Horst, "Würzburger Student schreibt an Hermann Hesse," *Göttinger Universitätszeitung*, June 10, 1949, p. 14.

822 Kusche, Lothar, "Zwischen Denken und Fühlen," *BZ am Abend* (Berlin), July 2, 1952, p. 3.

823 Langgässer, Elisabeth, "Weisheit des Herzens. Zu Hermann Hesses *Krieg und Frieden*," *Deutsche Zeitung und Wirtschaftszeitung* (Stuttgart), Oct. 8, 1949, p. 15.

824 Lazare, Christopher, "A Measure of Wisdom. *Siddhartha*," *NYT Book Review*, Dec. 2, 1951, p. 52.

825 Leuteritz, Gustav, "Der deutsche Humanist Hermann Hesse," *Die Frau von heute*, 7 (July 4, 1952), 18.

826 ———, "Fern dem deutschen Wirrsal," *Berliner Ztg.*, July 2, 1947, p. 3.

827 ———, "Der Zauberer von Montagnola," *Tägliche Rundschau* (Berlin), Nov. 26, 1946.

828 Lewalter, C. E., "Gedanken über Hermann Hesse zu seinem 75 Geburtstag," *Die Zeit*, 7, No. 27 (1952), 4.

829 Luma, "Ein heutiger Romantiker," *Der Deutschen-Spiegel*, 5 (Oct. 26, 1928), 1767-70.

830 MacDonald, Dwight, "Books," *New Yorker*, Jan. 23, 1954, p. 98.

831 Mann, Thomas, "Hermann Hesse, liberator of a stifling provincialism," *SRL*, Jan. 3, 1948, pp. 5-7. See 146.

832 Matzig, R. B., "Hermann Hesse als Lyriker," *National-Ztg.* (Basel), No. 291, 1947.

833 Mauer, Otto, "Maria oder Diana? Zu *Narziss und Goldmund*," *Die Zeit im Buch*, No. 10-11, 1949.

834 Meuer, Adolf, "Friedenspreis für Hermann Hesse," *Die Kultur*, 3, No. 53 (1954-55), 5.

835 Middleton, Drew, "A literary letter from Germany," *NYT Book Review*, July 31, 1949, p. 2.

836 Mieg, H. P., "Dem Maler Hermann Hesse," *Basler Nachrichten*, Sonntagsblatt No. 26, 1946.

837 Morris, A. S., "The Will to perish. *Demian*," *NYT Book Review*, Feb. 1, 1948, p. 6.

838 Ohff, Heinz, "Hermann Hesse auf der Bühne," *Das ganze Deutschland* (Heidelberg), 5, No. 15 (1953), 5.

839 Otto, Heinrich, "Hermann Hesse als Künstler und Mahner," *Das andere Deutschland*, 14, No. 6 (1952), 6.

840 Pfeifer, Martin, "Fünfzig Jahre, *Unterm Rad*," *Berliner Ztg.*, August 13, 1955.

841 ———, "Hermann Hesse in Montagnola," *Pulsschlag* (Zwickau), Oct. 1956, p. 10.

842 ———, "Hermann-Hesse-Literatur in der DDR," *Liberal-Demokratische Ztg.* (Halle), July 3, 1955, p. 5.

843 ———, "Wir Freunde des Friedens stehen zu unserem Glauben. Zu Hermann Hesses Geburtstag am 2. Juli," *Der Morgen*, July 1, 1952, p. 6.

844 ———, "Hermann Hesse und Thomas Mann," *Die Union* (Dresden), Aug. 25, 1955, p. 4.

845 Pfeifle, L., "Hermann Hesse zu seinem 50. Geburtstag," *Württemberg Lehrerzeitung*, 87 (1927).

846 Pick, Robert, "Cryptic Game of Beads," *SRL*, Oct. 15, 1949, pp. 15-16.

847 ———, "*Demian*," *SRL*, Jan. 24, 1948, p. 18.

848 ———, "*Magister Ludi*," *SRL*, Oct. 15, 1949, pp, 15-16.

849 ———, "Nobel Prize Winner Hesse," *SRL*, Dec. 7, 1946, pp. 38-40.

850 Plant, Richard, "*Magister Ludi*," *NYT Book Review*, Oct. 30, 1949, p. 52.

851 Porst, Peter, "Wo bleiben die Werke von Hermann Hesse und Thomas Mann?" *Sonntag* (Berlin), 6, No. 46 (1951), 4, 9.

852 Porterfield, A. W., "Mozart still lives. *Steppenwolf*," *NYHT Books*, Sept. 8, 1929, p. 4.

853 Pröhl, Grete, "Stille Liebe zu Hermann Hesse," *Die Brücke zur Welt* (Sonntagsbeilage zur *Stuttgarter Ztg.*), Oct. 8, 1955.

854 Randall, A. W. G., "*Narziss und Goldmund*," *SRL*, Dec. 27, 1930, p. 492.

855 Redman, B. R., "*Steppenwolf*," *SRL*. March 29, 1947, p. 30.

856 Reifferscheidt, F. M., "Hermann Hesse und Thomas Mann," *Deutsche Woche* (München), 2, No. 28 (1952), 13.

857 Reimann, R., "Hermann Hesse und der Surrealismus," *Echo der Woche. Unabhängige Wochenzeitung*, 2, No. 43 (1948), 9.

858 Reuter, Gabrielle, "Hermann Hesse: Gesammelte Werke," *NYT Book Review*, Sept. 25, 1927, pp. 10, 30.

859 Roch, Herbert, "Hermann Hesse: *Die Gedichte*," *Sonntag* (Berlin), March 7, 1948, p. 10.

860 ——, "Hermann Hesse, Träger des Nobelpreises für Literatur," *Der Horizont*, 1, No. 27 (1946), 22-23.

861 Rolland, Romain, "Besuch bei Hermann Hesse," *Geistiges Frankreich*, 6, No. 281 (1952).

862 Roman, F., "Hermann Hesse," *Die Wochenpost* (Stuttgart), 2, No. 27 (1947), 4.

863 Rousseaux, André, "Hermann Hesse, le loup et l'homme," *Le Figaro Littéraire* (Paris), March 5, 1949, p. 2.

864 Rupp, Lisel, "*Gedichte des Malers* von Hermann Hesse," *Schwäbischer Merkur*, Feb. 25, 1921.

865 Schäfer, Wilhelm, "Hermann Hesse," *Schwabenspiegel* (Beil. z. *Württ. Ztg.*), 2 (1908), 170-172.

866 Schmid, Max, "Ein Grundproblem der Werke Hermann Hesses," *Neue Züricher Ztg.*, No. 407, 1946.

867 Schonauer, Franz, "Der Dichter der Suchenden. Friedenspreis für Hermann Hesse," *Christ und Welt*, 8, No. 41 (1955), 12.

868 Schröder, Rudolf Alex., "Hermann Hesse zum 75. Geburtstag," *Neue Literarische Welt*, 3 (July 10, 1952), 1-2.

869 ——, "In Montagnola auf einer Bank. Zu Hermann Hesses 75. Geburtstag," *Christ und Welt*, 5, No. 27 (1952), 10.

870 Schüddekopf, J., "*Das Glasperlenspiel*. Zu Hesses neuem Roman," *Rheinischer Merkur*, 2, No. 4 (1947), 5-6.

871 Schussen, Wilhelm, "*Musik des Einsamen* von Hermann Hesse," *Propyläen* (Beil. z. *Münchener Ztg.*), 12 (1915), 308-309.

872 Setz, K., "Hermann Hesse und seine Schwabenheimat," *Schwabenspiegel* (Beil. z. *Württ. Ztg.*), 21 (1927), 205.

873 Shuster, G. N., "A Commentary on the Soul of an Artist," *NYHT Weekly Book Review*, March 16, 1947, p. 1.

874 Sieveling, G., "Hermann Hesse und wir Jüngsten," *Neue Züricher Ztg.*, Feb. 22, 1921.

875 Smith, B., "*Steppenwolf*," *NY World*, Oct. 27, 1929, p. 11.

876 Stange, C. N., "Anstoss und Überlegung," *Basler Nachrichten*, Sonntagsblatt No. 26, 1947.

877 Sulser, W. G., "Geschenk an den Fünfzigjährigen," *Sonntagsblatt des Bund* (Bern), July 3, 1927.

878 Taylor, R. A., "*Steppenwolf*," *Spectator*, May 18, 1929, pp. 790-793.

879 Tetzner, Lisa, "Erinnerung. Hermann Hesse zum 50. Geburtstag," *Der Schacht*, 3 (July 6, 1927), 943-944.

880 Tr., "Hermann Hesse 70 Jahre," *Neues Deutschland* (Berlin), July 2, 1947, p. 3.

881 Uhlig, Helmut, "Stunden mit einem Dichter," *Tribüne* (Berlin), July 2, 1947.

882 Walter, H., "Hermann Hesse," *Die Wochenpost* (Stuttgart), 1, No. 6 (1946), 6.

883 Werner, Alfred, "Nobel Prize Winner," *NYT Book Review*, Dec. 8, 1946, pp. 6, 56-57.

884 Wick, K., "Hermann Hesse," *Vaterland* (Luzern), No. 152, 1947.

885 Wiegler, Paul, "Der andere Hesse," *Das Deutsche Wort*, 3, No. 27 (1927), 1.

886 Wunder, Günther, "*Hermann Hesse: Goethepreisträger,*" *National-Ztg.* (Basel), No. 407, 1946.

887 W. A. N., "*Demian,*" *Boston Transcript*, April 14, 1923, p. 5.

888 Zinniker, Otto, "Besuch in Montagnola," *National-Ztg.* (Basel), No. 131, 1948.

889 Zweig, Stefan, "Ein deutscher Dichter," *Köln Tagebl.*, Oct. 24, 1915.

890 ———, "Hermann Hesses neue Gedichte: *Musik des Einsamen,*" *Basler Nachrichten*, Feb. 28, 1915.

891 ———, "Ein Roman von Hermann Hesse: *Peter Camenzind,*" *Die Freistadt* (München), 6, No. 14 (1904), 270.

892 ———, "Selbstbesinnungsschriften von Künstlern. Hermann Hesse: *Blick ins Chaos,*" *Basler Nachrichten*, July 27, 1922.

893 ———, "Der Weg Hermann Hesses," *Neue Freie Presse* (Wien), Feb. 6, 1923, 1-3.

894 "*Demian,*" *NYT Book Review*, April 8, 1923, p. 14.

895 "Deutsches Telegramm an Hesse," *National-Ztg.* (Berlin), July 3, 1954, p. 7.

896 "Dem Dichter des *Glasperlenspiels,*" *Sächsische Neueste Nachrichten* (Dresden), July 10, 1952, p. 4.

897 "Dem Dichter Hermann Hesse zum 75. Geburtstag," *Mitteldeutsche Tageszeitung, Freiheit* (Halle), July 2, 1952, 6.

898 "390000 neue Bücher an einem Tag! Thomas Mann und Hermann Hesse für unsere Werktätigen," *Vorwärts* (Berlin), 62 (May 5, 1952), Ausg. A. p. 4.

899 "Erste Auflage der Werke von Thomas Mann und Hermann Hesse bereits vergriffen," *Vorwärts* (Berlin), 62 (May 12, 1952), Ausg. A. p. 5.

900 "Wir Freunde des Friedens und der Wahrheit," *Sächsische Ztg.* (Dresden), July 2, 1952, p. 5.

901 "Grosser Erfolg der Werke von Thomas Mann und Hermann Hesse. Die ersten Ausgaben in der DDR vergriffen," *Sonntag* (Berlin), 7, No. 19 (1952), 1.

902 "Die Heimkehr," *Theaterdienst* (Berlin), 8, No. 17 (1953), 11.

903 "Hermann Hesse," *The Bulletin* (Bonn), 3, No. 40 (Oct. 6, 1955), 3.

904 "Hermann Hesse—Leben und Werk," *Neues Deutschland* (Berlin), 7 (May 10, 1952), Ausg. A. p. 4.

905 "Hermann Hesse 77 Jahre," *Tägliche Rundschau* (Berlin), July 2, 1954, p. 4.

906 "Hermann Hesse's *Briefe*," *The Times Literary Supplement*, Dec. 28, 1951, p. 838.

907 "Hermann Hesses Mariabronn," *Neue Literarische Welt*, 4, No. 15 (1953), 8.

908 "Hesse und Raabe," *Rheinischer Merkur*, 5, No. 47 (1950), 8.

909 "Im Widerstand gegen zwei Weltkrankheiten. Zur Verleihung des Friedenspreises des deutschen Buchhandels an Hermann Hesse," *Parlament* (Hamburg), 5, No. 40 (1955), 10.

910 "Minister Wandel begrüsst zum Tag des Buches die Herausgabe der Werke von Thomas Mann und Hermann Hesse," *Neues Deutschland* (Berlin), 7 (May 10, 1952), Ausg, A. p. 4.

911 "The Novels of Hermann Hesse," *The Times Literary Supplement*, Dec. 19, 1952, p. 835.

912 "*Siddhartha*," *Nation*, Nov. 17, 1951, p. 430.

913 "*Steppenwolf*," *Bookman*, Oct., 1929, xxii.

914 "Der Streit um Hermann Hesse," *Das ganze Deutschland*, 4, No. 3 (1952), 5.

915 "Telegramm an Hermann Hesse" by the 3. Deutscher Schriftsteller-kongress, *Tägliche Rundschau* (Berlin), May 29, 1952, p. 4.

916 "The Wolf Man," *NYT Book Review*, Sept. 29, 1929, p. 7.

DOCTORAL DISSERTATIONS, UNLESS OTHERWISE INDICATED

These works have not been published. The starred items are available in the *Westdeutsches Hermann Hesse-Archiv*, Cologne. Items lacking dates have not yet been completed:

GERMANY

917 Adenauer, Charlotte, "Eine zeitmorphologische Untersuchung des Romans *Ritter der Gerechtigkeit* von Stefan Andres" (Bonn, 1951), 115 pp. (*Demian* discussed in chapters 6 and 7).

918 Arnz, Käthe, "Die Natursymbolik in den Werken Hermann Hesses" (Staatsexamensarbeit, Köln), 1952.

919 Baaten, Heta, "Der Romantiker Hermann Hesse. Eine geistesgeschichtliche Untersuchung seiner Werke auf dem Hintergrunde der pietistischen Tradition seiner Familie" (Münster, 1932). See 24.

920 Bärhausen, Eugen, "Der Dualismus von Geist und Sinnlichkeit in Hermann Hesses Werk" (Freie Universität Berlin, 1952), 195 pp.

*921 Baumer, Franz, "Das magische Denken in der Dichtung Hermann Hesses. Versuch einer Wesensschau seiner Epik," (München, 1951), 193 pp. (microfilm in University of Calif., Berkeley).

*922 Berger, Johann, "Die Angst im Werke Hermann Hesses" (Innsbruck, 1938), 102 pp.

923 Böhme, Siegfried, "Die Entwicklung und Wandlung des Existenzgedankens im Werk Hermann Hesses" (Freie Universität Berlin, 1950).

924 Bormann, Elisabeth, "Das Bild des Bürgers im Werk Hermann Hesses" (Staatsexamensarbeit, Frankfurt a. M.).

925 Böttcher, Margot, "Aufbau und Form von Hermann Hesses *Steppenwolf, Morgenlandfahrt* und *Glasperlenspiel*" (Berlin, 1948), 57 pp.

*926 ———, "Erschliessung von Hermann Hesses Spätwerk—insbesondere des magischen Gehalts—durch Formanalyse" (Berlin, 1951), 85 pp.

*927 Dahrendorf, Malte, "Hermann Hesses *Demian*. Sein Problemgehalt, seine Grundlagen und seine Stellung im Gesamtwerk des Dichters" (Staatsexamensarbeit, Hamburg, 1953), 111 pp.

928 ———, "Der Entwicklungsroman bei Hermann Hesse," (Hamburg, 1955), 308 pp.

929 Erhart, Ilse, "Die Lyrik Hermann Hesses" (Wien, 1936).

930 Fourmanoir, Annie, "Über den Einfluss des Orients auf das Werk Hermann Hesses" (Heidelberg, 1954).

931 Fritz, Walter Helmut, "Die Bedeutung der Imaginationskräfte für das Dichten Hermann Hesses" (Heidelberg).

*932 Fuchs, Karl, "Hermann Hesses Bild des Menschen. Nach dem epischen Werk des Dichters" (Erlangen, 1949), 128 pp.

*933 Götting, Wilhelm, "Das Kunstproblem in der Dichtung Hermann Hesses" (Staatsexamensarbeit, Köln, 1950), 116 pp.

*934 Hackelsberger-Bergengruen, Luise, "Individuum und Umwelt im Werke Hermann Hesses" (Bern, 1950), 193 pp.

935 Hammes, Karl, "Gehalt und Gestalt in Hermann Hesses Jugendromanen" (Bonn, 1950).

936 Hirsch, Willi, "Hermann Hesse und das Christentum" (Akzessarbeit, Theologische Fakultät, Bern, 1943).

937 Hoyer, Karl Heinz, "Die Landschaft im Prosawerk Hermann Hesses" (Freie Universität Berlin, 1954), 176 pp.

938 Kegel, Gerhard, "Schönheit und Krisis der ästhetischen Existenz. Kritische Betrachtungen im Anschluss an Hermann Hesses *Glasperlenspiel*" (Leipzig, 1950), 83 pp. (in Schiller-Museum, Marbach).

*939 Kempfes, Werner, "Hermann Hesses lyrischer Stil" (Staatsexamensarbeit, Köln, 1950), 116 pp.

940 Kirchberger, Hubert, "Das Bild des Menschen in Hermann Hesses Roman *Das Glasperlenspiel*" (Staatsexamensarbeit, Jena, 1949).

941 Kirchhoff, Gerhard, "Das Bild des Menschen in Hermann Hesses Dichtung" (Freiburg i. Br., 1951), 310 pp.

942 Kleiter, Hildegard, "Besonderheiten und Entwicklung des Stils bei Hermann Hesse" (München).

943 Knell, Elisabeth, "Die Kunstform der Erzählungen und Novellen Hermann Hesses" (Wien, 1938), 141 pp.

944 Langlo, Otto, "Hesse und die Romantik" (Kiel).

945 Lehner, Hans Horst, "Nachwirkungen der deutschen Romantik auf die Prosadichtung Hermann Hesses" (Würzburg, 1954), 265 pp.

946 Liepelt-Unterberg, Maria, "Das Polaritätsgesetz in der Dichtung. Am Beisp. v. Hermann Hesses *Steppenwolf*" (Bonn, 1951), 70 pp.

*947 Lizounat, Michelle, "Indische Religionen bei Hermann Hesse" (Bonn, 1952), 94 pp.

948 Matthias, Klaus, "Die Musik bei Thomas Mann und Hesse" (Kiel, 1956), 352 pp.

949 Mauer, Gerhard, "Hermann Hesse und die deutsche Romantik" (Tübingen, 1955), 219 pp.

950 Mentgen, Marie, "Die Gedichte des Dichters Hermann Hesse in der Komposition" (Staatsexamensarbeit, Musik Hochschule, Köln, 1954).

951 Moenikes, G., "Sprachliche Ausdruckskräfte in Hermann Hesses *Glasperlenspiel*" (Prüfungsarbeit für den Realschullehrerkurs Pädag. Akademie, Köln, 1955), 62 pp.

952 Overberg, Marianne, "Die Bedeutung der Zeit in Hermann Hesses *Demian*" (Bonn, 1948), 109 pp. (in Schiller-Museum, Marbach).

953 Peter, Maria, "Das Kulturproblem bei Hermann Hesse" (Freiburg i. Br., 1948), 110 pp.

*954 Pfeifer, Martin, "Verseinlagen in modernen Prosadichtungen, hauptsächlich dargelegt an Werken Hermann Hesses" (Staatsexamensarbeit, Jena, 1950), 137 pp.

*955 ———, "Hermann Hesses Kritik am Bürgertum" (Jena, 1952), 133 pp.

956 Pielow, Winfried, "Die Erziehergestalten der grossen deutschen Bildungsromane von Goethe bis zur Gegenwart: *Wilhelm Meister, Nachsommer, Grüner Heinrich, Glasperlenspiel* (Münster, 1951), 133 pp.

*957 Poestges, Friedhelm, "Hermann Hesse und die Empfindsamkeit" (Köln, 1955), 208 pp.

958 Pohlmann, Gisela, "Das Problem der Wirklichkeit bei Hermann Hesse" (Münster, 1951), 228 pp.

959 Protzer, Heinz, "Hermann Hesse und die Psychoanalyse" (Köln).

*960 Rastfeld, Carin, "Die Mittel der Menschengestaltung in der Prosadichtung Hermann Hesses" (a rejected Staatsexamensarbeit, Köln, 1953), 64 pp.

961 Schepler, Hans-Jürgen, "Begriffsbestimmung der Neuromantik mit besonderer Berücksichtigung der dichterischen Gestalten im Werke Hermann Hesses und Ricarda Huchs" (Freie Universität, Berlin).

*962 Spreen, Otfried, "Struktur des Psychologischen im Roman (dargestellt an Hermann Hesses *Steppenwolf*). Eine morphologisch-methodologische Untersuchung" (Bonn, 1951), 96 pp.

963 Unseld, Siegfried, "Hermann Hesse. Anschauung vom Beruf des Dichters" (Tübingen, 1952), 232 pp.

964 Wagner, Marianne, "Zeitmorphologischer Vergleich von Hermann Hesses *Demian, Siddhartha, Der Steppenwolf, Narziss und Goldmund* zur Aufweisung typischer Gestaltzüge" (Bonn, 1953), 194 pp.

*965 Wasserscheid, Rosemarie, "Die Gestaltung der Landschaft in Hermann Hesses Prosadichtung" (Staatsexamensarbeit, Köln, 1951), 105 pp.

966 Wassner, Hermann, "Über die Bedeutung der Musik in den Dichtungen von Hermann Hesse" (Heidelberg, 1953), 145 pp.

967 Zelder, Georg, "Mundartliche Einflüsse in der Sprache Hermann Hesses" (Breslau, 1922), 109 pp.

UNITED STATES

968 Beyers, John M., "Anxiety in the Works of Hermann Hesse" (University of Southern California).

969 Boardman, Ruth, "The Vagabond in Hermann Hesse's Prose Works" (M.A., Ohio State University, 1950), 42 pp.

970 Boersma, Clarence, "The Educational Ideal in the Major Works of Hermann Hesse" (University of Michigan, 1948), 308 pp. (University Microfilms, Publication No. 1186, Ann Arbor, Michigan).

971 Brunner, John W., "Hermann Hesse. The Man as revealed in his Works" (Columbia).

972 Dawson, A. A., "Hermann Hesse. Growth of a poet" (M.A., Southern Methodist University, 1949). A translation of Max Schmid's *Hermann Hesse. Weg und Wandlung* (Zürich, 1947), 240 pp.

973 Fickert, Kurt J., "The problem of the artist and the philistine in the work of Hermann Hesse" (New York University, 1952), 195 pp.

974 Frendote, Christine, "*Das Glasperlenspiel* und *Wilhelm Meister*" (M.A., Buffalo).

975 Gould, Loyal N., "Romantic Elements in the characters of H. Hesse" (University of North Carolina, 1955).

976 Halpert, Inge David, "Hermann Hesse and Goethe" (M.A., Columbia, 1949).

977 Heller, Peter, "The Writer's Image of the Writer. A study in the ideologies of six German authors: 1918—1933, Mann, Hesse, Toller, Grimm, Brecht, Jünger" (Columbia, 1951), 372 pp. (University Microfilms, Publication No. 2819, Ann Arbor, Michigan).

978 Henze, Amanda Roost, "A translation of *Siddhartha*" (M.A., University of Southern California, 1936).

979 Kilchenmann, Ruth J., "Wandel in der Gestaltung der Natur in Hesses Werken" (University of Southern California, 1956).

980 Koerber, Ruth, "Hermann Hesse as a critic of modern Life" (M.A., Nebraska, 1933), 56 pp.

981 Land, S. L., "Hermann Hesse. His development up to 1914" (B.A., Harvard, 1942), 27 pp.

982 Larson, R. C., "The Dream as a Literary Device in Five Novels by Hermann Hesse: *Unterm Rad, Rosshalde, Demian, Steppenwolf, Narziss und Goldmund* (B.A., Yale, 1949), 122 pp.

983 Lund, H. G., "Hermann Hesse since 1928" (B.A., Harvard, 1941), 26 pp.

984 Maier, Emanuel, "The Psychology of C. G. Jung in the Works of Hermann Hesse" (New York University, 1953), 171 pp.

985 McCormick, John O., "Thomas Wolfe, André Malraux, Hermann Hesse: a study in creative vitality" (Harvard, 1951).

986 Mihailovitch, Vasa, "Das Leid in Hermann Hesses Werk" (M.A., Wayne University, 1957).

987 Mileck, Joseph, "Hermann Hesse. A Study" (Harvard, 1950), 490 pp.

988 Mullett, Frederic M., "The Vagabond Theme in the Fiction of Hermann Hesse" (M.F.S., University of Maryland, 1950), 72 pp.

989 Rich, Doris E., "Der Deutsche Entwicklungsroman am Ende der

Bürgerlichen Kultur, 1892-1924" (Radcliffe, 1940) Hesse, pp. 32-52.

990 Sanger, Harold H., "Changes in the Concept of Personality in the Works of Hermann Hesse" (Princeton).

991 Stern, Peter, "Hermann Hesse: *Der Steppenwolf*" (B.A., Harvard, 1950), 80 pp.

992 Ziolkowski, Th. J., "Hermann Hesse and Novalis" (Yale, 1956).

FRANCE

(Diplôme d'études supérieures, unless otherwise indicated)

993 Bruckner, Mr., "Einsamkeit und Zusammenleben bei Hermann Hesse" (Bordeaux, 1947), 150 pp.

994 Cornille, Miss, "La Personalité de Hermann Hesse d'après ses romans de jeunesse jusqu'en 1914" (Sorbonne, 1950), 115 pp.

995 Fourmanoir, Annie, "L'Orient dans la vie et l'oeuvre de Hermann Hesse" (Paris, 1954), 114 pp.

996 Hatterer, Georges, "Hermann Hesses Weltanschauung und ihre künstlerische Verwirklichung im *Glasperlenspiel*" (Bésançon, 1950), 100 pp.

997 Lizounat, Michelle, "Le bouddhisme chez Hermann Hesse" (Bordeaux, 1951).

998 Lorrain, Miss, "Étude des Poésies de Hermann Hesse" (Sorbonne, 1950), 155 pp.

999 Robert, L., "L'humanisme de Hermann Hesse" (Toulouse, 1950), 120 pp.

1000 Sagave, Pierre Paul, "Le déclin de la bourgeoisie allemande d'après le roman, 1890-1933" (Thèse principale pour le Doctorat ès lettres, Sorbonne, 1949), 535 pp. (Hesse is one of seven writers considered: *Peter Camenzind, Demian* and *Steppenwolf*).

ENGLAND

1001 Benn, Maurice, "An Interpretation of the Work of Hermann Hesse" (M.A., University of London, 1948), 211 pp.

1002 Leibholz, R. N., "The Construction of Hesse's Short Stories" (rejected doctoral thesis, Oxford).

CANADA

1003 McBroom, Robert Riddick, "The nature problem in Hermann Hesse" (M.A., Toronto, 1934).

SWEDEN

1004 Ljungerud, Ivar, "Bemerkungen zur modernen deutschen Dichtersprache unter besonderer Berücksichtigung der Sprache Thomas Manns, Hermann Hesses und Hans Carossas" (Lund, 1948).

NOTES

A Bio-Bibliographical Sketch

1 Fifty years passed before Finckh was to give his version of this summer of 1899 (*Die Verzauberung* [Ulm, 1950], 136 pp.).
2 Bruno, the oldest of Hesse's three sons was born during this period. Heiner and Martin were born after the new house was built.
3 From May, 1916, to November, 1917, Hesse had seventy-two consultations with Dr. J. B. Lang, a student of C. G. Jung.
4 Since this prize was intended for authors just beginning their careers, Hesse returned the award. His pseudonym, Emil Sinclair, had not immediately been associated with him.
5 Maria Bernoulli eventually recovered from her illness; in 1954 she was living in Bern with her son Martin.

Hesse and his Art

1 Unless otherwise indicated, the dates in parentheses are those of publication, not of composition.
2 *Gerbersau* (1949), 2 vols.
3 Only two of Hesse's poems exhibit some of the patriotic bravado of the traditional *Kriegslied*: *"Dem Daheimgebliebenen"* (Feb. 1915) in the second edition of *Unterwegs* (1915), and "An den Kaiser," the prologue to a *Kaiserfeier* held by the German colony in Bern (*Süddeutsche Ztg.*, Feb. 4, 1915).
4 See, *e.g.*, "Klein und Wagner," *Weg nach Innen*, p. 346.
5 For the genesis of "Media in Vita" and a discussion of Sankhya philosophy, see "Aus einem Tagebuch des Jahres 1920," *Corona*, 3 (1932), 207.
6 *Krisis. Ein Stück Tagebuch* (1928), 85 pp. This very limited edition of forty-five poems, of which only sixteen are included in the *Gedichte* (1942), is the poetic counterpart of *Steppenwolf* (1927). Both works were written in the course of 1926.
7 See "Aus einem Tagebuch des Jahres 1920," *Corona*, 3 (1932), 197.
8 After *Krisis*, Hesse reverts to free verse only occasionally (about a dozen times), and then, characteristically, in the distraught state of illness (*e.g.*, "Krank im Hotelzimmer," p. 338), in bitter discord with himself (*e.g.*, "Widerlicher Traum," p. 358), in sharp disparagement of our age (*e. g.*, "Das Lied von Abels Tod," p. 354), or in tense thought (*e.g.*, "Besinnung," p. 376).
9 The idyl, *Stunden im Garten* (1936, 63 pp.), the poetic episode, *Der lahme Knabe. Eine Erinnerung aus der Kindheit* (1937, 17 pp.), both written in Greek hexameters, and *Rückblick*, the autobiographical fragment in free verse written in 1937 but not published until 1951 (*Neue Schweizer Rundschau*, 19 [1951], 78-81), are not included in this average.
10 See "Ein Stückchen Theologie," *Neue Rundschau*, 43, i (1932), 738-739.

Hesse and his Age

1 "Über die ästhetische Erziehung des Menschen," *Schillers Werke* (Säkular Ausgabe), Vol. 12, 32-33.

2 *Heinrich von Ofterdingen, Novalis Schriften,* ed. Paul Kluckhohn, Vol. 1, 251.

3 See footnote 3 of "Hesse and his Art."

4 "Apologie des Krieges," *März,* 9 (May 1915), 167-168.

5 *Au-Dessus de la Mêlée* (1916), p. 128.

6 Literary contributions extend from the beginning of the century to 1933.

7 See G. Sieveling, "Hermann Hesse und wir Jüngsten," *Neue Züricher Ztg.,* Feb. 22, 1921.

8 *Neue Rundschau,* 31, ii (1920), 1109.

9 R. B. Matzig, *Hermann Hesse in Montagnola,* p. 48.

10 Jörn Oven, "Hermann Hesse: *Siddhartha," Schöne Literatur,* 24, (1923), 332.

11 Gustav Hecht, "Offener Brief an Hermann Hesse," *Deutsches Volkstum,* 1929, ii, p. 611. But that "antideutsch" was substituted for "antilutherisch," Hecht's censure of Hesse is the very criticism Hesse himself had once directed against Angelus Silesius (*Betrachtungen,* p. 234).

12 Having accepted his membership in the newly established Prussian Academy of Writers in the autumn of 1926 with considerable reluctance, Hesse anxiously awaited the first opportune occasion to tender his resignation (*Briefe* [1951], p. 7). This opportunity presented itself four years later. Thomas Mann's subsequent intercession proved of no avail; Hesse's reply was curt and unequivocal: "der letzte Grund meines Unvermögens zur Einordnung in eine offizielle deutsche Korporation ist mein tiefes Misstrauen gegen die deutsche Republik. Dieser haltlose und geistlose Staat . . ." *Briefe,* p. 57.

13 Gustav Zeller, "Offener Brief an Hermann Hesse," *Psychische Studien,* 47 (1920), 627.

14 *Jüdische Herkunft und Literaturwissenschaft* (1925), p. 136.

15 "Thomas Mann, Hermann Hesse und wir Jungen," *Die Umschau,* 2 (1947), 611-615.

16 "Hermann Hesse, *Peter Camenzind* und das *Glasperlenspiel," Die Sammlung,* 3 (1948), 597-609.

17 "Versuch einer Rechtfertigung," *Krieg und Frieden,* pp. 223-225. For these same reasons Hesse refused to comply with communistically inclined Anna Seghers' request that he support the Congress of Vienna (Dec. 1952), and its plea for peace (Bodo Uhse, "Literatur und Nation," *Aufbau,* 9 [1953], 507).

Hesse and his Critics

1 For more about Hesse and his family background see: *Aus Dr. Hermann Gunderts Briefnachlass* (1900), 422 pp. Johannes Hesse, *Aus Dr. Hermann Gunderts Leben* (Calw, 1894), 368 pp. Hermann Hesse,

"Alemannisches Bekenntnis," *Alemannen-Buch*, ed. Hesse (1919), pp. 7-9; family background and early years. Monika Hunnius, *Mein Onkel Hermann. Erinnerungen an Alt-Estland* (1921), 126 pp.; reference is to Hesse's grandfather in Weissenstein. Hermann und Adele Hesse, *Zum Gedächtnis unseres Vaters* (1930), 85 pp. Adele Gundert, *Maria Hesse. Ein Lebensbild in Briefen und Tagebüchern* (1934), 283 pp. Heta Baaten, *Die pietistische Tradition der Familie Gundert und Hesse* (1934), 42 pp. Ida Frohnmeyer, "In Erinnerung," *Die Ernte* (1941), pp. 65-72; about Hesse's father. *Friedrich Gundert. Zum Gedächtnis* (1946), 111 pp.; six very informative letters by a close relative to Hesse, 1944-46. Ludwig Finckh, *Schwäbische Vettern* (1948), 15 pp. Ludwig Finckh, "Die Ahnen des Dichters Hermann Hesse," *Genealogie und Heraldik*, 3 (1951), 1-2. Robert Arthur von Lemm, "Die väterliche Seite der Ahnen Hermann Hesses," *Genealogie und Heraldik*, 3 (1951), 94-95.

2 Other items of biographical interest: Gertrud Fink, *Ludwig Finckh. Leben und Werk* (1936); Hesse-Finckh relationship in Gaienhofen, pp. 13, 18-19, 22, 31-35. Horst Kliemann, "Hermann Hesse und München," *Weihnachten mit Büchern* (1947), pp. 7-10. Ernst Rheinwald, "Hermann Hesse in Calw," a speech given in Calw by an old schoolmate upon the occasion of Hesse's seventieth birthday; a copy of the eleven typed sheets is available in the Hesse Archives in Cologne. Otto Hartmann, "Ansprache z. Morgenfeier am 30. 6. 1947 in Calw"; these nine typed pages by another old schoolmate, dealing with Hesse in Maulbronn, are also available in the Hesse Archives. Erich Scheurmann, "Begegnung mit Hermann Hesse," *Deutsche Presse-Korrespondenz* (Hannover-Kirchrode, June 1951), pp. 11-12; Hesse in Gaienhofen. Gotthilf Hafner, "Hermann Hesses Anfänge," *Welt und Wort*, 7 (1952), 229-230; Hesse in Tübingen. Theo. Baeschlin, "Begegnung mit Hermann Hesse," *Du. Schweizerische Monatsschrift*, 13 (Feb. 1953), 30-31; Hesse's years in Basel. Hans Kägi, "Begegnung mit Hermann Hesse," *Du. Schweizerische Monatsschrift*, 13 (Feb. 1953), 36; more of Gaienhofen years. Ludwig Finckh, "Hesse-Erinnerungen aus Gaienhofen," a thirty page typed manuscript; a rough draft, but very informative; available in the Hesse Archives.

3 To these may be added three more unpublished, and one unfinished dissertation: Johann Berger, "Die Angst im Werke Hermann Hesses" (Innsbruck, 1938), 102 pp.; Otfried Spreen, "Struktur des Psychologischen im Roman (dargestellt an Hermann Hesses Steppenwolf)" (Bonn, 1951), 96 pp.; Emanuel Maier, "The Psychology of C. G. Jung in the works of Hermann Hesse" (New York University, 1953), 171 pp.; Heinz Protzer, "Hermann Hesse und die Psychoanalyse" (Köln).

4 Jean-Éduard Spenlé, "Les Derniers Romans de Hermann Hesse," *Mercure de France*, 185 (1926), 74-87; Emma Maria Probizer, "L'India antica elle opere di due moderni poeti tedeschi," *Nuova Antologia*, 258 (1928), 96-103; Johannes Malthaner, "Hermann Hesses *Siddhartha*," *Germann Quarterly*, 25 (1952), 103-109.

5 Paulus Lambrecht, "*Siddhartha*," *Vivos Voco*, 3 (1923), 260; Adolf Saager, "Zu Hermann Hesses *Siddhartha*," *Wissen und Leben*, 17

(1924), 560-562; "Hermann Hesse. *Siddhartha,*" *Velhagen u. Klasings Monatshefte,* 38 (1924), 574.

6 Here Schröder broaches an aspect of Hesse's art which has not yet received the attention it deserves. Mimi Jehle touches lightly upon two of Hesse's many *Märchen (Augustus* and *Iris),* describing them as poetically realistic, novel in their very personal implications, and exceptional in their symbolism; unfortunately no attempt is made to develop these contentions ("Das moderne deutsche Kunstmärchen," *Journal of English and Germanic Philology,* 33 [1934] 457-458). See also, H. Missenharter, "Hermann Hesse: Märchen," *Der deutsche Bund,* 1 (1919), 135-138 (a review of *Märchen,* 1919).

7 Otto Zoff, "Über Hermann Hesse," *Wieland,* 6 (May 1920), 11-12; Walter über Wasser, "Der Maler Hermann Hesse," *Die Schweiz,* 24 (1920), 511-515; W. Rz., "*Elf Aquarelle aus dem Tessin,*" *Die Schweiz,* 24 (1920), 711; Karl Scheffler, "Zwei Besprechungen über Hermann Hesse als Maler," *Kunst und Künstler,* 19 (1920-21); P. Gey, "Der Dichter malt," *Daheim,* 64, No. 7 (1927); Gunter Böhmer, "Malausflug mit Hermann Hesse," *Bodenseebuch,* (1936); H. P. Mieg, "Dem Maler Hermann Hesse," *Basler Nachrichten,* Sonntagsblatt No. 26, 1947.

8 See H. Kliemann, K. H. Silomon, *Hermann Hesse. Eine bibliographische Studie* (1947), pp. 71-72.

9 See Kliemann/Silomon, items 44, 47, 68; *Briefe,* pp. 12, 296-300; *Hesse/Rolland. Briefe,* pp. 48-49.

10 *Elf Aquarelle aus dem Tession* (1921); *Aquarelle aus dem Tessin* (1955), 12.

11 *Wanderung* (1920), 14; *Gedichte des Malers* (1920), 10; Sinclairs *Notizbuch* (1923), 4; *Jahreszeiten* (1931), 10; *Aus vielen Jahren. Gedichte, Erzählungen und Bilder* (1949), 2; *Hesse/Rolland. Briefe* (1954) 8; *Piktors Verwandlungen* (1954), 17.

12 Josef Ponten, *Die luganische Landschaft* (Stuttgart, 1926), 6; Josef Ponten, *Die letzte Reise* (Lübeck, 1926), 2; *Friedrich Gundert. Zum Gedächtnis* (Stuttgart, 1946), 2; Kliemann/Silomon, *Eine bibliographische Studie* (1947), 4.

13 *Die Schweiz,* 24 (1920), 511-515 (6); *Wieland,* 6 (May 1920), (9); *Ikarus,* 40, i (1925-26), 160-169; *Westermanns Monatshefte,* 94, ii (1953-54), 19 (1); *Du. Schweizerische Monatsschrift,* 13 (Feb. 1953), (2); *The American-German Review,* Oct.-Nov., 1956 (1).

14 Albert Welti, Gemälde und Radierungen (Berlin, 1917), 51 pp.; *Ausstellung Cuno Amiet* (Bern, 1919), 13 pp.; Frans Masereel, *Die Idee* (München, 1927); Frans Masereel, *Geschichte ohne Worte* (Leipzig, 1933), 69 pp.; *Ernst Morgenthaler* (Zürich, 1936), 23 pp.; *Gartenfreuden* (Zürich, 1950), 16 pp.

15 For remarks by Hesse about his own painting see: *Briefe,* pp. 13, 298; "Kurzgefasster Lebenslauf," *Traumfährte,* p. 117; "Traumgeschenk," *Späte Prosa,* p. 48; *Aquarelle aus dem Tessin* (1955).

16 That Hesse ever experienced such a conflict is very doubtful (see *Hesse/Rolland. Briefe,* p. 49); painting was a diversion which afforded respite, not additional conflict (see *Traumfährte,* p. 116).

17 *E.g., Hermann Lauscher* (1920), p. 52; *Schön ist die Jungend* (1916),

pp. 74, 88; *Weg nach Innen* (1931), p. 388; *Nürnberger Reise*, p. 78; *Bilderbuch*, pp. 181-182; *Betrachtungen*, pp. 70, 100, 133, 164, 212-223, 249-250, 274; *Steppenwolf* (1931), pp. 23, 102; *Gedenkblätter* (1947), p. 83; *Dank an Goethe*, 94 pp.; *Krieg und Frieden* (1949), pp. 17, 176, 208-212; Kliemann/Silomon, items 150, 189, 215; "Goethes Briefe," *Die Rheinlande*, 4 (1904) 589-590 (some unflattering remarks about Goethe); see bibliography for Hesse's many reviews dealing with Goethe.

18   That Hesse, like Keller, is a "Dichter des Bürgertums," is questioned by H. R. Schmid (*Hermann Hesse*, p. 98). Refuting Bühner, he maintains that the bourgeois world is only a foil in Hesse's tales, and that these *Novellen* are primarily concerned with the lonely outsider.

19   Neither Ball nor H. R. Schmid makes more than a few general remarks about *Steppenwolf;* Anni Carlsson devotes six pages to it (Ball, [1947], pp. 251-256); best of the studies is the brochure of R. B. Matzig (*Der Dichter und die Zeitstimmung* [1944], 51   pp.) and M. Schmid's analysis (pp. 73-96). P. M. Pasinetti criticizes *Steppenwolf* severely in his "Novels from three Languages," *Sewanee Review*, 56 (1948), 171-174. André Rousseaux's "Hermann Hesse, Le Loup et L'Homme" (*Littératur du Vingtième Siècle* [1953], pp. 134-142) is an interesting survey. Seymour L. Flaxman's article (*"Der Steppenwolf*. Hesse's Portrait of the Intellectual," *Modern Language Quarterly*, 15 [1954], 349-358) is primarily a descriptive portrayal of Haller, with only passing notice of the problems the novel poses. Though rather unavailable, mention might also be made of pertinent dissertations: Peter Stern, "Hermann Hesse: Der Steppenwolf," (B.A., Harvard, 1950), 80 pp.; Margot Böttcher, "Aufbau und Form von Hermann Hesses *Steppenwolf, Morgenlandfahrt* und *Glasperlenspiel*" (Berlin, 1948), 57 pp.; Maria Liepelt-Unterberg, "Das Polaritätsgesetz in der Dichtung. Am Beisp. v. Hermann Hesses *Steppenwolf*" (Bonn, 1951), 70 pp.; Otfried Spreen, "Struktur des Psychologischen im Roman, dargestellt an Hermann Hesses *Steppenwolf*" (Bonn, 1951), 96 pp.

20   The studies of Helga Groth ("Hermann Hesse," *Dichter des Humanismus im heutigen Deutschland* [1939], pp. 91-133) and S. R. Townsend ("The German Humanist Hermann Hesse," *Modern Language Forum*, 32 [1947], 1-12 are misleading in their titles. Both are excellent surveys of Hesse's life and of his art, but neither actually dwells upon the suggested theme of humanism. In his book, *Le roman allemand contemporain et la crise de l'esprit* (1940), Maurice Boucher devotes one chapter to Hesse, "Les soubresauts de l'humanisme." Unfortunately, the book was suppressed by the Nazis, and only its proofs are available (at the Sorbonne among other places). Only one dissertation dealing expressly with Hesse's humanism has yet been written: L. Robert, "Humanism de Hermann Hesse" (Toulouse, 1950), 120 pp.

21   Relevant to Hesse and Nietzsche: *Faust und Zarathustra* (1909), 32 pp.; *Demian; Zarathustras Wiederkehr;* "Eigensinn," *Betrachtungen; Kurgast* (1925), p. 36; *Nürnberger Reise*, pp. 63, 79; *Steppenwolf* (1931), pp. 20, 38; *Betrachtungen*, p. 133; *Gedenkblätter* (1947), pp. 82-83, 296; *Glasperlenspiel* (1943), Vol. 2, 132-133; *Traumfährte*, p.

47; *Eine Bibliothek der Weltliteratur* (1946), p. 79; *Briefe*, pp. 203-204. See also: Ball (index); H. R. Schmid, pp. 115-116; Kunze, pp. 21-22, 26; M. Schmid, pp. 58, 231; Matzig (1947), pp. 18, 23-24, 44.

22 Relevant to Hesse and Schopenhauer: *Peter Camenzind* (1905), p. 107; "Klein und Wagner," *Weg nach Innen* (1931), pp. 265, 342; "Die Brüder Karamasoff," *Betrachtungen; Siddhartha*: "Kleines Bekenntnis," *Jahrbuch der Schopenhauer-Gesellschaft* (1938); *Bibliothek der Weltliteratur* (1946), p. 59; see also: Ball (index); H. R. Schmid, pp. 184, 188.

23 See *Briefe*, pp. 176, 183, 202, 211, 218, 220, 234, 252, 323, 362, 417. A very brief but suggestive study of this problem is made by J. F. Angelloz, "L'Oeuvre de Hermann Hesse," *Critique*, May 1949, pp. 388-391.

24 See *Briefe*, pp. 49, 56, 113, 114, 116, 124, 263, 267, 268, 303, 386, 392; *Nürnberger Reise*, pp. 119-120; *Glasperlenspiel* (1943), Vol. 1., 212, 272, 332-333, 360, 451; *Zwei Briefe* (1945), 7 pp; Kliemann/Silomon, item 137:20, 21; "Thomas Manns *Königliche Hoheit, März*, 4, i (1910), 281-283 (rather negative remarks); Thomas Mann, "Dem sechzigjährigen Hermann Hesse," *Neue Literatur*, 38 (1937), 424-426; Thomas Mann, "Hermann Hesse," *Neue Rundschau*, 1947, pp. 245-250; Thomas Mann, *Die Entstehung des Dr. Faustus* (1949), pp. 68-69; *Dank an Hesse. Reden und Aufsätze* (1952), pp. 119-120.

25 For very recent, pertinent remarks about *Camenzind* by Hesse himself see, "Gruss an die französischen Studenten zum Thema der diesjährigen Agrégation," *Katalog der Buchhandlung Martin Flinker* (1951), pp. 9-12.

26 Elster's introduction to *Im Pressel'schen Gartenhaus* is a briefer version of this survey.

27 In the subsequent issue of *Aufbau* (8 [1952], 863-864), Mayer apologizes very weakly for this blatant error, and in a republication of his article (*Studien zur deutschen Literaturgeschichte* [1954], pp. 225-240), the necessary corrections are made.

28 A. Meuer's "Demiurg oder der Untergang. Der andere Hermann Hesse" "*Zwiebelfisch*, 25, No. 4 [1946-48], 3-7) was not available for examination.

29 For a better understanding of Hesse and in defense of his attitude, see *Briefe*, pp. 85-89, 91-92, 94-96, 111-113, 123-124, 128-129, 202, 204, 241-243, 350-356, 369-372, 418-419. Grappin seems to have given little heed to this material.

30 In a study of Rolland and Hesse the following should not be neglected: Romain Rolland, *Au-Dessus de la Mêlée* (1916), p. 128, "Besuch bei Hermann Hesse," *Geistiges Frankreich*, 6, No. 281 (1952); Hermann Hesse, "Romain Rolland, *Jean Christof*," *Berl. Tageblatt*, May 4, 1915, *Weg nach Innen* (1931), p. 433, *Dank an Goethe* (1946), p. 15, *Krieg und Frieden* (1949), pp. 7-8, *Hermann Hesse. Alle Bücher dieser Welt* (1950), p. 68, *Briefe*, p. 94; Hesse dedicated the first part of *Siddhartha* and *Krieg und Frieden* to Rolland, and it was at the request of Rolland that he wrote his essay "Dank an Goethe" in 1932; *Hesse/Rolland. Briefe*, 118 pp.; see also, Hansgerhard Weiss, *Romain*

Rolland (1948), pp.. 85-87, Werner Ilberg, *Traum und Tat. Romain Rolland in seinem Verhältnis zu Deutschland und zur Sowjet-Union* (1950), p. 57, Karl Ude, "Hermann Hesse und Frankreich," *Welt und Wort,* 10 (1955), 104, and Gotthilf Hafner, "Frankreich und Hesse," *Welt und Wort,* 10 (1955), 172.

31 Three dissertations have dealt with the problem and one is in progress: Ruth Koerber, "Hermann Hesse as a critic of modern Life" (M.A., Nebraska, 1933), 56 pp.; Maria Peter, "Das Kulturproblem bei Hermann Hesse" (Freiburg i. Br., 1948), 110 pp.; Martin Pfeifer, "Hermann Hesses Kritik am Bürgertum" (Jena, 1952), 133 pp.; Elisabeth Bormann, "Das Bild des Bürgers im Werk Hermann Hesses" (Staatsexamensarbeit, Frankurt a. M.). Pierre Paul Sagave's doctoral thesis is also pertinent to the problem: "Le déclin de la bourgeoisie allemande d'après le roman, 1890-1933" (Sorbonne, 1949), 535 pp. (Hesse is one of seven writers considered).

32 Five dissertations have dealt with the problem: Robert Riddick Mc-Broom, "The nature problem in Hermann Hesse" (M.A., Toronto, 1934); Rosemarie Wasserscheid, "Die Gestaltung der Landschaft in Hermann Hesses Prosadichtung" (Staatsexamensarbeit, Köln, 1951), 105 pp.; Käthe Arnz, "Die Natursymbolik in den Werken Hermann Hesses" (Staatsexamensarbeit, Köln, 1952), Karl Heinz Hoyer, "Die Landschaft im Prosawerk Hermann Hesses" (Freie Universität Berlin, 1954), 176 pp.; Ruth J. Kilchenmann, "Wandel in der Gestaltung der Natur in Hesses Werken" (University of Southern California, 1956). In her *Hermann Hesse. Naturliebe, Menschenliebe, Gottesliebe* (1956, 143 pp.) Käte Nadler devotes an entire chapter to Hesse and nature (pp. 15-50).

33 By 1954 Erich Weiss, director of the *Hesse-Archiv* in Cologne, had already listed more than two hundred and sixty-eight poems set to music, some of them as many as a dozen times, and "Im Nebel" twenty times. For very brief bibliographies of compositions see: Kliemann/Silomon, pp. 68-70; Martin Pfeifer, *Bibliographie der im Gebiet der DDR seit 1945 erschienenen Schriften von und über Hermann Hesse* (1952), p. 14; and Pfeifer's supplement of 1955, pp. 54-58. Only one dissertation has dealt with this subject: Marie Mentgen, "Die Gedichte des Dichters Hermann Hesse in der Komposition" (Staatsexamensarbeit, Musik Hochschule Köln, 1954); see also: Friedrich Welter, *Justus H. Wetzel* (1931), pp. 34-36.

34 "Nocturne," *Kleiner Garten* (1919); "Musik," *Die Schweiz,* 19 (1915), 147-150; "Kirchenkonzert," *Deutsche Interniertenzeitung,* Dec. 25, 1918, pp. 11-12; *Mozarts Opern. Programmschrift des Züricher Stadttheaters vom 29. Oktober, 1932;* "Erinnerungen an Othmar Schoeck," *Gedenkblätter;* "Alte Musik," *Betrachtungen;* "Musikalische Notizen," *Neue Schweizer Rundschau,* 15 (1948), 598-616; *Engadiner Erlebnisse* (1953), pp. 17-25; "Ferienberichte und Erinnerungen," *Neue Züricher Ztg.,* Aug. 27, 1954, pp. 3-4; *Kleine Festgabe für Fritz Brun* (1941), pp. 33-34; "Notizblätter um Ostern" (1954), *Beschwörungen,* pp. 234-236, also 247-251 and 285-288.

35 Two dissertations have treated the theme: Hermann Wassner,

"Über die Bedeutung der Musik in den Dichtungen von Hermann Hesse" (Heidelberg, 1953), 145 pp; Klaus Matthias, "Die Musik bei Thomas Mann und Hermann Hesse" (Kiel, 1956), 352 pp. Two other pertinent items were published too recently for consideration: Helmut Reinhold, "Hermann Hesses Morgenlandfahrt mit Mozart," *Geist und Zeit*, 1, No. 5 (1956), 86-99; George Schoolfield, *The Figure of the Musician in German Literature* (1956), pp. 136-137, 147-150, 156-158, 190-194; Werner Dürr, *Hermann Hesse. Vom Wesen der Musik in der Dichtung* (1927), 120 pp.

36 Otto Basler's more recent remarks are characterized by similar enthusiastic generalities. He would have Hesse's art so permeated by the spirit of music, that he speaks of the "musikalische Logik, die dem Werkorganismus von Hesses Schaffen innewohnt," "Hermann Hesses Weg zum *Glasperlenspiel*," *Schweizer Annalen*, 1 (1944), 639.

37 Unlike Müller-Blattau, Walter Dirks perceives an ominous warning in both novels. *Faustus* witnesses the dangers of music become a demonic force, and *Glasperlenspiel*, the bankruptcy of music which has become a religion ("Die Musik und die Vollkommenheit," *Frankfurter Hefte*, 4 [1949], 245-246.

38 Hesse would hardly appreciate this intimate association with Heidegger and his existentialism. When, upon occasion of a visit in Montagnola in the summer of 1954, conversation turned to Heidegger, Hesse could only shake his head slowly in an obvious expression of antipathy. For a further association of Hesse and Heidegger see Hans Jaeger, "Heidegger's Existential Philosophy and Modern German Literature," *Publications of the Modern Language Association*, 67 (1952), 655, 670, 673, 676-677.

39 Berta Berger maintains that even *Siddhartha* and *Narziss und Goldmund* continue to be autopsychoanalytical studies ("Hermann Hesse. Die Darstellung des seelischen Chaos," *Der Moderne Deutsche Bildungsroman* [1942], pp. 47-53.

40 In "Traumtheater" (*National-Ztg.*, Basel, April 24-25, 1948), Hesse mentions that he had even been in the habit of recording his dreams and interpreting them according to the methods of psychoanalysis which were then in vogue. Psychoanalysis had obviously made a deep impression upon him: "Das Kennenlernen einiger psychoanalytischer Bücher und der praktischen Psychoanalyse selbst, das ich erlebt hatte, war mehr als nur eine Sensation gewesen, es war eine Begegnung mit wirklichen Mächten." See also "Nächtliche Spiele," *Beschwörungen*, p. 84.

41 Hesse acclaimed Freud and his psychoanalysis as early as 1914. In his review of Kurt Wolff's *Nervöse Leute*, he writes: "Er stützt sich ganz auf Dr. Adler in Wien, verschweigt aber, dass Adler selbst sein ganzes Fundament Sigmund Freud verdankt. Freud und seine Psychoanalyse haben erbitterte Gegner, und gewiss ist Freuds Methode noch mit subjektiven Vorurteilen behaftet, aber der Weg zur Erkennung und Heilung der Nervosität ist von ihm gezeigt, daran ist kaum mehr zu zweifeln." *Die Propyläen* (Beil. z. *Münchener Ztg.*), 12 (1914), 186.

42 By 1934 Hesse's attitude toward psychoanalysis had become less favorable. Like Rilke (*Briefe* 1907-14 [1939], p. 190), he had become convinced that treatment might well end an artist's career: "Eben darum ist ja die Psychoanalyse für Künstler so sehr schwierig und gefährlich, weil sie dem, der es ernst nimmt, leicht das ganze Künstlertum zeitlebens verbieten kann" (a letter to C. G. Jung, *Briefe*, p. 145).

43 The earliest psychological study of Hesse (Cesco Como, "Hermann Hesse. Eine psychische Studie," *Deutsche Heimat*, 6 [1903], 1669-74), was not available for examination.

44 Only two dissertations have dealt specifically with this problem: Maria Liepelt-Unterberg, "Das Polaritätsgesetz in der Dichtung. Am Beisp. v. Hermann Hesses *Steppenwolf*" (Bonn, 1951), 70 pp.; Eugen Bärhausen, "Der Dualismus von Geist und Sinnlichkeit in Hermann Hesses Werk" (Freie Universität Berlin, 1952), 195 pp.

45 Notwithstanding, Hesse has always been somewhat suspicious of conversions, and has never quite approved of them (see *Briefe*, pp. 150, 162, 420-421).

46 Two dissertations have dealt with Hesse and the East: Michelle Lizounat, "Indische Religionen bei Hermann Hesse" (Bonn, 1952), 94 pp.; Annie Fourmanoir, "Über den Einfluss des Orients auf das Werk Hermann Hesses" (Heidelberg, 1954). Gerhard Mayer's *Die Begegnung des Christentums mit den asiatischen Religionen im Werk Hermann Hesses* (1956, 181 pp.) promises a thorough treatment of Hesse and the Orient.

47 One minor student project has treated this theme: Willi Hirsch, "Hermann Hesse und das Christentum" (Akzessarbeit, Theologische Fakultät, Bern, 1943). See also Käte Nadler, "Gottesliebe," *Hermann Hesse. Naturliebe, Menschenliebe, Gottesliebe* (1956), pp. 91-142.

48 The numbers preceding the page references refer to "Works about Hesse" in the Bibliography.

49 For other references to Knecht's death see *Briefe*, pp. 231, 355.

50 *Glasperlenspiel* is hardly unique in its mystery of names. Almost every one of Hesse's prose works from his most insignificant tale to his major novels indulges in this intriguing hide-and-seek. A major investigation of these names and their allusions must eventually become part of Hesse studies.

51 Any future study should not fail to take into consideration Hesse's many references to the novel in his *Briefe*, pp. 96, 117, 125, 141-142, 148, 222, 226-227, 229-232, 234, 259, 264, 269-270, 287, 290, 314 355, 385; see also *Beschwörungen*, pp. 237-238.

52 O. Engel, *Hermann Hesse. Dichtung und Gedanke*, pp. 54-57; M. Schmid, *Hermann Hesse. Weg und Wandlung*, pp. 201-209; G. Hafner, *Hermann Hesse. Werk und Leben* (1954), pp. 76-79; J. F. von Hecker, *Hermann Hesse*, 56-59; W. Kramer, *Hermann Hesses Glasperlenspiel und seine Stellung in der geistigen Situation unserer Zeit*, pp. 14-18; W. Schwinn, *Hermann Hesses Altersweisheit und das Christentum*, pp. 14-15; W. Kohlschmid, *Zeitwende*, 19 (1947), 220-223. Sidney M. Johnson's very recent article ("The Autobiographies in Hermann Hesse's *Glasperlen-*

spiel," German Quarterly, 24 [1956], 160-171) is the first more detailed study of the *Lebensläufe.*

53 The best study, to date, is that of C. M. Konheiser-Barwanietz, *Hermann Hesse und Goethe* (1954), pp. 67-86.

54 J. Müller-Blattau (*Geistige Welt,* 4, No. 1 [1949], 29-34), A. Dornheim (*Revista de Estudios Musicales* [Mendoza], 1 [1949], pp. 131-172), Walter Dirks (*Frankfurter Hefte,* 4 [1949], 245-246), and G. W. Field (*University of Toronto Quarterly,* 24 [1955], 175-190) have considered the two novels in terms of their music. K. Schmid (*Hermann Hesse und Thomas Mann,* 48 pp.) delves into the humanism each represents. R. A. Schröder (*Neue Schweizer Rundschau,* 20 [1952], 140-142) finds *Glasperlenspiel* the maturer, the more pleasing of the two. Note Mann's remarks about Hesse's work: *Die Entstehung des Doktor Faustus* (1949), pp. 68-69; *Neue Rundschau,* 1947, p. 237. Hesse remarks upon *Dr. Faustus* in his *Briefe,* pp. 269-270.

55 Eight of these eleven poems appear in Suhrkamp's edition of the *Gedichte* (1947), and all eleven in Fretz & Wasmuth's third edition (1947). Two, more recent poems (written in 1947 and 1950) were added to the *Gedichte* of the *Gesammelte Dichtungen* of 1952. Other later poems which are not included in the *Gedichte* of 1942: "Drei Gedichte," *Neue Schweizer Rundschau,* 16 (1948), 29-31; *Heute und Morgen* (Düsseldorf), 7 (1952), 577 (three poems); "Die Gedichte eines Jahres," *Neue Schweizer Rundschau,* 22 (1954), 293-296 (four poeme written in 1953-54).

It might be pointed out that item ninety-three of the one hundred and fifty-two poems listed in Kliemann/Silomon, a poem which appears in *Klingsors letzter Sommer,* is not by Hesse but by Goethe. To this list of Hesse's poems Silomon might have added "Wenn mich dein Bild im Traum besucht," which was published in Ludwig Finckh's *Fraue du, du Süsse* (1900), and again in Finckh's *Verzauberung* (1950), (see Finckh, *Schwäbische Vettern* [1948], p. 11). "Süsser Narrheit voll gemacht," of *Verzauberung,* is probably also by Hesse (for the close friendship between Hesse and Finckh at the turn of the century, see Gotthilf Hafner, "Hermann Hesses Anfänge," *Welt und Wort,* 7 [1952], 229-230).

56 For an insight into Hesse's attitude toward his own, and poetry in general, see: "Gespräch über die Neutöner," *Blick ins Chaos,* pp. 30-43; "Schlechte Gedichte," *Betrachtungen,* pp. 93-99; "Sprache," *Betrachtungen,* pp. 45-52; *Neue Rundschau,* 36 (1925); 220; *Briefe,* pp. 218, 220, 232, 234; *Betrachtungen,* p. 172; "Aus einem Brief," *Krieg und Frieden* (1949), pp. 165-168; "Briefwechsel zu einem Gedicht," *Neue Züricher Ztg.,* Jan. 17, 1954, p. 4; "Begegnungen mit Vergangenem," *Beschwörungen,* pp. 184-193. "Wiederbegegnung mit zwei Jugendgedichten," *Westermanns Monatshefte,* No. 9 (1956), pp. 27-28.

57 Only two dissertations have dealt specifically with Hesse's poetry: Ilse Erhart, "Die Lyrik Hermann Hesses" (Wien, 1936); Miss Lorrain, "Étude des Poésies de Hermann Hesse" (Sorbonne, 1950), 155 pp.

58   W. Kunze, "Hermann Hesses Lyrik," *Weimarer Blätter*, 4 (1922), 323-328; E. Lissauer, "Zu Hermann Hesses Lyrik," *Das Literarische Echo*, 24 (1922), 730-733; H. Federmann, "Hermann Hesses Neue Gedichte," *Hochland*, 29 (1931-32), 558-560; Johannes Edfelt, "Nattens Tröst," *Strövtåg* (1941), pp. 44-54; C. W. Park, "Note on Hermann Hesse's Verse," *Poetry*, 70 (1947), 206-208; U. Seyffarth, "Hermann Hesse: Die Gedichte," *Welt und Wort*, 3 (1948), 83-84; G. Schwarz, "Hermann Hesse in seinem Gedicht," *Welt und Wort*, 4 (1949), 171-174; R. Drews, "Hermann Hesses Verse," *Die Weltbühne* (Berlin), 7 (1952), 882-883; Ball (1947), see index; G. Hafner, *Hermann Hesse* (1947), pp. 13-15, 62-71; A. Goes, *Rede auf Hermann Hesse* (1946), pp. 31-33.

59   Attention should also be drawn to the following articles which were not available for examination: "Hermann Hesse. Ensayo sobre la lírica sustancial," *Boletín del Instituto de Estudios Germánicos* (Universidad de Buenos Aires, 1939-40), pp. 151-168; Francesco Delbono, "Beitrag zur Lyrik Hermann Hesses," *Italienische Kulturnachrichten*, 1954, No. 41-42, pp. 37-42; Eberhard Hilscher, "Der Lyriker Hermann Hesse," *Neue Deutsche Literatur*, 4, No. 9 (1956), 109-118; "Die Lyrik. Ernte eines reichen Lebens," *Schriftsteller der Gegenwart* (1956), pp. 84-95.

Hesse Archives in Europe

1   *Der Umgang mit Büchern* (appeared in *Moderne Kultur. Ein Handbuch der Lebensbildung und des guten Geschmacks*, ed. Ed. Heyck [Stuttgart, 1907], Vol. 2); *Hans Dierlamms Lehrzeit* (a very rare item published in Berlin in 1916 as volume eight of the *Feldbücher* by the Künstlerdank-Ges.); *Der Weg zur Kunst* (published also as *Die Legende vom Dichter* and then later as *Der Dichter* in *Märchen*); *Verrede eines Dichters zu seinen ausgewählten Werken* (written in 1921, published in *Betrachtungen*); *Tragisch* (written in 1922, published in *Träumfährte*).

2   According to good authority, the *Westdeutsches Hermann Hesse-Archiv* of Cologne was sold to the *Schiller Nationalmuseum*, September, 1957.

INDEXES

INDEX

HESSE'S WORKS
(Articles and Reviews not included)

Abends, 227.
Abendwolken, 223.
Alle Bücher dieser Welt, 11, 222.
Alte Geschichten, 219.
Am Weg, 8, 9, 154, 164, 219, 220.
Anton Schievelbeyns Ohnfreiwillige Reisse Nachher Ostindien, 219, 228.
Aquarelle aus dem Tessin (1955), 223, 301.
Aufzeichnungen eines Herrn im Sanatorium, 12.
Aus dem Tagebuch eines Entgleisten, 221
Aus einem Notizbuch, 221.
Aus Indien, 8, 173, 175, 178, 219, 221, 267.
Aus Kinderzeiten, 164, 219.
Aus vielen Jahren, 11, 222, 301.
Ausgewählte Gedichte (1921), 10, 219.
Aventiure, 227.

Begegnungen mit Vergangenem, 222.
Bei den Massageten, 223, 231.
Berg und See, 12, 222.
Bericht aus Normalien, 222.
Berthold, 8, 101, 221, 276.
Beschwörungen, 12, 199, 213, 223, 232, 240, 268, 304, 305.
Betrachtungen, 9, 10, 47, 66, 86, 96, 142, 146, 147, 153, 166, 177, 178 220, 223, 238, 242, 268, 299, 302, 303, 304, 307, 308.
Eine Bibliothek der Weltliteratur, 10, 74, 99, 124, 173, 178, 220, 303.
Bilderbuch, 8, 10, 35, 97, 101, 146, 147, 178, 220, 256.
Blick ins Chaos, 10, 55, 70, 74, 82, 115, 131, 139, 140, 141, 147, 164, 167, 169, 220, 282, 291, 307.
Blütenzweig, 11, 221.
Boccaccio, 8, 219.
Die Braut, 229.
Briefe (1951), 12, 48, 54, 55, 74, 97, 106, 143, 144, 145, 147, 148, 153, 155, 156, 157, 164, 173, 175, 177, 178, 184, 186, 187, 188, 199, 213, 222, 223, 254, 260, 266, 292, 299, 303, 306, 307.

Dank an Goethe, 12, 98, 221, 276, 302, 303.

Danksagung und moralisierende Betrachtung, 221
Demian, 9, 14, 20, 21, 22, 30, 35, 36, 45, 46, 56, 61, 62, 63, 64, 65, 69, 70, 74, 76, 77, 78, 81, 82, 83, 84, 85, 86, 87, 91, 92, 96, 99, 101, 106, 107, 108, 115, 121, 123, 128, 131, 132, 134, 135, 138, 142, 145, 147, 148, 149, 150, 154, 158, 159, 160, 162, 163, 166, 168, 169, 170, 172, 175, 178, 198, 199, 219, 229, 242, 259, 261, 270, 275, 286, 287, 288, 289, 291, 293, 295, 297, 298.
Die Dichter, 229.
Diesseits, 8, 112, 114, 129, 130, 131, 147, 154, 164, 219, 223, 227, 266, 272, 286.
Doktor Knölges Ende, 228.

Elf Aquarelle aus dem Tessin, 220, 301.
Emil Kolb, 5.
Engadiner Erlebnisse, 223.
Erinnerung an André Gide, 12, 125, 222.
Das erste Abenteuer, 227.
Der Europäer, 221, 271.

Fabulierbuch, 8, 12, 86, 96, 146, 221, 223, 227, 228.
Faust und Zarathustra, 219.
Festliches Tessin, 223.
Feuerwerk, 12, 39, 139, 147, 221.
Flötentraum, 220.
Franz v. Assisi, 8, 64, 150, 177, 219.
Freunde, 12, 61, 154, 222, 227.
Frühe Prosa, 11, 222.
Eine Fussreise, 219, 227.

Garibaldi, 164.
Gedenkblätter, 12, 95, 97, 114, 146, 151, 152, 173, 176, 178, 188, 221, 302, 304.
Gedichte (1912), 7, 129, 192, 206, 219.
Gedichte (1942), 11, 81, 115, 151, 178, 192, 193, 211, 221, 267, 269, 280, 282, 290, 298, 307.
Gedichte des Malers, 10, 220, 290, 301.
Gedichte und Prosa (1956), 223.
Geheimnisse, 222.

Gerbersau, 11, 15, 46, 112, 222, 298.
Gertrud, 8, 15, 30, 36, 61, 68, 77, 78, 101, 107, 128, 130, 133, 151, 152, 154, 173, 199, 219, 260, 281.
Gesammelte Dichtungen, 11, 93, 218, 223, 271, 307.
Gesammelte Schriften, 218, 223.
Gesammelte Werke, 218, 260.
Geselle Zbinden, 225.
Glasperlenspiel, 11, 13, 28, 30, 36, 37, 38, 53, 56, 60, 63, 65, 66, 70, 80, 81, 82, 83, 84, 85, 88, 89, 91, 92, 94, 98, 100, 102, 103, 106, 107, 108, 109, 110, 115, 117-118, 119, 121, 123, 124, 129, 135, 136, 141, 143, 146, 147, 152, 153, 154, 155, 156, 157, 160, 165, 168, 169, 170, 171, 172, 176, 177, 178-192, 193, 198, 199, 221, 240, 250, 252, 253, 256, 257, 258, 259, 260, 261, 265, 266, 267, 268, 269, 270, 271, 272, 273, 274, 275, 276, 278, 280, 281, 282, 285, 286, 287, 289, 290, 291, 293, 295, 296, 297, 299, 302, 303, 305, 306.
Castalia, 28, 37, 38, 51, 56, 65, 66, 80, 94, 100, 110, 111, 117, 138, 146, 152, 153, 155, 156, 179, 180, 181, 182, 183, 184, 186, 187, 188, 190, 191, 266, 267, 275, 282.
Knecht's death, 80, 101, 109, 110, 111, 165, 180, 183-186, 187, 189, 266, 267, 306.
Lebensläufe, 110-111, 179, 180, 191-192, 272, 306-307.
Tito episode, 180, 183, 184, 185, 188.
Glück, 11, 222.
Grossväterliches, 222.

Eine Handvoll Briefe, 12, 222.
Hans Amstein, 227.
Hans Dierlamms Lehrzeit, 219, 308.
Haus der Träume, 9, 221.
Haus zum Frieden, 8, 11, 126, 222, 253.
Heimkehr, 9, 229, 242.
Herbstliche Erlebnisse, 222
Hermann Hesse (Auszüge), 221.
Hermann Hesse. Eine Auswahl, 11, 223.
Hermann Hesse/Romain Rolland. Briefe, 12, 144, 223, 226, 301.
Hermann Lauscher, 7, 14, 15, 30, 36, 61, 68, 76, 77, 98, 101, 113, 114, 129, 130, 147, 148, 151, 154, 164, 206, 219, 301.
Herr Piero, 228.

Im Pressel'schen Gartenhaus, 9, 131, 220, 242, 256, 282, 303.
In der alten Sonne, 5, 112, 219.
In einer kleinen Stadt, 229.
Italien, 10, 220.

Jahreszeiten, 221, 301.
Jugendgedichte, 11, 222.

Karl Eugen Eiselein, 14, 113.
Das Kind. Eine thebaische Legende, 225.
Kinderseele, 9, 81, 107, 148, 164, 242, 257.
Klein und Wagner, 10, 11, 21, 22, 36, 56, 64, 74, 81, 82, 84, 85, 86, 87, 91, 99, 101, 102, 107, 162, 169, 298, 303.
Kleine Betrachtungen, 12, 221, 238.
Kleine Welt, 11, 130, 221, 223.
Kleiner Garten, 9, 96, 220.
Klingsors letzter Sommer, 10, 21, 22, 30, 36, 56, 69, 70, 81, 84, 85, 86, 87, 96, 115, 134, 165, 166, 169, 172, 220, 227, 230, 296, 307.
Knulp, 5, 8, 9, 30, 36, 37, 46, 61, 78, 101, 107, 114, 129, 130, 178, 219, 242, 261, 268, 276.
Eine Konzertpause, 222.
Krieg und Frieden, 12, 35, 40, 41, 42, 43, 44, 51, 52, 89, 99, 117, 141, 142, 143, 147, 169, 178, 222, 223, 226, 239, 288, 299, 302, 303, 307.
Krisis, 10, 21, 25-26, 27, 32, 81, 86, 107, 115, 132, 160, 220, 298.
Kurgast, 10, 21, 22, 30, 36, 66, 81, 86, 107, 126, 132, 154, 164, 166, 169, 170, 171, 177, 220, 256, 274.
Kurzgefasster Lebenslauf, 68, 97, 132, 147, 151, 242, 301.

Ladidel, 5, 113, 154, 242.
Der lahme Knabe, 11, 149, 223, 298.
Lateinschüler, 154, 242.
Legende, 227.
Legende vom indischen König, 227.
Die Legende vom verliebten Jüngling, 227.
Lektüre für Kriegsgefangene, 219.
Lektüre für Minuten, 11, 223.
Eine Liebesgeschichte, 227.
Lieblingslektüre, 220.
Die Lieder der deutschen Romantik, 153.
Der Lindenbaum, 153.

Magie des Buches, 220.

Mahnung, 11, 221.
Maler Brahm, 96, 227.
Märchen, 9, 101, 220, 224, 277, 308.
Marmorsäge, 112, 242.
Das Meisterbuch, 114.
Morgenlandfahrt, 10, 11, 28, 37, 60, 61, 81, 83, 86, 91, 92, 95, 97, 98, 102, 107, 108, 109, 121, 135, 138, 154, 207, 221, 250, 257, 260, 270, 276, 277, 281, 282, 287.
Musik des Einsamen, 9, 153, 192, 219, 271, 290, 291.

Nachbarn, 5, 8, 14, 15, 112, 113, 114, 129, 130, 147, 164, 178, 219, 221, 279.
Narziss und Goldmund, 10, 28, 29, 30, 37, 61, 63, 66, 81, 83, 84, 85, 87, 102, 105, 107, 108, 121, 134, 135, 138, 148, 154, 159, 160, 162, 163, 166, 167, 168, 170, 171, 172, 175, 188, 198, 220, 261, 268, 274, 276, 279, 282, 288, 289, 290, 292, 295, 296, 305.
Neue Gedichte (1937), 11, 221.
Der Novalis, 221.
Nürnberger Reise, 10, 30, 81, 96, 114, 169, 220, 274, 302, 303.

Die Offizina Bodoni in Montagnola, 220.

Pater Mathias, 173, 178.
Peter Camenzind, 7, 15, 30, 36, 46, 61, 64, 65, 68, 77, 78, 96, 101, 105, 107, 111, 113, 120, 124, 128, 129, 130, 131, 132, 134, 135, 143, 146, 147, 150, 154, 158, 181, 219, 226, 257, 258, 260, 261, 266, 270, 278, 280, 287, 291, 297, 299, 303.
Der Pfirsichbaum und andere Erzäh-lungen, 12, 97, 221.
Piktors Verwandlungen, 213, 220, 266, 301.

Rigi-Tagebuch, 221.
Robert Aghion, 173, 174, 178, 219.
Romantische Lieder, 6, 17, 18, 68, 107, 129, 192, 219.
Rosshalde, 9, 15, 20, 30, 36, 61, 68, 77, 78, 96, 101, 107, 128, 133, 134, 154, 188, 219, 267, 278, 296.
Rückblick, 230, 250.

Schön ist die Jugend, 8, 147, 164, 215, 238, 301.
Schweizerische Gesamt-Ausgabe, 218.

Siddhartha, 10, 21, 22, 30, 36, 47, 51, 61, 63, 66, 74, 76-79, 81, 83, 85, 86, 91, 92, 102, 106, 107, 108, 120, 121, 128, 132, 134, 135, 149, 154, 160, 166, 168, 178, 198, 199, 220, 250, 256, 261, 274, 275, 277, 278, 283, 287, 288, 292, 295, 296, 299, 300, 303, 305.
Sinclairs Notizbuch, 9, 166, 220, 301.
Späte Prosa, 12, 114, 149, 222, 223, 266, 271, 280, 285, 301.
Statt eines Briefes, 222.
Steppenwolf, 10, 21, 22, 27, 28, 30, 35, 36, 37, 48, 52, 56, 60, 61, 63, 70, 81, 82, 83, 84, 85, 86, 87, 88, 91, 92, 98, 102, 107, 108, 115-116, 121, 123, 124, 132, 134, 135, 136, 138, 141, 145, 147, 152, 153, 154, 158, 162, 166, 170, 198, 199, 220, 250, 253, 260, 261, 269, 277, 278, 279, 281, 282, 286, 287, 289, 290, 292, 293, 294, 295, 296, 297, 298, 302, 306.
Die Stimmen und der Heilige, 222.
Stufen der Menschwerdung, 222.
Eine Stunde hinter Mitternacht, 6, 14, 15, 17, 20, 22, 68, 77, 82, 101, 128, 129, 152, 154, 219, 267, 279, 280.
Stunden im Garten, 11, 94, 221, 223, 298.

Taedium vitae, 227.
Tagebuchblatt, 223.
Der Trauermarsch, 223.
Traumfährte, 10, 22, 44, 45, 68, 95, 96, 97, 151, 178, 221, 269, 279, 301, 308.
Trost der Nacht, 10, 220.

Umwege, 5, 8, 61, 112, 113, 114, 147, 154, 173, 178, 219, 221.
Unterm Rad, 5, 8, 15, 46, 61, 62, 63, 65, 68, 77, 101, 104, 107, 113, 128, 129, 130, 131, 146, 154, 158, 188, 219, 261, 266, 267, 289, 296.
Unterwegs, 8, 9, 219, 298.

Die Verlobung, 5, 227, 242.
Die Verlobung und andere Erzäh-lungen, 11, 222.
Verse im Krankenbett, 10, 220.
Vom Baum des Lebens, 11, 192, 221.

Walter Kömpff, 5, 178.
Ein Wandertag vor hundert Jahren, 228.
Wanderung, 10, 97, 146, 147, 153, 154, 220, 301.

Weg nach Innen, 10, 86, 220, 302, 303.
Wege zu Hermann Hesse, 11.
Weltverbesserer, 61.
Der Wolf und andere Erzählungen, 223.

Zarathustras Wiederkehr, 9, 20, 43, 46, 74, 85, 141, 142, 143, 148, 220, 229, 286, 302.
Der Zauberbronnen, 153.

Zum Gedächtnis unseres Vaters, 10, 220.
Zum Sieg, 219.
Zwei Aufsätze, 221.
Zwei Idyllen, 11, 92, 149, 223, 271.
Zwei Märchen, 219.
Zwischen Sommer und Herbst, 221.
Der Zwerg, 223, 242.
Der Zyklon, 9, 219, 220
Der Zyklon und andere Erzählungen, 220.

INDEX OF SUBJECTS

The American-German Review, 126, 253, 301.

Archives, 125, 203-207, 211, 273, 283, 293, 300, 304, 308.

Awards, 7, 9, 12-13, 51, 104, 124, 126, 179, 196, 197, 199, 226, 252, 254, 255, 267, 270, 272, 275, 276, 282, 283, 284, 288, 289, 290, 291.

Berliner Tageblatt, 10.

Bibliography, 126-127, 134, 192, 204, 205, 208-213, 217-297, 277.

Bildungsroman, 120, 189, 229, 255, 258, 266, 293, 295, 296.

Bonniers Litterära Magasin, 12, 48.

Bookdealer, 6, 7, 59, 124, 224, 228, 278.

Bourgeois world, 15, 20, 24, 25, 34-56, 61, 64, 83, 94, 108, 116, 118, 119, 130, 136, 138, 139, 145-146, 170, 197, 272, 293, 296, 297, 302, 304.

Brahmanism, 78.

Braille, 249.

Buddhism, 78, 132, 138, 297.

Casa Bodmer, 11.

Casa Camuzzi, 9-10, 11, 25.

Catholicism, 173, 175, 176, 186-187.

Childhood, 16, 17, 18, 23, 26, 29, 32, 61, 63, 68, 69, 73, 83, 89, 105, 147-150, 151, 165, 194, 274.

Classicism, 22, 33, 47, 70, 75, 76, 98, 152, 155, 156, 170, 198.

Communism, 45, 48, 54-55, 140, 175, 232, 299.

Death, 6, 16, 17, 19, 23, 24, 25, 26, 27, 32, 33, 38, 42, 43, 44, 56, 73, 84, 88, 101, 102, 130, 171, 193, 194, 225, 228, 231, 278, 289.

Decadence, 14, 22, 29, 67, 70, 71, 77, 82, 121, 163, 193.

Deutsche Beiträge, 93.

Deutsche Internierten-Zeitung, 9, 148, 203.

Doppelgänger motif, 94, 138, 158.

Dreams, 23, 32, 70, 76, 85, 103, 148, 160, 161, 166, 225, 229, 232, 296, 305.

Du. Schweizerische Monatsschrift, 126, 253, 301.

Editor, Hesse as, 8, 9, 10, 40, 44, 60, 73, 105, 124, 148, 153, 197, 203, 208, 209, 210, 212, 233, 236.

Educational ideal, 61-66, 95, 100, 103, 107, 122-123, 179, 226, 250, 253, 261, 267.

Eigensinn, 20, 43, 44, 65, 70, 109, 115, 151.

Essayist, Hesse as, 40-44, 46, 47, 51, 73, 89, 97, 114, 116-117, 141, 142, 143, 146, 151, 154, 178, 224-232.

Existentialism, 159, 161, 172, 183, 272, 290, 305.

Expressionism, 22, 115, 116, 134, 236, 259, 260, 287, 290.

Family, 3-13, 20, 59-60, 66, 73, 89, 90, 99, 105, 114, 125, 126, 145, 176, 177, 204, 205, 206, 271, 274, 298, 299-300.

Fear, 25, 38, 69, 90, 148, 165, 225, 293, 296.

Flux, 16, 24, 26, 32, 33, 61, 171, 184.

Frankfurter Zeitung, 10.

Friendship, 16.

Geist and *Natur,* 20, 21, 23, 24, 25, 28, 32, 61, 78, 79, 81, 83, 84, 85, 86, 87, 88, 89, 91, 92, 98, 99, 106, 107, 108, 109, 110, 115, 116, 117, 118, 120, 121, 122, 136, 137, 156, 158, 160, 164, 166-173, 180, 184, 185, 194, 265, 274, 293, 306.

Geist and *Seele,* 82-88, 95, 101, 125, 164, 166-167, 168, 185.

Heimat, 16, 17, 18, 23, 24, 26, 32, 83, 87, 91, 135, 171, 172, 194.

Hinduism, 78, 232.

Humanism, 118-119, 120, 138, 169, 180, 185, 257, 281, 285, 288, 297, 302.

Humor, 15, 21, 25, 27, 63, 88, 102, 130, 146, 152, 168, 193.

Impressionism, 163.

Inadequacy, 25, 68, 130.

Individualism, 26, 27, 28, 29, 30, 37, 43, 44, 50, 52, 61, 63, 64, 65, 66, 68, 70, 85, 91, 95, 106, 117, 122, 123, 124, 125, 132, 139, 140, 144, 146, 158, 165, 167, 169, 172, 173, 186, 255, 294.

Introversion, 15, 30, 71-72, 165, 250, 268.

Jews, 48-49, 50, 53, 255, 267, 299.

Künstlerroman, 8, 9, 73.

Legends, 101, 225, 227.
Letters (by Hesse), 12, 106, 125, 147, 204, 205, 206, 207, 222, 223, 238-241.
Loneliness, 8, 16, 20, 24, 29, 30, 32, 33, 43, 63, 68, 85, 88, 132, 134, 137, 165, 172, 173, 193, 225, 297.
Love, 16, 18, 19, 24, 27, 28, 30, 32, 36, 38, 43, 68, 70, 76, 77, 78, 87, 89, 106, 107, 117, 121, 124, 130, 142, 164, 165-166, 167, 171, 172, 180, 182, 186, 193, 194, 286.

Märchen, 73, 93, 101, 102, 103, 219, 220, 221, 272, 301.
März, 8, 44, 45, 60, 233-235.
Meditation, 22, 27, 61, 63, 80, 83, 88, 89, 91, 99, 102, 117, 118, 119, 151, 182.
Modern age, 19, 20, 29, 34-56, 63, 95, 109, 139-147, 150, 151, 163, 174, 179, 180, 184, 185, 272, 296.
Music, 25, 32, 37, 38, 63, 76, 94, 95, 100, 116, 119, 126, 131, 151-157, 176, 178, 190, 192, 193, 204, 211, 212, 225, 226, 227, 229, 230, 231, 239, 250, 256, 259, 260, 261, 266, 268, 274, 277, 280, 289, 294, 295, 304-305.
Mutter ·Eva, 63, 84-85, 86, 99, 101, 121, 159, 164, 172, 176.

Nature, 12, 15, 16, 17, 23, 27, 30, 31, 32, 35, 36, 38, 61, 68, 69, 73, 83, 88, 89, 90, 95, 100, 101, 106, 107, 112, 113, 118, 119, 125, 126, 129, 130, 135, 139, 149, 150-151, 187, 194, 225, 226, 227, 228, 230, 232, 250, 280, 293, 294, 295, 297, 304.
Butterflies, 125, 150, 228, 231.
Garden motif, 95, 150, 187, 228, 272.
Water motif, 101, 102, 135, 150.
Nazis, 48, 49, 50, 51, 54, 61, 128, 132, 133, 136, 141, 143, 144, 163, 189, 218, 302.
Neue Rundschau, 8, 10, 12, 203, 236-237.
Neue Schweizer Rundschau, 12, 93.
Neue Züricher Zeitung, 10, 12, 27, 40.
Nirvana, 21, 24, 74, 82, 91, 152.

Orient, 4, 8, 18, 20, 24, 29, 63, 72, 73, 74, 76, 78, 81, 90, 94, 96, 99, 118, 119, 121, 124, 139, 143, 172, 173,

174, 185, 228, 250, 265, 293, 297, 306.
Outsider, 14, 17, 20, 30, 36, 68, 113, 121, 124, 146, 165, 169, 194, 296, 302.

Pacifism, 9, 40-44, 45, 46, 52, 53, 136, 144-145, 229, 231, 257, 287.
Painting, 10, 85, 95-97, 126, 150, 154, 204, 205, 206, 207, 211, 223, 227, 232, 233, 270, 272, 279, 281, 283, 301.
Pietism, 3, 59, 73, 114-115, 173, 176.
Poetry, 6, 7, 10, 11, 15-20, 22-27, 30, 31-32, 33, 40, 73, 79, 81, 88, 96, 105, 107, 116, 122, 126, 128, 135, 152, 153, 171-172, 180, 192-195, 197, 204, 206, 211, 212, 226, 230, 231, 232, 233, 240, 245, 246, 247, 248, 249, 252, 255, 265, 266, 268, 271, 272, 274, 275, 277, 280, 286, 289, 293, 294, 297, 298, 304, 307-308.
Politics, 34, 40, 42, 44, 45, 48, 49, 51, 52-54, 89, 116-117, 136, 138, 143, 146, 151, 185, 241, 283, 288.
Propyläen (supplement of Münchener Zeitung), 203.
Prose style, 14-15, 21-22, 28-29, 30, 31, 33, 47, 60, 71, 73, 75, 76, 79, 80, 94, 104, 107, 112-113, 116, 124, 129, 132, 133, 135, 136, 153-154, 156-157, 160, 161, 162-163, 166, 179-180, 181, 182-183, 185, 189-192, 197, 288, 294, 295, 297, 301.
Protestantism, 170, 173, 175.
Psychology, 9, 22, 25, 26, 27, 29, 30, 33, 49, 59, 60, 66, 67, 68, 69, 70, 71, 72, 82, 83, 84, 85, 86, 90, 91, 92, 107, 116, 119, 126, 130, 132, 135, 136, 138, 147, 148, 152, 158-165, 170, 172, 180, 181, 207, 225, 237, 254, 267, 268, 272, 287, 295, 298, 300, 305-306.

Realism, 15, 20, 22, 60, 93, 107, 112.
Relativity, 55, 56, 64, 70, 74, 77, 118, 139, 141, 167.
Religion, 3, 4, 5, 25, 28, 32, 34, 35, 38, 39, 42, 43, 55, 61, 65, 72, 73, 74, 76, 79, 80, 88, 89, 90, 107, 108, 114, 117-118, 131, 151, 158, 163, 164, 167, 170, 172, 173-178, 179, 181, 186, 194, 229, 230, 231, 236, 250, 267, 287, 293, 294, 306.
Reviewer, Hesse as, 8, 9, 10, 12, 114, 204, 205, 211, 233-238.
Die Rheinlande, 8, 203.

Romanticism, 7, 14, 15, 17, 20, 22, 26, 29, 30, 33, 35, 46, 60, 62, 67, 70, 72, 73, 75, 76, 90, 93, 98, 100-103, 107, 108, 112, 114, 118, 119, 124, 125, 130, 131, 133, 138, 149, 150, 152, 153, 155, 159, 175, 189, 193, 194, 199, 230, 250, 251, 274, 276, 289, 294, 295.

Sankhya, 24, 298.
Service, 21, 38, 64, 66, 70, 77, 89, 91, 95, 110, 111, 117, 123, 135, 164, 165, 167, 181, 182, 184, 186.
Simplicissimus, 8, 44, 203, 231.
Space, 37, 83, 84, 171.

Theosophy, 173.
Time, 29, 37, 82, 84, 120, 158, 171, 190, 294.
Translations, 196, 198, 208, 210, 211, 243-249.

Unity, 21, 26, 27, 61, 63, 64, 75, 78, 79, 80, 82, 83, 90, 91, 92, 95, 98, 101, 102, 106, 132, 137, 150, 158, 167, 168, 170, 175, 177, 278.
Untergang, 29, 37-38, 55-56, 74, 107, 116, 138, 139-141, 153, 225, 276, 294, 303.

Vivos Voco, 10, 45, 47, 148, 203, 236.

Wanderer, 16, 17, 26, 30, 32, 36, 105, 131, 193, 224, 225, 228, 229, 231, 232, 234, 280, 296.
War, 18-20, 34, 39-42, 44, 46, 47, 50, 51, 53, 55, 59, 62, 74, 90, 106, 128, 130, 138, 140, 141, 142, 143, 144, 146, 148, 151, 185, 194, 203, 224, 226, 228, 231, 232, 235, 238, 239, 267, 273, 278, 281, 286.
Weg nach Innen (self-knowledge, self realization), 10, 20, 22, 24-26, 27, 30, 33, 41, 43, 62, 63, 66, 74, 77, 78, 84, 89, 91, 92, 106, 107, 115, 117, 121, 122, 134-135, 145-146, 158, 159, 162, 165, 169, 172, 174, 182, 275.
Women, 63, 69, 73, 76, 84-85, 86, 87, 99, 101, 107, 121, 151, 159, 163, 164, 172, 176, 186, 187, 276.

Youth, 16, 17, 29, 43, 45, 46, 47, 50, 51, 61, 62, 63, 66, 67, 89, 101, 122, 128, 131, 142, 143, 147-150, 165, 193, 224, 225, 274, 278.

INDEX OF NAMES

Abenius, Sigrid, 246.
Aburi, H., 285.
Abusch, Alex., 262.
Ackerknecht, E., 265.
Ackermann, W., 265.
Adenauer, C., 293.
Adler, Alfred, 69, 82, 305.
Adolph, Rudolf, 111, 123, 252.
Akiyama, Rokurobê, 243.
Alker, Ernst, 262.
Allason, B., 247.
Almquist, C. J. L., 235.
Alter, Georg, 204-205, 206.
Amégu, G. y, 265.
Amiet, Cuno, 96, 207, 301.
Amrhein, M., 285.
Anderle, H., 265.
Andréä, J. V., 94.
Andres, Stefan, 293.
Andrews, R. C., 194-195, 265.
Angelloz, J. F., 111, 121-122, 195, 252, 254, 265, 303.
Anselm, F., 265.
Aram, Kurt, 44, 60.
Aretz, Karl, 255.
Argentina, 196.
Arnz, K., 293, 304.
Ascher, Anita, 242.
Ashton, E. B., 244.
Assisi, St. Francis of, 38, 77, 130, 150, 173.
Auerheimer, R., 265.
Augustin, E., 265.

Baaten, Heta, 72, 90, 111, 114-115, 177, 252, 293, 300.
Bach, Joh. Seb., 88, 153, 155, 156, 157.
Bach, R., 265.
Bachofen, Joh. Jacob, 255.
Bad Boll, 6.
Baden, 9, 10, 126, 254.
Baeschlin, Alfredo, 226, 254.
Baeschlin, Th., 265, 300.
Bahr, Hermann, 238, 255.
Baldus, A., 265.
Ball, Hugo, 59-61, 66, 67, 68, 71, 73, 76, 90, 92, 96, 104, 105, 113, 114, 117, 126, 128, 133, 134, 154, 157, 236, 250, 255, 265, 285, 302, 303.
Ball-Hennings, Emma, 255, 266, 273, 285.
Ballesteros y de Torres, L. L., 245.
Balzac, Honoré de, 234.
Bärhausen, E. 293, 306.
Barnstorff, Hermann, 197, 198.
Bartels, Adolf, 50, 255, 262.

Baseggio, C., 247.
Basel, 3, 4, 6, 7, 59, 60, 232, 234, 300.
Baser, Fr., 266.
Basler, Otto, 60, 104, 117, 143, 157, 182, 184, 188, 207, 250, 252, 255, 266, 285, 305.
Bauer, P., 266.
Bauer, Rector, 6, 188.
Baumer, Franz, 72, 104, 111, 252, 293.
Bäumer, Gertrud, 131, 139-141, 266.
Becher, H., 266.
Becher, Joh. R., 255.
Beck, Adolf, 171-173, 175, 255.
Beer, Johannes, 50, 262.
Beethoven, Ludwig van, 46, 153, 155, 157, 235.
Behrens, Ada, 255.
Benn, Gottfried, 226.
Benn, Maurice, 170, 266, 297.
Bennet, E. K., 255.
Benz, Richard, 126, 240, 254, 266.
Berg, Adele von, 60.
Berger, Berta, 255, 305.
Berger, J., 293, 300.
Bergholter, J., 285.
Bern, 8, 9, 12, 39, 59, 96, 111, 207, 231, 298.
Berna, J., 239, 266.
Bernecker, G., 266.
Bernoulli, C. A., 255.
Bernoulli, Maria, 7, 9, 151, 298.
Bernt, Alois, 262.
Bernus, A. von, 239.
Bétemps, René, 134, 246, 266.
Beyers, J. M., 296.
Bezold, K., 285.
Bick, Ignatz, 255.
Biedermeier, 234.
Bierbaum, Otto, 239, 279.
Biese, Alfred, 262.
Binz, Arthur F., 255.
Birrer, E., 249, 266.
Biscardo, R., 247.
Bithell, Jethro, 262.
Black Forest, 3, 188.
Blanchot, M., 266.
Blei, Franz, 255.
Bleuler, Eugen, 71.
Bloch, Ernst, 49.
Blomberg, E., 246.
Blum, B., 285.
Blümel, Otto, 96.
Blumenthal, Marie-Louise, 184, 266.
Blumhardt, Christoph, 6, 60.
Blumhardt, Joh. Christoph, 60.
Boardman, R., 296.

Bock, Hans-Joachim, 211, 285.
Bock, Werner, 255.
Böckmann, Paul, 136, 137, 168-169, 170, 182, 190, 256, 266, 280.
Bode, Helmut, 88-89, 193, 250.
Bodmann, Emanuel von, 234.
Bodmer, H. C., 10, 11, 207.
Boeckh, Joachim, 255.
Boehme, Jakob, 244.
Boeninger, H. S., 198.
Boer-Breijer, B. H. den, 248.
Boersma, Clarence, 62-65, 66, 123, 296.
Böhm, H., 266.
Böhme, Gerhart, 131, 266,
Böhme, S., 266. 293.
Böhmer, Emil, 155, 266.
Böhmer, Gunter, 96, 207, 223, 256, 301.
Bollnow, O. F., 134, 160, 183, 255, 266.
Bonitz, Amalie, 65, 178, 267.
Bonsels, Waldemar, 174, 259.
Bonwit, Marianne, 267.
Bormann, E., 293, 304.
Bott, Hans, 240, 261.
Botta, P., 267.
Böttcher, Margot, 252, 293, 302.
Böttger, F., 267.
Boucher, Maurice, 256, 267, 302.
Boyer, J., 65.
Braem, Helmut M., 256.
Braemer, Edith, 65, 267.
Brahms, Johannes, 153, 154.
Brand, Guido K., 50, 256.
Brandeweiler, H., 285.
Braunschweig, 12.
Brazil, 6.
Brecht, Bertolt, 296.
Bredel, Willi, 137, 262, 267.
Bremgarten, 154, 188, 207.
Brenner, A., 247.
Brentano, Bettina, 273.
Brentano, Clemens, 73, 101, 102, 233, 235.
Brod, Max, 53, 267.
Bronson, J., 285.
Brown, T. K., 244.
Bruckner, 297.
Bruder, E., 267.
Brüll, O., 267.
Brümmer, Franz, 224.
Brun, Fritz, 238.
Brunner, J. W., 296.
Buber, Martin, 238.
Bucherer, Max, 96.
Buchwald, Reinhard, 93, 149-150, 223, 256, 267, 285.
Bühner, K. H., 111, 112-114, 128, 252, 302.

Burano, 18.
Burckhardt, Jakob, 63, 89, 90, 99, 107, 187, 226, 235.
Burger, Otto Heinz, 262, 285.
Busch, Wilhelm, 225.
Busse, Carl, 192-193, 206, 257, 267.

Cahn, Alfredo, 246.
Calw, 3, 4, 5, 6, 12, 59, 94, 154, 188, 206, 300.
Canada, 297.
Cannstatt, 6.
Carlsson, Anni (Rebenwurzel), 60, 95, 111, 120, 123, 128, 135, 136, 137, 138, 178, 189-190, 193, 250, 252, 267, 285, 302.
Carossa, Hans, 124, 226, 253, 256, 261, 267, 271, 272, 285, 297.
Casanova, 227, 229.
Caspar, G., 285.
Cast, G. C., 65-66, 267.
Cervantes, Miguel de, 234.
Ceylon, 8, 18.
Chastain, A., 267.
Chemnitz, E. W., 286.
Chen, Chuan, 256.
Chiles, J. A., 242.
China, 18, 44, 74, 90, 91, 92, 99, 107, 134, 156, 167, 173, 177, 178, 179, 188, 190, 196, 233, 234, 237, 248.
Chioggia, 18.
Chopin, 88, 152, 153, 155.
Cohn, Hilde, 183, 185, 189, 267.
Coleman, P., 244.
Colleville, Maurice, 176-177, 240, 267.
Cologne, 154, 187, 188, 203, 204.
Colombo, 18.
Como, Cesco, 267, 306.
Cornille, 297.
Coster, Charles de, 233.
Craven, T., 286.
Creighton, B., 244.
Cube, H., 268.
Curtius, E. R., 135, 150, 193, 256, 268.
Cysarz, Herbert, 268.

Dahrendorf, M., 293.
Dante, 37.
David-Schwarz, H., 162, 268.
Davidsen, A., 247.
Dawson, A. A., 251, 296.
Debruge, Suzanne, 129, 166, 195, 254, 268.
Dehorn, W., 163, 164, 268.
Deike, G., 286.

Delage, Jos., 246, 268.
Delbono, F., 286, 308.
Delmas, Fernand, 246.
Denmark, 196, 247.
Deubel, W., 286.
Diamond, Wm., 242.
Diederichs, Eugen, 233.
Dirks, W., 268, 305, 307.
Doderer, Otto, 268.
Dornheim, Alfredo, 120, 156-157, 178, 268, 307.
Dorpat, 3.
Dostoyevsky, Feodor, 55, 63, 64, 74, 120, 140, 141, 158, 164, 255, 259, 269.
Drews, Richard, 139, 268, 308.
Drewsen, S., 247.
Dschuang Dsi, 92.
Dubois, Julie, 3, 187.
Dunlap, G. 244.
Dürr, Erich, 268.
Dürr, Werner, 250, 305.
Durumann, Safinaz, 171, 268.
Dutton, W. M., 242.
Duwe, Willi, 50, 262.

Eckmann, Otto, 86.
Edfelt, Johannes, 247, 256, 308.
Eggebrecht, Axel, 262, 286.
Eggeling, H. F., 242.
Egger, Eugen, 256.
Ehrenberg, H., 269.
Eichbaum, Gerda, 256.
Eichendorff, Josef von, 29, 73, 101, 119, 131, 234.
Eickhorst, William, 256.
Eilenberg, J. H., 197.
Eloesser, Arthur, 48, 262.
Elster, H. M., 131, 132-134, 256, 262, 269, 303.
Emerson, R. W., 66.
Engel, Edward, 262.
Engel, Hans, 155, 269.
Engel, M., 286.
Engel, Otto, 79-80, 104, 155, 176, 182, 183, 186, 189, 190, 193, 250, 252, 269, 306.
Engelmann, Susanne, 257.
England, 196, 283.
Eppelsheimer, Hanns W., 262.
Epping, F., 286.
Erba, Annie dell, 245.
Erhart, L., 293, 307.
Erler, I., 286.
Erné, Nino, 134, 141, 195, 269.
Esslingen, 6.
Estonia, 3, 59, 258.
Eulenberg, Heda, 125, 254, 256.
Eulenberg, Herbert, 235.

Ewers, Hanns Heinz, 258.
Eyberg, J., 286.
Eyck, H. A. van, 286.

Faber du Faur, Curt von, 183, 191, 269.
Fabian, E., 269.
Faesi, Robert, 120, 256, 269, 286.
Fankhauser, Alfred, 257.
Farrelly, J., 286.
Fechter, Paul, 262.
Federmann, H., 269, 308.
Feinhals, 188.
Feuerbach, Ludwig A., 173, 235.
Fichte, J. G., 46, 82.
Fickert, K. J., 296.
Fiechtner, H., 269.
Field, G. W., 120, 157, 178, 269, 307.
Finckh, Ludwig, 7, 60, 105, 125, 126, 204, 206, 230, 235, 240, 252, 253, 257, 261, 267, 269, 286, 298, 300, 307.
Fink, Gertrud, 257, 300.
Finland, 196, 248.
Fischer, J. M., 269.
Fischer, S., 59, 218, 229.
Fizaine, Mag., 246.
Flaubert, Gustave, 94.
Flaxman, S. L., 269, 302.
Flinker, Martin, 226.
Floeck, Oswald, 262.
Florence, 18.
Flügel, H., 269.
Folgia, Giuseppi, 96.
Foltin, Lore, 242.
Fontana, O. M., 269.
Fontane, Th., 119.
Foram, M. N., 269.
Forst, John, 257.
Förster, F., 286.
Fourmanoir, A., 293, 297, 306.
France, 40, 196, 226, 236, 240, 246, 268, 271, 281, 283, 297, 304.
Frank, Bruno, 235.
Frankfurt a. M., 12, 218.
Franulic, Lenka, 257.
Frauwallner, E., 264.
Freemantle, Anne, 286.
Frendote, C., 296.
Frenzel, C. O., 270.
Frerking, J., 134, 257.
Fretz & Wasmuth, 218.
Freud, Sigmund, 22, 49, 62, 66, 69, 72, 82, 158, 159, 161, 162, 163, 172, 232, 305.
Frey, Emmy, 270.
Freyberger, L., 182, 190, 270.
Fricke, G., 264.
Fried, A. H., 145.

Friederici, H., 270.
Friedmann, Hermann, 256, 260.
Frisch, M., 286.
Fritsch, O., 286.
Fritz, W. H., 293.
Fröbel, Friedrich, 122.
Frohnmeyer, Ida, 257, 300.
Fuchs, Hella, 104, 252.
Fuchs, K., 270, 293.
Fuss, K., 286.

Gaienhofen, 7, 8, 59, 60, 76, 92, 96, 111, 112, 114, 151, 204, 221, 300.
Gardner, A., 242.
Geffert, Heinrich, 61, 123, 150, 179, 250.
Geheeb, C., 270.
Geijerstam, Gustav von, 233.
Geissendorfer, Th., 242.
Geissler, Max, 262.
Georg, B., 270.
George, Stefan, 133, 237.
Georgi, Arthur, 126, 254, 270.
Gerbersau, 5.
Gerhard, I., 270.
Germany, 18-19, 39-54, 116, 118, 119, 120, 133, 135, 136-147, 152, 178, 181, 184, 196, 197, 203-206, 207, 239, 293-295.
East Germany, 93, 127, 128, 137-139, 212, 240, 251, 289, 291, 292, 299.
Geroe-Tobler, M., 230.
Gerstner, Hermann, 50.
Gey, P., 270, 301.
Geyh, K. W., 270.
Gide, André, 12, 115, 124, 125, 175, 222, 246, 253, 255, 257, 258, 270, 286, 287.
Giebisch, H., 264.
Ginster, Ria, 230.
Gjellerup, Karl, 278.
Gnamm, Dr., 270.
Gnefkow, Edmund, 89-92, 93, 107, 177, 250.
Goebbels, P. J., 49.
Goebel, Heinrich, 224.
Goern, Hermann, 95-97, 270, 287.
Goes, Albrecht, 103, 125, 181, 247, 265, 303.
Goethe, 12, 18, 37, 41, 47, 51, 63, 65, 80, 83, 97-100, 102, 107, 116, 120, 131, 140, 143, 162, 179, 182, 184, 186, 188, 189, 190, 192, 221, 228, 234, 237, 250, 255, 258, 259, 276, 295, 302, 303, 307.
Gömöri, Eugen, 225.
Goodloe, Jane, 242.

Göppert-Spanel, Dr., 164-165, 270.
Göppingen, 6, 188.
Görres, Joseph, 73.
Gotthelf, Jeremias, 235.
Götting, W., 293.
Gould, L. N., 72, 296.
Gowan, B. L., 270.
Grabert, W., 262.
Graef, Hermann, 253.
Graf, O. M., 93, 278.
Gran, Bjarne, 248.
Grappin, Pierre, 143-144, 270, 303.
Grebert, L., 287.
Gregori, Aristides, 246.
Greece, 195, 248.
Grenzmann, Wilhelm, 184, 257.
Griese, W. H., 270.
Grill, Julius, 237.
Grillparzer, Franz, 119.
Grimm, Hans, 296.
Grolmann, Adolf von, 257.
Groothoff, H. H., 183, 186, 190, 271.
Gross, Harvey, 185, 244, 271.
Groth, Helge, 257, 302.
Grünberg, K., 271.
Guder, E., 271.
Guilland, A., 271.
Gündel, B., 271.
Gundert, Adele, 206, 230, 257, 300.
Gundert, Friedrich, 261, 300, 301.
Gundert, Hermann, 3, 4, 6, 59, 98, 105, 114, 257, 261, 299.
Gundert, Joh. Christian, 114.
Gundert, Marie (H. H.'s mother), 3, 4, 5, 105, 126, 254, 257.
Gundert, Paul, 59.
Günnel, P., 271.
Günther, G., 271.
Gutkind, C. S., 287.

Haas, Joseph, 258.
Hackelsberger-Bergengruen, L., 294.
Haering, A., 287.
Hafkesbrink, Hanna, 242.
Hafner, Gotthilf, 104, 105-106, 107, 128, 129, 239, 250, 252, 271, 300, 306, 307, 308.
Haga, Mayumi, 243, 244.
Hager, Wilhelm, 204, 206.
Halpert, I. D., 296.
Halsband, R., 287.
Hammer, F., 287.
Hammerich, C., 247, 257.
Hammes, K., 294.
Händel, G. F., 155, 157.
Hänsel, L., 271.
Hannington, Bishop, 4.
Hara, Kenchû, 243.

Hartley, L. P., 287.
Hartmann, Otto, 222, 300.
Hartmann, R., 287.
Hartmann, Ursula, 257.
Hartung, L., 271.
Hartung, R., 271.
Hartung, Wilhelm, 130, 271.
Hartwich, O., 105, 130, 257.
Hatterer, G., 297.
Hauptmann, Gerhard, 163.
Hauser, Arnold, 257.
Hauser, Ernst, 259.
Haussmann, Conrad, 60.
Haussmann, Konrad, 231.
Haussmann, Walter, 94, 222, 271.
Haydn, F. J., 37, 157.
Hecht, Gustav, 142, 271, 279, 299.
Heckenhauer, 6.
Hecker, Joachim von, 104, 108-111, 252, 306.
Hedinger-Henrici, P., 65, 175, 271.
Hees, M., 287.
Hegel, Friedrich, 107.
Heidegger, Martin, 159, 172, 272, 305.
Heidenstam, Verner von, 233.
Heilbut, Ivan, 123-124, 252.
Heine, Heinrich, 279.
Heinemann, Karl, 262.
Heiney, Donald W., 257.
Heinzel, E., 264.
Heise, W., 271.
Heiseler, B. von, 271.
Heisterbach, Cäsarius von, 227, 234.
Heiting, Ingeborg, 67, 163-164, 257.
Helbing, C., 272.
Heller, Peter, 146-147, 166-167, 272, 296.
Hellmann, Julia, 7, 206, 240.
Hendriksen, Jörgen, 257.
Henze, A. R., 296.
Heraclitus, 77, 194.
Hering, G. F., 272.
Hermann-Neisse, Max, 125, 253.
Herrigel, H., 287.
Hertel, W., 287.
Hertig, H., 247.
Herzog, F. M., 287.
Hesse, Bruno, 9, 96, 207, 298.
Hesse, Heiner, 9, 207, 298.
Hesse, Hermann (H. H.'s grandfather), 3, 114, 300.
Hesse, Hermannus, (16th century humanist), 188.
Hesse, Johannes, 3, 4, 5, 6, 9, 114, 257, 299.
Hesse, Martin, 8, 9, 207, 298.
Hesse, Marulla, 230.
Hesse, Ninon (Ausländer), 11, 207, 220.

Heuschele, Otto, 272.
Heuss, Theodor, 94, 206, 240, 257, 258, 261, 272, 287.
Hildebrandt, K., 247.
Hill, Claude, 135, 136-137, 145-146, 147, 197, 242, 272, 287.
Hilscher, E., 272, 308.
Hippe, Robert, 195, 272.
Hippel, Th. G., 234.
Hirsau, 188.
Hirsch, F. E., 287.
Hirsch, W., 294, 306.
Hitler, Adolph, 11, 45, 51, 106, 140, 144.
Hoerschelmann, Rolf v., 258.
Hofer, Karl, 96.
Hoffmann, E. T. A., 14, 73, 101, 102, 153, 236.
Hoffmann, F. J., 161.
Hofmannsthal, Hugo von, 163.
Holbein, Hans, 234.
Hölderlin, Friedrich, 47, 73, 86, 94, 101, 103.
Holland, 196, 248.
Holm, Korfiz, 258.
Holmberg, N., 247.
Holmberg, Olle, 258.
Hornung, E., 272.
Horst, K. A., 258.
House, R. T., 244.
Hoyer, K. H., 294.
Huber, Hans, 104, 106, 107, 252.
Huch, Ricarda, 149, 233, 256, 287, 295.
Hudson, Stephen, 244.
Humm, R. J., 272.
Hungary, 195, 248.
Hunnius, A., 272.
Hunnius, Monika, 258, 300.

I Ging, 92, 191.
Ihlenfeld, Kurt, 258.
Ilberg, Wernher, 258.
Ilg, Paul, 239.
India, 3, 4, 24, 25, 59, 73, 74, 79, 91, 92, 107, 131, 173, 174, 177, 178, 227, 231, 257, 270, 278, 306.
Irvine, L. L., 287.
Isenberg, Karl (H. H.'s stepbrother), 151.
Isenberg, Karl (H. H.'s nephew), 187.
Isenberg, Th., 151.
Ishinaka, Shôji, 243.
Italy, 18, 20, 196, 224, 231, 235, 243-244, 258.

Jacobson, Anna, 124, 252, 272.
Jaeger, Hans, 198, 272, 305.

Jancke, O., 272.
Japan, 177, 196, 197, 239, 243-244.
Jehle, Mimi, 150-151, 272, 301.
Jenssen, Christian, 50, 262.
Jente, Richard, 197.
Jerven, Walter, 258.
Johnson, S. M., 272, 306.
Joho, W., 287.
Jokusch, Robert, 126, 254.
Jonas, K. W., 93, 210-212, 241, 273.
Jordan, Max, 174-175, 238, 273.
Josselin de Jong, K. H. R. de, 248.
Joyce, James, 115.
Jung, C. G., 69, 71, 82, 91, 160, 162, 163, 236, 298, 300, 306.
Jünger, Ernst, 258, 267, 296.
Jursch, Hanna, 226.
Jursch, Ilse, 226.

Käge, H., 254, 273, 300.
Kafka, Franz, 48, 162, 198, 237, 238.
Kalenter, O., 288.
Kant, Immanuel, 46, 75, 246.
Kantorowicz, A., 288.
Kappstein, Th., 131, 273.
Kasack, Hermann, 259, 267.
Kayser, Rudolf, 132, 273.
Keckeis, Gustav, 132, 273.
Kegel, G., 294.
Kehr, Charlotte, 258.
Keller, Gottfried, 5, 12, 15, 36, 46, 93, 112-114, 129, 130, 131, 173, 229, 233, 235, 302.
Kellermann, B., 288.
Kempfes, W., 294.
Kepler, Joh., 94.
Kesten, Hermann, 244.
Keyserling, Hermann, 174, 259.
Kiener, H., 258.
Kiessig, M., 288.
Kilchenmann, R. J., 197, 296, 304.
Kirchenberger, H., 294.
Kirchheim unter der Teck, 6-7.
Kirchhoff, Gerhard, 93, 111, 123, 184, 190, 250, 252, 294.
Klabund, 46, 149, 273.
Klages, Ludwig, 82, 83, 86, 88, 172.
Klaiber, Th., 113, 129, 131, 258, 273.
Klee, Paul, 97.
Klein, Johannes, 258.
Klein, T., 288.
Kleiter, H., 294.
Klie, B., 273.
Kliemann, Horst, 93, 126, 192, 204, 205, 209-211, 212, 224, 249, 250, 252, 258, 273, 300, 301, 302, 303, 307.
Kloter, Karl, 125, 253.
Kluckhohn, Paul, 255.

Knab-Grzimek, F., 273.
Knell, E., 294.
Knodt, K. E., 273.
Koch, Franz, 50, 262.
Koenig, Robert, 262.
Koerber, R., 296, 304.
Köge, H. H., 273.
Kohlschmid, Werner, 108, 111, 176, 179-181, 183, 186, 190, 191, 193, 258, 273, 306.
Koischwitz, Otto, 242.
Kolb, Walter, 104.
Kolbenheyer, E. G., 163.
Koller, Gottfried, 177, 179, 190-191, 273.
Konheiser-Barwanietz, C. M., 97-100, 250, 307.
König, O., 288.
Korn, Karl, 273.
Kornthal, 206.
Korrodi, Eduard, 225, 254, 273, 274, 288.
Korrodi, Otto, 125, 253.
Kosch, Wilhelm, 262.
Köstlin, H. A., 131, 274.
Kraeger, Heinrich, 258.
Krafft, Joh., 288.
Kramer, Walter, 111, 123, 253, 306.
Kraus, Fritz, 183, 274, 288.
Krauss, R., 288.
Kretschmer, Ernst, 71, 90.
Kretschmer, Max, 134, 258.
Krezdorn, Franz, 264.
Krieg, W., 274.
Krklec, P. G., 249.
Kronenberger, L., 288.
Krug, 240.
Krüger, H., 288.
Krüger, Herm. Anders, 262.
Kubczak, Viktor, 225.
Kubin, Alfred, 96.
Kuhlmann, Gerhard, 167-168, 274.
Kuhn, Alfred, 104, 113, 128, 192-193, 253.
Kunimatsu, Kôji, 244.
Kunstmann, Lisa, 155, 274.
Kunze, Johanna M. L., 76-79, 177, 250, 303.
Kunze, Wilhelm, 132, 274, 308.
Kurth, Rudolf, 150, 274.
Kusch, E., 274.
Kusche, L., 274, 288.
Kutzbach, K. A., 263.

Laaths, E., 263.
Lagerlöf, Selma, 224.
Lambert, Jean, 246.
Lambrecht, P., 274, 300.

Land, S. L., 296.
Lang, J. B., 60, 298.
Lang, Martin, 263.
Lang, Renée, 258.
Lange, Horst, 239.
Lange, I. M., 274.
Lange, Victor, 263.
Langen, Albert, 44, 60.
Langenbucher, Helmut, 50.
Langenmaier, Theodor, 50.
Langgässer, Elisabeth, 143, 298.
Langlo, Otto, 72, 294.
Lanuza, E. G., 274.
Lao-Tse, 92, 237.
Larese, Franz, 239.
Largiader, M., 274.
Laroches, 60.
Larson, R. C., 296.
Laserstein, K., 274.
Lasne, René, 246.
Lass, Jeanette Agnese, 3, 60.
Laux, Karl, 258.
Lavalette, Robert, 263.
Lazare, C., 288.
Lechner, Hermann, 263.
Leese, Kurt, 259.
Lehner, H. H., 72, 274, 294.
Leibholz, M., 245.
Leibholz, R. N., 297.
Leins, Hermann, 240, 261.
Lemm, R. A., 274, 300.
Lemp, Armin, 207, 208-209, 212, 251, 259.
Lenau, Nikolaus, 102.
Lennartz, Franz, 50, 263.
Lenz, H., 274.
Leonardi, E., 248.
Leschnitzer, Franz, 139, 275.
Lesser, J., 275.
Lessing, G. E., 119.
Lestiboudois, Herbert, 259, 275.
Leuteritz, G., 275, 288.
Leuthold, Heinrich, 234, 237.
Levander, Hans, 104, 107, 128, 253, 275.
Lewalter, C. E., 95, 289.
Lewisohn, Adele, 244.
Lewisohn, Ludwig, 245.
Leyen, Fr. von der, 263.
Li-Tai-Po, 92, 134.
Libal, E., 275.
Liepelt-Unterberg, M., 294, 302, 306.
Lieser, Fr., 66, 123, 275.
Liliencron, Detlev von, 235.
Linden, Walter, 50, 263.
Lindquist, Axel, 240.
Lindley, Denver, 245.
Lingelbach, H., 275.
Lissauer, E., 275, 308.

Litt, Th., 184, 259, 275.
Livingstone, David, 4.
Livorno, 18.
Lizounat, M., 294, 297, 306.
Ljungerud, I., 297.
Loerke, Oskar, 259.
Loomis, C. Grant, 249.
Lorenzen, Hermann, 66, 111, 122-123, 253, 275.
Lorrain, 297, 307.
Lü Bu We, 156, 157.
Lübeck, 3.
Lublinski, Samuel, 259.
Lugano, 53.
Lukáč, E. B., 249.
Lund, H. G., 296.
Lunding, E., 275.
Lundquist, Arthur, 256.
Lüth, P. E. H., 263.
Lützkendorf, E. A. F., 72-74, 76, 103, 150, 177, 250.

Måås, Kerstin, 246.
Maass, J., 275.
MacDonald, D., 289.
McBroom, R. R., 297, 304.
McLain, Wm., 242.
McCormick, J. O., 296.
Mächler, Robert, 126, 254.
Maeterlinck, Maurice, 133.
Magnat, G. E., 259.
Mahrholz, Werner, 263.
Maier, E., 296, 300.
Maier, Hans, 259, 275.
Majut, Rudolf, 263.
Malabar, 3, 4.
Malaya, 8.
Mallorca, 226.
Malmberg, B., 246.
Malthaner, Joh., 275, 300.
Mann, Erika, 259.
Mann, Klaus, 244.
Mann, Otto, 256, 260.
Mann, Thomas, 36, 50, 87, 94, 115, 118-120, 121, 124, 135, 136, 143, 155, 156, 157, 160, 162, 163, 175, 178, 182, 187, 189, 192, 198, 226, 232, 233, 241, 244, 253, 255, 256, 259, 260, 261, 269, 273, 275, 276, 279, 281, 286, 289, 290, 291, 292, 294, 296, 297, 299, 303, 305, 307.
Manner, E. L., 248.
Manzanares, Manuel, 245.
Marbach, 205-206, 207.
Marck, Siegfried von, 259.
Martens, Kurt, 263.
Marti, E. O., 276.
Marti, Fritz, 259.
Martin, Jacques, 246.

Martini, Fritz, 95, 263, 276.
Marx, H. K., 55.
Masereel, Frans, 301.
Matheson, William, 207.
Mathies, M. E., 276.
Matthias, K., 294, 305.
Matzig, R. B., 76, 80-81, 92, 111, 115-116, 154, 182, 195, 250, 253, 276, 289, 299, 302, 303.
Mauer, Gerhard, 72, 294.
Mauer, O., 289.
Mauerhofer, Hugo, 67, 71, 72, 158, 250.
Maulbronn, 6, 59, 111, 140, 188, 223, 300.
Maurer, K. W., 242, 245, 276.
Maurer, L., 276.
Maury, G., 246.
Mauthner, Fritz, 234.
Mayer, Gerhard, 250, 306.
Mayer, Hans, 120, 136, 138-139, 184, 259, 276, 303.
Medici, Lorenzo, 18.
Melchinger, S., 276.
Mentgen, M., 294, 304.
Meridies, Wilhelm, 149, 229, 276.
Mersmann, H., 276.
Metelmann, Ernst, 128, 134, 208, 209, 276, 277, 296.
Meuer, A., 271, 289, 303.
Meyer, C. F., 87, 272.
Meyer, R. M., 263.
Meyer, Th. A., 276.
Meyer-Benfey, H., 131, 276.
Michael, W. F., 242.
Middleton, D., 289.
Mieg, H. P., 289, 301.
Mihailovitch, V., 296.
Mila, M., 247.
Mileck, Joseph, 172, 195, 197, 242, 276, 277, 296.
Missenharter, H., 277, 301.
Mjöberg, Jöran, 259.
Moenikes, G., 294.
Moilliet, Louis, 60, 96, 188.
Montagnola, 9, 13, 20, 51, 59, 76, 80, 81, 96, 99, 106, 124, 148, 188, 206, 207, 250.
Monteverdi, Claudio, 157.
Moras, Joachim, 258.
Mordell, Albert, 161.
Morgan, B. Q., 261.
Morgenstern, Christian, 235, 236.
Morgenthaler, Ernst, 96, 207, 277.
Mörike, Eduard, 73, 94, 102, 111, 119, 233, 236, 237.
Morris, A. S., 289.
Moser, Joachim H., 259.
Mozart, W. A., 37, 83, 116, 152, 154,
155, 157, 225, 229, 260, 278, 289, 304, 305.
Mueller, Gustav E., 245, 259, 277.
Mühlenberger, Josef, 95, 277.
Müller, Ernst, 94.
Müller, Lotte, 259.
Müller-Blattau, J., 120, 155-156, 178, 277, 305, 307.
Müller-Seidel, W., 277.
Mullett, F. M., 296.
Mumbauer, Joh., 50, 263.
München, 97, 204, 225, 258.
Münsterberg, M., 245.
Münzel, Uli, 126, 254.

Nadler, Josef, 50, 263.
Nadler, Käte, 250, 304, 306.
Näf, Hans, 277.
Natorp, Paul, 259.
Naumann, Hans, 50, 263.
Naumann, Walter, 94, 169-170, 277.
Nestele, K., 277.
Nestle, Wilhelm, 182, 277.
Nicolai, Friedrich, 119.
Nietzsche, Friedrich, 20, 21, 38, 39, 43, 47, 63, 64, 74, 75, 85, 87, 94, 119, 135, 156, 158, 187, 226, 302.
Nordau, Max, 72.
Norton, W. W., 242.
Norway, 196, 248.
Novalis, 38, 63, 72, 73, 95, 101, 102, 153, 189, 199, 233, 299.

Oepke, Albrecht, 131, 174, 259, 277.
Oetinger, F. C., 94.
Ohff, H., 289.
Olbrich, Wilhelm, 264.
Opitz, F., 277.
Östergaard, C. V., 247.
Österling, A., 246, 247.
Otto, Berthold, 122.
Otto, H., 289.
Oven, Jörn, 52, 149, 277, 299.
Overberg, M., 294.

Padua, 18.
Paeschke, Hans, 258.
Paoli, R., 248.
Paquet, Alfons, 258.
Park, C. W., 277, 308.
Park, Rosemary, 242.
Pary, Juliette, 246.
Pasinetti, P. M., 278, 302.
Paulsen, Wolfgang, 259.
Peebles, W. C., 242.
Penzoldt, Ernst, 94, 278.
Peppard, M. B., 197, 278.

Perrot, 5, 6, 187.
Pestalozzi, 122.
Peter, M., 294, 304.
Peters, Eric, 164, 245, 278.
Petry, Karl, 263.
Pfau, Reinhold, 205-206.
Pfeifer, Martin, 93, 127, 212, 253, 278, 285, 289, 294, 304.
Pfeiffer, Joh., 193, 260, 278.
Pfeifle, L., 289.
Pfisterer, Pastor, 6.
Phelps, L. R., 242.
Pick, R., 289.
Pielow, W., 294.
Pinette, Jorge, 246.
Pintó, Alfonso, 246.
Piot, André, 246.
Pistor, M., 278.
Plant, R., 289.
Plato, 226.
Plümacher, Walter, 74-76, 251.
Pocar, E., 247, 248.
Poestges, F., 295.
Pöggeler, Fr., 278.
Pohlmann, G., 295.
Polgar, Alfred, 49.
Polockoj, A. S., 249.
Pongs, Hermann, 175-176, 184, 259.
Ponten, Josef, 301.
Porst, P., 289.
Porterfield, A. W., 289.
Portugal, 196.
Prescott, F. C., 161.
Priday, N. H., 244.
Probizer, E. M., 278, 300.
Pröhl, G., 289.
Protzer, H., 295, 300.
Prussia, 44, 299.
Purcell, H., 155, 157.

Raabe, Wilhelm, 12, 233, 292.
Rabuse, Georg, 246.
Railo, E., 248.
Rainalter, E. H., 278.
Randall, A. W. G., 290.
Rang, Bernhard, 260, 278.
Rasch, W., 278.
Rastfeld, C., 295.
Rathenau, Walter, 260.
Rauch, Karl, 149, 278.
Raum, C., 247.
Rauscher, U., 278.
Read, Herbert, 161.
Redman, B. R., 290.
Reich, Willi, 260.
Reifferscheidt, F. M., 290.
Reimann, R., 290.
Rein, Heinz, 260, 263.
Reindl, L. E., 95.

Reinhold, H., 278, 305.
Reinke-Ortmann, S., 278.
Reisse, M., 278.
Renner, Ludwig, 96.
Reuter, E., 278.
Reuter, G., 290.
Rheinwald, Ernst, 206, 222, 300.
Riboni, Denise, 171, 246, 278.
Rich, D. E., 296.
Richey, Margaret, 245.
Richter, Georg, 104, 106, 107, 253.
Richter, Jean Paul, 47, 73, 101, 102, 103, 236, 237.
Richter, Rudolf, 260.
Riemann, Robert, 263.
Rilke, R. M., 236, 237, 260, 261, 272, 306.
Ringer, P., 279.
Robert, L., 297, 302.
Robison, A., 245.
Roch, Herbert, 145, 260, 279, 290.
Rockenbach, M., 279.
Röder, Gerhard, 260.
Rodin, Auguste, 235.
Röhl, Hans, 263.
Rolland, Romain, 41, 52, 53, 124, 143-145, 237, 260, 261, 270, 290, 303.
Roman, F., 290.
Rose, Ernst, 198, 279.
Rosner, Hilda, 244, 245.
Röttger, F., 279.
Rousseau, J. J., 122.
Rousseaux, André, 260, 290, 292.
Ruiz, Jesús, 245.
Rupp, L., 290.
Ruprecht, Erich, 260.
Russell, Bertrand, 175.
Russia, 3, 54-55, 59, 64, 74, 139-141, 167, 185, 233, 249, 304.
Russo, W., 279.
Rychner, Max, 125, 254, 260.

Saager, A., 274, 300.
Sabais, H. W., 260.
Sagara, Morio, 243.
Sagave, P. P., 297, 304.
Salinger, Hermann, 245.
Salzer, Anselm, 263.
Samuel, Richard, 260.
Sander, E., 279.
Sanger, H. H., 297.
Satô, Kôichi, 243, 260.
Savill, Mervyn, 244, 245.
Scarlotti, A., 157
Schacht, R., 279.
Schäfer, Wilhelm, 279, 290.
Schall, Franz, 142, 188, 279.
Schall, Pastor, 6.

Schandorf, F., 247.
Schandorf, K., 247.
Scheffler, H., 279.
Scheffler, K., 279, 301.
Scheler, Max, 40, 235.
Schelling, F. W. J., 94, 119.
Schepler, H. J., 295.
Scherer, Wilhelm, 264.
Schestow, 238.
Scheuermann, Erich, 96, 279, 300.
Schiller, 34, 46, 47, 75, 94, 157, 205, 299.
Schlegel, F., 72, 101, 102.
Schleiermacher, 101, 102.
Schmid, F. D., 131, 279.
Schmid, H. R., 66-70, 71, 76, 82, 83, 88, 105, 114, 128, 150, 153, 158, 161, 164, 172, 193, 208, 251, 302, 303.
Schmid, Karl, 93, 111, 118-120, 253, 279, 307.
Schmid, Max, 82-88, 155, 172, 184-185, 195, 251, 259, 290, 296, 303, 306.
Schmid-Gruber, R., 131, 279.
Schmidt, Erich, 234.
Schmitt, F., 264.
Schneider, G., 279.
Schneider, Hermann, 255.
Schneider, Manfred, 264.
Schneider, Marcel, 120, 279.
Schnitzler, A., 163.
Schoeck, Othmar, 126, 151-152, 153, 207, 280, 304.
Schöfer, Wolfgang von, 52, 108, 111, 128, 143, 149, 181-182, 183, 190, 280.
Scholz, Wilhelm von, 234, 280.
Scholz-Wülfing, P., 280.
Schonauer, F., 290.
Schönberg, Arnold, 157.
Schoolfield, George, 260, 305.
Schopenhauer, 21, 64, 74, 99, 119, 225, 226, 303.
Schott, R., 280.
Schouten, H., 280.
Schrempf, Christoph, 178, 229, 232.
Schröder, Ed., 280.
Schröder, Rud. Alex., 93, 260, 271, 280, 290, 301.
Schubert, F., 153.
Schüddekopf, J., 290.
Schuh, W., 280.
Schühle, E., 280.
Schultz de Mantovani, F., 280.
Schultze, F., 280.
Schulz-Behrend, G., 242.
Schumann, Hildegard, 242.
Schumann, Otto, 264.
Schussen, Wilhelm, 125, 253, 260, 290.

Schuster, W., 264.
Schuwerack, W., 280.
Schwarz, Egon, 197.
Schwarz, Georg, 260, 280, 308.
Schweter, W., 280.
Schwinn, Wilhelm, 111, 117-118, 175, 179, 186, 253, 306.
Schworm, Karl, 50.
Seghers, Anna, 299.
Seidel, Ina, 282.
Seidl, F., 280.
Seidlin, Oskar, 120, 158-161, 163, 172, 182, 189, 190, 245, 260, 280.
Seki, Taisuke, 243, 244.
Setz, K., 290.
Seyffarth, U., 280, 308.
Shaftesbury, 157.
Shomaker, C. B., 242.
Shuster, G. N., 124, 252, 290.
Siedler, W. J., 281.
Sieveling, G., 149, 290, 289.
Silesius, Angelus, 177, 299.
Silfverstolpes, G. M., 247.
Silomon, K. H., 93, 108, 126, 192, 210-211, 222, 224, 250, 252, 301, 302, 303, 307.
Silvio, Enea, 234.
Simon, Alfred, 221.
Singapore, 18.
Skou-Hansen, T., 247.
Smith, B., 290.
Socrates, 37, 159.
Soergel, Albert, 264.
Sousa Marques, M. de, 248.
Spain, 54, 196, 197, 245-246.
Spengler, Oswald, 55, 56, 111, 141, 236.
Spenlé, Édouard, 132, 281, 300.
Spezia, 18.
Spiero, Heinrich, 261.
Spinoza, 226.
Spreen O., 295, 300, 302.
Stalin, 54.
Stange, C. H., 290.
Steen, Albert, 261, 281.
Steffen, Albert, 239.
Steffens, Henrik, 233.
Stein, G., 281.
Steinbüchel, Theodor, 261.
Stern, P., 297, 302.
Stetten, 6.
Stifter, A., 113, 119, 189.
Stilling, Heinrich, 233.
Stirner, Karl, 96.
Stoecklin, Niklaus, 96.
Stolpe, S., 246.
Stolz, H., 281.
Storm, Th., 114, 224, 237.
Strachan, W. J., 245.

Straub, E., 261.
Strauss, Emil, 237.
Strauss, Richard, 280, 281.
Strauss und Torney, Lulu von, 132, 281.
Strich, Fritz, 75, 136, 137, 261.
Strindberg, Joh. August, 238.
Sturzenegger, Hans, 96.
Stuttgart, 3, 47, 93, 105, 112, 205, 206.
Suhrkamp, Peter, 93, 212, 215, 261.
Sulser, W. G., 290.
Sumatra, 8, 18.
Süskind, W. E., 149.
Swabia, 3, 13, 47, 59, 73, 89, 94, 113, 119, 125, 129, 206, 222, 224, 285.
Sweden, 196, 246-247, 297.
Switzerland, 39, 49, 136, 197, 203, 206-207, 238.
Szczesny, G., 120, 135, 136, 281.

Takahashi, Kenji, 243.
Takahashi, Yoshitaka, 261.
Talatscheri, 3.
Taylor, R. A., 290.
Tenschert, R., 281.
Tetzner, L., 290.
Tezuka, Tomio, 243.
Thackeray, Wm. M., 235.
Thiele, Guillermo, 157, 281.
Thieme-Becker, 97, 258.
Thiess, F., 281.
Thimus, Albert Freiherr von, 187-188.
Thoma, Ludwig, 44, 60.
Thomas, R. H., 260.
Thomas-San-Galli, W. A., 131, 155, 281.
Thomsen, A., 247.
Thoreau, H. D., 62.
Thu-Fu, 92, 134.
Thurm, H, G., 52, 120, 143, 149, 281.
Tieck, Ludwig, 29, 101.
Toller, Ernst, 296.
Töpffer, Rudolphe, 235.
Topsöe, S., 247.
Townsend, S. R., 281, 302.
Transvaal, 233.
Trog, H., 281.
Tübingen, 6, 59, 98, 300.
Türke, K., 281.

Über Wasser, W., 281, 301.
Ude, K., 281, 304.
Uemura, Toshio, 243.
Uenuira, T., 281.
Uhlig, H., 281, 291.
Uhlmann, A. M., 281.

Uhse, B., 282, 299.
Unger, W., 282.
United States of America, 54-55, 93, 197-199, 203, 211, 296-297.
Unseld, Siegfried, 93, 126, 127, 212-213, 253, 295.
Urach, 111.

Venice, 18.
Vesper, Will, 48-49, 143, 238, 282.
Verstegen, G. H. A., 248.
Vietsch, E. von, 180, 183, 282.
Vietta, E., 182, 183, 282.
Villon, François, 270.
Vinci, Leonardo da, 233.
Vogeler, Heinrich, 96.
Vogelpohl, Wilhelm, 264.
Volkart, D., 282.
Vortriede, 282.

Wackernagels, 59.
Wagner, Christian, 235.
Wagner, Fernando, 261.
Wagner, Gisela, 66, 282.
Wagner, M., 295.
Wagner, Richard, 46, 119, 153, 154, 162.
Waldhausen, A., 105, 113, 129-130, 282.
Waiblinger, W., 102.
Walter, H., 291.
Walzel, Oskar, 264.
Wantoch, H., 282.
Wassermann, Jakob, 268.
Wasserscheid, R., 295-304.
Wassmer, Max, 188, 207.
Wassner, H., 295, 304.
Weber, Ernst, 261.
Weber, Marta, 261.
Weber, Werner, 195, 240, 254, 282.
Weibel, Kurt, 72, 100-103, 252.
Weimar, K. C., 242.
Weiss, Erich, 125, 203-204, 304.
Weiss, E. R., 96.
Weiss, Hansgerhard, 261, 303.
Weissenstein, 3, 59, 300.
Welter, Friedrich, 261, 304.
Welti, Albert, 8, 96, 235.
Wenger, Lisa, 9, 92.
Wenger, Ruth, 9, 92.
Wennerberg, Ira, 247.
Werfel, Franz, 258, 267.
Werner, A., 282, 291.
Werner, B. E., 282.
Werner, Zacharias, 101.
Wetzel, Justus H., 261.
Whitman, Walt, 62.
Wick, K., 291.

Widner, T., 282.
Wiechert, E., 163, 261.
Wiedner, L., 282.
Wiegand, H., 128, 282.
Wiegler, Paul, 239, 261, 264, 282, 291.
Wieland, Christoph Martin, 225.
Wieser, M., 264.
Wieser, Sebastian, 130, 173-174, 282.
Wilhelm, Richard, 191, 237.
Wilhelm, II, 44, 54.
Wilson, Colin, 261.
Winston, Richard, 245.
Wistinghausen, K. von, 282.
Witkop, Philipp, 134, 261, 264, 282.
Wolf, Hugo, 153, 154.
Wolfenstein, A., 282.
Wolff, Kurt, 237, 305.
Wolff, G. M., 242.
Wölfflin, Heinrich, 75.
Woltereck, Richard, 40, 45.
Wood, R. C., 126, 253, 282.
Worbs, Erich, 261.
Wrobel, I., 283.

Wunder, G., 291.
Wurster, Gotthold, 261.
Württemberg, 3, 6, 47, 187, 205, 206.
Würzburg, 225.
Wüstenberg, H. L., 111, 116-117, 253, 283.
Wyss, H. A., 283.

Yamoto, Kunitarô, 244.

Zarek, Otto, 131, 283.
Zeidler, Kurt, 261.
Zelder, Georg, 128, 295.
Zeller, Gustav, 131, 140-141, 142, 283, 299.
Zeydel, Ed. H., 242.
Zinniker, O., 291.
Ziolkowski, Th. J., 72, 297.
Zoff, O., 283, 301.
Zohn, Harry, 242.
Zola, E., 94.
Zürich, 9, 93, 207, 218.
Zweig, Stefan, 7, 49, 163, 291.